OXFORD WORLD'S

OCCASIONAL, CRIT[...]
POLITICAL WRITING

JAMES JOYCE was born on 2 February 1882 in Dublin, eldest of ten surviving children born to Mary Jane ('May') Murray and John Joyce. Joyce's father was then a Collector of Rates but the family, once prosperous, had just begun its slow decline into poverty. Educated first at the Jesuit Clongowes Wood and Belvedere Colleges, Joyce entered the Royal University (now University College, Dublin) in 1898. Four years later Joyce left Dublin for Paris with the intention of studying medicine but soon his reading turned more to Aristotle than physic. His mother's illness in April 1903 took him back to Dublin. Here he met and, on 16 June 1904, first stepped out with Nora Barnacle, a young woman from Galway. In October they left together for the Continent. Returning only thrice to Ireland—and never again after 1912—Joyce lived out the remainder of his life in Italy, Switzerland, and France.

The young couple went first to Pola, but soon moved to Trieste where Joyce began teaching English for the Berlitz School. Except for seven months in Rome, the Joyces stayed in Trieste for the next eleven years. Despite disputes with recalcitrant publishers, severe eye problems, and the pressures of a growing family (both a son and a daughter were born), Joyce managed to write the poems that became *Chamber Music* (1907), as well as *Dubliners* (1914). He also began, abandoned, began again, and completed *A Portrait of the Artist as a Young Man* (1916). By the time the family moved to Zurich in July 1915, he had also begun *Ulysses*. Over the next seven years, first in Zurich, later in Paris, *Ulysses* progressed. Partial serial publication in the *Little Review* (1917–18) brought suppression, confiscation, and finally conviction for obscenity. The first copies arrived in Joyce's hands on 2 February 1922, his fortieth birthday.

The acclaim publication brought placed Joyce at the centre of the literary movement only later known as Modernism, but he was already restlessly pushing back its borders. Within the year he had begun his next project, known only mysteriously as *Work in Progress*. This occupied him for the next sixteen years, until in 1939 it was published as *Finnegans Wake*. By this time, Europe was on the brink of war. When Germany invaded France the Joyces left Paris, first for Vichy then on to Zurich. Here Joyce died on 13 January 1941 after surgery for a perforated ulcer. He was buried in Fluntern Cemetery.

KEVIN BARRY is Professor of English Literature at the National University of Ireland, Galway. He is the author of *Language, Music and the Sign* (Cambridge University Press, 1987) and has written on Joyce, the history of aesthetics, and on modern Irish literature. He is a founder and editor of the *Irish Review*.

OXFORD WORLD'S CLASSICS

*For over 100 years Oxford World's Classics have brought
readers closer to the world's great literature. Now with over 700
titles—from the 4,000-year-old myths of Mesopotamia to the
twentieth century's greatest novels—the series makes available
lesser-known as well as celebrated writing.*

*The pocket-sized hardbacks of the early years contained
introductions by Virginia Woolf, T. S. Eliot, Graham Greene,
and other literary figures which enriched the experience of reading.
Today the series is recognized for its fine scholarship and
reliability in texts that span world literature, drama and poetry,
religion, philosophy and politics. Each edition includes perceptive
commentary and essential background information to meet the
changing needs of readers.*

OXFORD WORLD'S CLASSICS

JAMES JOYCE

Occasional, Critical, and Political Writing

Edited with an Introduction and Notes by
KEVIN BARRY

Translations from the Italian by
CONOR DEANE

OXFORD
UNIVERSITY PRESS

OXFORD
UNIVERSITY PRESS

Great Clarendon Street, Oxford OX2 6DP

Oxford University Press is a department of the University of Oxford.
It furthers the University's objective of excellence in research, scholarship,
and education by publishing worldwide in

Oxford New York

Athens Auckland Bangkok Bogotá Buenos Aires Calcutta
Cape Town Chennai Dar es Salaam Delhi Florence Hong Kong Istanbul
Karachi Kuala Lumpur Madrid Melbourne Mexico City Mumbai
Nairobi Paris São Paulo Shanghai Singapore Taipei Tokyo Toronto Warsaw

with associated companies in Berlin Ibadan

Oxford is a registered trade mark of Oxford University Press
in the UK and in certain other countries

First published as an Oxford World's Classics paperback 2000

British Library Cataloguing in Publication Data

Data available

ISBN 0–19–283353–7

3 5 7 9 10 8 6 4 2

Typeset in Ehrhardt
by RefineCatch Limited, Bungay, Suffolk
Printed in Great Britain by
Clays Ltd, St Ives plc

CONTENTS

Contents vii

INTRODUCTION

A reader may take different paths through this gathering of Joyce's minor writings. These materials cover, albeit unequally, forty years of Joyce's life. They are diverse and might be grouped in several ways. Sections might be devised under such headings as aesthetics, Irish history, European drama, the literature of England. This Introduction answers certain thematic requirements by drawing together this miscellany in three of its aspects: the politics of Joyce's journalism; Joyce's strategic theory of art; and, linking both of these, Joyce's analysis of Irish cultural history.

The order preferred here for the texts in English is that of simple chronology and, indeed, a chronological order reveals most in so far as it measures the decisive changes and revisions that take place in Joyce's consciousness before the composition of *Ulysses*. The inter-relations between all of Joyce's writings constitute one aspect of their power and complexity. Within the juvenile essays the reader can detect motives which shape Joyce's major work: a matriculation essay in defence of the study of languages measures 'the effect of external influences on the very words of a race'; a childhood essay on subjugation proclaims the aversion to violence which Joyce, citizen of a country and of a continent immersed for much of his life in war, will always maintain.

In contrast to these continuities we may detect in the essays of the young Joyce attitudes which the creator of Leopold Bloom would abandon. In the 1899 essay 'Royal Hibernian Academy "Ecce Homo"' Joyce betrays an adolescent anti-Semitism in his description of a painting of a crowd of Jews witnessing Christ's passion:

Her child is clambering about her knees, her infant hoisted on her shoulder. Not even these are free from the all pervading aversion and in their small beady eyes twinkles the fire of rejection, the bitter unwisdom of their race.

The reader can also discover important changes in Joyce's publicly stated opinions and politics. The few years that separate Joyce, the reviewer of the *Daily Express*, from Joyce, the lecturer and journalist in Trieste, display a reversal in his argument with Irish nationalism.

Instead of mocking Arthur Griffith and Sinn Féin, as he had done in the *Daily Express*, Joyce in Trieste derives much of the principle and the detail of his analysis of Ireland, past and present, from Griffith's writings. Change again is evident between Joyce's caricature, in his attack on Lady Gregory's *Poets and Dreamers* (1903), of the senile and passionless storytellers of the Gaelic tradition and his recognition of the inadequacy of that representation of the west of Ireland in a later, more complex portrait of an island storyteller whom he describes as a sceptical and stylish artificer named 'O'Flaherty, the name which the young Oscar Wilde proudly had printed on the cover of his first book' ('The Mirage of the Fisherman of Aran', 1912). It is possible, therefore, to observe in these occasional writings the complication of Joyce's intelligence and his discarding of received opinion.

Journalism and Politics

In an uncollected letter of 25 March 1914 to a socialist Genoese publisher, Angelo Fortunato Formiggini, James Joyce proposed that they produce together a book on Ireland for Italian readers. The book would include the nine articles which Joyce had contributed to *Il Piccolo della Sera* between 1907 and 1912. In order to concentrate their political purpose, Joyce collected his Triestine journalism under a thematic heading without respect for the chronology of composition or of first publication. Joyce's proposed volume rearranges the sequence of his Triestine articles in order to emphasize their insistence on Irish autonomy and the inadequacies of such Home Rule as was offered by Westminster. His purpose is to state the case of Ireland to an international audience which, he claimed, had been systematically misinformed through the agencies of the British press. The title of the proposed volume and its first essay was to be 'L'Irlanda alla sbarra': 'Ireland at the Bar' or, one might say, Ireland in the dock. The Appendix to this volume includes these nine essays in the original Italian and in the sequence Joyce had proposed to Formiggini:

This year the Irish problem has reached an acute phase, and indeed, according to the latest news, England, owing to the Home Rule question, is on the brink of civil war.

The publication of a volume of Irish essays would be of interest to the Italian public.

These essays (nine) which I wrote, were published during the last seven years as signed editorials in the *Piccolo della Sera* of Trieste. The titles are:

    i. Ireland at the Bar (this could be the title of the small volume)

    ii. Home Rule Comes of Age

    iii. The Home Rule Comet

    iv. Bernard Shaw and censorship (Shaw, as is well known, is an Irishman)

    v. The City of the Tribes: Italian memories in an Irish port

    vi. The Mirage of the Fisherman of Aran

    vii. Oscar Wilde (he too is an Irishman)

    viii. Fenianism (i.e. the separatist movement)

    ix. The Shadow of Parnell.

I am an Irishman (from Dublin): and though these articles have absolutely no literary value, I believe they set out the problem sincerely and objectively.

Looking forward to your kind reply on the subject, I tender my respectful greetings,

James Joyce

Joyce's letter to Formiggini is his penultimate throw in a campaign which he had initiated seven years previously, not only in his journalism but also in public lectures to be given at the Università Popolare, Trieste, to counteract the assumption, published from London, that 'the Irish are the incapable and unbalanced cretins we read about in the leading articles in the *Standard* and the *Morning Post*'. The particular occasion of the proposal to publish his own articles in book form was the crisis of the Third Home Rule Bill, a crisis precipitated by the refusal of senior military officers at the Curragh Camp in Ireland in March 1914 to move against Unionist opponents to Home Rule and by the sympathetic response which this 'mutiny' received at the War Office in London.

Giorgio Melchiori has recently suggested that Joyce further intended to publish a collection of these essays for an English-speaking audience. His evidence is based on typescripts gathered together in the *James Joyce Archive* by Hans Walter Gabler. These typescripts include Italian versions and translations into English of certain articles, in whole and in part. The translations had been attributed by Gabler to Stanislaus Joyce, although recurrent errors in the translations ('Eminet' for Emmet, police 'office' for police station) make this attribution doubtful. Professor Melchiori writes:

The typescripts of the Italian texts are accompanied by English translations. The articles on Shaw (4) and Wilde (7), 'Ireland at the Bar' (1), and 'The City of the Tribes' (5) are translated in full, with handwritten corrections but no cuts; 'The Mirage of the Fisherman of Aran' (6) and 'The Shadow of Parnell' are also translated in full, but possible cuts are marked on the typescript; the other three are only partially translated: several sentences are omitted from 'Fenianism' (8) and 'Home Rule Comes of Age' (2), while only the last two paragraphs of 'The Home Rule Comet' (3) are preserved in the English version.

More significantly, six of the Italian typescripts bear pencilled figures on their first pages. 'Ireland at the Bar' is marked '1' (also in the translation), 'The Shadow of Parnell' '5' (also in the translation), 'The City of the Tribes' bears a hardly decipherable '2', while 'Fenianism', 'The Home Rule Comet' and 'Home Rule Comes of Age' are marked '4a', '4b' and '4c' respectively.

My conclusion: the copies and translations were made after the failed attempt to place the book with Formiggini. The intention was to address this time an English audience. The more literary pieces (on Shaw and Wilde) were set aside as independent essays. The rest were meant to be a report in five parts on the state of Ireland:

1. 'Ireland at the Bar' (in full, as introduction);
2. 'The City of the Tribes' (in full);
3. 'The Mirage of the Fisherman of Aran' (with some cuts);
4. A conflation of parts of 'Fenianism', 'The Home Rule Comet' and 'Home Rule Comes of Age', bringing up to date their political implications;
5. 'The Shadow of Parnell' (shorn of outdated parts, as conclusion).[1]

In order to understand the status of Joyce's Triestine journalism within his life and work, we need to reckon with at least three propositions. First, there is the certainty that Joyce intended to publish in a single volume his Triestine journalism for an Italian audience. Second, there is the probability that he intended to publish, in a separate single volume, translations and adaptations of these articles for an English-speaking audience. Third, there is the indisputable

---

[1] I am grateful to Professor Melchiori for permission to quote this letter from our correspondence during the preparation of this edition. For the text of Joyce's letter to Formiggini, see Giorgio Melchiori, 'The Language of Politics and the Politics of Language', *James Joyce Broadsheet*, 4 (Feb. 1981), 1.

fact that he allowed both proposed collections of these writings to lapse. In the long run Joyce decided not to proceed, against whatever odds, to book publication. That choice is in sharp contrast with Joyce's determination against all the odds to ensure publication of, for example, *Dubliners*. Any judgement on the status of the Triestine journalism must take account of both the intention and the failure to publish in book form for a wider audience.

The proposed title and first essay of both intended volumes, 'Ireland at the Bar', gives notice of Joyce's intention to defend Ireland's national character against its criminalization by England. 'Ireland cannot appeal to the modern conscience of England or abroad. The English newspapers act as interpreters [. . .] So the Irish figure as criminals, with deformed faces, who roam around at night with the aim of doing away with every Unionist.' Such a process had its origins in the first half of the nineteenth century and had continued and intensified during the Land War after 1879 and in the London *Times* enquiry into Parnellism and crime. Thomas Bartlett, in his *The Fall and Rise of the Irish Nation* (Dublin, 1992), outlines the manner in which Westminster justified its assertion that Ireland is 'not to be governed as England is'. Parliamentary claims that the Irish Catholic populace practised 'unnatural and unprecedented savagery' and wallowed in crime 'worse than in the most savage country in any age in the world', not only justified military rule but also, as a byproduct, confirmed a sense of 'otherness' or distinctness which strengthened the Catholics' claim to be a separate nation. Joyce's proposed volume of essays on Ireland would oppose both these claims: that the Irish are criminally violent in character and that the nation belongs to Catholicism. In this manner Joyce contradicts the international press and prevents, in his words, the English journalists 'disposing of the most complicated questions of colonial politics'.

Joyce was satisfied with his contributions to *Il Piccolo della Sera* and commented to his brother Stanislaus, 'I may not be the Jesus Christ I once fondly imagined myself, but I think I must have a talent for journalism.' Several of Joyce's most important characters— Leopold Bloom, Gabriel Conroy, and Robert Hand—work for newspapers. In *Ulysses* it is part of Stephen Dedalus's self-esteem that he is close to newspapermen. Joyce's contrast between Robinson Crusoe and John the Evangelist, and his contrast between the medieval and the post-renaissance mind, specify that it is the journalistic spirit that defines modernity. 'If the Renaissance did nothing else, it did much in creating within ourselves and our art a sense of pity for every being that lives and hopes and dies and deludes itself. In this at least we excel the ancients: in this the popular journalist is greater than the theologian.' Joyce valued newspapers because they provide a materialist history of social life. For him, as for his younger contemporary Walter Benjamin, two things are essential for knowledge of the city: walking its streets and reading its newspapers. Streets and newspapers give the world as material circumstance. That is why Joyce, as he explained in a letter of 1906 to his brother Stanislaus, plagued 'reluctant relatives at home to send [. . .] papers or cuttings from them'. He justified his demands by citing Ibsen: no one, according to Ibsen, could properly understand *A Doll's House* if they had not 'been in Norway when the Paris fashion journals first began to be on sale in Christiania.'

Joyce's attitude to the vocation of journalist vacillated between that of opportunist, persuader, and publicist. Cash for writing (if not writing for cash) always appealed to the younger Joyce. So too did the free rail pass and other perks of the journalist's trade. He proposed far more articles to the editors of newspapers than they were ever willing to accept. Reluctant editors have deprived us of the articles Joyce offered to write on Sarah Bernhardt, the Paris Carnival, and the Dublin Exhibition. His proposal for an interview with Caruso was refused by the *Irish Times*, the *Daily Express*, and Nora's favourite paper, the *Mail*. He wrote to his father, 'I am seriously thinking of entering the church if I find editors [. . .] so very stubborn as they appear to be.' Chance also let him down: a visit to Clifden in County Galway to interview Marconi failed because Marconi was not there and his radio station was not open.

Joyce did not lack persistence. As we see from his promotion of the declining career of John Sullivan, the French-Irish tenor whom he had befriended, he well knew how to play the publicist. 'From a Banned Writer to a Banned Singer' is the culmination of a persistent exercise in public relations. Distinctions, nevertheless, could be applied. 'A writer,' he remarked to Djuna Barnes, 'should never write about the extraordinary. That is for the journalist.' Such an opinion comes a little later in Joyce's life. His motive as a journalist in Trieste appears to have been that of sustained, deeply felt, and deliberate persuasion. It is the work of a political writer.

Joyce's journalism divides itself into two main periods. The first is his reviewing for the *Daily Express* during his stay in Paris in 1902 and 1903. The second comprises his articles written in Trieste between 1907 and 1912. These two periods are radically different from each other in so far as the second reverses the values of the first. The fond view of the emigrant cannot explain this difference, given that Joyce was equally an emigrant in both. The two periods are separated by the writing of 'The Dead' with its ironic portrait of that other *Daily Express* reviewer, Gabriel Conroy. When Joyce was writing 'The Dead' he was preparing his first articles for *Il Piccolo della Sera*. The differences between the two newspapers are the measure of the differences apparent in Joyce as he moves from Dublin under English rule to Trieste under Austrian rule. The *Daily Express* took as its policy the reconciliation of 'the rights and impulses of Irish nationality with the demands and obligations of imperial dominions'. It is accordingly derided by Miss Ivors as a West British rag (although the *Daily Express* was more complex than that). *Il Piccolo della Sera* was nationalist in its politics in so far as it supported the irredentist Italians of Trieste against demands and obligations imposed by their Austrian masters.

Joyce's reviews for the *Daily Express* do state a definite politics. Indeed, it is his very first review in December 1902 which is most specifically contradicted by the politics of his journalism after 1907. The object of Joyce's antipathy is William Rooney, an activist in the Gaelic League and co-founder with Arthur Griffith of Cumann na nGaedheal and of the *United Irishman*. Rooney had died at the age of 28 and Griffith did not delay in collecting, editing, introducing, and publishing his *Poems and Ballads*. On the title-page of the book Rooney is designated as *Fear na Muintire* (Man of the People), one of his pseudonyms in the *United Irishman*. Griffith asserts in the introduction that 'Rooney was the greatest Irishman I have known or whom I expect to know. I do not claim him as the greatest of Ireland's men of genius. Such a claim would be absurd. He was a man of genius, deep learning and ardent patriotism. [. . .] he had established between his soul and the soul of Ireland a perfect communion'.[2]

With these words Griffith summarizes the requirement of

---

[2] William Rooney, *Poems and Ballads*, Dublin: United Irishman ([1902]), p. x.

nationalism most troublesome to Joyce. The concept of a spirit or
soul of the nation defines cultural nativism as the only effective
means by which Ireland might survive British cultural dominance. It
is precisely this essentialism which Joyce resists. His modes of
resistance and differentiation include: a rhetoric of disdain; an eclectic aesthetic theory of distance developed in the Paris notebook; a
judgement that William Rooney's patriotic verse lacks 'even the first
quality of beauty, the quality of integrity, the quality of being
separate and whole'; an aesthetic practice of formal realism in the
composition of the 'Epiphanies'; a separation effected between
patriotism and aesthetics in the arguments of *Stephen Hero*.

This resistance to essentialism, to an identity between self and
nation, extends backwards to the considerable uncertainty of Joyce's
essay on James Clarence Mangan of 1902. Joyce is content both to
repeat John Mitchel's romantic estimate of Mangan and to detect its
inadequacy: 'Mangan is the type of his race. History encloses him so
straitly that even his fiery moments do not set him free from it'.[3]
Resistance to this mantrap is something which Joyce can reflect on
with greater equanimity in his Triestine lectures and journalism,
including his revised version of the Mangan essay of 1907. A con-
trolling theme in those Triestine writings (controlled not merely by
means of a perspective lent by distance but also through a wider
reading both of Irish history and of Italian political theory) is that of
the divided and adulterated histories of Ireland and not of her singular and virginal soul.

The flavour of Joyce's review of William Rooney can be caught in
his judgement that the poems are 'a false and mean expression of a
false and mean idea'. Even if Griffith thinks that these verses will
'enkindle the young men of Ireland to hope and activity, Mr. Rooney
has been persuaded to great evil'. It is no surprise that Griffith
struck back in the face of such abuse. He published Joyce's review in
the *United Irishman* as an *advertisement* for the book. His only
emendation was the addition of a single word. Joyce had written (in
an idiom to be taken up by Stephen Dedalus) that Rooney 'might
have written well if he had not suffered from one of those big words

---

[3] For a history of Mangan's reputation see David Lloyd, *Nationalism and Minor
Literature: James Clarence Mangan and the Emergence of Irish Cultural Nationalism*,
Berkeley: University of California Press (1988).

which make us so unhappy.' Griffith merely inserted the unspoken word: patriotism.[4]

Joyce was unabashed. His review of Stephen Gwynn's *Today and Tomorrow in Ireland* maintains his chill refusal of the patriots. However, it adds an equally chill refusal of the imperialists. 'Give Ireland the status of Canada and Mr. Gwynn becomes an Imperialist at once', comments Joyce in the first of his several condemnations (repeated, for example, in his review 'Colonial Verses') of whatever nations supported Britain in the Boer War. Gwynn occupies a position doubly removed from that of Joyce: too Gaelic for the Irish Parliamentary Party and too mild for the *United Irishman*. E. V. Longworth, the editor of the *Daily Express*, found the review negative and sought to ameliorate it by the addition of a sentence of his own: 'The volume, admirably bound and printed, is a credit to the Dublin firm [Hodges Figgis] to whose enterprise its publication is due'. Joyce was not amused and wrote to Stanislaus: 'I wrote nothing in my review [. . .] about the printing and binding. My little editor must have added that [. . .]' Joyce meditated revenge. He concluded another of his more scathing reviews, 'For the rest, the binding of the book is as ugly as one could reasonably expect.' That was the end of it. Longworth not only sacked him but also threatened to kick him down a flight of stairs. Joyce never reviewed a book again.

Joyce lost not only a convenient job at the *Daily Express* but also put at risk the sympathy of the person whose influence had secured the job for him. Lady Gregory, at Joyce's request, had asked Longworth to send him books for review in Paris. Some months later Longworth had sent Joyce a review copy of Lady Gregory's *Poets and Dreamers: Studies and Translations from the Irish*. Joyce bit the hand that fed him. Under the title 'The Soul of Ireland' (quoting Griffith in revenge for Griffith's quoting him) Joyce contrived, in the words of Buck Mulligan, to 'slate her drivel to Jaysus'. Longworth hesitated to print the review. Finally he did print it, but again with one telling addition: Joyce's initials. The normal practice of the *Daily Express* was that all reviews were anonymous, but Longworth contrived to distance himself from Joyce's opinions.

All this plays upon several ironies in 'The Dead'. It is Gabriel Conroy's initials that betray him to Miss Ivors as a writer at the

[4] *United Irishman*, 20 Dec. 1902.

Daily Express. The argument which Joyce detects in Lady Gregory, about the nobility of the West of Ireland on the one hand and the ignobility of Britain on the other, is what animates Miss Ivors' politics of nativism. Again it is the binary exclusiveness of this argument—the innocence of the Gaelic West balanced against the perfidy of Britain—which troubles Joyce and prompts him to contrast its insistence with the 'delicate scepticism' on a similar theme which distinguishes Yeats's manner in *The Celtic Twilight.*

It is in the subtext of this review of Lady Gregory that Joyce indicates his terms (dramatized in 'The Dead') for an analysis of a colonial relationship that requires more than a caricature of opposites. Lady Gregory had cited as the epigraph to her book Walt Whitman's 'A Song for Occupations':

> Will you seek afar off? you surely come back at last,
> In things best known to you finding the best, or as good as the best,
>
> In folks nearest to you finding the sweetest, strongest, lovingest,
> Happiness, knowledge, not in another place but this place, not
>   for another hour but this hour

Against this demand, paraphrased by Miss Ivors, of 'A Song for Occupations' Joyce in his review selects, with whatever irony, Whitman's 'Song of Myself':

> With music strong I come, with my cornets and drums,
> I play not marches for accepted victors only, I play marches
>   for conquer'd and slain persons.
> Have you heard that it was good to gain the day?
> I also say it is good to fall, battles are lost in the same spirit in
>   which they are won.
>
> I beat and pound for the dead,
> I blow through my embouchures my loudest and gayest for them.
>
> Vivas to those who have fail'd![5]

[5] The presence in 'The Dead' of the grand old lady of Coole Park and her *Poets and Dreamers* does not end here. One popular interpretation has reinstated her: John Huston in his film of the story allows the insertion of a translation by Lady Gregory of a Gaelic lament first published in *Poets and Dreamers*:

> You promised me a thing that was hard for you, a ship of gold under a silver mast;
> twelve towns with a market in all of them; and a fine white court by the side of the sea.
> You promised me a thing that is not possible, that you would give me gloves of the
> skin of a fish; that you would give me shoes of the skin of a bird, and a suit of the
> dearest skin in Ireland.

The reviews for the *Daily Express* reflect something of the variety in Joyce's reading at this time. Nevertheless, the blandness of much of what Longworth sent him leaves many of the reviews—whether about current fiction or about philosophy—opinionated and parasitic. Pieces on books about Aristotle, Giordano Bruno, Shakespeare, or George Meredith, disappoint. One or two pieces betray a livelier attention. The energy Joyce invests in Marcelle Tinayre's novel, *La Maison du péché*, is strongly felt, no doubt because she, with her horror of Jansenism and with 'a finer sympathy with Catholicism [. . .] a lover of life and of the fair shows of the world', helps him to measure the distance that will emerge between his own fiction and the fashionable 'politico-religious' novel of Huysmans. On another occasion, faced with a book on the Burmese by 'one of the conquerors of this people', Joyce is fascinated with the quietism of Buddhism in Burma, 'a suave philosophy which does not know that there is anything to justify tears and lamentations. The courtesies of life are not neglected; anger and rudeness of manners are condemned; the animals themselves are glad to be under masters'. Only an implicit contrast can be made between such a response to subjugation and its opposite which Joyce had questioned some months earlier in his essay on Mangan: 'An eager spirit would cast down with violence the high traditions of Mangan's race—love of sorrow for the sake of sorrow and despair and fearful menaces—but where their voice is a supreme entreaty to be borne with forbearance seems only a little grace; and what is so courteous and so patient as a great faith?'

In the face of these disparate and implicit themes of the *Daily Express* reviews the coherent intensification of purpose in the *Piccolo della Sera* articles becomes all the more evident. The editor of this newspaper, Roberto Prezioso, to whom Joyce taught English and talked about Ireland and 'the ignorance that existed about Ireland on the continent',[6] requested articles from him that would strike not

Clive Hart has commented that, although this insertion in the film is justifiable as artistic licence in its anticipating and strengthening Gretta's memory of her own youth, 'Joyce would have hated the introduction into his story of a passage of Celtic revival literature' (*Joyce, Huston, and the Making of The Dead*, Gerrards Cross: Colin Smythe (1988), 13). It is certain that Joyce, the reviewer at the *Daily Express* in 1902 and 1903, would have hated such an insertion a great deal more than Joyce, the columnist of *Il Piccolo della Sera* in 1907. And 1907 is the date of the composition of 'The Dead'.

[6] John McCourt, 'Joyce on National Deliverance: The View from 1907 Trieste,' *Prospero: Rivista di Culture Anglo-Germaniche*, 5, (1998), 27–46; this quotation from Stanislaus's Triestine diary is given on p. 37.

only at the British empire that ruled Ireland but also at the Austrian
empire that ruled Trieste. Joyce obliged. Although, in so far as these
articles educate their Triestine readers, they educate them only
about Ireland. By contrast with the contributions to the *Daily
Express* four years previously, almost all of Joyce's material on this
theme is now drawn from Arthur Griffith's writings in the *United
Irishman* and, after its demise in 1906, its successor *Sinn Féin*. The
policies of Sinn Féin appeal to Joyce for at least two reasons. First,
trade replaces violence in Griffith's policy of separation from Britain. Second, consuls in foreign ports and capitals replace the Irish
members of parliament at Westminster. Joyce agrees with Griffith
that the results might be an Ireland not only more prosperous but
also more accurately represented abroad. 'Either *Sinn Féin* or
Imperialism will conquer the present Ireland', Joyce wrote to Stanislaus. Griffith, to whom Joyce sent these Triestine articles, responded
in kind: some years later it was his newspaper alone which agreed
to print in full Joyce's open letter, 'A Curious History', about the
publishers' censorship of *Dubliners*.

Triestines grasped the intention of Joyce's journalism. Alessandro
Francini Bruni (a friend of Joyce, albeit a sceptical one) remembered
'a valuable and powerful contributor to our newspaper', whose
articles were written in his usual densely packed and vigorous style.
Though veiled in steely coldness, they are intense pieces treating
various burning issues related to his native Ireland. I recall well such
titles as "The Last Fenian", "Home Rule Comes of Age", and "Ireland at the Bar".[7] The author of *Dubliners* was faced with a double
embarrassment by the child of some of his Triestine friends, when
she mocked him to his face about Ireland. 'I felt humiliated,' he
wrote to Stanislaus, 'at the little Galatti girl sneering at my impoverished country.' Charles Joyce, in an exchange of letters with his
brother Stanislaus in 1912, recalled that when confronted by the
assertion that *Dubliners* is not a book which betters its author's country or people, 'Jim replied that he was probably the only Irishman
who wrote leading articles for the Italian press and that all his
articles in "Il Piccolo" were about Ireland and the Irish people.'

That is an exaggeration. The Triestine lectures and articles are

[7] Willard Potts (ed.), *Portraits of the Artist in Exile: Recollections of James Joyce
by Europeans*, Dublin: Wolfhound Press, Seattle: University of Washington Press
(1979), 43.

peculiarly abstract and political: whatever about Ireland, there is little in them about the Irish people. From 'Ireland: Island of Saints and Sages' to 'The City of the Tribes', and 'The Mirage of the Fisherman of Aran' Joyce's enquiries, unlike those which flourish in *A Portrait of the Artist as a Young Man*, *Dubliners*, and *Ulysses*, are peculiarly immaterialist. His hagiography is culled from the reference shelves of a library; his statistics derive from Arthur Griffith's editorials; his version of the Maamtrasna murders is the shreds of a story told by his wife Nora; an account of Galway is almost wholly lifted from the footnotes of James Hardiman's history of the city; analysis of Parnell derives from a recent biography; his account of a boat-trip to the Aran islands is again laced with citations from Hardiman and also from an official booklet on the Galway Harbour scheme. None of this diminishes either Joyce's purpose or the eloquent structure of his argument,[8] but the contrast remains apparent between his vague ignorance of the complex of social life beyond the Pale and his unparalleled intimacy within it. Despite some efforts to journey West (not to speak of North or South) Joyce remains in his own words 'The lazy Dubliner who does not travel much and knows his country only by hearsay'.

The recurrent design of Joyce's lectures and journalism at Trieste is their criss-crossing of previous antinomies such that we see a transformation of Joyce's consciousness in the collapsing inward of previously sustained stereotypes, even those of self and nation. The criss-crossing, reversing, or overcoming of opposites is explicit: the Aran storyteller is a displaced Wildean; Italy is in Galway; Ireland, both medieval and modern, is in Europe; Dante's *Divine Comedy* is a belated version of St Fursa's *Vision*; Christopher Columbus is a belated discoverer of America; Great Wyrley in England is the scene of barbaric agrarian maimings, and the crime rate in Ireland is the lowest in Europe; a seventeenth-century provincial cleric named Joyce had mapped his native city so elaborately that his text 'resembles more than anything a topographical symphony'; Dublin's Abbey Theatre emerges from its 'Day of the Rabblement' to produce a play banned in London; before Defoe there was no English literature; Oliver Cromwell was a Celt; the triumph of William of Orange

---

[8] For the rhetorical structure of Joyce's articles see Cinzia Giglioni, 'James Joyce Giornalista del "Piccolo della Sera"', unpub. thesis, Università degli Studi di Milano, 1997.

'signifies a crisis of race, an ethnic revenge' by the Germanic upon
the English: the English, 'that hybrid race which lives a tough life on
a small island in the northern sea'. Joyce's writings during his Triestine years revel in these inversions. West and East, past and present,
precursor and afterword, interchange and merge.

On their first appearance in English the articles in *Il Piccolo della
Sera* were characterized by Ellsworth Mason as displaying Joyce as
'an Irish apologist'. They have often served to identify a moment in
Joyce's life in which he appears, in Mason's words, to be 'at one with
the Citizen in Barney Kiernan's pub.'[9] Some have exaggerated the
status of the Triestine writings and their continuity with Joyce's later
fiction,[10] some have deliberately altered the texts in order to excise
Joyce's ironies and 'political incorrectness' where these prove
recalcitrant to consistent and edifying interpretation.[11] When we
notice, however, the recurrent motif of inversion with which these
Triestine writings make play, we notice that they are a part of a
process by which Joyce transforms himself between 1907 and 1914
into a comic writer. Joyce's early fiction is in a tragic mode composed
out of the inherited polarities against which he reacts. The year 1914
is the moment when he began writing *Ulysses* and proposed to publish these articles which, he insisted, 'have absolutely no literary
value.' At that moment polarities are dispersed or merged. There-
after he writes in that mode which his aesthetics since 1903 had
recommended as the higher mode of art: the comic.

A Theory of Art

The *nego* (I deny) and the *non serviam* (I shall not serve) of Stephen
Dedalus, taken with the 'scrupulous meanness' which characterizes
the style of *Dubliners*, are defining negatives peculiarly at odds with
the aesthetic committed to paper in Paris in 1903 and in Pola in 1904.
These notes on aesthetic principles are included, to some extent,
both in *Stephen Hero* and in *Portrait*. The manner in which they
appear, in particular the deflationary context of *Portrait*, renders

[9] Ellsworth Mason, 'James Joyce's Shrill Note—the *Piccolo della Sera* Articles,'
Twentieth-Century Literature, 2/3 (Oct. 1956), 115–39.
[10] See Emer Nolan, *James Joyce and Nationalism*, London: Routledge (1995), 96 ff.,
120 ff.
[11] See the excisions made by Vincent Cheng, *Joyce, Race and Empire*, Cambridge:
Cambridge University Press (1995), 5.

them subject to an increasing irony that can be understood to subvert them. The notes on aesthetics appear as a development of (even a reaction to) the conflict within the Mangan essay. Joyce wrestles with Mangan precisely because Mangan is, in the idiom of romanticism, a poet of sorrow.

The identification that Joyce expresses between himself and Mangan derives from Joyce's continuing anxiety to analyse the conflicts within successive Irish literary renascences, an analysis of which only a fragment of a lecture survives. In that fragment (here collected in translation for the first time) Joyce identifies the literary moment as an accompanying reaction to a political clash within nationalism itself, a clash between those who do and those who do not support physical force: the first is the detachment of Young Ireland from Daniel O'Connell in 1848; the second after the Fenian debacle of 1867; the third in Joyce's own day since the death of Parnell. To wrestle with Mangan is to wrestle with part of himself. To detach himself from Mangan, to define not the sorrowful but the impersonal joy of art, he needs to have recourse elsewhere: to Aristotle and Aquinas, to Coleridge and Shelley, to Flaubert and Mallarmé, to D'Annunzio and Ibsen. The use he makes of these writers, unlike the later more expansive essays on Defoe and Blake, is to extract from them the structure of an aesthetic which can tolerate simultaneously the sensitivity of the artist and the separateness of the art. This eclectic process is a deliberate opportunism announced in *Stephen Hero*: Stephen refuses 'oaths to his patria and this refusal resulted in a theory of art'.

There are two other elements which intensify Joyce's identification with and struggle against Mangan: the first is the death of Joyce's favourite brother, George, at the age of 15, weeks before Joyce delivered his paper on Mangan who had suffered the similar death of a sister; the second is Joyce's fear of being consumed by his father and Mangan's image of his own father as a human boa-constrictor. According to Stanislaus this essay 'bore witness to a determined struggle to impose an elegance of thought on the hopeless distortion of the life that surrounded him'. The family's economic plight had fully expressed itself in this most appalling waste of George's death, a moment recorded and returned to more often than any other in Joyce's 'Epiphanies'. The characterization of Mangan borders continuously on that of Stephen Dedalus. It is of

Mangan that Joyce writes: 'This purely defensive reserve is not without dangers for him, and in the end it is only his excesses that save him from indifference.'

Stanislaus informs us of how widely read Joyce was in the poets of _The Nation_ but it is Mangan, and Mangan alone, whom Joyce selects as an epitome. In this he follows a romantic fashion and displays throughout the essay the impression which inherited ideas about Mangan as a _poète maudit_ have made upon him. It is this same image of Mangan from which he wishes to free himself. Therefore, he contrasts Mangan with many other writers from Leopardi to Poe, from Goethe to Leonardo. Without jettisoning his inheritance Joyce defines Mangan's limitation: 'All his poetry remembers wrong and suffering [. . .] the poet who hurls his anger against tyrants would establish upon the future an intimate and far more cruel tyranny.' It is for this reason that the 1902 Mangan essay concludes with a cele-bration of that quality decisive also in the subsequent notes on aes-thetics: the 'life of earth' in the later Ibsen, _splendor veri_ in Plato and Flaubert, the silver laughter of the esoterics, the 'holy spirit of joy'.

Joyce's quasi-scholastic definitions of art have received some scholarly attentions. All emphasize the mixture of Thomism and nineteenth-century aestheticism through which the early Joyce, it is argued, severed art from life.[12] That severance, Umberto Eco insists, is not healed until in the act of writing _Ulysses_ Joyce confronts 'real events, nothing less than the whole of society and culture'. The materials gathered together in this volume indicate, however, that even the early Joyce had become aware of the _tactical_ usefulness of an aesthetic as a formal distance between deprivation and sorrow, between experience and violence. It is an aesthetic which explicitly resists the ineffectualness of a quasi-Pateresque aestheticism or, indeed, the dependence upon Wagner's more energetic aestheticism that had been so evident in 'Drama and Life'. Joyce's theory of art in the Paris and Pola notebooks does retain the phrase 'for an aesthetic end' and he does ignore the functionalism of Aquinas whose ideas of art have more to do with the art of farming than with the art of poetry. Joyce, however, retains the phrase 'for an aesthetic end' to

---

[12] Umberto Eco's _Opera Aperta_, Milan: Bompiani (1962) followed upon the researches of William T. Noon's _Joyce and Aquinas_, New Haven: Yale University Press (1957). Both are superseded by the broader enquiries of Jacques Aubert's _Introduction à l'esthétique de James Joyce_, Paris: Didier (1973).

define a condition of *stasis* uniquely induced by art. Art is severed from history or from 'real events' only in so far as this *stasis* is preferred by Joyce to the more common condition in which 'we cannot or will not conceive of the past in any other than its iron memorial aspect'.

The reader of Joyce's aesthetics might do worse than notice a contrast between two different sets of terms both of which describe movement: rhythm, process, or fluidity, on the one hand; excitement, desire, and appetite, on the other. Excitement, desire, and appetite are, in Joyce's terms, appropriate to both the pornographer and the didact. Rhythm, process, and fluidity are appropriate to the artist *and also* to the nature of real events. The past can be defined by Joyce as early as 1904 as 'a fluid succession of presents' and that perception itself derives from the apparently dry aesthetic of the Paris notebook:

It is false to say that sculpture, for instance, is an art of repose if by that be meant that sculpture is unassociated with movement. Sculpture is associated with movement in as much as it is rhythmic; for a work of sculptural art must be surveyed according to its rhythm and this surveying is an imaginary movement in space.

The formal realism of Joyce's 'Epiphanies', the exacting realism of *Exiles* and of *Dubliners*, the analytical realism of *Portrait*, each discovers in 'real events' a fluid shape that remains imperceptible to almost all of those who fictively live out those events. Any critique of those works which suggests, as Eco does, that they allow 'real events' to slip out of view must fail to remain persuasive. An examination of Joyce's aesthetics may, therefore, defend an assertion that Joyce is not a modernist. That assertion is based on the ways in which Joyce excludes himself from two defining elements of a modernist aesthetic: first, the abstraction of aesthetic perception into a formal, or bodiless, moment of intelligibility; second, the assumption that the world of 'real events' is a chaotic and ugly mass which only the creative artist can oppose.

The idea of aesthetic perception as a formal and ascetic moment of intelligibility, modelled upon the merely visual perception of things, is modernism's inheritance from the Enlightenment. Kant's definition of disinterested perception requires first of all the suppression of the four senses other than sight. The *Critique of*

Judgement warns that, in the face of a work of art, 'we must avoid coming too near just as much as remaining too far away'. The measure of our distance is the requirement of the eye. Kant compares the intrusive and dispersed behaviour of music to a man impolitely flourishing a perfumed handkerchief: the one, like the other, 'scatters its influence abroad to an uncalled-for extent'. Lionel Trilling, in his essay on 'The Fate of Pleasure', has argued that this modern and ascetic aesthetic derives from the Enlightenment's critique of luxury as an index of power. However, Kant's idea of taste excludes the poor as well as the rich:

Hunger is the best sauce; and people with a healthy appetite relish everything, so long as it is something they can eat. Such delight, consequently, gives no indication of taste having anything to say to the choice. Only when men have got all they want can we tell who among the crowd has taste or not.

Joyce refuses to accept this presumption that aesthetic experience is beyond the reach of those who are poor or hungry.

The aesthetic of modernism uncritically sustained Kant's immaculate concept of aesthetic perception: from Mallarmé to Yeats modernism expresses its distaste for the squalid and imbecile exteriority of an actual world and places against it the self-sufficient and isolated creation of the art-work. The purism of modernism and its origin in the Enlightenment is summarized by, for example, Ozenfant in the following terms: 'I call ART everything that takes us out of real life and tends to ELEVATE us. Such a definition would include among the major arts the art of pure speculation.' Frank Lentricchia notices that, within such an antithetical logic, if the real *could* of itself be beautiful there would be no need for the *creative* artist.[13] The vacuity of 'real events', however, constitutes the demand of pure modernism.

Joyce's opposition to these modernist values is so great as to require almost no comment. The lectures on 'Realism and Idealism in English Literature: Daniel Defoe and William Blake' dramatize that opposition. The apparent Kantianism of Joyce's notes on aesthetics has often been remarked. Joyce seems to argue both for a

---

[13] Amédé Ozenfant, *The Foundations of Modern Art*, New York: Dover Publications (1952), p. xiv; Frank Lentricchia, *After the New Criticism*, London: Athlone Press (1980), 54–5.

disinterested aesthetic perception and for that perception to be occasioned by neither need nor excess. Few things allow us more distinctly to separate Joyce from Stephen than a contrast between the profusion of the senses (oral, aural, and olfactory) in Joyce's writing and Stephen's Kantian interpretation of Aquinas' use of the word for sight, *visa*,

to cover esthetic apprehensions of all kinds, whether through sight or hearing or through any other avenue of apprehension. This word, though it is vague, is clear enough to keep away good and evil which excite desire and loathing.

Rest, arrest, and *stasis* are the consequence of this aesthetic self-consciousness. In this sense comedy is no more than the formally self-sufficient work of art (even tragedy is 'formally' comic) and the joy it occasions is no more than our correspondent perception of it. However, in Joyce's notes on aesthetics, comedy is more than that in so far as it is not self-sufficient but refers us to 'whatever is substantial or accidental, general or fortuitous, in human fortunes'. When Joyce comes to dramatize these notes in *Portrait* we cannot but notice how they are repeatedly interrupted by the substance and accidence of human fortune, of hunger and need: the results of exams, a feed of curry, the basket of a butcher's boy, the inconvenient rain of 'this miserable God-forsaken island'.

Cultural History

Joyce's analysis of previous literary revivals in Ireland is, in part, a strategy by which he comes to terms with his own priorities. In order to distance himself from the behaviour of his national contemporaries, with their projects of either a Gaelic or an Anglo-Irish literary revival, he contrived that aloof disdain which he both practised and mocked. That disdain has often been exaggerated. 'The Day of the Rabblement' may be its most public moment but even that is undermined by Joyce himself in Epiphany 17. The alert reader of Joyce's letters, the perceptive reader of *Dubliners*, the sympathetic reader of Joyce's poetry, must question the extent of that attitude of Dedalean pride. A consequence of Joyce's attitude, nevertheless, has been the impression that he was severely different from his Irish contemporaries both in his knowledge and his intentions. The individualism of the heretic seems to be Joyce's early style, but that style masks the fact that Joyce was one heretic among others.

It may therefore come as a surprise to the reader of Joyce's early writing to notice, for example, how his ideas about drama and the repertoire of European dramatists overlap with those celebrated in the pages of *Bealtaine*, the magazine of the Irish Literary Theatre, edited by W. B. Yeats. It may also come as a surprise to notice some overlap of Joyce's version of nationalism not only with that of Arthur Griffith but also with that of the magazine *Dana: An Irish Magazine of Independent Thought* to which Joyce offered his essay 'A Portrait of the Artist'. Because it quite legitimately refused that incoherent effusion (while accepting Joyce's poetry) *Dana* has been consigned to a marginal note in the *inferno* of Joyce studies. It should be noticed, however, that Joyce chose *Dana* as an appropriate journal in which to publish his essay no doubt because of his agreement with its editorial preference to 'receive and print contributions in prose and verse which are the expression of the writer's individuality'.

Joyce's cultivated isolation requires some scepticism. In his university days Joyce had represented himself as the only man for Ibsen in Dublin. He wrote to Ibsen himself that 'I have sounded your name defiantly through the college where it was either unknown or known faintly or darkly'. It is as well for Joyce's credibility that Ibsen is unlikely to have seen *Bealtaine* for there he would have discovered in its first issue of 1899 an essay by C. H. Herford, reprinted from the *Daily Express*, on 'The Scandinavian Dramatists'. Herford notices how the 'extraordinary vogue of the Norwegian drama' must be attributed to Norway's 'dramatist of extraordinary power', Henrik Ibsen. In the subsequent issue Yeats ridicules the rabble who think Ibsen 'immoral', and George Moore, wondering why *Hedda Gabler* did not cover its cost, proposes nevertheless 'a European masterpiece, like Ibsen's' should be produced each autumn. Joyce could argue that these early international ideas of the Irish theatre had not been sustained. He could also have noticed that, no less than George Bernard Shaw and William Archer in London, C. H. Herford in Dublin had anticipated his own judgements about Ibsen's corrosive and inward heroism:

The complete emancipation of the Norwegian stage may be dated from 1860. Characteristically enough, Ibsen's career as implacable critic of the

Norwegian people dates from the same year [. . .] an audacious assault upon the ruling conventions of love-making and marriage in the name of an idealism at once heroic and fanatical. Ibsen was too solitary and self-centred a nature to comply submissively with the Nationalist formula when it had ceased to be a battle-cry. The battle won, it was inevitable that he who held that 'no one is so strong as the man who stands alone,' should go his own way and work out his own ideal. An artist of the first rank can, indeed, rarely take any other course.

This could almost be Joyce, but it is in fact Herford. Both value the corrosive autonomy of the artist. Herford and Joyce are separated merely by the timetables they adopt. Herford places the emancipation of the nation prior to that of the artist. Joyce does not. His comments on Ibsen and his essay on 'Ibsen's New Drama' celebrate the late, but exclude the early, Ibsen. Herford, with others in *Bealtaine*, celebrates both.

This is not merely an exceptional coincidence of critical value between Joyce and his Dublin contemporaries. Joyce's international and cult status has concealed the ways in which his work is part of an articulate and broad debate within the Irish literary revival. Furthermore, in his political and critical writings gathered here Joyce disguises his dialogue with others who seek to open up a space within colonized nationalism. It is Joyce's style to address us as if his text were a monologue, but this is an affectation. Herford's essay is itself a contribution to a celebrated debate in the *Daily Express* between W. B. Yeats and John Eglinton (the pseudonym of W. K. Magee) about what should be the subject of a national drama—contemporary lives or epic traditions?—a debate in which the disputants focus on Ibsen's *Peer Gynt* and Wagner's *Lohengrin*.

From 'Ibsen's New Drama' and 'The Day of the Rabblement' to 'Ireland: Island of Saints and Sages' and 'A Curious History' Joyce's journalism intervenes in controversies of the day. Apart from Yeats and Joyce, the main agents of this debate were, on the one hand, D. P. Moran and his *Philosophy of Irish Ireland* (Dublin, 1905) and, on the other hand, the radical humanist John Eglinton and the socialist Frederick Ryan, co-editors of *Dana* (1904–5). Joyce's essay of 1907, 'Ireland: Island of Saints and Sages', effectively subverts the *Philosophy of Irish Ireland*:

Our civilization is an immense woven fabric in which very different elements are mixed, in which Nordic rapacity is reconciled to Roman law, and new Bourgeois conventions to the remains of a Siriac religion. In such a fabric, it is pointless searching for a thread that has remained pure, virgin and uninfluenced by other threads nearby.

John Eglinton's volume, *Bards and Saints* (Dublin, 1906), equally rejects Irish nativism. Others also sought to resist the tendencies of Irish nationalist culture to become as exclusive as D. P. Moran intended it to be. A defence of these cultural renegades—for example, Thomas Kettle, James Connolly, Thomas McDonagh, and R. W. Lynd—and a re-presentation of their work, the diversity of which was overwhelmed by Easter 1916, has been effected by Luke Gibbons.[14] At the centre of the controversy an exclusivist Irish Ireland opposed a broadening of the literary revival beyond national boundaries, the eliciting of divisions and differences within Irish life, an emphasis on its metropolitan Europeanism, an insistence on cultural criticism. The titles of several articles in *Dana* summarize its convergence with the essays and lectures of Joyce reproduced here: 'Empire and Liberty'. 'On Language and Political Ideas', 'On the Possibility of a Thought Revival in Ireland', 'The Island of Saints', 'Political and Intellectual Freedom'. *Dana* irreverently opposed what passed for religious and national sentiments. Its contributors perceived such sentiments to be a suppression of a new Irish culture that could be forceful, complex, and independent. Their venture did not thrive and the magazine ceased publication within a year.

Amid these emancipatory endeavors there remains one important difference between Joyce and the editors of *Dana*, and it can be detected even in the magazine's first editorial:

Man and nature—what more do we want? The difficulty is to begin: and to make a beginning is especially difficult in a country like Ireland, where our bards and prophets have never learned to deal directly and as men with the elements of human nature, and to dispense with traditional methods and traditional themes.

Joyce's writing, in particular the discursive writing collected in this volume, shares some of its intentions with *Dana*'s enlightenment project but remains different from it to the degree that Joyce is a perverse traditionalist. Dominic Manganiello has demonstrated how

---

[14] Seamus Deane (ed.), *The Field Day Anthology of Irish Writing*, 3 vols., Derry: Field Day Publications (1991), ii. 950–1020.

Italian socialist and anarchist writers inform Joyce's analysis of social and institutional life.[15] It remains true, however, that Joyce in his essays and lectures about Ireland does not allow *their* analysis to constitute the terms of *his* analysis, an analysis in terms of nation and empire. It remains equally true that, while he participates in the emancipatory project of such Dublin contemporaries as John Eglinton and Frederick Ryan, Joyce refuses their enlightenment and modernist intention 'to dispense with traditional methods and traditional themes'. His minor and his major writings remain immersed in those methods and themes. The historiographer Carl Schorske has recently investigated the changing place of history in nineteenth- and twentieth-century cultures. He identifies the modernist way of thinking *without* history and the nineteenth-century way of thinking *with* history as different ways of trying to address the problems of modernity.[16] Were we to accept this distinction we would discover in Joyce something of a nineteenth-century (rather than a wholly modernist) frame of mind.

Thinking *with* history also placed Joyce in an uneasy relationship with his Triestine audience. Richard Ellmann has indicated that the Triestines who attended Joyce's lecture at the Università Popolare were modernist, anti-clerical, and agnostic. A careful reading of Joyce's hesitations with this audience suggests that Ellmann was right. For Joyce cautiously and wittily persuades his audience that, although in 'Ireland, Island of Saints and Sages' he is defending the dignity of early Christian Ireland and her ecclesiastical history, he is not naïve in his judgement of either its historical reality or its sentimental value. He refuses, nevertheless, to jettison it. He addresses his Triestine audience as 'you [who have been] fed over the past years on a diet of scepticism'. One aspect of that scepticism had been the new history of Guglielmo Ferrero whose *Grandezza e Decadenza di Roma* had introduced a journalistic and irreverent approach to the past, in opposition to German idealist historiography. Ferrero had no time for the great-man-decisive-crisis view of history, no time for history as high politics or as a Hegelian–Carlylean conflict of destiny and will. Manners, needs, luxuries, changes in the standard of

[15] *Joyce's Politics*, London: Routledge & Kegan Paul (1980), 67–114.
[16] *Thinking with History: Explorations in the Passage to Modernism*, Princeton: Princeton University Press (1998).

living—these modes of explanation interested Ferrero. We know (not least from recent work such as that of Robert Spoo[17]) how indebted to Ferrero's materialist history Joyce was. But we know too that, for good tactical reasons, he did not wish in his lecture on the island of saints and sages to indulge Ferrero's disrespectful style towards a lost *grandezza d'Irlanda* (if not its present *decadenza*). Therefore, Joyce tells his audience that he is up to speed with his reading of Ferrero, but that the evidence from the reviled German historians (whatever their inaccuracies about early Rome) cannot be denied to early medieval Ireland, 'when the island was a true centre of intellectualism and sanctity, that spread its culture and stimulating energy throughout the continent.'

In his Triestine writings, Joyce thinks *with* history. That way of thinking is an old-fashioned caution to several of his Dublin, no less than European, contemporaries. His practice is neither to reverence the past nor to eliminate its complexity. Sporting with the past, abusing it, always implicated in it, Joyce's major writings, facilitated by the minor writings gathered here, refuse to jettison history while they release the present from its grip.

[17] *James Joyce and the Language of History*, New York: Oxford University Press (1994), 27–37.

TRANSLATOR'S INTRODUCTION

The translations of James Joyce's Italian writings collected in this volume are new translations and, therefore, it is as well to make some brief observations on the peculiarities of Joyce's Italian and the special problems his use of that language entails. In 1907 Joyce was writing an Italian that was often ungrammatical and clumsy. By 1909, however, and particularly by 1912 he had become a reasonably accomplished stylist in the language. The translator, therefore, is faced with the task of rendering works of varying quality and proficiency into a single, constant, and fluent style. Yet, in a sense, efforts at consistency are misplaced, for the reader naturally loses all sense of the organic development of Joyce's style from 1907 to 1912, though he is at least spared Joyce's linguistic blunders. Further, where a translator rightly feels that his English prose cannot match Joyce's, he might console himself none the less that he papers over the many grammatical, idiomatic, and stylistic cracks in Joyce's early Italian.

The lectures to the Università Popolare of Trieste pose another problem. Joyce did not trust his Italian sufficiently to deliver his lectures from notes, and so he wrote the texts out in full. Yet they remain lectures, not finished essays. The mode of argument and the overall flow of these pieces are more suited to the spoken than to the written word. Allowances have to be made for this in a written translation and I have occasionally changed the punctuation or order where sense demands.

It would have been at best pointless, and at worst irritating, for the reader had I remarked upon every oddity of syntax, spelling, grammar, and vocabulary in the early lectures or the articles in *Il Piccolo della Sera*. Joyce's Italian in 1907 was faulty enough, but no more so than might be expected of any young student of a foreign language. What is interesting, however, is the nature of some of his errors; Joyce had a tendency to use Dantesque archaicisms and Latinate vocabulary. Whether or not he was aware of the odd effects in his Italian, the original Italian texts provide an interesting insight into the literary and semantic influences behind his work. Unfortunately, the idiosyncrasies and archaicisms, whether intentional or not, are

rendered invisible in the translation. In short, some of the strange
flavour of Joyce's Italian prose has unavoidably been lost.

The Mangan lecture brings these translation problems to a head.
In the original paper on Mangan delivered in 1902 to the University
College Literary and Historical Society and published in the University magazine, *St Stephen's*, Joyce used a self-conscious, over-
wrought style that is influenced by Walter Pater. By 1907, when he
intended to deliver his lecture on the same subject before an Italian
audience (a quixotic enough gesture in itself), his view of Mangan
had altered. The first part of the lecture is more or less new and
reflects the modification of his opinion of Mangan since his original
paper in 1902. He is now more critical of his subject, more incisive
and lucid in his expression. This is not simply because he has moved
on from the high-flown rhetoric of youth, but because he is more
carefully composing and expressing his thoughts in a foreign tongue.

The second part of the lecture, however, is for the most part lifted
directly from his 1902 version. In this case, then, Joyce is translating
his own work. This leads to three distinct problems. In the first
place, there is the inevitable distortion that occurs in translating
one's thoughts into a foreign language. The influence of Joyce's
mother-tongue occasionally overwhelms his ear for Italian idiom. In
other words, his lecture sounds like what it is, a translation. The
second problem is that, as anyone familiar with the 1902 paper will
know, the original English is itself particularly ornate and studied.
Joyce seems to have made few allowances for this when he came to
revise it in 1907. The third problem is that there is only one solution
to the other two—namely, to return to the 1902 text wherever Joyce
is simply translating rather than modifying. Although there is no
alternative to this, it is an unsatisfactory solution in that it fails to
reflect the flaws of Joyce's Italian. It is not that I wish to underline
his failings; indeed, as I have already said, my practice in these translations has been to eliminate petty errors without even footnoting
them. Readers of the early 1902 paper on Mangan may enjoy the
eloquence and pomp of Joyce's Pateresque periods where the Italian
audience hear only an eccentric and strangely flawed (but not always
inelegant) Italian. Conversely, however, where Joyce interrupts his
earlier paper to add new observations or wry comments, an Italian
might notice a more natural flow to the style where an English reader
will register only a sudden simplification or even deterioration. So

the consequence of returning to the original has been to create a translation that is rather like a photographic negative of the original. My aim has been to disguise the fine shift in style as much as possible. On the other hand I did not attempt at any point to imitate the style of Joyce's original.

Finally, the articles in *Il Piccolo della Sera* are notably simpler and more accessible than the lectures, probably because they were written for a more general audience. Here Joyce adopts a more direct style, shorter periods, and simpler concepts. All the same, this has not prevented him from his usual allusiveness or from sprinkling his articles with the occasional Latin word or phrase. In the case of 'The City of the Tribes', the article ends on a strange and ambiguous note, to some extent reminiscent of the way the stories in *Dubliners* come to a close. For the most part, however, the articles are direct, polemical, and even journalistic. I do not think they require further comment.

NOTE ON THE TEXTS

The manuscripts and typescripts of a large proportion of the texts collected here can be located in *The James Joyce Archive*, edited by Michael Groden and others (63 volumes, New York, 1977–80). Previous editions of these texts include *The Critical Writings of James Joyce* edited by Ellsworth Mason and Richard Ellmann (New York: Viking, 1959); *Scritti Italiani*, edited by Giorgio Melchiori and others (Milan: Mondadori, 1979); *James Joyce: Œuvres*, vol. 1, edited by Jacques Aubert (Paris: Gallimard, 1982); *Daniel Defoe by James Joyce*, edited by Joseph Prestcott, *University of Buffalo Studies*, (1964); *James Joyce in Padua*, edited by Louis Berrone (New York: Random House, 1977). Corrections have silently been made to some errors of transcription that appear in earlier editions; inconsistent spellings and punctuation have been retained. I am indebted to previous editors for certain annotations and for the location of non-manuscript sources. My own researches have been assisted by many who offered information or responded to enquiries: Giorgio Melchiori, Louis Dupré, Fritz Senn, John McCourt, Kevin Whelan, Aoife Feeney, Herman Rasche, Patrick Sheeran, Máirín Ní Dhonnchadha, Frank Callanan, Riana O'Dwyer, John O'Hanlon, Seamus Deane, Donncha O hAodha, Gearóid O Tuathaigh, Colm Luibhéid, John O'Meara, Pascale McGarry, Carla de Petris, Seán Ryder, Una Bradley. I wish to thank Donna Monroe for her invaluable assistance. Translations from the Italian are by Conor Deane; all other translations are my own. I am grateful to the library staff of National University of Ireland, Galway, University College Dublin, the National Library of Ireland, Trinity College Dublin, Yale University, Cornell University, University of Buffalo, and University of Padua. I acknowledge the generous support of the Millennium Research Fund of the National University of Ireland, Galway.

The editor and publishers would like to thank the following institutions for permission to reproduce copyright material in their possession: Cornell University Library (Department of Rare Books); University of Buffalo (The Poetry/Rare Books Collection); Yale University Library (The Beinecke Rare Book and Manuscript Library).

SELECT BIBLIOGRAPHY

Bibliography

Cohn, Alan M., and Kain, Richard M. (comps.), 'Supplemental James
Joyce Checklist' (now 'Current James Joyce Checklist'), *James Joyce
Quarterley*, 1– (1964–).

Deming, Robert H. (ed.), *A Bibliography of James Joyce Studies* (1964; 2nd
edn., Boston: Hall, 1977).

Slocum, John J., and Cahoon, Herbert, *A Bibliography of James Joyce
(1882–1941)* (1953: repr. Westport, Conn.: Greenwood Press, 1971).

Biography

Ellmann, Richard, *James Joyce* (1959; rev. edn. 1982; corr. New York:
Oxford University Press, 1983). (This is *the* landmark biography,
though it can usefully be supplemented by the other works in the
following list.)

Banta, Melissa, and Silverman, Oscar (eds.), *James Joyce's Letters to Sylvia
Beach* (Bloomington, Ind.: Indiana University Press, 1987).

Beach, Sylvia, *Shakespeare and Company* (1959; repr. London: Plantin,
1987).

Gorman, Herbert, *James Joyce: A Definitive Biography* (1939; repr.
London: John Lane and Bodley Head, 1941).

Joyce, Stanislaus, *The Complete Dublin Diary of Stanislaus Joyce* (Ithaca,
NY: Cornell University Press, 1971).

Joyce, Stanislaus, *My Brother's Keeper: James Joyce's Early Years*, ed.
Richard Ellmann (London: Faber & Faber, 1958).

Lidderdale, Jane, and Nicholson, Mary, *Dear Miss Weaver: Harriet Shaw
Weaver, 1876–1961* (New York: Viking, 1970).

Maddox, Brenda, *Nora: A Biography of Nora Joyce* (London: Hamish
Hamilton, 1988).

O Laoi, Pádhraic, *Nora Barnacle Joyce: A Portrait* (Galway: Kennys,
1983).

Potts, Willard (ed.), *Portraits of the Artist in Exile: Recollections of James
Joyce by Europeans* (1979; repr. New York: Harcourt Brace, 1986).

Pound, Ezra, *Pound/Joyce: The Letters of Ezra Pound to James Joyce, with
Pound's Essays on Joyce*, ed. Forrest Read (1967; repr. London: Faber &
Faber, 1968).

Power, Arthur, *Conversations with James Joyce*, ed. Clive Hart (1974; repr.
Chicago: University of Chicago Press, 1982).

Editions and Other Works

Dubliners, with Introduction and Notes by Terence Brown (Harmondsworth: Penguin Books, 1992).

Finnegans Wake (London: Faber, New York: Viking, 1939).

The Letters of James Joyce, vol. i ed. Stuart Gilbert (London: Faber, New York: Viking, 1957, revised 1966); vols. ii and iii ed. Richard Ellmann (London: Faber, New York: Viking, 1966).

Poems and Exiles, ed. J. C. C. Mays (Harmondsworth: Penguin Books, 1992).

A Portrait of the Artist as a Young Man, ed. Chester G. Anderson and Richard Ellmann (New York: Viking, 1964).

Stephen Hero, ed. with Introduction by Theodore Spencer, revised edition with additional material and Foreword by John J. Slocum and Herbert Cahoon (London: Cape, 1956).

Ulysses, ed. Hans Walter Gabler and others (Harmondsworth: Penguin Books, 1986).

James Joyce: Poems and Shorter Writings, ed. Richard Ellmann, A. Walton Litz, and John Whittier-Ferguson (London: Faber & Faber, 1991).

Selected Letters of James Joyce, ed. Richard Ellmann (New York: Viking, 1975).

The Critical Writings of James Joyce, ed. Ellsworth Mason and Richard Ellmann (London: Faber & Faber, 1959).

The James Joyce Archive, ed. Michael Groden (63 vols.; New York and London: Garland, 1977–80).

Groden, Michael (ed.), *James Joyce's Manuscripts: An Index to the James Joyce Archive* (New York and London: Garland, 1980).

Criticism and Related Writings

Attridge, Derek, *Peculiar Language: Literature as Difference from the Renaissance to James Joyce* (London: Methuen, 1988).

—— (ed.), *The Cambridge Companion to James Joyce* (Cambridge: Cambridge University Press, 1990).

—— and Ferrer, Daniel (eds.), *Post-Structuralist Joyce: Essays from the French* (Cambridge: Cambridge University Press, 1984).

Aubert, Jacques, *Introduction à l'esthétique de James Joyce* (Paris: Didier, 1973).

—— *The Aesthetics of James Joyce* (Baltimore: Johns Hopkins University Press, 1992).

—— and Jolas, M., *Joyce and Paris*, Papers from the Fifth International James Joyce Symposium (Paris: Editions du CNRS, 1979).

Beja, Morris, *et al.*, (eds.), *James Joyce: The Centennial Symposium* (Urbana and Chigaco: University of Illinios Press, 1986).

Borach, Georges, 'Conversations with James Joyce', trans. and ed. Joseph Prescott, *College English*, 15 (Mar. 1954), 325–7.

Bowen, Zack, and Carens, James F. (eds.), *A Companion to Joyce Studies* (Westport, Conn., and London: Greenwood Press, 1984).

Brown, Malcolm, *The Politics of Irish Literature: From Thomas Davis to W. B. Yeats* (London: George Allen & Unwin, 1972).

Brown, Richard, *James Joyce and Sexuality* (Cambridge: Cambridge University Press, 1985).

Budgen, Frank, *James Joyce and the Making of 'Ulysses'* (1934; reissued London: Oxford University Press, 1972).

Cheng, Vincent, *Joyce, Race and Empire* (Cambridge: Cambridge University Press, 1995).

Cixous, Hélène, *The Exile of James Joyce* (1968), trans. Sally A. J. Purcell (New York: David Lewis, 1972).

Clery, Arthur, *Dublin Essays* (Dublin: Maunsel, 1919).

Deane, Seamus, *Celtic Revivals: Essays in Modern Irish Literature* (London: Faber, 1985).

—— 'Joyce and Nationalism', in Colin MacCabe (ed.) *James Joyce: New Perspectives* (London: Harvester, 1982).

Deming, Robert H. (ed.), *James Joyce: The Critical Heritage* (2 vols.; London: Routledge & Kegan Paul, 1970).

Eco, Umberto, *Opera Operta* (Milan: Bompiani, 1962).

—— *The Open Work* (Cambridge, Mass.: Harvard University Press, 1989).

—— *The Middle Ages of James Joyce* (London: Hutchinson Radius, 1989).

Eglinton, John (W. K. Magee), *Bards and Saints* (Dublin: Maunsel, 1906).

—— and Ryan, Frederick (eds.), *Dana: An Irish Magazine of Independent Thought* (May 1904–April 1905; repr. New York: Lemma Publishing Corporation, 1970).

Ellmann, Richard, *The Consciousness of Joyce* (London: Faber, 1977).

Flood, Jeanne A., 'Joyce and the Maamtrasna Murders', *James Joyce Quarterly*, 28/4 (Summer 1991), 879–88.

Garvin, John, *James Joyce's Disunited Kingdom and the Irish Dimension* (Dublin: Gill & Macmillan, 1976).

Gibbons, Luke, 'Constructing the Canon: Versions of National Identity', in Seamus Deane (ed.), *The Field Day Anthology of Irish Writing*, 3 vols. (Derry: Field Day Publications, 1991), ii. 950–1020.

Giglioni, Cinzia, 'James Joyce Giornalista del "Piccolo della Sera"', unpub. thesis, Università degli Studi di Milano, 1997.

Goldman, Arnold, *The Joyce Paradox: Form and Freedom in his Fiction* (London: Routledge & Kegan Paul, 1966).

Hart, Clive, *Joyce, Huston, and the Making of The Dead* (Gerrards Cross: Colin Smythe, 1988).

Herr, Cheryl, *Joyce's Anatomy of Culture* (Urbana and Chicago: University of Illinois Press, 1986).

Jameson, Fredric, '*Ulysses* in History', in W. J. McCormack and Alistair Stead (eds.), *James Joyce and Modern Literature* (London: Routledge & Kegan Paul, 1982).

Kelly, John, 'The Fall of Parnell and the Rise of Irish Literature: An Investigation', *Anglo-Irish Studies*, 2 (1976), 1–23.

Kenner, Hugh, *Dublin's Joyce* (1956; repr. New York: Columbia University Press, 1987).

—— *Joyce's Voices* (Berkeley and Los Angeles: University of California Press, 1978).

Kershner, R. B., *Joyce, Bakhtin, and Popular Literature* (Chapel Hill: University of North Carolina Press, 1989).

Leerssen, Joep, *Remembrance and Imagination: Patterns in the Historical and Literary Representation of Ireland in the Nineteenth Century* (Cork: Cork University Press, 1996).

—— '1798: The Recurrence of Violence and Two Conceptualizations of History', *Irish Review*, 22 (Summer 1998), 37–45.

Lentricchia, Frank, *After the New Criticism* (London: Athlone Press, 1980).

Levin, Harry, *James Joyce: A Critical Introduction* (1941; rev. edn. New York: New Directions, 1960).

Lloyd, David, *Nationalism and Minor Literature: James Clarence Mangan and the Emergence of Irish Cultural Nationalism* (Berkeley: University of California Press, 1988).

Lyons, F. S. L., *Culture and Anarchy in Ireland 1890–1939* (Oxford: Clarendon Press, 1979).

MacCabe, Colin, *James Joyce and the Revolution of the Word* (London: Macmillan, 1978).

—— (ed.), *James Joyce: New Perspectives* (Brighton: Harvester Press, 1982).

McCourt, John, 'Joyce on National Deliverance: The View from 1907 Trieste', *Prospero: rivista di culture anglo-germaniche*, 5 (Trieste, 1998), 27–48.

MacDonagh, Oliver, *States of Mind: A Study of Anglo-Irish Conflict 1780–1980* (London: George Allen & Unwin, 1983).

Manganiello, Dominic, *Joyce's Politics* (London: Routledge & Kegan Paul, 1980).

—— 'The Politics of the Unpolitical in Joyce's Fictions', *James Joyce Quarterly*, 29/2 (Winter 1992), 241–58.

Mason, Ellsworth, 'James Joyce's Shrill Note—the *Piccolo della Sera* Articles', *Twentieth-Century Literature*, 2/3 (Oct. 1956), 115–39.

Melchiori, Giorgio, 'The Language of Politics and the Politics of Language', *James Joyce Broadsheet*, 4 (Feb. 1981), 1.

—— (ed.), *Joyce in Rome: The Genesis of 'Ulysses'* (Rome: Bulzoni, 1984).

Moran, D. P., *The Philosophy of Irish Ireland* (Dublin: James Duffy & Co., 1905).

Nadel, Ira B., *Joyce and the Jews: Culture and Texts* (Iowa City: University of Iowa Press, 1989).

Nolan, Emer, *James Joyce and Nationalism* (London: Routledge, 1995).

Noon, William T., *Joyce and Aquinas* (New Haven: Yale University Press, 1957).

Ozenfant, Amédé, *The Foundations of Modern Art*, trans. John Rodker (New York: Dover Publications, 1952).

Parrinder, Patrick, *James Joyce* (Cambridge: Cambridge University Press, 1984).

Paseta, Senia, *Before the Revolution: Nationalism, Social Change and Ireland's Catholic Élite, 1879–1922* (Cork: Cork University Press, 1999).

Peake, C. H., *James Joyce: The Citizen and the Artist* (London: Edward Arnold, 1977).

Platt, L. H., 'Joyce and the Anglo-Irish Revival: The Triestine Lectures', *James Joyce Quarterly*, 29/2 (Winter 1992), 262–4.

Rabaté, Jean-Michel, *Joyce Upon the Void: The Genesis of Doubt* (New York: St Martin's Press, 1991).

Renan, Ernest, *The Poetry of the Celtic Races, and Other Studies* (1896; reissued New York: Kennikat Press, 1970).

Riquelme, John Paul, *Teller and Tale in Joyce's Fiction: Oscillating Perspectives* (Baltimore and London: Johns Hopkins University Press, 1983).

Schorske, Carl, *Thinking with History: Explorations in the Passage to Modernism* (Princeton: Princeton University Press, 1998).

Scott, Bonnie Kime, *Joyce and Feminism* (Brighton: Harvester, 1984).

Senn, Fritz, 'History as Text in Reverse', *James Joyce Quarterly*, 28/4 (Summer 1991), 765–75.

—— *Nichts Gegen Joyce: Joyce Against Nothing*, ed. Franz Cavigelli (Zurich: Haffmans Verlag, 1983).

—— *Joyce's Dislocations: Essays on Reading as Translation*, ed. John Paul Riquelme (Baltimore and London: Johns Hopkins University Press, 1984).

Spoo, Robert, *James Joyce and the Language of History* (New York: Oxford University Press, 1994).

Valente, Joseph, *James Joyce and the Problem of Justice* (Cambridge: Cambridge University Press, 1995).

Further Reading in Oxford World's Classics

James Joyce, *Ulysses*, ed. Jeri Johnson.
—— *A Portrait of the Artist as a Young Man*, ed. Jeri Johnson.
—— *Dubliners*, ed. Jeri Johnson.
Empire Writing: An Anthology of Colonial Literature, 1870–1918, ed. Elleke Boehmer.
J. M. Synge, *The Playboy of the Western World and Other Plays*, ed. Ann Saddlemyer.

A CHRONOLOGY OF JAMES JOYCE

1882 (2 Feb.) Born James Augustine Joyce, eldest surviving son of John Stanislaus Joyce ('John'), a Collector of Rates, and Mary Jane ('May') Joyce née Murray, at 41 Brighton Square West, Rathgar, Dublin. (May) Phoenix Park murders. (Aug.) Maamtrasna murders. (Dec.) Execution of Myles Joyce.

1884 First of many family moves, to 23 Castlewood Avenue, Rathmines, Dublin. (17 Dec.) John Stanislaus Joyce ('Stanislaus') born.

1886 Gladstone's Home Rule bill defeated.

1887 Family (now four children: three boys, one girl) moves to 1 Martello Terrace, Bray, south of Kingstown (now Dun Laoghaire). JJ's uncle, William O'Connell, moves in with family, as does Mrs 'Dante' Hearn Conway, who is to act as a governess.

1888 (1 Sept.) JJ enrols at Clongowes Wood College, near Sallins, County Kildare, a Jesuit boys' school.

1889 After his first communion, JJ becomes altar boy. (At his later confirmation, also at Clongowes, JJ takes 'Aloysius' as his saint's name.) Given four strikes on the back of the hand with a pandybat for use of 'vulgar language'. (24 Dec.) Captain O'Shea files for divorce from Katherine ('Kitty') O'Shea on grounds of her adultery with Charles Stewart Parnell, MP, leader of the Irish Home Rule Party.

1890 Parnell ousted as leader of Home Rule Party.

1891 (June) JJ removed from Clongowes as family finances fade. John Joyce loses job as Rates Collector (pensioned off at age of 42). (6 Oct.) Parnell dies. JJ writes 'Et Tu, Healy', identifying Tim Healy, Parnell's lieutenant, with Brutus and indicting Ireland's rejection of Parnell as treachery.

1892 Family (now eight children: four boys, four girls) moves to Blackrock, then into central Dublin.

1893 Children sent to the Christian Brothers School on North Richmond Street. (6 Apr.) JJ and his brothers enter Belvedere College, Jesuit boys' day-school, fees having been waived. Last Joyce child born (family now four boys, six girls). Gaelic League founded.

1894 JJ travels to Cork with John Joyce, who is disposing of the last of the family's Cork properties. Family moves to Drumcondra. JJ wins first of many Exhibitions for excellence in state examinations. (Summer) Trip to Glasgow with John Joyce. Family moves again, to

North Richmond Street. JJ reads Lamb's *Adventures of Ulysses* and writes theme on Ulysses as 'My Favourite Hero'.

1895 JJ enters the Sodality of the Blessed Virgin Mary.

1896 JJ chosen prefect of the Sodality, attends retreat, later claims to have begun his 'sexual life' in this, his fourteenth year.

1897 JJ wins prize for best English composition in Ireland for his age group.

1898 JJ begins to read Ibsen, attends and reviews plays. Leaves Belvedere. (Sept.) Enters Royal University (now University College, Dublin). Writes essay on subjugation. Family continues to move from house to house.

1899 JJ writes essay on 'The Study of Languages'. (8 May) Attends première of Yeats's *The Countess Cathleen*, refuses to sign students' letter of protest to the *Freeman's Journal* against the play. (Sept.) Writes essay on Munkácsy's *Ecce Homo* on exhibition at the Royal Hibernian Academy.

1900 (20 Jan.) JJ delivers paper 'Drama and Life' before the university Literary and Historical Society. (1 Apr.) JJ's review of Ibsen's *When We Dead Awaken*, 'Ibsen's New Drama', published in *Fortnightly Review*. Ibsen responds with pleasure. JJ visits London, attends Music Hall, writes prose and verse plays, poems, begins to keep 'epiphany' notebook.

1901 JJ writes 'The Day of the Rabblement', an attack on the Irish Literary Theatre and its narrow nationalism, and publishes it privately in a pamphlet with Francis Skeffington's essay arguing for equality for women.

1902 (Feb.) JJ delivers paper to Literary and Historical Society praising the Irish poet James Clarence Mangan and advocating literature as 'the continual affirmation of the spirit'. (Mar.) JJ's brother George dies. JJ leaves university and registers for the Royal University Medical School. (Oct.) Meets Yeats and, later, Lady Gregory. Leaves Medical School and (1 Dec.) departs for Paris, ostensibly to study medicine. Passes through London where Yeats introduces him to Arthur Symons. Reviews books for Dublin *Daily Express*. Returns to Dublin for Christmas.

1903 JJ meets Oliver St John Gogarty. (17 Jan.) Returns to Paris by way of London. Giving up on medical school, spends days in Bibliothèque Nationale, nights in Bibliothèque Sainte-Geneviève. Writes notes on aesthetics. (Mar.) Meets Synge. (11 Apr.) Returns to Dublin due to mother's illness; she dies (13 Aug.). JJ continues to contribute short pieces to the *Daily Express*, the *Irish Times*, and the *Speaker*.

1904 JJ writes essay 'A Portrait of the Artist', first seeds of later novel *A Portrait of the Artist as a Young Man*. Begins writing stories, which will become *Dubliners*, and publishes three in the *Irish Homestead*. Begins work on *Stephen Hero*. Writes and publishes poems which will be collected later as *Chamber Music*. Leaves the family home, takes rooms in Dublin, teaches at Clifton School, Dalkey. Joins Gogarty (for one week) in the Martello Tower, Sandycove. Writes 'The Holy Office', a satirical poem about the contemporary Dublin literary scene. (10 June) Meets Nora Barnacle and on 16 June first goes out with her. (8 Oct.) JJ and Nora leave Dublin together for the Continent, first to Zurich, then to job with the Berlitz School in Pola where JJ will teach English. Writes further notes on aesthetics.

1905 JJ and Nora move to Trieste, where JJ teaches English for Berlitz School. (27 July) Son, Giorgio, born. *Chamber Music* submitted to (and refused by) four publishers in Dublin and London. First version of *Dubliners* submitted to Grant Richards, Dublin publisher, who contracts to publish it, but later withdraws. Stanislaus moves to Trieste (where he stays until his death in 1955).

1906 (July) Family moves to Rome where JJ accepts abortive job in bank. (30 Sept.) JJ writes to Stanislaus, 'I have a new story for Dubliners in my head. It deals with Mr. Hunter'; later (13 Nov.) identifies it: 'I thought of beginning my story *Ulysses*.' Begins 'The Dead' instead.

1907 (Jan.) Riots at the Abbey Theatre over J. M. Synge's *The Playboy of the Western World*. (7 Feb.) JJ writes to Stanislaus: '*Ulysses* never got any forrader than the title.' (Mar.) Family returns to Trieste. Death of John O'Leary, the subject of the first article JJ writes for *Il Piccolo della Sera* on Ireland. (Apr.) Lectures on 'Ireland, Island of Saints and Sages', at the Università del Popolare in Trieste. (May) Elkin Matthews (London) publishes *Chamber Music*. First essay on Home Rule published in *Il Piccolo della Sera*. (July) JJ contracts rheumatic fever and is hospitalized; beginnings of his eye troubles. (26 July) Daughter, Lucia, born. Scraps the 26 chapters of *Stephen Hero* and begins to rework entirely as *Portrait*. (Sept.) Essay on Maamtrasna murders, 'Ireland at the Bar', published in *Il Piccolo della Sera*. Completes 'The Dead'.

1908 JJ completes first three chapters of *Portrait*, but then sets them aside. Family troubles and continued poverty.

1909 Friendship with Ettore Schmitz (Italian author 'Italo Svevo'), whose high opinion of *Portrait* fragments spurred JJ to revise and continue. (Mar.) JJ writes article on Oscar Wilde for *Il Piccolo della Sera*. (Apr.) Revised *Dubliners* sent to Maunsel & Co. in Dublin. (July) JJ and Giorgio go to Dublin and Galway. JJ signs contract with Maunsel & Co. and meets old acquaintances. One, Vincent Cosgrave, who had also wooed Nora, claimed that she had been unfaithful to JJ with him. JJ's '1909 Letters' to Nora written as result, first, of his doubting and, later, of his reconciliation with, her. (Sept.) Essay on Bernard Shaw appears in *Il Piccolo della Sera*. JJ, Giorgio, and JJ's sister Eva return to Trieste. (Oct.) JJ returns to Dublin as agent for Triestine consortium to open first cinema in Dublin. (20 Dec.) The 'Volta' cinema opens.

1910 (2 Jan.) JJ returns to Trieste with another sister, Eileen. 'Volta' fails. Publication of *Dubliners* delayed. (Dec.) Second essay on Home Rule published in *Il Piccolo della Sera*.

1911 Continuing delay of *Dubliners*. JJ writes open letter, published in Arthur Griffiths's *Sinn Féin*, complaining of his mistreatment at the hands of his publishers. Home Rule passed in House of Commons, defeated in Lords.

1912 JJ lectures on Blake and Defoe at the Università Popolare. (Apr.) For the purpose of taking Italian state examinations for teachers at Padua JJ writes essays on Dickens and on the Renaissance. (May) Essay on Parnell published in *Il Piccolo della Sera*. Nora and Lucia travel to Ireland, followed quickly by JJ and Giorgio. (JJ's last trip to Ireland.) (Aug., Sept.) Essays on Galway, 'The City of the Tribes' and 'The Mirage of the Fisherman of Aran', published in *Il Piccolo della Sera*. Essay on 'Politics and Cattle Disease' published in *Freeman's Journal*. Negotiations with Maunsel & Co. finally fail; proofs destroyed. JJ writes broadside 'Gas from a Burner' in response and publishes it on his return to Trieste (15 Sept.). JJ begins his (twelve) *Hamlet* lectures at the Università. Begins writing poetry again.

1913 JJ continues *Hamlet* lectures. Grant Richards again shows interest in *Dubliners*. Ezra Pound writes (having been told by Yeats of JJ).

1914 JJ revises *Portrait*, sends first chapter and *Dubliners* to Pound. Pound asks to publish poem ('I Hear an Army') in Imagist anthology in USA, and begins serialization of *Portrait* (beginning 2 Feb.) in the *Egoist* (originally called the *New Freewoman* and edited by

Dora Marsden and Rebecca West). Under demand of publishing, JJ finishes last two chapters. (June) Harriet Shaw Weaver takes over editorship of *Egoist*. (15 June) Grant Richards publishes *Dubliners*. (Aug.) World War I begins. JJ writes *Giacomo Joyce*. (Nov.) JJ drafts notes for *Exiles*. Begins *Ulysses*.

1915 (9 Jan.) Stanislaus arrested, interned in Austrian detention centre for remainder of war. *Exiles* completed. (15 May) Italy enters war. (June) In return for a pledge of neutrality, Joyce family allowed to leave Austrian Trieste and move to neutral Swiss Zurich. Through the intercession of Yeats and Pound, JJ awarded a grant (£75) from the Royal Literary Fund. *Ulysses* in progress.

1916 Easter Rising in Dublin. (Aug.) JJ granted £100 from the British Civil List (again at Pound's instigation). (Dec.) B. W. Huebsch (New York) publishes *Dubliners* and *Portrait*. JJ writes 'A Notebook of Dreams'—record of Nora's dreams with JJ's interpretations.

1917 (Feb.) English edition of *Portrait* published by Egoist Press. JJ suffers eye troubles which lead to his first eye operation (Aug.). (Feb.) Harriet Shaw Weaver begins anonymous benefaction to JJ; her financial support will continue until (and beyond) JJ's death (when she pays for his funeral). (Oct.) Family goes to Locarno for winter. *Ulysses* continues; first three chapters ('Telemachia') written and sent to Pound. JJ contracts with Weaver to publish *Ulysses* serially in the *Egoist*.

1918 (Jan.) Family returns to Zurich. Pound sends 'Telemachia' to Jane Heap and Margaret Anderson, editors of the *Little Review*. Serial publication begins with March issue. Under pressure of serialization, JJ continues writing. (May) *Exiles* published by Grant Richards. JJ receives financial gift from Mrs Harold McCormick. JJ forms theatrical group, the English Players, with Claud Sykes, and writes programme notes for the plays. First performance: *The Importance of Being Earnest*. JJ meets Frank Budgen. Further eye troubles. (11 Nov.) Armistice signed. By New Year's Eve, *Ulysses* drafted through episode 9, 'Scylla and Charybdis'.

1919 (Jan.) Irish War of Independence begins. Publication of *Ulysses* continues in *Little Review*. January (first part of 'Lestrygonians') and May (first half of 'Scylla and Charybdis') issues confiscated and burned by US Postal Authorities. *Egoist* publishes edited versions of four episodes (2, 3, 6, and 10). (7 Aug.) *Exiles* performed (unsuccessfully) in Munich. Mrs McCormick discontinues financial support, ostensibly because JJ refused to be psychoanalysed by her analyst, Carl Jung. (Oct.) Family returns to Trieste.

1920 (June) JJ and Pound meet for the first time. (July) Family moves to Paris. JJ meets Adrienne Monnier and Sylvia Beach, later T. S. Eliot and Wyndham Lewis and, later still, Valery Larbaud. (Sept.) JJ sends first *Ulysses* 'schema' to Carlo Linati. *Ulysses* composition and serialization continue. January (second half of 'Cyclops') and July–August (second half of 'Nausicaa') issues of the *Little Review* confiscated by US Postal Authorities. (20 Sept.) Complaint lodged by the New York Society for the Suppression of Vice, specifically citing 'Nausicaa' issue. What was to be the final *Little Review* instalment of *Ulysses* (first part of 'Oxen of the Sun') published in Sept.–Dec. issue.

1921 (Feb.) Editors of *Little Review* convicted of publishing obscenity; publication ceases. Sylvia Beach offers to publish *Ulysses* under the imprint of Shakespeare and Company (her Paris bookshop), to be printed in Dijon by Maurice Darantière, to be funded by advance subscription. JJ agrees. Episodes sent seriatim to printers; JJ continues to compose while also adding to and correcting returned proofs. Manuscript of episode 15, 'Circe', thrown in fire by typist's outraged husband. (29 Oct.) JJ 'completes' 'Ithaca' (last episode to be drafted), continues correction and addition. (7 Dec.) Valery Larbaud delivers lecture on *Ulysses* at Shakespeare and Company; uses another 'schema' of the book provided by Joyce (the 'Gilbert schema'). (Dec.) Treaty granting southern Ireland dominion status signed, the war having ended in July.

1922 (2 Feb.) First two copies of *Ulysses* delivered by express train from Dijon in time for celebration of JJ's fortieth birthday. Irish Civil War. (1 Apr.) Nora and children visit Ireland where their train is fired upon by troops. Return to Paris. JJ's eye troubles recur. (Aug.) Family travels to England where JJ meets Harriet Weaver for the first time. (Sept.) Return to Paris and trip to Côte d'Azure.

1923 (Mar.) JJ begins *Work in Progress* (working title of *Finnegans Wake*). (May) Irish Civil War ends.

1924 (Apr.) First fragments from *Work in Progress* published in *transatlantic review*. French translation of *Portrait* published.

1927 (June) Instalments of *Work in Progress* begin to be published in Eugene Jolas's *transition*. (July) *Pomes Penyeach* published by Shakespeare and Company.

1928 *Anna Livia Plurabelle* published in New York.

1929 (Feb.) French translation of *Ulysses* published by Adrienne Monnier's *La Maison des Amis des Livres*. Samuel Beckett *et al.* publish *Our Exagmination Round his Factification* . . . as *aide d'explication* and defence of *Work in Progress*. *Tales Told of Shem and Shaun* published in Paris. Roth's pirated edition of *Ulysses* published in New York.

1930 Publication of Stuart Gilbert's *James Joyce's 'Ulysses'*, critical study of *Ulysses*, written with JJ's assistance. *Haveth Childers Everywhere* published in Paris and New York.

1931 (May) French translation (completed with JJ's assistance) of *Anna Livia Plurabelle* published in *Nouvelle Revue*. (4 July) JJ and Nora Barnacle married in London to ensure the inheritance of their children. (29 Dec.) John Joyce dies.

1932 (15 Feb.) Son, Stephen James Joyce, born to Giorgio and Helen Joyce. JJ writes 'Ecce Puer'. Lucia's first breakdown and stay in Maillard clinic. Essay on John Sullivan, 'From a Banned Writer to a Banned Singer', published in the *New Statesman and Nation*. The Odyssey Press edition of *Ulysses*, 'specially revised . . . by Stuart Gilbert', published in Hamburg.

1933 Lucia's initial hospitalization in Nyon near Zurich. (6 Dec.) Judge John M. Woolsey, US District Court, delivers opinion that *Ulysses* is not obscene and can be published in the USA.

1934 Random House publishes US edition of *Ulysses*. Lucia again hospitalized. JJ returns to *Work in Progress*. *The Mime of Mick Nick and the Maggies*, published in The Hague. Frank Budgen's *James Joyce and the Making of 'Ulysses'* (written with JJ's assistance) published in London. Lucia under the care of Carl Jung.

1935 Publication of Limited Editions Club edition of *Ulysses* with illustrations by Henri Matisse.

1936 (Oct.) Bodley Head publishes *Ulysses* in London. (Dec.) *Collected Poems* published in New York.

1937 (June) JJ speaks at Paris PEN Congress on the moral right of authors. (Oct.) *Storiella She is Syung* published in London.

1938 (13 Nov.) Finishes *Finnegans Wake*. Douglas Hyde becomes Eire's first president.

1939 (Jan.) Yeats dies. (4 May) *Finnegans Wake* is published in London and New York, though advance copy reaches JJ in time for his 57th birthday on 2 Feb. (1 Sept.) Germany invades Poland; two days later France and Great Britain declare war on Germany. Family leaves Paris for St Gérard-le-Puy, near Vichy. Herbert Gorman's biography, commissioned and abetted by JJ, published in New York.

1940 France falls to the Nazis. Family moves to Zurich.

1941 (13 Jan.) JJ dies after surgery on a perforated ulcer, buried in Fluntern cemetery, Zurich, without the last rites of the Catholic Church. Nora dies in 1951, buried separately in Fluntern, though both bodies were reburied together in 1966.

OCCASIONAL, CRITICAL,
AND
POLITICAL WRITING

TRUST NOT APPEARANCES

AMDG[1]

There is nothing so deceptive and for [all] that so alluring as a good surface. The sea, when beheld in the warm sunlight of a summer's day; the sky, blue in the faint and amber glimmer of an Autumn sun, are pleasing to the eye: but, how different the scene, when the wild anger of the elements has waked again the discord of Confusion, how different the ocean, choking with froth & foam, to the calm, placid sea, that glanced and rippled merrily in the sun. But the best examples of the fickleness of appearances are:—Man and Fortune. The cringing, servile look; the high and haughty mien alike conceal the worthlessness of the character. Fortune that glittering bauble, whose brilliant shimmer has allured and trifled with both proud and poor, is as wavering as the wind. Still however, there is a 'something' that tells us the character of man. It is the eye. The only traitor that even the sternest will of a fiendish villian [sic] cannot overcome. It is the eye that reveals to man the guilt or innocence, the vices or the virtues of the soul. This is the only exception to the proverb 'Trust not appearances'. In every other case the real worth has to be searched for. The garb of royalty or of democracy are but the shadow that a 'man' leaves behind him. 'Oh! how unhappy is that poor man that hangs on princes' favours'.[2] The fickle tide of ever-changing Fortune brings with it—good and evil. How beautiful it seems as the harbinger of good and how cruel as the messenger of ill! The man who waits on the temper of a King is but a tiny craft in that great ocean. Thus we see the hollowness of appearances. The hypocrite is the worst kind of villian [sic] yet under the appearance of virtue he conceals the worst of vices. The friend, who is but the fane of fortune, fawns and grovells [sic] at the feet of wealth. But the man, who has no ambition, no wealth, no luxury save Contentment cannot hide the joy of happiness that flows from a clear conscience & an easy mind.

LDS.

James A. Joyce

[SUBJUGATION]

[The first half page of the manuscript is missing.]

—both questions of moment and difficult to answer. And although it is, in the main, evident that the conquest gained in a righteous war, is itself righteous, yet it will not be necessary to digress into the regions of political economy, etc, but it will be as well to bear in mind, that all subjugation by force, if carried out and prosecuted by force is only so far successful in breaking mens' [*sic*] spirits and aspirations. Also that it is, in the extreme, productive of ill-will and rebellion, that it is, again, from its beginning in unholy war, stamped with the stamp of ultimate conflict. But indeed it seems barbaric to only consider subjugation, in the light of an oppressing force, since we shall see that more often is it an influence rather than a positive power, and find it better used than for the vain shedding of blood.

In the various grades of life there are many homely illustrations of its practice—none the truer, that they are without blaze or notoriety, and in the humblest places. The tiller who guides the plough through the ground, and breaks the 'stubborn glebe'[1] is one. The gardener who prunes the wayward vine or compels the wild hedge into decent level, subjugating the savage element in 'trim gardens'[2], is another. Both of these represent subjugation by force; but the sailor's method is more diplomatic. He has no plough to furrow the resisting wind, nor no knife to check the rude violence of storm. He cannot, with his partial skill, get the better of its unruliness. When Æolus has pronounced his fiat, there is no direct countermanding his order. That way the sailor cannot overcome him; but by veering, and patient trial, sometimes using the strength of the Wind, sometimes avoiding it, now advancing and now retreating, at last the shifting sails are set for a straight course, and amid the succeeding calm the vessel steers for port. The miller's wheel which although it restrains the stream yet allows it to proceed on its own way, when it has performed the required service, is an useful example. The water rushing in swift stream, is on the higher mountains a fierce power both to excite emotion and to flood the fields. But the magic miller changes its humour, and it proceeds on its course, with all its tangled locks in orderly crease, and laps its waves, in placid resignation, on the banks that slope soberly down from suburban villas. And more, its strength has been utilised for commercial ends, and it helps to feed, with fine flour and bread, no longer the poetical but the hungry.

After these subjugations of the elements, we come to the subjugation of animals. Long ago in Eden responsible Adam had a good time. The birds of the air and the beasts of the field, ministered to his comfort. At his feet slept the docile lion, and every animal was his willing servant. But when sin arose in Adam—before only a latent evil—and his great nature was corrupted and broken, there were stirred up also among beasts the unknown dregs of ferocity. A similar revolt took place among them against man, and they were no longer to be friendly servants but bitter foes to him. From that hour, in greater or less degree, more in one land than another, they have struggled against him and refused him service. Aided often by great strength they fought successfully. But at length by superior power, and because he was man and they were but brutes, they, at least to a great extent, were overcome. Some of them, as the dog, he made the guardians of his house; others, as the horses and oxen, the helpmates of his toils. Others again he could not conquer but merely guard against, but one race in particular threatened by its number and power, to conquer him; and here it may be as well to follow the fate of it and see how a superior power intervened to preserve for man his title, not in derision, of lord of the creation and to keep him safe from the fear of mammoth and of mastodon. The Zoo elephants are sorry descendants of those mighty monsters who once traversed the sites of smoky cities; who roamed in hordes, tameless and fearless, proud in their power, through fruitful regions and forests, where now are the signs of busy men and the monuments of their skill and toil; who spread themselves over whole continents and carried their terror to the north and south, bidding defiance to man that he could not subjugate them; and finally in the wane of their day, though they knew it not, trooped up to the higher regions of the Pole, to the doom that was decreed for them. There what man could not subdue, was subdued, for they could not withstand the awful changes that came upon the earth. Lands of bright bloom, by degrees, lost all beauty and promise. Luxuriance of trees and fulness of fruit gradually departed, and were not, and stunted growth of shrub and shrivelled berries that no suns would ripen, were found in their

room. The tribes of the Mammoth were huddled together, in strange
wonder, and this devastation huddled them still closer. From oases,
yet left them, they peered at the advancing waves, that locked them
in their barren homes. Amid the gradual ice and waters, they eked
out the days of the life of their vanity and when nothing remained
for them but death, the wretched animals died in the unkind cold of
enduring winter, and to-day their colossal tusks and ivory bones, are
piled in memorial mounds, on the New Siberian Islands. This is all
of them that is left, that man may have good by their death, whom he
was not able to make his slaves when they lived, to tempt his greed
across the perilous, Polar seas, to those feasts of the wealth of bygone
times, that are strewn and bleaching beneath the desolate sky, white
and silent through the song of the changeless waves, and on the
verge of the eternal fathoms. What a subjugation has this been—
how awful and how complete! Scarce the remembrance of the
mammoth remains and no more is there the fear of the great woolly
elephant but contempt of his bulk and advantage of his unweildiness
[*sic*].

It is generally by intercourse with man, that animals have been
tamed and it is noticeable that the domestic tabby and the despised
pig rage in distant lands, with all their inbred fierceness and
strength. These with others are subjugated by constant war, or
driven from familiar haunts, and then their race dies out as the bison
of America is dying. Gradually all common animals are subdued to
man's rule, becoming once again his servants and regaining something of former willingness, in the patient horse and faithful dog. In
some instances the vain-glory and conscious victory of the three
spears is observed.[3] Thus, in the swampy marshes of South America,
the venomous snakes are lulled into deadness, and lie useless and
harmless, at the crooning of the charmer and in shows and circuses
before large crowds, broken-spirited lions and in the streets the
ungraceful bears are witnesses to the power of man.

It may be that the desire to overcome and get the mastery of
things, which is expressed in man's history of progress, is in a great
measure responsible for his supremacy. Had it been that he possessed no such desire, the trees and vegetation would have choked
the sunlight from him, barring all passage; the hills and seas would
have been the bounds of his dwellings; the unstemmed mountain-
stream would always snatch away his rude huts and the ravaging

hungry beasts stamp on the ashes of his fire. But his superior mind overcame all obstacles, not however universally, for in those places where his visits were seldom, the lower creation has usurped his Kingdom, and his labour must be anew expended in hunting the savage tiger through the jungles and forests of India, and in felling the trees in Canadian woods.

The next important subjugation is that of race over race. Among human families the white man is the predestined conqueror. The negro has given way before him, and the red men have been driven by him out of their lands and homes. In far New Zealand the sluggish Maoris in conceded sloth, permit him to portion out and possess the land of their fathers. Everywhere that region and sky allow, he has gone. Nor any longer does he or may he practise the abuse of subjugation—slavery, at least in its most degrading forms or at all so generally. Yet slavery only seems to have appealed to the conscience of men when most utterly base and inhuman and minor offences never troubled them. Happily this could not continue and now any encroachment on the liberties of others whether by troublesome Turk or not, is met with resolute opposition and just anger. Rights when violated, institutions set at nought, privileges disregarded, all these, not as shibboleths and war-cries, but as deep-seated thorough realities, will happily always call forth, not in foolish romantic madness nor for passionate destruction, but with unyielding firmness of resistance, the energies and sympathies of men to protect them and to defend them.

Hitherto we have only treated of man's sub-

[one half page of the manuscript is missing]

often when a person gets embarked on a topic which in its vastness almost completely swallows up his efforts, the subject dwarfs the writer; or when a logician has to treat of great subjects, with a view to deriving a fixed theory, he abandons the primal idea and digresses into elaborate disquisitions, on the more inviting portions of his argument. Again in works of fancy, a too prolific imagination literally flys [*sic*] away with the author, and lands him in regions of loveliness unutterable, which his faculties scarcely grasp, which dazzles his senses, and defies speech, and thus his compositions are beautiful indeed, but beautiful with the cloudiness and dream-beauty of a visionary. Such a thing as this often affects poets of high, fanciful temper, as Shelley,[4] rendering their poetry vague and misty. When however the gift—great and wonderful—of a poetic sense, in sight and speech and feeling, has been subdued by vigilance and care and has been prevented from running to extremes, the true and superior spirit, penetrates more watchfully into sublime and noble places, treading them with greater fear and greater wonder and greater reverence, and in humbleness looks up into the dim regions, now full of light, and interprets, without mysticism, for men the great things that are hidden from their eyes, in the leaves of the trees and in the flowers, to console them, to add to their worship, and to elevate their awe. This result proceeds from the subjugation of a great gift, and indeed it is so in all our possessions. We improve in strength when we husband it, in health when we are careful of it, in power of mental endurance when we do not over-tax it. Otherwise in the arts, in sculpture and painting, the great incidents that engross the artist's attention would find their expression, in huge shapelessness or wild daubs; and in the ear of the rapt musician, the loveliest melodies outpour themselves, madly, without time or movement, in chaotic mazes, 'like sweet bells jangled, out of tune and harsh'.[5]

It has been pointed out what an influence this desire of man to overcome has exerted over the Kingdom of animals and vegetation, and how it not merely destroys and conquers the worse features but betters and improves what is good. There are spots on this earth, where licence of growth holds absolute sway, where leaves choke the light and rankness holds the soil, where there are dangerous reptiles and fierce beasts, all untamed, amid surroundings of great beauty, in colour and fertility, but overshadowed by the horror of savage unrule. But the coming of man in his onward way, shall alter the face of things, good himself rendering good his own dominions. As has been written—'when true servants of Heaven shall enter these Edens and the Spirit of God enter with them, another spirit will also be breathed into the physical air; and the stinging insect and venomous snake and poisonous tree, pass away before the power of the regenerate human soul'—This is the wished subjugation that must come in good time. And meanwhile we have considered the power of overcoming man, against the lowest races of the world, and his influence in the subjugation of his own mental faculties, and there remains for us to consider the manifold influence of his desire to conquer, over his human instincts, over his work and business and over his reason.

In the sagas of Norway, in ancient epics in the tales of 'Knights and barons bold'[6] and to-day in the stories of Hall Caine,[7] we have abundant examples of the havoc that men's passions make, when they are allowed to spend their force in Bersirk freedom. Of course in conventional life there are fewer instances of such characters as Thor, Ospakar, Jason, and Mylrea[8] as in those savage places which were once their homes. Modern civilisation will not permit such wholesale licence, as the then state of affairs gave occasion to. The brood of men now, in towns and cities, is not of fierce passion, at least not to such an extent as to make men subserve their rages. The ordinary man has not so often to guard against fits of demon's anger, though the Vendetta is still common in Southern Europe but mankind has quite as many opportunities of subjugating himself or herself as before. The fretful temper, the base interpretation, the fool's conceitedness, the fin-de-siècle sneer, the gossiping, the refusal of aid, the hurting word and worthless taunt, together with ingratitude and the forgetting of friends—all these are daily waiting for us to subjugate. Above all, the much-maligned, greatest charity, so distinct from animal profusion and reckless liberality, that charitable deeds do not wholly constitute; but which springs from inner wells of gentleness and goodness; which is shy of attributing motives; 'which interprets everything for the best'; which dictates, from emotions of Heaven's giving, the sacrifice of all that is dear, in urgent need, which has its being and beauty from above; which lives and thrives in the atmosphere of thoughts, so upraised and so serene that they will not suffer themselves to be let down on earth among men, but in their own delicate air 'intimate their presence and commune with themselves'—this utter unselfishness in all things, how does it on the contrary, call for constant practice and worthy fulfilling!

Again in the case of man's mission, marked out for him from the gate of Eden, labour and toil, has not subjugation a direct influence, with advantage both to the world and to the man himself. 'Foul jungles' says Carlyle[9] 'are cleared away, fair seedfields rise instead and stately cities, and withal the man

[*one half page of the manuscript is missing*]

greater difficulty for some to subjugate their reason, than their passions. For they pit the intellect and reason of men, with their vain theorisings, against the superhuman logic of belief. Indeed to a rightly constituted mind the bugbears of infidelity have no terrors and excite no feeling save contempt. Men have passions and reason, and the doctrine of licence is an exact counterpart of the doctrine of freethinking. Human reason has no part in wisdom, if it fulfils not the whole three attributes given by the inspired writer, if it is not 'pudica, pacifica et desursum'—chaste, peaceful and from above.[10] How can it thrive if it comes not from the seat of Wisdom but has its source elsewhere? And how can earthly intellects, if they blind their eyes to wisdom's epithets 'pudica, pacifica et desursum' hope to escape that which was the stumbling-block with Abelard and the cause of his fall.[11]

The essence of subjugation lies in the conquest of the higher. Whatever is nobler and better, or reared upon foundations more solid, than the rest, in the appointed hour, comes to the appointed triumph. When right is perverted into might, or more properly speaking, when justice is changed to sheer strength, a subjugation ensues—but transient not lasting. When it is unlawful, as too frequently in the past it has been, the punishment invariably follows in strife through ages. Some things there are no subjugation can repress and if these preserve, as they do and will, the germs of nobility, in good men and saintly lives, they preserve also for those who follow and obey, the promise of after victory and the solace and comfort of active expectation. Subjugation is 'almost of the essence of an empire and when it ceases to conquer, it ceases to be'. It is an innate part of human nature, responsible, in a great way, for man's place. Politically it is a dominant factor and a potent power in the issues of nations. Among the faculties of men it is a great influence, and forms part of the world's laws, unalterable and for ever—subjugation with the existence also of freedom, and even, within its sight, that there may be constant manifestation of power over all, bringing all things under sway, with fixed limits and laws and in equal regulation, permitting the prowl

[*one half page of the manuscript is missing*]

power for force and of persuasion for red conquest, has brought about the enduring rule foretold, of Kindness over all the good, for ever, in a new subjugation.

—The End—

written by
Jas. A. Joyce
27/9/98

Note—
the insertions in pencil are chiefly omissions in writing out.

THE STUDY OF LANGUAGES

In the church of San' Maria Novella there are seven figures by Memmi, named the seven earthly Sciences.[1] Reading from right to left, the first is the 'Art of Letters' and the seventh 'Arithmetic'. The first is oftener called Grammar, because it refers more directly to that branch of 'Letters'. Now the artist's idea in this arrangement was to shew the gradual progress from Science to Science, from Grammar to Rhetoric, from Rhetoric to Music and so on to Arithmetic. In selecting his subjects he assumes two things. First he assumes that the primary Science is Grammar, that is, that Science which is the first and most natural one to man, and also that Arithmetic is the last, not exactly as the culmination of the other six, but rather as the final, numbered expression of man's life. Secondly, or perhaps first, he assumes that Grammar, or Letters, is a Science. His first assumption classes, if it does nothing more, Grammar and Arithmetic together as the first and last things in human knowledge. His second assumption, as we have said, makes Grammar a science. Both of these assumptions are directly opposed to the opinions of many illustrious followers of Arithmetic, who deny that 'Letters' is a science, and seem or affect to regard it as a totally different thing from Arithmetic. Literature is only at the root a science, that is in its Grammar and Characters, but such conduct is most senseless on the part of the Arithmeticians.

We hope that they will grant that it is essential for a man, who wishes to communicate in the ordinary way with his fellow-man, that he should know how to speak. We, on our part, will admit that, for the building of an intellectual man, his most important study is that of Mathematics. It is the study which most developes his mental precision and accuracy, which gives him a zest for careful and orderly method, which equips him, in the first place, for an intellectual career. We, the pluralised essayist, say this, who were never an ardent votary of the subject, rather from disinclination to taskwork than because of a rooted aversion to it. In this we are supported by the great lights of the age, though Matthew Arnold has his own little opinion about the matter, as he had about other matters.[2] Now while the advocates of more imaginative pursuits fully recognise the paramount importance of a mathematical education, it is deplorable that so many followers of the more rigid course, having assimilated unto themselves, a portion of the rigidity of that course, and a share of its uncompromising theorems, affect to regard the study of languages as altogether beneath them, and merely a random, occasional sort of study. Linguists must be allowed to make protest against such treatment and surely their defence is worthy of consideration.

For that which ennobles the study of Mathematics in the eyes of the wise, is the fact that it proceeds with regular course, that it is a science, a knowledge of facts, in contradistinction to literature, which is in the more elegant aspect of it, imaginary and notional. This draws a line of stern demarcation between the two; and yet as Mathematics and the Sciences of Numbers partake of the nature of that beauty which is omnipresent, which is expressed, almost noiselessly, in the order and symmetry of Mathematics, as in the charms of literature; so does literature in turn share in the neatness and regularity of Mathematics.[3] Moreover we do not, by any means, suffer such a premiss to pass unchallenged, but before taking up the cudgels on behalf of Language and Literature, we wish it to be understood that we admit that the most important study for the mind is Mathematics, and our vindication of Literature will never venture to put it before Mathematics in that respect.

The statement the study of Languages is to be despised since it is imaginary and does not deal with facts nor deals in a precise way with ideas, is absurd. First, because the study of any language must begin at the beginning and must advance slowly and carefully, over ascertained ground. The Grammar of a language, its orthography and etymology are admitted as known. They are studies in the same manner as tables in Arithmetic, surely and accurately. Some will admit this but go on to say that thus far a language is to be approved of, but that the higher parts of syntax and style and history, are fanciful and imaginative. Now the study of languages is based on a mathematical foundation, and sure of its footing, and in consequence both in style and syntax there is always present a carefulness, a carefulness bred of the first implantings of precision. So they are no mere flourishings of unkempt, beautiful ideas but methods of correct expression ruled and directed by clear regulations, sometimes of facts, sometimes of ideas. And when of ideas their expression elevated from the hardness, which is sufficient for 'flat unraised'[4]

statements, by an over-added influence of what is beautiful in pathetic phrases, swelling of words, or torrents of invective, in tropes and
varieties and figures, yet preserving even in moments of the greatest
emotion, an innate symmetry.

Secondly even if we [were] disposed to admit, which we are far
from doing, that unwarrantable 'since' of the mathematicians we
should not admit that poetry and imagination, though not so deeply
intellectual, are to be despised and their names to be cast out, totally.
Are our libraries to contain only works of Science? Are Bacon and
Newton to monopolise our shelves? and no place be found for Shakespeare and Milton? Theology is a Science, yet will either Catholic or
Anglican, however profound and learned, taboo poetry from their
studies, and the one banish a living, constant element of his Church
and the other forbid the 'Christian Year'?[5] The higher grades of
language, style, syntax, poetry, oratory, rhetoric, are again the cham-
pions and exponents, in what way soever, of Truth. So in the figure
of Rhetoric in Santa Maria's church Truth is seen reflected in a
Mirror. The notion of Aristotle and his school, that in a bad cause
there can be true oratory, is utterly false. Finally, if they claim,
Science advances more the civilization of the world, there must be
some restriction imposed. Science may improve yet demoralise.
Witness Dr Benjulia.[6] Did the great Science of Vivisection improve
him? 'Heart and Science'! yes, there is great danger in heartless
science, very great danger indeed, leading only to inhumanity. Let it
not be our case to stand like him, crushed and broken, aloof from
sympathy at the door of his laboratory, while the maimed animals
flee away terrified between his legs, into the darkness.[7] Do not think
that Science, human or divine, will effect on the one hand a great
substantial change for good in men and things, if it merely consults
the interests of men in its own interests, and does good to them it
may do good to itself, and in everything passes over that first, most
natural aspect of man, namely, as a living being, and regard him as an
infinitely small actor, playing a most uninteresting part in the drama
of worlds. Or on the other hand, if it proceeds, when directed
towards divine objects, as a contrivance useful for extracting hard,
rational inferences, ever induce in man an uplifting of trust and
worship.

Having thus got rid of the obnoxious mathematicians, something
is to be said about the study of languages and there chiefly in the

study of our own. First, in the history of words there is much that indicates the history of men, and in comparing the speech of to-day day with that of years ago, we have a useful illustration of the effect of external influences on the very words of a race. Sometimes they have changed greatly in meaning, as the word 'villain' because of customs now extinct, and sometimes the advent of an overcoming power may be attested by the crippled diction, or by the complete disuse of the original tongue, save in solitary, dear phrases, spontaneous in grief or gladness. Secondly, this knowledge tends to make our language purer and more lucid, and therefore tends also to improve style and composition. Thirdly, the names we meet in the literature of our language are handed down to us, as venerable names, not to be treated lightly but entitled beforehand to our respect. They are landmarks in the transition of a language, keeping it inviolate, directing its course straight on like an advancing way, widening and improving as it advances but staying always on the high road, though many byways branch off it at all parts and seem smooth to follow. Thus these names, as those of the masters of English, are standards for imitation and reference, and are valuable because their use of the language was also based on their study of it, and is for that reason deserving of great and serious attention. Fourthly, and this is the greatest of all, the careful study of the language, used by these men, is almost the only way to gain a thorough knowledge of the power and dignity, that are in the elements of a language and further to understand, as far as nature allows, the feelings of great writers, to enter into their hearts and spirits, to be admitted, by privilege, into the privacy of their proper thoughts. The study of their language is useful as well, not merely to add to our reading and store of thought, but to add to our vocabulary and imperceptibly to make us sharers in their delicateness or strength. How frequently it happens that when persons become excited, all sense of language seems to forsake them, and they splutter incoherently and repeat themselves, that their phrases may have more sound and meaning. Look, how great the difficulty that many have in expressing their most ordinary ideas in correct English. If it were only to rectify these errors which exist amongst us, the study of our language should recommend itself to us. How much more so, then, when it not alone cures these defects, but works such wonderful changes in our speech by the mere contact with good diction and introduces us to beauties, which cannot here be enlarged on but obtain only passing mention, to which our former ignorance or negligence denied us access.

Lest we should seem to dwell overlong [on] our own language let us consider the case of the classics. In Latin—for the writer acknowledges humbly his ignorance of Greek—a careful and well-directed study must be very advantageous. For it acquaints us with a language, which has a strong element in English, and thus makes us know the derivations of many words, which we then apply more correctly and which have therefore a truer meaning for us. Again Latin is the recognised language of scholars and philosophers, and the weapon of the learned; whose books and thoughts are only open, through the medium of translation. Further, it is astonishing that Latin is like Shakespeare in everyone's mouth, without his seeming, in the least, to recognise the fact. Quotations are constantly employed, even by those who are not Latin scholars and common convenience would prompt us to study it. Then also it is the uniform language of the ritual of the Church. Moreover it is for those who study it a great help intellectually, for it has some terse expressions, that are more forcible than many of our similar expressions. For instance a single Latin phrase or word is so complex in meaning, and enters into the nature of so many words, and has yet a delicate shade of its own, that no single word in English will properly represent. Thus Vergil's Latin is said to be so idiomatic as to defy translation. Evidently careful rendering of such language into suitable English must be a great exercise in judgment and expression, if we were to count nothing else. But Latin besides being in its degraded form the language of schoolmen, is in a better form the language of Lucretius, Vergil, Horace, Cicero, Pliny and Tacitus, all of whom are great names and who have withstood dislodgment from their high seats for thousands of years—a fact which is sufficient in itself to gain them a reading. They are moreover interesting as the writers in a vast Republic, the greatest and vastest the world has seen, a Republic which during five hundred years was the home of nearly all the great men of action in that time, which made its name heard from Gibraltar to Arabia, and to the stranger-hating Briton, everywhere a name of power, and everywhere with conquest in its army's van.

[*The manuscript ends here.*]

ROYAL HIBERNIAN ACADEMY
'ECCE HOMO'

Munkacsy's picture which has been exhibited in the principal cities of Europe, is now on view at the Royal Hibernian Academy.[1] With the other two pictures 'Christ before Pilate' and 'Christ on Calvary' it forms almost a complete trilogy of the later portion of the Passion. Perhaps what strikes one most in the picture under consideration is the sense of life, the realistic illusion. One could well fancy that the men and women were of flesh and blood, stuck into silent trance, by the warlock's hand. Hence the picture is primarily dramatic, not an execution of faultless forms, or a canvas reproduction of psychology. By drama I understand the interplay of passions; drama is strife, evolution, movement, in whatever way unfolded. Drama exists as an independent thing, conditioned but not controlled by its scene. An idyllic portrait or an environment of haystacks do not constitute a pastoral drama, no more than rhodomontade, and a monotonous trick of 'tutoyer'[2] build up a tragedy. If there be only quiescence in one, or vulgarity in the second, as is generally the case, then in neither one nor the other is the note of true drama sounded for a moment. However subdued the tone of passions may be, however ordered the action or commonplace the diction, if a play, or a work of music, or a picture concerns itself with the everlasting hopes, desires and hates of humanity, or deals with a symbolic presentment of our widely related nature, albeit a phase of that nature, then it is drama. Maeterlinck's[3] characters may be, when subjected to the search-light of that estimable torch, common sense, unaccountable, drifting, fate-impelled creatures—in fact, as our civilisation dubs them, uncanny. But in whatever dwarfed and marionette-like a manner, their passions are human, and so the exposition of them is drama. This is fairly obvious when applied to a stage subject but when the word drama is in an identical way, applied to Munkacsy, it may need perhaps an additional word of explanation.

In the statuary art the first step towards drama was the separation of the feet. Before that sculpture was a copy of the body, actuated by only a nascent impulse, and executed by routine. The infusion of life, or its semblance, at once brought soul into the work of the artist, vivified his forms and elucidated his theme. It follows naturally from the fact that the sculptor aims at producing a bronze or stone model of man, that his impulse should lead him to the portrayal of an instantaneous passion. Consequently although he has the advantage of the painter, in at the first glance deceiving the eye, his capability to be a dramatist is less broad than the painter's. His power of moulding can be equalised by the painter's backgrounds and skilful disposition of shades, and while in such a manner naturalism is produced on an areal canvas, the colours, which add another life, help his theme to its expression in a very much completer and clearer whole. Moreover, and this applies markedly in the present case, as the theme becomes loftier or more extended, it can manifestly obtain more adequate treatment in a large picture than in the crowding of colourless, perfectly-modelled statues in a tableau. Notably then does the difference hold in the instance of 'Ecce Homo' where some seventy figures are limned on one canvas. It is a mistake to limit drama to the stage; a drama can be painted as well as sung or acted, and 'Ecce Homo' is a drama.

In addition, it is much more deserving of the comment of a dramatic critic than the majority of the pieces which are directly under his notice in the theatre. To speak of the technical point of an art-work such as this is, to my thinking, somewhat superfluous. Of course the draping, and the upraised hands, and outstretched fingers reveal a technique and a skill, beyond criticism. The narrow yard is a scene of crowded figures, all drawn with a master's faithfulness. The one blemish is the odd, strained position of the governor's left hand. It gives one the impression of being maimed or crippled from the manner in which the cloak conceals it. The background is a corridor, opened on the spectator, with pillars upholding a verandah, on which the eastern shrubs show out against a sapphire sky. At the right hand and in the extreme corner, as you face the picture, a stairway of two flights, say some twenty steps in all leads to a platform which is thus almost at right angles to the line of the pillars. The garish sunlight falls directly over this platform leaving the rest of the court partly in the shade. The walls are decorated and at the back of the piazza is a narrow doorway crowded with Roman soldiery. The first half of the mob, that is, those next underneath the platform, is enclosed between the pillars and a swinging chain in the foreground, which is parallel to them. A decrepit street cur, the only animal in the picture, is crouching by it. On the platform in front of the soldiers, stand two figures. One has his hands bound in front and is standing facing the rabble, his fingers just touching the balustrade. A red mantle is so placed about the shoulders as to cover the entire back and a little of the foreshoulders and arms. The whole front of the figure is thus exposed to the waist. A crown of irregular, yellowish thorns is on the temples and head and a light, long reed barely supported between the clasped hands. It is Christ. The other figure is somewhat nearer the populace and leans a little towards them over the balustrade. The figure is pointing at Christ, the right arm in the most natural position of demonstration, and the left arm extended in the peculiar, crippled way I have already noticed. It is Pilate. Right underneath these two main figures, on the paved yard, is the tossing, tumbling Jewish rabble. The expressions conveyed in the varying faces, gestures, hands and opened mouths are marvelous. There is the palsied, shattered frame of a lewd wretch; his face is bruted animalism, feebly stirred to a grin. There is the broad back and brawny arm and tight clenched fist, but the face of the muscular 'protestant' is hidden.[4] At her [*sic*] feet, in the angle where the stairway bends a woman is kneeling. Her face is dragged in an unwholesome pallor but quivering with emotion. Her beautifully rounded arms are displayed as a contrast of writhing pity against the brutality of the throng. Some stray locks of her copious hair are blown over them and cling to them as tendrils. Her expression is reverential, her eyes are straining up through her tears. She is the emblem of the contrite, she is the new figure of lamentation as against the severe, familiar types, she is of those, the sorrowstricken, who weep and mourn but yet are comforted. Presumably, from her shrinking pose, she is a magdalen. Near her is the street dog, and near him a street urchin. His back is turned but both arms are flung up high and apart in youthful exultation, the fingers pointing outwards, stiff and separate.

In the heart of the crowd is the figure of a man, furious at being jostled by a well clad Jew. His eyes are squinting with rage, and an execration foams on his lips. The object of his rage is a rich man, with that horrible cast of countenance, so common among the sweaters of modern Israël. I mean, the face whose line runs out over the full forehead to the crest of the nose and then recedes in a similar curve back to the chin, which, in this instance is covered with a wispish, tapering beard. The upper lip is raised out of position, disclosing two long, white teeth, while the whole lower lip is trapped. This is the creature's snarl of malice. An arm is stretched forth in derision, the fine, snowy linen falling back upon the forearm. Immediately behind is a huge face, with features sprawled upon it, the jaws torn asunder with a coarse howl. Then there is the half profile and figure of the triumphant fanatic. The long gaberdine falls to the naked feet, the head is erect, the arms perpendicular, raised in conquest. In the extreme end is the bleared face of a silly beggar. Everywhere is a new face. In the dark hoods, under the conical headresses [*sic*], here hatred, there the mouth gaping open at its fullest stretch, the head thrown back on the nape. Here an old woman is hastening away, horrorstruck, and there is a woman of comely appearance but evidently a proletariat. She has fine, languid eyes, full features and figure, but marred with crass stupidity and perfect, if less revolting bestiality. Her child is clambering about her knees, her infant hoisted on her shoulder. Not even these are free from the all pervading aversion and in their small beady eyes twinkles the fire of rejection, the bitter unwisdom of their race. Close by are the two figures of John and Mary. Mary has fainted. Her face is of a grey hue, like a sunless dawn, her features rigid but not drawn. Her hair is jet black, her hood white. She is almost dead, but her force of anguish keeps her alive. John's arms are wound about her, holding her up, his face is half feminine in its drawing, but set in purpose. His rust coloured hair falls over his shoulders, his features express solicitude and pity. On the stairs is a rabbi, enthralled with amazement, incredulous yet attracted by the extraordinary central figure. Round about are the soldiers. Their mien is self-possessed contempt. They look on Christ as an exhibition and the rabble as a pack of unkennelled animals. Pilate is saved from the dignity his post would have given him, by the evidence that he is not Roman enough to spurn them. His face is round, his skull compact, the hair cropped short on it. He is shifting, uncertain of his next move, his eyes wide open in mental fever. He wears the white and red Roman toga.

It will be clear from all this that the whole forms a wonderful picture, intensely, silently dramatic, waiting but the touch of the wizard wand to break out into reality, life and conflict. As such too much tribute cannot be paid to it, for it is a frightfully real present-ment of all the baser passions of humanity, in both sexes, in every gradation, raised and lashed into a demoniac carnival. So far praise must be given, but it is plain through all this, that the aspect of the artist is human, intensely, powerfully human. To paint such a crowd one must probe humanity with no scrupulous knife. Pilate is self-seeking, Mary is maternal, the weeping woman is penitent, John is a strong man, rent inside with great grief, the soldiers bear the impress of the stubborn unideality of conquest; their pride is uncompromising for are they not the overcomers? It would have been easy to have made Mary a Madonna and John an evangelist but the artist has chosen to make Mary a mother and John a man. I believe this treatment to be the finer and the subtler. In a moment such as when Pilate said to the Jews, Behold the man, it would be a pious error but indubitably, an error to show Mary as the ancestress of the devout, rapt madonnas of our churches. The depicting of these two figures in such a way in a sacred picture, is in itself a token of the highest genius. If there is to be anything superhuman in the picture, anything above and beyond the heart of man, it will appear in Christ. But no matter how you view Christ, there is no trace of that in his aspect. There is nothing divine in his look, there is nothing superhuman. This is no defect of hand on the part of the artist, his skill would have accomplished anything. It was his voluntary position. Van Ruith[5] painted a picture some years ago of Christ and the traders in the temple. His intention was to produce elevated reprimand and divine chastisement, his hand failed him and the result was a weak flogger and a mixture of loving kindness and repose, wholly incompatible with the incident. Munkacsy on the contrary would never be under the power of his brush, but his view of the event is humanistic. Consequently his work is drama. Had he chosen to paint Christ as the Incarnate Son of God, redeeming his creatures of his own admirable will, through insult and hate, it would not have been drama, it would have been Divine Law, for drama deals with man. As it is from the artist's conception, it is powerful drama, the drama of the thrice told revolt of humanity against a great teacher.

The face of Christ is a superb study of endurance, passion, I use the word in its proper sense, and dauntless will. It is plain that no thought of the crowd obtrudes itself on his mind. He seems to have nothing in common with them, save his features which are racial. The mouth is concealed by a brown mustache, the chin and up to the ears overgrown with an untrimmed but moderate beard of the same colour. The forehead is low and projects somewhat on the eyebrows. The nose is slightly Jewish but almost aquiline, the nostrils thin and sensitive. The eyes are of a pale blue colour, if of any, and as the face is turned to the light, they are lifted half under the brows, the only true position for intense agony. They are keen, but not large, and seem to pierce the air, half in inspiration, half in suffering. The whole face is of an ascetic, inspired, whole souled, wonderfully passionate man. It is Christ, as the Man of Sorrows, his raiment red as of them that tread in the winepress. It is literally Behold the Man.

It is this treatment of the theme that has led me to appraise it as a drama. It is grand, noble tragic but it makes the founder of Christianity, no more than a great social and religious reformer, a personality, of mingled majesty and power, a protagonist of a world-drama. No objections will be lodged against it on that score by the public, whose general attitude when they advert to the subject at all, is that of the painter, only less grand and less interested. Munkacsy's conception is as much greater than theirs, as an average artist is greater than an average greengrocer, but it is of the same kind, it is, to pervert Wagner, the attitude of the folk.[6] Belief in the divinity of Christ is not a salient feature of secular Christendom. But occasional sympathy with the eternal conflict of truth and error, of right and wrong, as exemplified in the drama at Golgotha, is not beyond its approval.

JAJ
Sept. 1899.

DRAMA AND LIFE

Although the relations between drama and life are, and must be of the most vital character, in the history of drama itself these do not seem to have been at all times, consistently in view. The earliest and best known drama, this side of the Caucasus, is that of Greece. I do not propose to attempt anything in the nature of a historical survey but cannot pass it by. Greek drama arose out of the cult of Dionysos, who, god of fruitage, joyfulness and earliest art, offered in his life-story a practical groundplan for the erection of a tragic and a comic theatre. In speaking of Greek drama it must be borne in mind that its rise dominated its form. The conditions of the Attic stage suggested a syllabus of greenroom proprieties and cautions to authors, which in after ages were foolishly set up as the canons of dramatic art, in all lands. Thus the Greeks handed down a code of laws which their descendants with purblind wisdom forthwith advanced to the dignity of inspired pronouncements. Beyond this, I say nothing. It may be a vulgarism, but it is literal truth to say that Greek drama is played out. For good or for bad it has done its work, which, if wrought in gold, was not upon lasting pillars. Its revival is not of dramatic but of pedagogic significance. Even in its own camp it has been superseded. When it had thriven over long in hieratic custody and in ceremonial form, it began to pall on the Aryan genius. A reaction ensued, as was inevitable; and as the classical drama had been born of religion, its follower arose out of a movement in literature. In this reaction England played an important part, for it was the power of the Shakespearean clique that dealt the deathblow to the already dying drama. Shakespeare was before all else a literary artist; humour, eloquence, a gift of seraphic music, theatrical instincts—he had a rich dower of these. The work, to which he gave such splendid impulse, was of a higher nature than that which it followed. It was far from mere drama, it was literature in dialogue. Here I must draw a line of demarcation between literature and drama.[1]

Human society is the embodiment of changeless laws which the whimsicalities and circumstances of men and women involve and overwrap. The realm of literature is the realm of these accidental manners and humours—a spacious realm; and the true literary artist concerns himself mainly with them. Drama has to do with the underlying laws first, in all their nakedness and divine severity, and only secondarily with the motley agents who bear them out. When so much is recognised an advance has been made to a more rational and true appreciation of dramatic art. Unless some such distinction be made the result is chaos. Lyricism parades as poetic drama, psychological conversation as literary drama, and traditional farce moves over the boards with the label of comedy affixed to it.

Both of these dramas having done their work as prologues to the swelling act,[2] they may be relegated to the department of literary curios. It is futile to say that there is no new drama or to contend that its proclamation is a huge boom [*sic*]. Space is valuable and I cannot combat these assertions. However it is to me day-clear that dramatic drama must outlive its elders, whose life is only eked by the most dexterous management and the carefullest husbanding. Over this New School some hard hits have been given and taken. The public is slow to seize truth, and its leaders quick to miscal [*sic*] it. Many, whose palates have grown accustomed to the old food, cry out peevishly against a change of diet. To these use and want is the seventh heaven. Loud are their praises of the bland blatancy of Corneille, the starchglaze of Trapassi's godliness, the Pumblechookian woodenness of Calderon.[3] Their infantile plot juggling sets them agape, so superfine it is. Such critics are not to be taken seriously but they are droll figures! It is of course patently true that the 'new' school masters them on their own ground. Compare the skill of Haddon Chambers and Douglas Jerrold, of Sudermann and Lessing.[4] The 'new' school in this branch of its art is superior. This superiority is only natural, as it accompanies work of immeasurably higher calibre. Even the least part of Wagner—his music—is beyond Bellini.[5] Spite of the outcry of these lovers of the past, the masons are building for Drama, an ampler and loftier home, where there shall be light for gloom, and wide porches for drawbridge and keep.

Let me explain a little as to this great visitant.[6] By drama I understand the interplay of passions to portray truth; drama is strife, evolution, movement in whatever way unfolded; it exists, before it takes form, independently; it is conditioned but not controlled by its scene. It might be said fantastically that as soon as men and women began life in the world there was above them and about them, a spirit, of which they were dimly conscious, which they would have had sojourn in their midst in deeper intimacy and for whose truth they became seekers in after times, longing to lay hands upon it. For this spirit is as the roaming air, little susceptible of change, and never left their vision, shall never leave it, till the firmament is as a scroll rolled away. At times it would seem that the spirit had taken up his abode in this or that form—but on a sudden he is misused, he is gone and the abode is left idle. He is, one might guess, somewhat of an elfish nature, a nixie, a very Ariel. So we must distinguish him and his house. An idylic [*sic*] portrait, or an environment of haystacks does not constitute a pastoral play, no more than rhodomontade and sermonising build up a tragedy. Neither quiescence nor vulgarity shadow forth drama. However subdued the tone of passions may be, however ordered the action or commonplace the diction, if a play or a work of music or a picture presents the everlasting hopes, desires and hates of us, or deals with a symbolic presentment of our widely related nature, albeit a phase of that nature, then it is drama. I shall not speak here of its many forms. In every form that was not fit for it, it made an outburst, as when the first sculptor separated the feet. Morality, mystery, ballet, pantomime, opera, all these it speedily ran through and discarded. Its proper form 'the drama' is yet intact. 'There are many candles on the high altar, though one fall.'[7]

Whatever form it takes must not be superimposed or conventional. In literature we allow conventions, for literature is a comparatively low form of art.[8] Literature is kept alive by tonics, it flourishes through conventions in all human relations, in all actuality. Drama will be for the future at war with convention, if it is to realise itself truly. If you have a clear thought of the body of drama, it will be manifest what raiment befits it. Drama of so wholehearted and admirable a nature cannot but draw all hearts from the spectacular and the theatrical, its note being truth and freedom in every aspect of it. It may be asked what are we to do, in the words of Tolstoï.[9] First, clear our minds of cant[10] and alter the falsehoods to which we have lent our support. Let us criticise in the manner of free people, as a free race, recking little of ferula and formula. The Folk is, I believe, able to do so much.[11] Securus judicat orbis terrarum,[12] is not too high a motto for all human artwork. Let us not overbear the weak, let us treat with a tolerant smile the state pronouncements of those matchless serio-comics—the 'litterateurs' [*sic*].[13] If a sanity rules the mind of the dramatic world there will be accepted what is now the faith of the few, then will be past dispute written up the respective grades of Macbeth and The Master Builder.[14] The sententious critic of the thirtieth century may well say of them—Between him and these there is a great gulf fixed.

There are some weighty truths which we cannot overpass, in the relations between drama and the artist. Drama is essentially a communal art and of widespread domain.[15] The drama—its fittest vehicle almost presupposes an audience, drawn from all classes. In an art-loving and art-producing society the drama would naturally take up its position at the head of all artistic institutions. Drama is moreover of so unswayed, so unchallengeable a nature that in its highest forms it all but transcends criticism. It is hardly possible to criticise The Wild Duck, for instance; one can only brood upon it as upon a personal woe.[16] Indeed in the case of all Ibsen's later work dramatic criticism, properly so called, verges on impertinence. In every other art personality, mannerism of touch, local sense, are held as adornments, as additional charms. But here the artist forgoes his very self and stands a mediator in awful truth before the veiled face of God.[17]

If you ask me what occasions drama or what is the necessity for it at all, I answer Necessity. It is mere animal instinct applied to the mind. Apart from his world-old desire to get beyond the flaming ramparts, man has a further longing to become a maker and a moulder. That is the necessity of all art.[18] Drama is again the least dependent of all arts on its material. If the supply of mouldable earth or stone gives out, sculpture becomes a memory, if the yield of vegetable pigments ceases, the pictorial art ceases. But whether there be marble or paints, there is always the artstuff for drama. I believe further that drama arises spontaneously out of life and is coeval with it. Every race has made its own myths and it is in these that early drama often finds an outlet. The author of Parsifal[19] has recognised this and hence his work is solid as rock. When the mythus passes over the borderline and invades the temple of worship, the possibilities of its drama have lessened considerably. Even then it struggles back to its rightful place, much to the discomfort of the stodgy congregation.

As men differ as to the rise, so do they as to the aims of drama. It is in most cases claimed by the votaries of the antique school that the drama should have special ethical aims, to use their stock phrase, that it should instruct, elevate, and amuse. Here is yet another gyve that the jailers have bestowed. I do not say that drama may not fulfil any or all of these functions, but I deny that it is essential that it should fulfil them. Art, elevated into the overhigh sphere of religion, generally loses its true soul in stagnant quietism. As to the lower form of this dogma it is surely funny. This polite request to the dramatist to please point a moral, to rival Cyrano, in iterating through each act 'A la fin de l'envoi je touche' is amazing.[20] Bred as it is of an amiable-parochial disposition we can but waive it. Mr Beoerly sacked with strychnine, or M. Coupeau in the horrors are nothing short of piteous in a surplice and dalmatic apiece.[21] However this absurdity is eating itself fast, like the tiger of story, tail first.

A yet more insidious claim is the claim for beauty. As conceived by the claimants beauty is as often anaemic spirituality as hardy animalism. Then, chiefly because beauty is to men an arbitrary quality and often lies no deeper than form, to pin drama to dealing with it, would be hazardous. Beauty is the swerga[22] of the aesthete; but truth has a more ascertainable and a more real dominion. Art is true to itself when it deals with truth. Should such an untoward event as a universal reformation take place on earth, truth would be the very threshold of the house beautiful.[23]

I have just one other claim to discuss, even at the risk of exhausting your patience. I quote from Mr Beerbohm Tree. 'In these days when faith is tinged with philosophic doubt, I believe it is the function of art to give us light rather than darkness. It should not point to our relationship with monkeys but rather remind us of our affinity with the angels.'[24] In this statement there is a fair element of truth which however requires qualification. Mr Tree contends that men and women will always look to art as the glass wherein they may see themselves idealised. Rather I should think that men and women seldom think gravely on their own impulses towards art. The fetters of convention bind them too strongly. But after all art cannot be governed by the insincerity of the compact majority but rather by those eternal conditions, says Mr Tree, which have governed it from the first. I admit this as irrefutable truth. But it were well we had in mind that those eternal conditions are not the conditions of modern communities. Art is marred by such mistaken insistence on its religious, its moral, its beautiful, its idealising tendencies. A single Rembrandt is worth a gallery full of Van Dycks.[25] And it is this doctrine of idealism in art which has in notable instances disfigured

manful endeavour, and has also fostered a babyish instinct to dive
under blankets at the mention of the bogey of realism. Hence the
public disowns Tragedy, unless she rattles her dagger and goblet,
abhors Romance which is not amenable to the laws of prosody, and
deems it a sad defect in art if, from the outpoured blood of hapless
heroism, there does not at once spring up a growth of sorrowful
blossoms. As in the very madness and frenzy of this attitude, people
want the drama to befool them, Purveyor supplies plutocrat with a
parody of life which the latter digests medicinally in a darkened
theatre, the stage literally battening on the mental offal of its patrons.

Now if these views are effete what will serve the purpose? Shall
we put life—real life—on the stage? No, says the Philistine chorus,
for it will not draw. What a blend of thwarted sight and smug commercialism. Parnassus and the city Bank divide the souls of the
pedlars. Life indeed nowadays is often a sad bore. Many feel like the
Frenchman[26] that they have been born too late in a world too old,
and their wanhope and nerveless unheroism point on ever sternly to
a last nothing, a vast futility and meanwhile—a bearing of fardels.[27]
Epic savagery is rendered impossible by vigilant policing, chivalry
has been killed by the fashion oracles of the boulevardes.[28] There is
no clank of mail, no halo about gallantry, no hat-sweeping, no roys-
tering! The traditions of romance are upheld only in Bohemia. Still I
think out of the dreary sameness of existence, a measure of dramatic
life may be drawn. Even the most commonplace, the deadest among
the living, may play a part in a great drama. It is a sinful foolishness
to sigh back for the good old times, to feed the hunger of us with the
cold stones they afford. Life we must accept as we see it before our
eyes, men and women as we meet them in the real world, not as we
apprehend them in the world of faery. The great human comedy in
which each has share, gives limitless scope to the true artist, today as
yesterday and as in years gone. The forms of things. as the earth's
crust, are changed. The timbers of the ships of Tarshish[29] are falling
asunder or eaten by the wanton sea; time has broken into the fast-
nesses of the mighty; the gardens of Armida[30] are become as treeless
wilds. But the deathless passions, the human verities which so found
expression then, are indeed deathless, in the heroic cycle, or in the
scientific age. Lohengrin,[31] the drama of which unfolds itself in a
scene of seclusion, amid half-lights, is not an Antwerp legend but a
world drama. Ghosts,[32] the action of which passes in a common

parlour, is of universal import—a deepset branch on the tree, Igdrasil [*sic*],[33] whose roots are struck in earth, but through whose higher leafage the stars of heaven are glowing and astir. It may be that many have nothing to do with such fable, or think that their wonted fare is all that is of need to them. But as we stand on the mountains today, looking before and after, pining for what is not, scarcely discerning afar the patches of open sky; when the spurs threaten, and the track is grown with briers, what does it avail that into our hands we have given us a clouded cane[34] for an alpenstock, or that we have dainty silks to shield us against the eager, upland wind? The sooner we understand our true position, the better; and the sooner then will we be up and doing on our way. In the meantime, art, and chiefly drama, may help us to make our resting places with a greater insight and a greater foresight, that the stones of them may be bravely builded, and the windows goodly and fair. '. . . what will you do in our Society, Miss Hessel?' asked Rörlund—'I will let in fresh air, Pastor '—answered Lona.[35]

Jas. A. Joyce
January. 10. 1900.

IBSEN'S NEW DRAMA

Twenty years have passed since Henrik Ibsen wrote *A Doll's House*, thereby almost marking an epoch in the history of drama. During those years his name has gone abroad through the length and breadth of two continents, and has provoked more discussion and criticism than that of any other living man. He has been upheld as a religious reformer, a social reformer, a Semitic lover of righteousness, and as a great dramatist. He has been rigorously denounced as a meddlesome intruder, a defective artist, an incomprehensible mystic, and, in the eloquent words of a certain English critic, 'a muck-ferreting dog'.[1] Through the perplexities of such diverse criticism, the great genius of the man is day by day coming out as a hero comes out amid the earthly trials. The dissonant cries are fainter and more distant, the random praises are rising in steadier and more choral chaunt. Even to the uninterested bystander it must seem significant that the interest attached to this Norwegian has never flagged for over a quarter of a century. It may be questioned whether any man has held so firm an empire over the thinking world in modern times. Not Rousseau; not Emerson; not Carlyle; not any of those giants of whom almost all have passed out of human ken. Ibsen's power over two generations has been enhanced by his own reticence. Seldom, if at all, has he condescended to join battle with his enemies. It would appear as if the storm of fierce debate rarely broke in upon his wonderful calm. The conflicting voices have not influenced his work in the very smallest degree. His output of dramas has been regulated by the utmost order, by a clockwork routine, seldom found in the case of genius. Only once he answered his assailants after their violent attack on *Ghosts*. But from *The Wild Duck* to *John Gabriel Borkman*, his dramas have appeared almost mechanically at intervals of two years. One is apt to overlook the sustained energy which such a plan of campaign demands; but even surprise at this must give way to admiration at the gradual, irresistible advance of this extraordinary man. Eleven plays, all dealing with modern life, have been published.[2] Here is the list: *A Doll's House, Ghosts, An Enemy of the People, The Wild Duck, Rosmersholm, The Lady from the Sea, Hedda Gabler, The Master Builder, Little Eyolf, John Gabriel Borkman*, and lastly—his new drama, published at Copenhagen, 19 December 1899—*When We Dead Awaken*. This play is already in process of translation into almost a dozen different languages—a fact which speaks volumes for the power of its author. The drama is written in prose, and is in three acts.

To begin an account of a play of Ibsen's is surely no easy matter. The subject is, in one way, so confined, and, in another way, so vast. It is safe to predict that nine-tenths of the notices of this play will open in some such way as the following: 'Arnold Rubek and his wife, Maja, have been married for four years, at the beginning of the play. Their union is, however, unhappy. Each is discontented with the other.' So far as this goes, it is unimpeachable; but then it does not go very far. It does not convey even the most shadowy notion of the relations between Professor Rubek and his wife. It is a bald, clerkly version of countless, indefinable complexities. It is as though the history of a tragic life were to be written down rudely in two columns, one for the pros and the other for the cons. It is only saying what is literally true, to say that, in the three acts of the drama, there has been stated all that is essential to the drama. There is from first to last hardly a superfluous word or phrase. Therefore, the play itself expresses its own ideas as briefly and as concisely as they can be expressed in the dramatic form. It is manifest, then, that a notice cannot give an adequate notion of the drama. This is not the case with the common lot of plays, to which the fullest justice may be meted out in a very limited number of lines. They are for the most part reheated dishes—unoriginal compositions, cheerfully owlish as to heroic insight, living only in their own candid claptrap—in a word, stagey. The most perfunctory curtness is their fittest meed. But in dealing with the work of a man like Ibsen, the task set the reviewer is truly great enough to sink all his courage. All he can hope to do is to link some of the more salient points together in such a way as to suggest rather than to indicate, the intricacies of the plot. Ibsen has attained ere this to such mastery over his art that, with apparently easy dialogue, he presents his men and women passing through different soul-crises. His analytic method is thus made use of to the fullest extent, and into the comparatively short space of two days the life in life of all his characters is compressed. For instance, though we only see Solness during one night and up to the following evening, we have in reality watched with bated breath the whole course of

his life up to the moment when Hilda Wangel enters his house. So in
the play under consideration, when we see Professor Rubek first, he
is sitting in a garden chair, reading his morning paper, but by degrees
the whole scroll of his life is unrolled before us, and we have the
pleasure not of hearing it read out to us, but of reading it for ourselves, piecing the various parts, and going closer to see wherever the
writing on the parchment is fainter or less legible.

As I have said, when the play opens, Professor Rubek is sitting in
the gardens of a hotel, eating, or rather having finished, his breakfast.
In another chair, close beside him, is sitting Maja Rubek, the Professor's wife. The scene is in Norway, a popular health resort near the
sea. Through the trees can be seen the town harbour, and the fjord,
with steamers plying over it, as it stretches past headland and river-
isle out to the sea. Rubek is a famous sculptor, of middle age, and
Maja, a woman still young, whose bright eyes have just a shade of
sadness in them. These two continue reading their respective papers
quietly in the peace of the morning. All looks so idyllic to the careless
eye. The lady breaks the silence in a weary, petulant manner by
complaining of the deep peace that reigns about them. Arnold lays
down his paper with mild expostulation. Then they begin to con-
verse of this thing and that; first of the silence, then of the place and
the people, of the railway stations through which they passed the
previous night, with their sleepy porters and aimlessly shifting lan-
terns. From this they proceed to talk of the changes in the people,
and of all that has grown up since they were married. Then it is but a
little further to the main trouble. In speaking of their married life it
speedily appears that the inner view of their relations is hardly as
ideal as the outward view might lead one to expect. The depths of
these two people are being slowly stirred up. The leaven of prospec-
tive drama is gradually discerned working amid the *fin-de-siècle*
scene. The lady seems a difficult little person. She complains of the
idle promises with which her husband had fed her aspirations.

MAJA. You said you would take me up to a high mountain and show
    me all the glory of the world.
RUBEK (*with a slight start*). Did I promise you that, too?

In short, there is something untrue lying at the root of their
union. Meanwhile the guests of the hotel, who are taking the baths,
pass out of the hotel porch on the right, chatting and laughing men

and women. They are informally marshalled by the inspector of the baths. This person is an unmistakable type of the conventional official. He salutes Mr. and Mrs. Rubek, enquiring how they slept. Rubek asks him if any of the guests take their baths by night, as he has seen a white figure moving in the park during the night. Maja scouts the notion, but the inspector says that there is a strange lady, who has rented the pavilion which is to the left, and who is staying there, with one attendant—a Sister of Mercy. As they are talking, the strange lady and her companion pass slowly through the park and enter the pavilion. The incident appears to affect Rubek, and Maja's curiosity is aroused.

MAJA (*a little hurt and jarred*). Perhaps this lady has been one of your models, Rubek? Search your memory.

RUBEK (*looks cuttingly at her*). Model?

MAJA (*with a provoking smile*). In your younger days, I mean. You are said to have had such innumerable models—long ago, of course.

RUBEK (*in the same tone*). Oh, no, little Frau Maja. I have in reality had only one single model. One and one only for everything I have done.

While this misunderstanding is finding outlet in the foregoing conversation, the inspector, all at once, takes fright at some person who is approaching. He attempts to escape into the hotel, but the high-pitched voice of the person who is approaching arrests him.

ULFHEIM's voice (*heard outside*). Stop a moment, man. Devil take it all, can't you stop? Why do you always scuttle away from me?

With these words, uttered in strident tones, the second chief actor enters on the scene. He is described as a great bear-killer, thin, tall, of uncertain age, and muscular. He is accompanied by his servant, Lars, and a couple of sporting dogs. Lars does not speak a single word in the play. Ulfheim at present dismisses him with a kick, and approaches Mr. and Mrs. Rubek. He falls into conversation with them, for Rubek is known to him as the celebrated sculptor. On sculpture this savage hunter offers some original remarks.

ULFHEIM. . . . We both work in a hard material, madam—both your husband and I. He struggles with his marble blocks, I daresay; and I struggle with tense and quivering bear-sinews. And we both of

us win the fight in the end—subdue and master our material. We
don't give in until we have got the better of it, though it fight
never so hard.

RUBEK (*deep in thought*). There's a great deal of truth in what you
say.

This eccentric creature, perhaps by the force of his own eccentricity, has begun to weave a spell of enchantment about Maja. Each
word that he utters tends to wrap the web of his personality still
closer about her. The black dress of the Sister of Mercy causes him
to grin sardonically. He speaks calmly of all his near friends, whom
he has dispatched out of the world.

MAJA. And what did you do for your nearest friends?
ULFHEIM. Shot them, of course.
RUBEK (*looking at him*). Shot them?
MAJA (*moving her chair back*). Shot them dead?
ULFHEIM (*nods*). I never miss, madam

However, it turns out that by his nearest friends he means his
dogs, and the minds of his hearers are put somewhat more at ease.
During their conversation the Sister of Mercy has prepared a slight
repast for her mistress at one of the tables outside the pavilion. The
unsustaining qualities of the food excite Ulfheim's merriment. He
speaks with a lofty disparagement of such effeminate diet. He is a
realist in his appetite.

ULFHEIM (*rising*). Spoken like a woman of spirit, madam. Come with
me, then! They [his dogs] swallow whole, great, thumping meat-
bones—gulp them up and then gulp them down again. Oh, it's a
regular treat to see them!

On such half-gruesome, half-comic invitation Maja goes out with
him, leaving her husband in the company of the strange lady who
enters from the pavilion. Almost simultaneously the Professor and
the lady recognise each other. The lady has served Rubek as model
for the central figure in his famous masterpiece, 'The Resurrection
Day'. Having done her work for him, she had fled in an unaccountable manner, leaving no traces behind her. Rubek and she drift into
familiar conversation. She asks him who is the lady who has just
gone out. He answers, with some hesitation, that she is his wife.

Then he asks if she is married. She replies that she is married. He asks her where her husband is at present.

RUBEK. And where is he now?

IRENE. Oh, in a churchyard somewhere or other, with a fine, handsome monument over him; and with a bullet rattling in his skull.

RUBEK. Did he kill himself?

IRENE. Yes, he was good enough to take that off my hands.

RUBEK. Do you not lament his loss, Irene?

IRENE (*not understanding*). Lament? What loss?

RUBEK. Why, the loss of Herr von Satow, of course.

IRENE. His name was not Satow.

RUBEK. Was it not?

IRENE. My second husband is called Satow. He is a Russian.

RUBEK. And where is he?

IRENE. Far away in the Ural Mountains. Among all his gold-mines.

RUBEK. So he lives there?

IRENE (*shrugging her shoulders*). Lives? Lives? In reality I have killed him.

RUBEK (*starts*). Killed—!

IRENE. Killed him with a fine sharp dagger which I always have with me in bed—

Rubek begins to understand that there is some meaning hidden beneath these strange words. He begins to think seriously on himself, his art, and on her, passing in review the course of his life since the creation of his masterpiece, 'The Resurrection Day'. He sees that he has not fulfilled the promise of that work, and comes to realise that there is something lacking in his life. He asks Irene how she has lived since they last saw each other. Irene's answer to this query is of great importance, for it strikes the keynote of the entire play.

IRENE (*rises slowly from her chair and says quiveringly*). I was dead for many years. They came and bound me—lacing my arms together at my back. Then they lowered me into a grave-vault, with iron bars before the loophole. And with padded walls, so that no one on the earth above could hear the grave-shrieks.

In Irene's allusion to her position as model for the great picture, Ibsen gives further proof of his extraordinary knowledge of women.

No other man could have so subtly expressed the nature of the relations between the sculptor and his model, had he even dreamt of them.

IRENE. I exposed myself wholly and unreservedly to your gaze [*more softly*] and never once did you touch me. . . .

*

RUBEK (*looks impressively at her*). I was an artist, Irene.
IRENE (*darkly*). That is just it. That is just it.

Thinking deeper and deeper on himself and on his former attitude towards this woman, it strikes him yet more forcibly that there are great gulfs set between his art and his life, and that even in his art his skill and genius are far from perfect. Since Irene left him he has done nothing but paint portrait busts of townsfolk. Finally, some kind of resolution is enkindled in him, a resolution to repair his botching, for he does not altogether despair of that. There is just a reminder of the will-glorification of *Brand*[3] in the lines that follow.

RUBEK (*struggling with himself uncertainly*). If we could, oh, if only we could . . .
IRENE. Why can we not do what we will?

In fine, the two agree in deeming their present state insufferable. It appears plain to her that Rubek lies under a heavy obligation to her, and with their recognition of this, and the entrance of Maja, fresh from the enchantment of Ulfheim, the first act closes.

RUBEK. When did you begin to seek for me, Irene?
IRENE (*with a touch of jesting bitterness*). From the time when I realised that I had given away to you something rather indispensable. Something one ought never to part with.
RUBEK (*bowing his head*). Yes, that is bitterly true. You gave me three or four years of your youth.
IRENE. More, more than that I gave you—spendthrift as I then was.
RUBEK. Yes, you were prodigal, Irene. You gave me all your naked loveliness—
IRENE. To gaze upon—
RUBEK. And to glorify. . . .

*

IRENE. But you have forgotten the most precious gift.

RUBEK. The most precious . . . what gift was that?

IRENE. I gave you my young living soul. And that gift left me empty within—soulless [*looks at him with a fixed stare*]. It was that I died of, Arnold.

It is evident, even from this mutilated account, that the first act is a masterly one. With no perceptible effort the drama rises, with a methodic natural ease it develops. The trim garden of the nineteenth-century hotel is slowly made the scene of a gradually growing dramatic struggle. Interest has been roused in each of the characters, sufficient to carry the mind into the succeeding act. The situation is not stupidly explained, but the action has set in, and at the close the play has reached a definite stage of progression.

The second act takes place close to a sanatorium on the mountains. A cascade leaps from a rock and flows in steady stream to the right. On the bank some children are playing, laughing and shouting. The time is evening. Rubek is discovered lying on a mound to the left. Maja enters shortly, equipped for hill-climbing. Helping herself with her stick across the stream, she calls out to Rubek and approaches him. He asks how she and her companion are amusing themselves, and questions her as to their hunting. An exquisitely humorous touch enlivens their talk. Rubek asks if they intend hunting the bear near the surrounding locality. She replies with a grand superiority.

MAJA. You don't suppose that bears are to be found in the naked mountains, do you?

The next topic is the uncouth Ulfheim. Maja admires him because he is so ugly—then turns abruptly to her husband saying, pensively, that he also is ugly. The accused pleads his age.

RUBEK (*shrugging his shoulders*). One grows old. One grows old, Frau Maja!

This semi-serious banter leads them on to graver matters. Maja lies at length in the soft heather, and rails gently at the Professor. For the mysteries and claims of art she has a somewhat comical disregard.

MAJA (*with a somewhat scornful laugh*). Yet, you are always, always an artist.

and again—

MAJA. . . . Your tendency is to keep yourself to yourself and—think
your own thoughts. And, of course, I can't talk properly to you
about your affairs. I know nothing about Art and that sort of
thing. [*With an impatient gesture.*] And care very little either, for
that matter.

She rallies him on the subject of the strange lady, and hints
maliciously at the understanding between them. Rubek says that he
was only an artist and that she was the source of his inspiration. He
confesses that the five years of his married life have been years of
intellectual famine for him. He has viewed in their true light his own
feelings towards his art.

RUBEK (*smiling*). But that was not precisely what I had in my mind.
MAJA. What then?
RUBEK (*again serious*). It was this—that all the talk about the artist's
vocation and the artist's mission, and so forth, began to strike me
as being very empty and hollow and meaningless at bottom.
MAJA. Then what would you put in its place?
RUBEK. Life, Maja.

The all-important question of their mutual happiness is touched
upon, and after a brisk discussion a tacit agreement to separate is
effected. When matters are in this happy condition Irene is descried
coming across the heath. She is surrounded by the sportive children
and stays awhile among them. Maja jumps up from the grass and
goes to her, saying, enigmatically, that her husband requires assistance to 'open a precious casket.' Irene bows and goes towards Rubek,
and Maja goes joyfully to seek her hunter. The interview which
follows is certainly remarkable, even from a stagey point of view. It
constitutes, practically, the substance of the second act, and is of
absorbing interest. At the same time it must be added that such a
scene would tax the powers of the mimes producing it. Nothing
short of a complete realisation of the two *rôles* would represent the
complex ideas involved in the conversation. When we reflect how
few stage artists would have either the intelligence to attempt it or
the powers to execute it, we behold a pitiful revelation.

In the interview of these two people on the heath, the whole
tenors of their lives are outlined with bold steady strokes. From the
first exchange of introductory words each phrase tells a chapter of

experiences. Irene alludes to the dark shadow of the Sister of Mercy which follows her everywhere, as the shadow of Arnold's unquiet conscience follows him. When he has half-involuntarily confessed so much, one of the great barriers between them is broken down. Their trust in each other is, to some extent, renewed, and they revert to their past acquaintance. Irene speaks openly of her feelings, of her hate for the sculptor.

IRENE (*again vehemently*). Yes, for you—for the artist who had so lightly and carelessly taken a warm-blooded body, a young human life, and worn the soul out of it—because you needed it for a work of art.

Rubek's transgression has indeed been great. Not merely has he possessed himself of her soul, but he has withheld from its rightful throne the child of her soul. By her child Irene means the statue. To her it seems that this statue is, in a very true and very real sense, born of her. Each day as she saw it grow to its full growth under the hand of the skilful moulder, her inner sense of motherhood for it, of right over it, of love towards it, had become stronger and more confirmed.

IRENE (*changing to a tone full of warmth and feeling*). But that statue in the wet, living clay, that I loved—as it rose up, a vital human creature out of these raw, shapeless masses—for that was our creation, our child. Mine and yours.

It is, in reality, because of her strong feelings that she has kept aloof from Rubek for five years. But when she hears now of what he has done to the child—her child—all her powerful nature rises up against him in resentment. Rubek, in a mental agony, endeavours to explain, while she listens like a tigress whose cub has been wrested from her by a thief.

RUBEK. I was young then—with no experience of life. The Resurrection, I thought, would be most beautifully and exquisitely figured as a young unsullied woman—with none of a life's experience—awakening to light and glory without having to put away from her anything ugly and impure.

With larger experience of life he has found it necessary to alter his ideal somewhat, he has made her child no longer a principal, but an

intermediary figure. Rubek, turning towards her, sees her just about
to stab him. In a fever of terror and thought he rushes into his own
defence, pleading madly for the errors he has done. It seems to Irene
that he is endeavouring to render his sin poetical, that he is penitent
but in a luxury of dolour. The thought that she has given up herself,
her whole life, at the bidding of his false art, rankles in her heart with
a terrible persistence. She cries out against herself, not loudly, but in
deep sorrow.

IRENE (*with apparent self-control*). I should have borne children into
the world—many children—real children—not such children as
are hidden away in grave-vaults. That was my vocation. I ought
never to have served you—poet.

Rubek, in poetic absorption, has no reply, he is musing on the old,
happy days. Their dead joys solace him. But Irene is thinking of a
certain phrase of his which he had spoken unwittingly. He had
declared that he owed her thanks for her assistance in his work. This
has been, he had said, a truly blessed *episode* in my life. Rubek's
tortured mind cannot bear any more reproaches, too many are
heaped upon it already. He begins throwing flowers on the stream, as
they used in those bygone days on the lake of Taunitz. He recalls to
her the time when they made a boat of leaves, and yoked a white
swan to it, in imitation of the boat of Lohengrin. Even here in their
sport there lies a hidden meaning.[4]

IRENE. You said I was the swan that drew your boat.
RUBEK. Did I say so? Yes, I daresay I did [*absorbed in the game*]. Just
see how the sea-gulls are swimming down the stream!
IRENE (*laughing*). And all your ships have run ashore.
RUBEK (*throwing more leaves into the brook*). I have ships enough in
reserve.

While they are playing aimlessly, in a kind of childish despair,
Ulfheim and Maja appear across the heath. These two are going to
seek adventures on the high tablelands. Maja sings out to her husband a little song which she has composed in her joyful mood. With
a sardonic laugh Ulfheim bids Rubek good-night and disappears
with his companion up the mountain. All at once Irene and Rubek
leap to the same thought. But at that moment the gloomy figure of
the Sister of Mercy is seen in the twilight, with her leaden eyes

looking at them both. Irene breaks from him, but promises to meet him that night on the heath.

RUBEK. And you will come, Irene?

IRENE. Yes, certainly I will come. Wait for me here.

RUBEK (*repeats dreamily*). Summer night on the upland. With you. With you. [*His eyes meet hers.*] Oh, Irene, that might have been our life. And that we have forfeited, we two.

IRENE. We see the irretrievable only when [*breaks off short*].

RUBEK (*looks inquiringly at her*). When?. . .

IRENE. When we dead awaken.

The third act takes place on a wide plateau, high up on the hills. The ground is rent with yawning clefts. Looking to the right, one sees the range of the summits half-hidden in the moving mists. On the left stands an old, dismantled hut. It is in the early morning, when the skies are the colour of pearl. The day is beginning to break. Maja and Ulfheim come down to the plateau. Their feelings are sufficiently explained by the opening words.

MAJA (*trying to tear herself loose*). Let me go! Let me go, I say!

ULFHEIM. Come, come! are you going to bite now? You're as snappish as a wolf.

When Ulfheim will not cease his annoyances, Maja threatens to run over the crest of the neighbouring ridge. Ulfheim points out that she will dash herself to pieces. He has wisely sent Lars away after the hounds, that he may be uninterrupted. Lars, he says, may be trusted not to find the dogs too soon.

MAJA (*looking angrily at him*). No, I daresay not.

ULFHEIM (*catching at her arm*). For Lars—he knows my—my methods of sport, you see.

Maja, with enforced self-possession, tells him frankly what she thinks of him. Her uncomplimentary observations please the bear-hunter very much. Maja requires all her tact to keep him in order. When she talks of going back to the hotel, he gallantly offers to carry her on his shoulders, for which suggestion he is promptly snubbed. The two are playing as a cat and a bird play. Out of their skirmish one speech of Ulfheim's rises suddenly to arrest attention, as it throws some light on his former life.

ULFHEIM (*with suppressed exasperation*). I once took a young girl—
lifted her up from the mire of the streets, and carried her in my
arms. Next my heart I carried her. So I would have borne her all
through life, lest haply she should dash her foot against a stone . . .
[*With a growling laugh.*] And do you know what I got for my
reward?

MAJA. No. What did you get?

ULFHEIM (*looks at her, smiles and nods*). I got the horns! The horns
that you can see so plainly. Is not that a comical story, madam
bear-murderess?

As an exchange of confidence, Maja tells him her life in
summary—and chiefly her married life with Professor Rubek. As a
result, these two uncertain souls feel attracted to each other, and
Ulfheim states his case in the following characteristic manner:—

ULFHEIM. Should not we two tack our poor shreds of life together?

Maja, satisfied that in their vows there will be no promise on his part
to show her all the splendours of the earth, or to fill her dwelling-
place with art, gives a half-consent by allowing him to carry her
down the slope. As they are about to go, Rubek and Irene, who have
also spent the night on the heath, approach the same plateau. When
Ulfheim asks Rubek if he and madame have ascended by the same
pathway, Rubek answers significantly.

RUBEK. Yes, of course [*with a glance at* MAJA]. Henceforth the
strange lady and I do not intend our ways to part.

While the musketry of their wit is at work, the elements seem to
feel that there is a mighty problem to be solved then and there, and
that a great drama is swiftly drawing to a close. The smaller figures
of Maja and Ulfheim are grown still smaller in the dawn of the
tempest. Their lots are decided in comparative quiet, and we cease to
take much interest in them. But the other two hold our gaze, as they
stand up silently on the fjaell,[5] engrossing central figures of bound-
less, human interest. On a sudden, Ulfheim raises his hand impressively towards the heights

ULFHEIM. But don't you see that the storm is upon us? Don't you
hear the blasts of wind?

RUBEK (*listening*). They sound like the prelude to the Resurrection Day. . . .

*

MAJA (*drawing* ULFHEIM *away*). Let us make haste and get down.

As he cannot take more than one person at a time, Ulfheim promises to send aid for Rubek and Irene, and, seizing Maja in his arms, clambers rapidly but warily down the path. On the desolate mountain plateau, in the growing light, the man and the woman are left together—no longer the artist and his model. And the shadow of a great change is stalking close in the morning silence. Then Irene tells Arnold that she will not go back among the men and women she has left; she will not be rescued. She tells him also, for now she may tell all, how she had been tempted to kill him in frenzy when he spoke of their connection as an episode of his life.

RUBEK (*darkly*). And why did you hold your hand?

IRENE. Because it flashed upon me with a sudden horror that you were dead already—long ago.

But, says Rubek, our love is not dead in us, it is active, fervent and strong.

IRENE. The love that belongs to the life of earth—the beautiful, miraculous life of earth—the inscrutable life of earth—that is dead in both of us.

There are, moreover, the difficulties of their former lives. Even here, at the sublimest part of his play, Ibsen is master of himself and his facts. His genius as an artist faces all, shirks nothing. At the close of *The Master Builder*, the greatest touch of all was the horrifying exclamation of one without, 'O! the head is all crushed in.' A lesser artist would have cast a spiritual glamour over the tragedy of Bygmester Solness.[6] In like manner here Irene objects that she has exposed herself as a nude before the vulgar gaze, that Society has cast her out, that all is too late. But Rubek cares for such considerations no more. He flings them all to the wind and decides.

RUBEK (*throwing his arms violently around her*). Then let two of the dead—us two—for once live life to its uttermost, before we go down to our graves again.

IRENE (*with a shriek*). Arnold!

RUBEK. But not here in the half-darkness. Not here with this hideous dank shroud flapping around us!

IRENE (*carried away by passion*). No, no—up in the light and in all the glittering glory! Up to the Peak of Promise!

RUBEK. There we will hold our marriage-feast, Irene—oh! my beloved!

IRENE (*proudly*). The sun may freely look on us, Arnold.

RUBEK. All the powers of light may freely look on us—and all the powers of darkness too [*seizes her hand*]—will you then follow me, oh my grace-given bride!

IRENE (*as though transfigured*). I follow you, freely and gladly, my lord and master!

RUBEK (*drawing her along with him*). We must first pass through the mists, Irene, and then—

IRENE. Yes, through all the mists, and then right up to the summit of the tower that shines in the sunrise.

> [*The mist-clouds close in over the scene.* RUBEK *and* IRENE, *hand in hand, climb up over the snowfield to the right and soon disappear among the lower clouds. Keen storm-gusts hurtle and whistle through the air.*
>
> [THE SISTER OF MERCY *appears upon the rubble-slope to the left. She stops and looks around silently and searchingly.*
>
> [MAJA *can be heard singing triumphantly far in the depths below.*
>
> MAJA. I am free! I am free! I am free!
> No more life in the prison for me!
> I am free as a bird! I am free!
>
> [*Suddenly a sound like thunder is heard from high up on the snowfield, which glides and whirls downwards with rushing speed.* RUBEK *and* IRENE *can be dimly discerned as they are whirled along with the masses of snow and buried in them.*

THE SISTER OF MERCY (*gives a shriek, stretches out her arms towards them, and cries*). Irene! [*Stands silent a moment, then makes the sign of the cross before her in the air, and says*], Pax Vobiscum!

> [MAJA'S *triumphant song sounds from still further down below.*

Such is the plot, in a crude and incoherent way, of this new drama. Ibsen's plays do not depend for their interest on the action, or on the incidents. Even the characters, faultlessly drawn though they be, are not the first thing in his plays. But the naked drama—either the perception of a great truth, or the opening up of a great question, or a great conflict which is almost independent of the conflicting actors, and has been and is of far-reaching importance—this is what pri marily rivets our attention. Ibsen has chosen the average lives in their uncompromising truth for the groundwork of all his later plays. He has abandoned the verse form, and has never sought to embellish his work after the conventional fashion. Even when his dramatic theme reached its zenith he has not sought to trick it out in gawds or tawdriness. How easy it would have been to have written *An Enemy of the People* on a speciously loftier level—to have replaced the *bourgeois* by the legitimate hero! Critics might then have extolled as grand what they have so often condemned as banal. But the surroundings are nothing to Ibsen. The play is the thing. By the force of his genius, and the indisputable skill which he brings to all his efforts, Ibsen has, for many years, engrossed the attention of the civilised world. Many years more, however, must pass before he will enter his kingdom in jubilation, although, as he stands to-day, all has been done on his part to ensure his own worthiness to enter therein. I do not propose here to examine into every detail of dramaturgy connected with this play, but merely to outline the characterisation.

In his characters Ibsen does not repeat himself. In this drama—the last of a long catalogue—he has drawn and differentiated with his customary skill. What a novel creation is Ulfheim! Surely the hand which has drawn him has not yet lost her cunning. Ulfheim is, I think, the newest character in the play. He is a kind of surprise-packet. It is as a result of his novelty that he seems to leap, at first mention, into bodily form. He is superbly wild, primitively impressive. His fierce eyes roll and glare as those of Yégof or Herne.[7] As for Lars, we may dismiss him, for he never opens his mouth. The Sister of Mercy speaks only once in the play, but then with good effect. In silence she follows Irene like a retribution, a voiceless shadow with her own symbolic majesty.

Irene, too, is worthy of her place in the gallery of her compeers. Ibsen's knowledge of humanity is nowhere more obvious than in his portrayal of women. He amazes one by his painful introspection; he seems to know them better than they know themselves. Indeed, if one may say so of an eminently virile man, there is a curious admixture of the woman in his nature. His marvellous accuracy, his faint traces of femininity, his delicacy of swift touch, are perhaps attributable to this admixture. But that he knows women is an incontrovertible fact. He appears to have sounded them to almost unfathomable depths. Beside his portraits the psychological studies of Hardy and Turgénieff, or the exhaustive elaborations of Meredith,[8] seem no more than sciolism. With a deft stroke, in a phrase, in a word, he does what costs them chapters, and does it better. Irene, then, has to face great comparison; but it must be acknowledged that she comes forth of it bravely. Although Ibsen's women are uniformly true, they, of course, present themselves in various lights.

Thus Gina Ekdal[9] is, before all else, a comic figure, and Hedda Gabler a tragic one—if such old-world terms may be employed without incongruity. But Irene cannot be so readily classified; the very aloofness from passion, which is not separable from her, forbids classification. She interests us strangely—magnetically, because of her inner power of character. However perfect Ibsen's former creations may be, it is questionable whether any of his women reach to the depth of soul of Irene. She holds our gaze for the sheer force of her intellectual capacity. She is, moreover, an intensely spiritual creation—in the truest and widest sense of that. At times she is liable to get beyond us, to soar above us, as she does with Rubek. It will be considered by some as a blemish that she—a woman of fine spirituality—is made an artist's model, and some may even regret that such an episode mars the harmony of the drama. I cannot altogether see the force of this contention; it seems pure irrelevancy. But whatever may be thought of the fact, there is small room for complaint as to the handling of it. Ibsen treats it, as indeed he treats all things, with large insight, artistic restraint, and sympathy. He sees it steadily and whole, as from a great height, with perfect vision and an angelic dispassionateness, with the sight of one who may look on the sun with open eyes.[10] Ibsen is different from the clever purveyor.

Maja fulfills a certain technical function in the play, apart from her individual character. Into the sustained tension she comes as a relief. Her airy freshness is as a breath of keen air. The sense of free, almost flamboyant, life, which is her chief note, counter-balances the austerity of Irene and the dulness of Rubek. Maja has practically the same effect on this play, as Hilda Wangel has on *The Master Builder*. But she does not capture our sympathy so much as Nora Helmer.[11] She is not meant to capture it.

Rubek himself is the chief figure in this drama, and, strangely enough, the most conventional. Certainly, when contrasted with his Napoleonic predecessor, John Gabriel Borkman, he is a mere shadow. It must be borne in mind, however, that Borkman is alive, actively, energetically, restlessly alive, all through the play to the end, when he dies; whereas Arnold Rubek is dead, almost hopelessly dead, until the end, when he comes to life. Notwithstanding this, he is supremely interesting, not because of himself, but because of his dramatic significance. Ibsen's drama, as I have said, is wholly independent of his characters. They may be bores, but the drama in which they live and move is invariably powerful. Not that Rubek is a bore by any means! He is infinitely more interesting in himself than Torvald Helmer or Tesman,[12] both of whom possess certain strongly-marked characteristics. Arnold Rubek is, on the other hand, not intended to be a genius, as perhaps Eljert Lovborg is.[13] Had he been a genius like Eljert he would have understood in a truer way the value of his life. But, as we are to suppose, the facts that he is devoted to his art and that he has attained to a degree of mastery in it—mastery of hand linked with limitation of thought—tell us that there may be lying dormant in him a capacity for greater life, which may be exercised when he, a dead man, shall have risen from among the dead.

The only character whom I have neglected is the inspector of the baths, and I hasten to do him tardy, but scant, justice. He is neither more nor less than the average inspector of baths. But he is that.

So much for the characterisation, which is at all times profound and interesting. But apart from the characters in the play, there are some noteworthy points in the frequent and extensive side-issues of the line of thought. The most salient of these is what seems, at first sight, nothing more than an accidental scenic feature. I allude to the environment of the drama. One cannot but observe in Ibsen's later work a tendency to get out of closed rooms. Since *Hedda Gabler* this tendency is most marked. The last act of *The Master Builder* and the last act of *John Gabriel Borkman* take place in the open air. But in this play the three acts are *al fresco*. To give heed to such details as these in the drama may be deemed ultra-Boswellian fanaticism. As a matter of fact it is what is barely due to the work of a great artist. And this feature, which is so prominent, does not seem to me altogether without its significance.

Again, there has not been lacking in the last few social dramas a fine pity for men—a note nowhere audible in the uncompromising rigour of the early eighties.[14] Thus in the conversion of Rubek's views as to the girl-figure in his masterpiece, 'The Resurrection Day', there is involved an all-embracing philosophy, a deep sympathy with the cross-purposes and contradictions of life, as they may be reconcilable with a hopeful awakening—when the manifold travail of our poor humanity may have a glorious issue. As to the drama itself, it is doubtful if any good purpose can be served by attempting to criticise it.[15] Many things would tend to prove this. Henrik Ibsen is one of the world's great men before whom criticism can make but feeble show. Appreciation, hearkening is the only true criticism. Further, that species of criticism which calls itself dramatic criticism is a needless adjunct to his plays. When the art of a dramatist is perfect the critic is superfluous. Life is not to be criticised, but to be faced and lived. Again, if any plays demand a stage they are the plays of Ibsen. Not merely is this so because his plays have so much in common with the plays of other men that they were not written to cumber the shelves of a library, but because they are so packed with thought. At some chance expression the mind is tortured with some question, and in a flash long reaches of life are opened up in vista, yet the vision is momentary unless we stay to ponder on it. It is just to prevent excessive pondering that Ibsen requires to be acted. Finally, it is foolish to expect that a problem, which has occupied Ibsen for nearly three years, will unroll smoothly before our eyes on a first or second reading. So it is better to leave the drama to plead for itself. But this at least is clear, that in this play Ibsen has given us nearly the very best of himself. The action is neither hindered by many complexities, as in *The Pillars of Society*, nor harrowing in its simplicity, as in *Ghosts*. We have whimsicality, bordering on extravagance, in the wild Ulfheim, and subtle humour in the sly contempt which Rubek and Maja entertain for each other. But Ibsen has striven to let the drama have perfectly free action. So he has not bestowed his wonted pains on the minor characters. In many of his plays these minor characters are matchless creations. Witness Jacob Engstrand,

Tönnesen, and the demonic Molvik![16] But in this play the minor characters are not allowed to divert our attention.

On the whole, *When We Dead Awaken* may rank with the greatest of the author's work—if, indeed, it be not the greatest. It is described as the last of the series, which began with *A Doll's House*— a grand epilogue to its ten predecessors. Than these dramas, excellent alike in dramaturgic skill, characterisation, and supreme interest, the long roll of drama, ancient or modern, has few things better to show.

James A. Joyce.

THE DAY OF THE RABBLEMENT

No man, said the Nolan, can be a lover of the true or the good unless he abhors the multitude;[1] and the artist, though he may employ the crowd, is very careful to isolate himself. This radical principle of artistic economy applies specially to a time of crisis, and today when the highest form of art has been just preserved by desperate sacrifices, it is strange to see the artist making terms with the rabblement. The Irish Literary Theatre is the latest movement of protest against the sterility and falsehood of the modern stage.[2] Half a century ago the note of protest was uttered in Norway, and since then in several countries long and disheartening battles have been fought against the hosts of prejudice and misinterpretation and ridicule. What triumph there has been here and there is due to stubborn conviction, and every movement that has set out heroically has achieved a little. The Irish Literary Theatre gave out that it was the champion of progress, and proclaimed war against commercialism and vulgarity. It had partly made good its word and was expelling the old devil, when after the first encounter it surrendered to the popular will. Now, your popular devil is more dangerous than your vulgar devil. Bulk and lungs count for something, and he can gild his speech aptly. He has prevailed once more, and the Irish Literary Theatre must now be considered the property of the rabblement of the most belated race in Europe.

It will be interesting to examine here. The official organ of the movement spoke of producing European masterpieces, but the matter went no further. Such a project was absolutely necessary. The censorship is powerless in Dublin, and the directors could have produced *Ghosts* or *The Dominion of Darkness*[3] if they chose. Nothing can be done until the forces that dictate public judgement are calmly confronted. But, of course, the directors are shy of presenting Ibsen, Tolstoy or Hauptmaun [*sic*],[4] where even *Countess Cathleen* is pronounced vicious and damnable. Even for a technical reason this project was necessary. A nation which never advanced so far as a miracle-play affords no literary model to the artist, and he must look abroad. Earnest dramatists of the second rank, Sudermaun [*sic*], Bypruson [*sic*], and Giocosa [*sic*],[5] can write very much better plays than the Irish Literary Theatre has staged. But, of course, the directors would not like to present such improper writers to the uncultivated, much less to the cultivated, rabblement. Accordingly, the rabblement, placid and intensely moral, is enthroned in boxes and galleries amid a hum of approval—*la bestia Trioufaute* [*sic*]—and those who think that Echegaray is 'morbid', and titter coyly when Mélisande lets down her hair,[6] are not sure but they are the trustees of every intellectual and poetic treasure.

Meanwhile, what of the artists? It is equally unsafe at present to say of Mr Yeats that he has or has not genius. In aim and form *The Wind among the Reeds* is poetry of the highest order, and *The Adoration of the Magi* (a story which one of the great Russians might have written) shows what Mr Yeats can do when he breaks with the half-gods. But an esthete has a floating will, and Mr Yeats's treacherous instinct of adaptability must be blamed for his recent association with a platform from which even self-respect should have urged him to refrain. Mr Martyn and Mr Moore are not writers of much originality. Mr Martyn, disabled as he is by an incorrigible style, has none of the fierce, hysterical power of Strindberg, whom he suggests at times; and with him one is conscious of a lack of breadth and distinction which outweighs the nobility of certain passages. Mr Moore, however, has wonderful mimetic ability, and some years ago his books might have entitled him to the place of honour among English novelists. But though *Vain Fortune* (perhaps one should add some of *Esther Waters*) is fine, original work,[7] Mr Moore is really struggling in the backwash of that tide which has advanced from Flaubert through Jakobsen[8] to D'Aununzio [*sic*]: for two entire eras lie between *Madame Bovary* and *Il Fuoco*. It is plain from *Celebates* [*sic*][9] and the latter novels that Mr Moore is beginning to draw upon his literary account, and the quest of a new impulse may explain his recent startling conversion. Converts are in the movement now, and Mr Moore and his island have been fitly admired. But however frankly Mr Moore may misquote Pater and Turgeuieff [*sic*] to defend himself, his new impulse has no kind of relation to the future of art.[10]

In such circumstances it has become imperative to define the position. If an artist courts the favour of the multitude he cannot escape the contagion of its fetishism and deliberate self-deception, and if he joins in a popular movement he does so at his own risk. Therefore, the Irish Literary Theatre by its surrender to the trolls has cut itself adrift from the line of advancement. Until he has freed himself from the mean influences about him—sodden enthusiasm and clever insinuation and every flattering influence of vanity and low ambition—no man is an artist at all. But his true servitude is that he inherits a will broken by doubt and a soul that yields up all its hate to a caress; and the most seeming-independent are those who are the first to reassume their bonds. But Truth deals largely with us. Elsewhere there are men who are worthy to carry on the tradition of the old master who is dying in Christiania. He has already found his successor in the writer of *Michael Kramer*, and the third minister will not be wanting when his hour comes. Even now that hour may be standing by the door.[11]

JAS. A. JOYCE
October 15th, 1901

JAMES CLARENCE MANGAN (1902)

'Memorial I would have . . . a constant presence with those that
love me.'[1]

It is many a day since the dispute of the classical and romantic
schools began in the quiet city of the arts, so that criticism, which
has wrongly decided that the classical temper is the romantic temper
grown older, has been driven to recognise these as constant states of
mind. Though the dispute has been often ungentle (to say no more)
and has seemed to some a dispute about names and with time has
become a confused battle, each school advancing to the borders of
the other and busy with internal strife, the classical school fighting
the materialism which attends it, and the romantic school to preserve
coherence, yet as this unrest is the condition of all achievement, it is
so far good, and presses slowly towards a deeper insight which will
make the schools at one. Meanwhile no criticism is just which avoids
labour by setting up a standard of maturity by which to judge the
schools. The romantic school is often and grievously misinterpreted,
not more by others than by its own, for that impatient temper which,
as it could see no fit abode here for its ideals, chose to behold them
under insensible figures, comes to disregard certain limitations, and,
because these figures are blown high and low by the mind that conceived them, comes at times to regard them as feeble shadows moving aimlessly about the light, obscuring it; and the same temper,
which assuredly has not grown more patient, exclaims that the light
is changed to worse than shadow, to darkness even, by any method
which bends upon these present things and so works upon them and
fashions them that the quick intelligence may go beyond them to
their meaning, which is still unuttered. Yet so long as this place in
nature is given us, it is right that art should do no violence to that
gift, though it may go far beyond the stars and the waters in the
service of what it loves. Wherefore the highest praise must be withheld from the romantic school (though the most enlightened of
Western poets[2] be thereby passed over), and the cause of the
impatient temper must be sought in the artist and in his theme. Nor
must the laws of his art be forgotten in the judgment of the artist, for

no error is more general than the judgment of a man of letters by the supreme laws of poetry. Verse, indeed, is not the only expression of rhythm, but poetry in any art transcends the mode of its expression; and to name what is less than poetry in the arts, there is need of new terms, though in one art the term 'literature' may be used. Literature is the wide domain which lies between ephemeral writing and poetry (with which is philosophy), and just as the greater part of verse is not literature, so even original writers and thinkers must often be jealously denied the most honourable title; and much of Wordsworth, and almost all of Baudelaire, is merely literature in verse and must be judged by the laws of literature. Finally, it must be asked concerning every artist how he is in relation to the highest knowledge and to those laws which do not take holiday because men and times forget them. This is not to look for a message but to approach the temper which has made the work, an old woman praying, or a young man fastening his shoe, and to see what is there well done and how much it signifies. A song by Shakespeare or Verlaine, which seems as free and living and as remote from any conscious purpose as rain that falls in a garden or the lights of evening, is discovered to be the rhythmic speech of an emotion otherwise incommunicable, at least so fitly. But to approach the temper which has made art is an act of reverence and many conventions must be first put off, for certainly the inmost region will never yield to one who is enmeshed with profanities.[3]

That was a strange question which the innocent Parsifal asked— 'Who is good?'[4] and it is recalled to mind when one reads certain criticisms and biographies, for which the influence of a modern writer, misunderstood as the worship of broad-cloth,[5] is answerable. When these criticisms are insincere they are humorous, but the case is worse when they are as sincere as such things can be. And so, when Mangan is remembered in his country (for he is sometimes spoken of in literary societies), his countrymen lament that such poetic faculty was mated with so little rectitude of conduct, surprised to find this faculty in a man whose vices were exotic and who was little of a patriot. Those who have written of him,[6] have been scrupulous in holding the balance between the drunkard and the opium-eater, and have sought to discover whether learning or imposture lies behind such phrases as 'from the Ottoman' or 'from the Coptic':[7] and save for this small remembrance, Mangan has been a stranger in his country, a rare and unsympathetic figure in the streets, where he is seen going forward alone like one who does penance for some ancient sin. Surely life, which Novalis has called a malady of the spirit,[8] is a heavy penance for him who has, perhaps, forgotten the sin that laid it upon him, a sorrowful portion, too, because of that fine artist in him which reads so truly the lines of brutality and of weakness in the faces of men that are thrust in upon his path. He bears it well for the most part, acquiescing in the justice which has made him a vessel of wrath, but in a moment of frenzy he breaks silence, and we read how his associates dishonoured his person with their slime and venom, and how he lived as a child amid coarseness and misery and that all whom he met were demons out of the pit and that his father was a human boa-constrictor.[9] Certainly he is wiser who accuses no man of acting unjustly towards him, seeing that what is called injustice is never so but is an aspect of justice, yet they who think that such a terrible tale is the figment of a disordered brain do not know how keenly a sensitive boy suffers from contact with a gross nature. Mangan, however, is not without some consolation, for his sufferings have cast him inwards, where for many ages the sad and the wise have elected to be. When someone told him that the account which he had given of his early life, so full of things which were, indeed, the beginnings of sorrows, was wildly overstated, and partly false, he answered—'Maybe I dreamed it.'[10] The world, you see, has become somewhat unreal for him, and he has begun to contemn that which is, in fine, the occasion of much error. How will it be with those dreams which, for every young and simple heart, take such dear reality upon themselves?[11] One whose nature is so sensitive cannot forget his dreams in a secure, strenuous life. He doubts them, and puts them from him for a time, but when he hears men denying them with an oath he would acknowledge them proudly, and where sensitiveness has induced weakness, or, as here, refined upon natural weakness, would even compromise with the world, and win from it in return the favour of silence, if no more, as for something too slight to bear a violent disdain, for that desire of the heart so loudly derided, that rudely entreated idea. His manner is such that none can say if it be pride or humility that looks out of that vague face, which seems to live only because of those light shining eyes and of the fair silken hair above it, of which he is a little vain. This purely defensive reserve is not without dangers for him, and in the end it is

only his excesses that save him from indifference.[12] Something has
been written of an affair of the heart between him and a pupil of his,
to whom he gave lessons in German,[13] and, it seems, he was an actor
afterwards in a love-comedy of three,[14] but if he is reserved with
men, he is shy with women, and he is too self-conscious, too critical,
knows too little of the soft parts of conversation, for a gallant. And in
his strange dress, in which some have seen eccentricity, and others
affectation—the high, conical hat, the loose trousers many sizes too
big for him, and the old umbrella, so like a bagpipes—one may see a
half-conscious expression of this.[15] The lore of many lands goes with
him always, eastern tales and the memory of curiously printed medieval books which have rapt him out of his time—gathered together
day by day and embroidered as in a web. He has acquaintance with
a score of languages, of which, upon occasion, he makes a liberal
parade, and has read recklessly in many literatures, crossing how
many seas, and even penetrating into Peristan, to which no road leads
that the feet travel. In Timbuctooese, he confesses with a charming
modesty which should prevent detractors, he is slightly deficient, but
this is no cause for regret. He is interested, too, in the life of the
seeress of Prevorst,[16] and in all phenomena of the middle nature and
here, where most of all the sweetness and resoluteness of the soul
have power, he seems to seek in a world, how different from that in
which Watteau[17] may have sought, both with a certain graceful
inconstancy, 'What is there in no satisfying measure or not at all.'[18]

His writings, which have never been collected and which are
unknown, except for two American editions of selected poems and
some pages of prose, published by Duffy,[19] show no order and sometimes very little thought. Many of his essays are pretty fooling when
read once, but one cannot but discern some fierce energy beneath the
banter, which follows up the phrases with no good intent, and there
is a likeness between the desperate writer, himself the victim of too
dexterous torture, and the contorted writing. Mangan, it must be
remembered, wrote with no native literary tradition to guide him,
and for a public which cared for matters of the day, and for poetry
only so far as it might illustrate these. He could not often revise what
he wrote, and he has often striven with Moore and Walsh[20] on their
own ground. But the best of what he has written makes its appeal
surely, because it was conceived by the imagination which he called,
I think, the mother of things, whose dream are we, who imageth us

to herself, and to ourselves, and imageth herself in us—the power before whose breath the mind in creation is (to use Shelley's image) as a fading coal.[21] Though even in the best of Mangan the presence of alien emotions is sometimes felt the presence of an imaginative personality reflecting the light of imaginative beauty is more vividly felt. East and West meet in that personality (we know how); images interweave there like soft, luminous scarves and words ring like brilliant mail, and whether the song is of Ireland or of Istambol [*sic*] it has the same refrain, a prayer that peace may come again to her who has lost her peace, the moonwhite pearl of his soul, Ameen.[22] Music and odours and lights are spread about her, and he would search the dews and the sands that he might set mother glory near her face. A scenery and a world have grown up about her face, as they will about any face which the eyes have regarded with love. Vittoria Colonna and Laura and Beatrice[23]—even she upon whose face many lives have cast that shadowy delicacy, as of one who broods upon distant terrors and riotous dreams, and that strange stillness before which love is silent, Mona Lisa[24]—embody one chivalrous idea, which is no mortal thing, bearing it bravely above the accidents of lust and faithlessness and weariness; and she whose white and holy hands have the virtue of enchanted hands, his virgin flower, and flower of flowers, is no less than these an embodiment of that idea. How the East is laid under tribute for her and must bring all its treasures to her feet! The sea that foams over saffron sands, the lonely cedar on the Balkans, the hall damascened with moons of gold and a breath of roses from the gulistan[25]—all these shall be where she is in willing service: reverence and peace shall be the service of the heart, as in the verses 'To Mihri':

> My starlight, my moonlight, my midnight, my moonlight,
> Unveil not, unveil not![26]

And where the music shakes off its languor and is full of the ecstasy of combat, as in the 'Lament for Sir Maurice FitzGerald', and in 'Dark Rosaleen', it does not attain to the quality of Whitman[27] indeed, but is tremulous with all the changing harmonies of Shelley's verse. Now and then this note is hoarsened and a troop of unmannerly passions echoes it derisively,[28] but two poems at least sustain the music unbroken, the 'Swabian Popular Song', and a translation of two quatrains by Wetzel.[29] To create a little flower,

Blake said,[30] is the labour of ages, and even one lyric has made Dowland immortal;[31] and the matchless passages which are found in other poems are so good that they could not have been written by anyone but Mangan. He might have written a treatise on the poetical art for he is more cunning in his use of the musical echo than is Poe,[32] the high priest of most modern schools, and there is a mastery, which no school can teach, but which obeys an interior command, which we may trace in 'Kathaleen-Ny-Houlahan', where the refrain changes the trochaic scheme abruptly for a line of firm, marching iambs.

All his poetry remembers wrong and suffering and the aspiration of one who has suffered and who is moved to great cries and gestures when that sorrowful hour rushes upon the heart. This is the theme of a hundred songs but of none so intense as these songs which are made in noble misery, as his favourite Swedenborg would say, out of the vastation of soul.[33] Naomi would change her name to Mara, because it has gone bitterly with her, and is it not the deep sense of sorrow and bitterness which explains these names and titles and this fury of translation in which he has sought to lose himself?[34] For he has not found in himself the faith of the solitary, or the faith, which in the middle age, sent the spires singing up to heaven, and he waits for the final scene to end the penance. Weaker than Leopardi,[35] for he has not the courage of his own despair but forgets all ills and forgoes his scorn at the showing of some favour, he has, perhaps for this reason, the memorial he would have had—a constant presence with those that love him—and bears witness, as the more heroic pessimist bears witness against his will to the calm fortitude of humanity, to a subtle sympathy with health and joyousness which is seldom found in one whose health is safe. And so he does not shrink from the grave and the busy workings of the earth so much as from the unfriendly eyes of women and the hard eyes of men. To tell the truth, he has been in love with death all his life, like another,[36] and with no woman, and he has the same gentle manner as of old to welcome him whose face is hidden with a cloud, who is named Azrael.[37] Those whom the flames of too fierce love have wasted on earth become after death pale phantoms among the winds of desire,[38] and, as he strove here towards peace with the ardour of the wretched, it may be that now the winds of peace visit him and he rests, and remembers no more this bitter vestment of the body.

Poetry, even when apparently most fantastic, is always a revolt against artifice, a revolt, in a sense, against actuality. It speaks of what seems fantastic and unreal to those who have lost the simple intuitions which are the tests of reality; and, as it is often found at war with its age, so it makes no account of history, which is fabled by the daughters of memory,[39] but sets store by every time less than the pulsation of an artery, the time in which its intuitions start forth, holding it equal in its period and value to six thousand years.[40] No doubt they are only men of letters who insist on the succession of the ages, and history or the denial of reality, for they are two names for one thing, may be said to be that which deceives the whole world. In this, as in much else, Mangan is the type of his race.[41] History encloses him so straitly that even his fiery moments do not set him free from it. He, too, cries out, in his life and in his mournful verses, against the injustice of despoilers, but never laments a deeper loss than the loss of plaids and ornaments. He inherits the latest and worst part of a legend upon which the line has never been drawn out and which divides against itself as it moves down the cycles.[42] And because this tradition is so much with him he has accepted it with all its griefs and failures, and has not known how to change it, as the strong spirit knows, and so would bequeath it: the poet who hurls his anger against tyrants would establish upon the future an intimate and far more cruel tyranny.[43] In the final view the figure which he worships is seen to be an abject queen upon whom because of the bloody crimes that she has done and of those as bloody that were done to her, madness is come and death is coming, but who will not believe that she is near to die and remembers only the rumour of voices challenging her sacred gardens and her fair, tall flowers that have become the food of boars. Novalis said of love that it is the Amen of the universe,[44] and Mangan can tell of the beauty of hate; and pure hate is as excellent as pure love. An eager spirit would cast down with violence the high traditions of Mangan's race—love of sorrow for the sake of sorrow and despair and fearful menaces—but where their voice is a supreme entreaty to be borne with forbearance seems only a little grace; and what is so courteous and so patient as a great faith?[45]

Every age must look for its sanction to its poetry and philosophy, for in these the human mind, as it looks backward or forward, attains to an eternal state. The philosophic mind inclines always to an

elaborate life—the life of Goethe or of Leonardo da Vinci; but the
life of the poet is intense—the life of Blake or of Dante—taking into
its centre the life that surrounds it and flinging it abroad again amid
planetary music.[46] With Mangan a narrow and hysterical nationality
receives a last justification, for when this feeble-bodied figure
departs dusk begins to veil the train of the gods, and he who listens
may hear their footsteps leaving the world. But the ancient gods, who
are visions of the divine names, die and come to life many times, and
though there is dusk about their feet and darkness in their indifferent eyes, the miracle of light is renewed eternally in the imaginative
soul. When the sterile and treacherous order is broken up, a voice or
a host of voices is heard singing, a little faintly at first, of a serene
spirit which enters woods and cities and the hearts of men, and of
the life of earth—*det dejlige vidunderlige jordliv det gaadefulde
jordliv*[47]—beautiful, alluring, mysterious.

Beauty, the splendour of truth,[48] is a gracious presence when the
imagination contemplates intensely the truth of its own being or the
visible world, and the spirit which proceeds out of truth and beauty
is the holy spirit of joy. These are realities and these alone give and
sustain life. As often as human fear and cruelty, that wicked monster
begotten by luxury, are in league to make life ignoble and sullen and
to speak evil of death the time is come wherein a man of timid
courage seizes the keys of hell and of death, and flings them far out
into the abyss, proclaiming the praise of life, which the abiding
splendour of truth may sanctify, and of death, the most beautiful
form of life.[49] In those vast courses which enfold us and in that great
memory which is greater and more generous than our memory,[50] no
life, no moment of exaltation is ever lost; and all those who have
written nobly have not written in vain, though the desperate and
weary have never heard the silver laughter of wisdom. Nay, shall not
such as these have part, because of that high, original purpose which
remembering painfully or by way of prophecy they would make
clear, in the continual affirmation of the spirit?[51]

James A. Joyce

AN IRISH POET

These are the verses of a writer lately dead, whom many consider the Davis of the latest national movement.[1] They are issued from headquarters, and are preceded by two introductions wherein there is much said concerning the working man, mutual improvement, the superior person, shady musical plays, etc. They are illustrative of the national temper, and because they are so the writers of the introductions do not hesitate to claim for them the highest honours. But this claim cannot be allowed, unless it is supported by certain evidences of literary sincerity. For a man who writes a book cannot be excused by his good intentions, or by his moral character; he enters into a region where there is question of the written word, and it is well that this should be borne in mind, now that the region of literature is assailed so fiercely by the enthusiast and the doctrinaire. An examination of the poems and ballads of William Rooney does not warrant one in claiming for them any high honours. The theme is consistently national, so uncompromising, indeed, that the reader must lift an eyebrow and assure himself when he meets on page 114 the name of D'Arcy MacGee.[2] But the treatment of the theme does not show the same admirable consistency. In 'S. Patrick's Day' and in 'Dromceat' one cannot but see an uninteresting imitation of Denis Florence M'Carthy and of Ferguson; even Mr T. D. Sullivan and Mr Rolleston have done something in the making of this book.[3] But 'Roilig na Riogh' [sic] is utterly lacking in the high distinctive virtue of 'The Dead at Clonmacnoise',[4] and Mr Rolleston, who certainly is not driven along by any poetic impulse, has written a poem because the very failure of the poetic impulse pleases in an epitaph. So much can careful writing achieve, and there can be no doubt that little is achieved in these verses, because the writing is so careless, and is yet so studiously mean. For, if carelessness is carried very far, it is like to become a positive virtue, but an ordinary carelessness is nothing but a false and mean expression of a false and mean idea.[5] Mr Rooney, indeed, is almost a master in that 'style', which is neither good nor bad. In the verses of Maedhbh he writes:

'Mid the sheltering hills, by the spreading waters,
They laid her down and her cairn raised
The fiercest-hearted of Erin's daughters—
The bravest nature that ever blazed.

Here the writer has not devised, he has merely accepted, mean
expressions, and even where he has accepted a fine expression, he
cannot justify his use of it. Mangan's Homeric epithet of 'wine-dark'
becomes in his paper a colourless and meaningless epithet, which
may cover any or all of the colours of the spectrum. How differently
did Mangan write when he wrote:

> Knowest thou the castle that beetles over
> The wine-dark sea!

Here a colour rises in the mind and is set firmly against the golden
glow in the lines that follow. But one must not look for these things
when patriotism has laid hold of the writer. He has no care then to
create anything according to the art of literature, not the greatest of
the arts, indeed, but at least an art with a definite tradition behind it,
possessing definite forms. Instead we find in these pages a weary
succession of verses, 'prize' poems—the worst of all. They were
written, it seems, for papers and societies week after week, and they
bear witness to some desperate and weary energy. But they have no
spiritual and living energy, because they come from one in whom the
spirit is in a manner dead, or at least in its own hell, a weary and
foolish spirit, speaking of redemption and revenge, blaspheming
against tyrants, and going forth, full of tears and curses, upon its
infernal labours. Religion and all that is allied thereto can manifestly
persuade men to great evil, and by writing these verses, even though
they should, as the writers of the prefaces think, enkindle the young
men of Ireland to hope and activity, Mr Rooney has been persuaded
to great evil. And yet he might have written well if he had not
suffered from one of those big words which make us so unhappy.
There is no piece in the book which has even the first quality of
beauty, the quality of integrity, the quality of being separate and
whole,[6] but there is one piece in the book which seems to have come
out of a conscious personal life. It is a translation of some verses by
Dr Douglas Hyde, and is called 'A Request', and yet I cannot believe
that it owes more than its subject to its original.[7] It begins:–

> In that last dark hour when my bed I lie on,
> My narrow bed of the deal board bare,
> My kin and neighbours around me standing,
> And Death's broad wings on the thickening air.

It proceeds to gather desolation about itself, and does so in lines of living verse, as in the lines that follow. The third line is feeble, perhaps, but the fourth line is so astonishingly good that it cannot be overpraised:—

> When night shall fall and my day is over
> And Death's pale symbol shall chill my face,
> When heart and hand thrill no more responsive,
> Oh Lord and Saviour, regard my case!

And when it has gathered about itself all the imagery of desolation, it remembers the Divine temptation, and puts up its prayer to the Divine mercy. It seems to come out of a personal life which has begun to realise itself but to which death and that realisation have come together. And in this manner, with the gravity of one who remembers all the errors of his members and his sins of speech, it goes into silence.

Poems and Ballads of William Rooney, 'The United Irishman,' Dublin.

GEORGE MEREDITH

Mr George Meredith has been included in the English men of letters series, where he may be seen in honourable nearness to Mr Hall Caine and Mr Pinero.[1] An age which has too keen a scent for contemporary values will often judge amiss, and, therefore, one must not complain when a writer who is, even for those who do not admire him unreservedly, a true man of letters,[2] comes by his own in such a strange fashion. Mr Jerrold in the biographical part of his book has to record a more than usual enormity of public taste, and if his book had recorded only this, something good would have been done; for it is certain that the public taste should be reproved, while it is by no means certain that Mr Meredith is a martyr. Mr Jerrold confesses his faith in novels and plays alike, and he will have it that 'Modern Love' is on the same plane with the 'Vita Nuova'.[3] No one can deny to Mr Meredith an occasional power of direct compelling speech (in a picture of a famine he wrote 'starving lords were wasp and moth')[4] but he is plainly lacking in that fluid quality, the lyrical impulse, which, it seems, has been often taken from the wise and given unto the foolish. And it is plain to all who believe in the tradition of literature that this quality cannot be replaced. Mr Meredith's eager brain, which will not let him be a poet, has, however, helped him to write novels which are, perhaps, unique in our time. Mr Jerrold subjects each novel to a superficial analysis, and by doing so he has, I think, seized a fallacy for his readers. For these novels have, for the most part, no value as epical art, and Mr Meredith has not the instinct of the epical artist. But they have a distinct value as philosophical essays, and they reveal a philosopher at work with much cheerfulness upon a very stubborn problem. Any book about the philosopher is worth reading, unless we have given ourselves over deliberately to the excellent foppery of the world,[5] and though Mr Jerrold's book is not remarkable, it is worth reading.

George Meredith: An Essay towards Appreciation. By Walter Jerrold.
London: Greening and Co. 3s. 6d.

TODAY AND TOMORROW IN IRELAND

In this book, the latest addition to the already formidable mass of modern Anglo-Irish literature, Mr Gwynn has collected ten essays from various reviews and journals, essays differing widely in interest, but for all of which he would claim a unity of subject. All the essays deal directly or indirectly with Ireland, and they combine in formulating a distinct accusation of English civilisation and English modes of thought. For Mr Gwynn, too, is a convert to the prevailing national movement, and professes himself a Nationalist, though his nationalism, as he says, has nothing irreconcilable about it. Give Ireland the status of Canada and Mr Gwynn becomes an Imperialist at once. It is hard to say into what political party Mr Gwynn should go, for he is too consistently Gaelic for the Parliamentarians, and too mild for the true patriots, who are beginning to speak a little vaguely about their friends the French.[1] Mr Gwynn, however, is at least a member of that party which seeks to establish an Irish literature and Irish industries. The first essays in his book are literary criticisms, and it may be said at once that they are the least interesting. Some are mere records of events and some seem written to give English readers a general notion of what is meant by the Gaelic revival. Mr Gwynn has evidently a sympathy with modern Irish writers, but his criticism of their work is in no way remarkable. In the opening essay he has somehow the air of discovering Mangan, and he transcribes with some astonishment a few verses from 'O'Hussey's Ode to the Maguire'. Few as the verses are, they are enough to show the real value of the work of the modern writers, whom Mr Gwynn regards as the voice of Celticism proper. Their work varies in merit, never rising (except in Mr Yeats's case) above a certain fluency and an occasional distinction, and often falling so low that it has a value only as documentary evidence. It is work which has an interest of the day, but collectively it has not a third part of the value of the work of a man like Mangan, that creature of lightning, who has been, and is, a stranger among the people he ennobled, but who may yet come by his own as one of the greatest romantic poets among those who use the lyrical form. Mr Gwynn, however, is more successful in those essays which are illustrative of the industrial work which has been set in movement at different points of Ireland. His account of the establishing of the fishing industry in the West of Ireland is extremely interesting, and so are his accounts of dairies, old-fashioned and new-fashioned, and of carpet-making. These essays are written in a practical manner, and though they are supplemented by many quotations of dates and figures, they are also full of anecdotes. Mr Gwynn has evidently a sense of the humorous, and it is pleasing to find this in a revivalist. He tells how, fishing one day, it was his fortune to meet with an old peasant whose thoughts ran all upon the traditional tales of his country and on the histories of great families. Mr Gwynn's instinct as a fisherman got the better of his patriotism, and he confesses to a slight disappointment when, after a good catch on an unfavourable day, he earned no word of praise from the peasant, who said, following his own train of thought, 'The Clancartys was great men, too. Is there any of them living?' The volume, admirably bound and printed, is a credit to the Dublin firm to whose enterprise its publication is due.[2]

'To-day and To-morrow in Ireland.' By Stephen Gwynn.
Dublin: Hodges Figgis, and Co. 5s.

A SUAVE PHILOSOPHY

In this book one reads about a people whose life is ordered according to beliefs and sympathies which will seem strange to us. The writer has very properly begun his account of that life by a brief exposition of Buddhism, and he sets forth so much of its history as illustrates its main principles. He omits some incidents which are among the most beautiful of the Buddhist legend—the kindly devas strewing flowers under the horse, and the story of the meeting of Buddha and his wife. But he States at some length the philosophy (if that be the proper name for it) of Buddhism. The Burmese people seem naturally adapted to follow such a wise passive philosophy. Five things are the five supreme evils for them—fire, water, storms, robbers, and rulers. All things that are inimical to human peace are evil. Though Buddhism is essentially a philosophy built against the evils of existence, a philosophy which places its end in the annihilation of the personal life and the personal will, the Burmese people have known how to transform it into a rule of life at once simple and wise. Our civilisation, bequeathed to us by fierce adventurers, eaters of meat and hunters, is so full of hurry and combat, so busy about many things which perhaps are of no importance, that it cannot but see something feeble in a civilisation which smiles as it refuses to make the battlefield the test of excellence. There is a Burmese saying—'The thoughts of his heart, these are the wealth of a man', and Mr Hall, who has lived in Burma for many years, draws a picture of Burmese life which shows that a happiness, founded upon peace of mind in all circumstances, has a high place in the Burmese table of values. And happiness abides among this people: the yellow-robed monks begging alms, the believers coming to tell their beads in the temple, tiny rafts drifting down the river on the night of some festival, each one bearing upon it a tiny lamp, a girl sitting at evening in the shadow of the eaves until the young men come 'courting'—all this is part of a suave philosophy which does not know that there is anything to justify tears and lamentations. The courtesies of life are not neglected; anger and rudeness of manners are condemned; the animals themselves are glad to be under masters who treat them as living beings worthy of pity and toleration. Mr Hall is one of the conquerors of this people, and as he does not think it a warrior people he cannot predict for it any great political future. But he knows that peace lies before it, and, perhaps in literature, or in some art, a national temper so serene and order-loving may achieve itself. He gives a version of the story of Ma Pa Da, which he calls 'Death the Deliverer', and this story itself is so pitiful that one would wish to know more of the Burmese popular tales. He gives elsewhere a rendering in prose of a Burmese love-song, which has, as may be seen, kept some of its charm, though it has lost, no doubt, much of its music:–

The moon wooed the lotus in the night, the lotus was wooed by the moon, and my sweetheart is their child. The flower opened in the night, and she came forth; the petals moved and she was born.

She is more beautiful than any flower; her face is as delicate as the dusk; her hair is as night falling over the hills; her skin is as bright as the diamond. She is very full of health, no sickness can come near her.

When the wind blows I am afraid, when the breezes move I fear. I fear lest the south wind take her, I tremble lest the breath of evening woo her from me—so light is she, so graceful.

Her dress is of gold, of silk and gold, and her bracelets are of fine gold. She has precious stones in her ears, but her eyes, what jewels can compare unto them?

She is proud, my mistress; she is very proud, and all men are afraid of her. She is so beautiful and so proud that all men fear her.

In the whole world there is none anywhere that can compare unto her.[1]

Mr Hall has written a most pleasing book in an easy and temperate style, a book which is full of interesting manners and stories. One is glad to see that even in these days of novels, religious and sensational, this book has run to four editions.

'The Soul of a People,' by H. Fielding Hall. London:
Macmillan and Co. 7s. 6d.

AN EFFORT AT PRECISION IN THINKING

He must be a hardy man who contends that the disputants in this book are common people. They are, happily for the peace of human animals, very uncommon people. For common people will not argue for any considerable time as to whether succession of appearances is or is not anything more than the appearance of succession. But these uncommon people, whose colloquies are recorded here at somewhat distressing length by Mr Austie [sic], argue about such subtleties with a precision which is more apparent than real. The speakers will seem more precise than they are, for at one time they dispute eagerly over certainty of thought, though certainty is not a habit of the mind at all, but a quality of propositions, and the speakers are really arguing about certitude, and more than once all the speakers are agreed that sense impressions mark the furthest limit of knowledge, and that 'reasonable belief' is an oxymoron—conclusions with which the man of the people, who is no philosopher, professes himself in loud accord. However, this book is an effort at precision in thinking, even if it does not always provoke that stimulated attention which one speaker calls a form of activity.

'Colloquies of Common People,' reported by James Austie [sic], K.C.
London: Smith, Elder and Co., 10s. 6d.

COLONIAL VERSES

These are colonial verses. The colonial Esau is asked on page 3 would he change his pottage for Jacob's birthright—a question which evidently expects the answer, No.[1] One piece is named 'Is Canada Loyal?' and Mr Wolley proclaims that it is loyal. His verse is for the most part loyal, and where it is not, it describes Canadian scenery. Mr Wolley says that he is a barbarian; he does not want the 'murmurous muddle' of the choir; he wants a 'clean-cut creed', 'plain laws for plain men'. There is a piece called 'Tableau', about a girl dreaming in a picture gallery. It begins: 'I wonder if it's really true that you are only paint.'

'Songs of an English Esau,' by Clive Phillips-Wolley. London: Smith, Elder and Co. 5s.

CATILINA

The French translators of this play have included in their preface some extracts from Ibsen's preface to the Dresden edition of 1875 and these extracts tell somewhat humorously the history of Ibsen's early years. The play was written in 1848, when Ibsen was twenty, a poor student working all day in a druggist's shop, and studying during the night as best he could. Sallust and Cicero, it seems, awakened his interest in the character of Catiline,[1] and he set to work to write a tragedy, in part historical and in part political, a reflection of the Norway of his day. The play was politely refused by the directors of the Christiania Theatre and by all the publishers. One of Ibsen's friends, however, published it at his own expense, fully convinced that the play would at once make the writer's name famous in the world. A few copies were sold and, as Ibsen and his friend were in need of money, they were glad to sell the remainder to a pork-butcher. 'For some days,' Ibsen writes, 'we did not lack the necessaries of life.' This is a sufficiently instructive history, and it is well to remember it when reading a play which Ibsen publishes simply that his work may be complete. For the writer of *Catilina* is not the Ibsen of the social dramas,[2] but, as the French translators joyfully proclaim, an ardent romantic exulting in disturbance and escaping from all formal laws under cover of an abundant rhetoric. This will not appear so strange when it is remembered that the young Goethe was somewhat given to alchemical researches, and as, to quote Goethe himself, the form in which a man goes into the shadows is the form which he moves among his posterity,[3] posterity will probably forget Ibsen the romantic as completely as it forgets Goethe and his athanor.

Yet, in some ways, this earlier manner suggests the later manner. In *Catilina* three figures are projected against the background of a restless and moribund society—Catiline, Aurelia, his wife, and Fulvia,[4] a vestal virgin. Ibsen is known to the general public as a man who writes a play about three people—usually one man and two women—and even critics, while they assert their admiration for Ibsen's 'unqualified objectivity', find that all his women are the same woman renamed successively Nora, Rebecca, Hilda, Irene—find, that is to say, that Ibsen has no power of objectivity at all. The critics, speaking in the name of the audience, whose idol is common sense, and whose torment is to be confronted with a clear work of art that reflects every obscurity like a mirror, have sometimes had the courage to say that they did not understand the system of three. They will be pleased to learn that some of the characters in *Catilina* are in as sorry a plight as themselves. Here is a passage in which Curius, a young relative of Catiline, professes his inability to understand Catiline's relations with Fulvia and Aurelia:

> CURIUS.   *Les aimerais-tu toutes deux á la fois?*
> *Vraiment je n'y comprends plus rien.*
> CATILINA.   *En effet c'est singulier et je n'y comprends*
> *Rien moi-même.*[5]

But perhaps that he does not understand is part of the tragedy, and the play is certainly the struggle between Aurelia, who is happiness and the policy of non-interference, and Fulvia, who is at first the policy of interference and who, when she has escaped from the tomb to which her sin had brought her, becomes the figure of Catiline's destiny. Very little use is made in this play of alarms and battles, and one can see that the writer is not interested in the usual property of romanticism. Already he is losing the romantic temper when it should be at its fiercest in him, and, as youth commonly brooks no prevention, he is content to hurl himself upon the world and establish himself there defiantly until his true weapons are ready to his hand. One must not take too seriously the solution of the drama in favour of Aurelia, for by the time the last act is reached the characters have begun to mean nothing to themselves and in the acted play would be related to life only by the bodies of the performers. And here is the most striking difference between Ibsen's earlier manner and his later manner, between romantic work and classical work. The romantic temper, imperfect and impatient as it is, cannot express itself adequately unless it employs the monstrous or heroic. In *Catilina* the women are absolute types, and the end of such a play cannot but savour of dogma—a most proper thing in a priest but a most improper in a poet. Moreover, as the breaking up of tradition, which is the work of the modern era, discountenances the absolute and as no writer can escape the spirit of his time, the writer of dramas must remember now more than ever a principle of all patient and perfect art which bids him express his fable in terms of his characters.

As a work of art *Catilina* has little merit, and yet one can see in it what the directors of the Christiania theatre and the publishers failed to see—an original and capable writer struggling with a form that is not his own. This manner continues, with occasional lapses into comedy, as far as *Peer Gynt*, in which, recognising its own limitations and pushing lawlessness to its extreme limit, it achieves a masterpiece. After that it disappears and the second manner begins to take its place, advancing through play after play, uniting construction and speech and action more and more closely in a supple rhythm, until it achieves itself in *Hedda Gabler*. Very few recognise the astonishing courage of such work and it is characteristic of our age of transition to admire the later manner less than the earlier manner. For the imagination has the quality of a fluid, and it must be held firmly, lest it become vague, and delicately, that it may lose none of its magical powers. And Ibsen has united with his strong, ample, imaginative faculty a pre-occupation with the things present to him. Perhaps in time, even the professional critic, accepting the best of the social dramas for what they are—the most excellent examples of skill and intellectual self-possession—will make this union a truism of professional criticism. But meanwhile a young generation which has cast away belief and thrown precision after it, for which Balzac[6] is a great intellect and every sampler who chooses to wander amid his own shapeless hells and heavens a Dante without the unfortunate prejudices of Dante, will be troubled by this pre-occupation, and out of very conscience will denounce a method so calm, so ironical. These cries of hysteria are confused with many others—the voices of war and statecraft and religion—in the fermenting vat. But Boötes, we may be sure, thinks nothing of such cries, eager as ever at that ancient business of leading his hunting-dogs across the zenith 'in their leash of sidereal fire'.[7]

THE SOUL OF IRELAND

Aristotle finds at the beginning of all speculation the feeling of wonder,[1] a feeling proper to childhood, and if speculation be proper to
the middle period of life it is natural that one should look to the
crowning period of life for the fruit of speculation, wisdom itself.
But nowadays people have greatly confused childhood and middle
life and old age; those who succeed in spite of civilisation in reaching
old age seem to have less and less wisdom, and children who are
usually put to some business as soon as they can walk and talk, seem
to have more and more 'common sense'; and, perhaps, in the future
little boys with long beards will stand aside and applaud, while old
men in short trousers play handball against the side of a house. This
may even happen in Ireland, if Lady Gregory has truly set forth the
old age of her country. In her new book she has left legends and
heroic youth far behind, and has explored in a land almost fabulous
in its sorrow and senility. Half of her book is an account of old men
and old women in the West of Ireland. These old people are full of
stories about giants and witches, and dogs and black-handled knives,
and they tell their stories one after another at great length and with
many repetitions (for they are people of leisure) by the fire or in the
yard of a workhouse. It is difficult to judge well of their charms and
herb-healing, for that is the province of those who are learned in
these matters and can compare the customs of countries, and,
indeed, it is well not to know these magical-sciences, for if the wind
changes while you are cutting wild camomile you will lose your
mind. But one can judge more easily of their stories. These stories
appeal to some feeling which is certainly not that feeling of wonder
which is the beginning of all speculation. The story-tellers are old,
and their imagination is not the imagination of childhood. The
story-teller preserves the strange machinery of fairyland, but his
mind is feeble and sleepy.[2] He begins one story and wanders from it
into another story, and none of the stories has any satisfying imaginative wholeness, none of them is like Sir John Daw's poem that cried
tink in the close.[3] Lady Gregory is conscious of this, for she often
tries to lead the speaker back to his story by questions, and when
the story has become hopelessly involved, she tries to establish

some wholeness by keeping only the less involved part; sometimes she listens 'half interested and half impatient'. In fine, her book, wherever it treats of the 'folk', sets forth in the fullness of its senility a class of mind which Mr Yeats has set forth with such delicate scepticism in his happiest book, 'The Celtic Twilight.'[4] Something of health and naturalness, however, enters with Raftery, the poet.[5] He had a terrible tongue, it seems, and would make a satirical poem for a very small offence. He could make love-poems, too (though Lady Gregory finds a certain falseness in the western love-poems), and repentant poems. Raftery, though he be the last of the great bardic procession, has much of the bardic tradition about him. He took shelter one day from the rain under a bush: at first the bush kept out the rain, and he made verses praising it, but after a while it let the rain through, and he made verses dispraising it. Lady Gregory translates some of his verses, and she also translates some West Irish ballads and some poems by Dr Douglas Hyde. She completes her book with translations of four one-act plays by Dr Douglas Hyde, three of which have for their central figure that legendary person, who is vagabond and poet, and even saint at times, while the fourth play is called a 'nativity' play. The dwarf-drama (if one may use that term) is a form of art which is improper and ineffectual, but it is easy to understand why it finds favour with an age which has pictures that are 'nocturnes', and writers like Mallarmé and the composer of 'Recapitulation'.[6] The dwarf-drama is accordingly to be judged as an entertainment, and Dr Douglas Hyde is certainly entertaining in the 'Twisting of the Rope',[7] and Lady Gregory has succeeded better with her verse-translations here than elsewhere, as these four lines may show:–

> I have heard the melodious harp
> On the streets of Cork playing to us:
> More melodious by far I thought your voice,
> More melodious by far your mouth than that.

This book, like so many other books of our time, is in part picturesque and in part an indirect or direct utterance of the central belief of Ireland. Out of the material and spiritual battle which has gone so hardly with her Ireland has emerged with many memories of beliefs, and with one belief—a belief in the incurable ignobility of the forces that have overcome her—and Lady Gregory, whose old men and women seem to be almost their own judges when they tell their wandering stories, might add to the passage from Whitman which forms her dedication, Whitman's ambiguous word for the vanquished—'Battles are lost in the spirit in which they are won.'[8]

J. J.

'Poets and Dreamers: Studies and Translations from the Irish.'
By Lady Gregory. Hodges Figgis, and Co.,
Dublin: John Murray, London.

THE MOTOR DERBY

INTERVIEW WITH THE FRENCH CHAMPION
(FROM A CORRESPONDENT)

Paris, Sunday.

In the Rue d'Anjou, not far from the Church of the Madeleine, is M. Henri Fournier's place of business. 'Paris-Automobile'—a company of which M. Fournier is the manager—has its headquarters there. Inside the gateway is a big square court, roofed over, and on the floor of the court and on great shelves extending from the floor to the roof are ranged motor-cars of all sizes, shapes, and colours. In the afternoon this court is full of noises—the voices of workmen, the voices of buyers talking in half-a-dozen languages, the ringing of telephone bells, the horns sounded by the 'chauffeurs' as the cars come in and go out—and it is almost impossible to see M. Fournier unless one is prepared to wait two or three hours for one's turn. But the buyers of 'autos' are, in one sense, people of leisure. The morning, however, is more favourable, and yesterday morning, after two failures, I succeeded in seeing M. Fournier.

M. Fournier is a slim, active-looking young man, with dark reddish hair. Early as the hour was our interview was now and again broken in upon by the importunate telephone.

'You are one of the competitors for the Gordon-Bennett Cup, M. Fournier?'

'Yes, I am one of the three selected to represent France.'[1]

'And you are also a competitor, are you not, for the Madrid prize?'[2]

'Yes.'

'Which of the races comes first—the Irish race or the Madrid race?'

'The Madrid race. It takes place early in May, while the race for the International Cup does not take place till July.'

'I suppose that you are preparing actively for your races?'

'Well, I have just returned from a tour to Monte Carlo and Nice.'

'On your racing machine?'

'No, on a machine of smaller power.

'Have you determined what machine you will ride in the Irish race?'

'Practically.'

'May I ask the name of it—is it a Mercedes?'

'No, a Mors.'

'And its horse-power?'

'Eighty.'

'And on this machine you can travel at a rate of—?'

'You mean its highest speed?'

'Yes.'

'Its highest speed would be a hundred and forty kilometres an hour.'

'But you will not go at that rate all the time during the race?'

'Oh, no. Of course its average speed for the race would be lower than that.'

'An average speed of how much?'

'Its average speed would be a hundred kilometres an hour, perhaps a little more than that, something between a hundred and a hundred and ten kilometres an hour.'

'A kilometre is about a half-mile, is it not?'

'More than that, I should think. There are how many yards in your mile?'

'Seventeen hundred and sixty, if I am right.'

'Then your half-mile has eight hundred and eighty yards. Our kilometre is just equal to eleven hundred yards.'

'Let me see. Then your top speed is nearly eighty-six miles an hour, and your average speed is sixty-one miles an hour?'[3]

'I suppose so, if we calculate properly.'

'It is an appalling pace! It is enough to burn our roads. I suppose you have seen the roads you are to travel?'

'No.'

'No? You don't know the course, then?'

'I know it slightly. I know it, that is, from some sketches that were given of it in the Paris newspapers.'

'But, surely, you will want a better knowledge than that?'

'Oh, certainly. In fact, before the month is over, I intend to go to Ireland to inspect the course. Perhaps I shall go in three weeks' time.'

'Will you remain any time in Ireland?'

'After the race?'

'Yes.'

'I am afraid not. I should like to, but I don't think I can.'

'I suppose you would not like to be asked your opinion of the result?'

'Hardly.'

'Yet, which nation do you fear most?'

'I fear them all—Germans, Americans, and English. They are all to be feared.'

'And how about Mr Edge?'

No answer.

'He won the prize the last time, did he not?'

'O, yes.'

'Then he should be your most formidable opponent?'

'O, yes . . . But you see, Mr Edge won, of course, but . . . a man who was last of all, and had no chance of winning might win if the other machines broke.'

Whatever way one looks at this statement it appears difficult to challenge its truth.

ARISTOTLE ON EDUCATION

This book is compiled from the first three books of the Ethics, and the tenth book, with some extracts from the Politics. Unfortunately, the compilation is not a complete treatise on education, nor is it even exhaustive so far as it goes. The Ethics is seized upon by admirers and opponents alike as the weak part of the peripatetic philosophy. The modern notion of Aristotle as a biologist—a notion popular among advocates of 'science'—is probably less true than the ancient notion of him as a metaphysician;[1] and it is certainly in the higher applications of his severe method that he achieves himself. His theory of education is, however, not without interest, and is subordinate to his theory of the state. Individualism, it would seem, is not easily recommended to the Greek mind, and in giving his theory of education Aristotle has endeavoured to recruit for a Greek state rather than to give a final and absolute solution to questions of the greatest interest. Consequently this book can hardly be considered a valuable addition to philosophical literature, but it has a contemporary value in view of recent developments in France,[2] and at the present time, when the scientific specialists and the whole cohort of Materialists are cheapening the good name of philosophy, it is very useful to give heed to one who has been wisely named 'maestro di color che sauno [sic]'.[3]

'Aristotle on Education.' Edited by John Burnet, Cambridge: At the University Press. 2s. 6d.

[A NE'ER-DO-WEEL]

After all a pseudonym library has its advantages; to acknowledge bad literature by signature is, in a manner, to persevere in evil.[1] 'Valentine Caryl's' book is the story of a gypsy genius, whose monologues are eked out by accompaniments on the violin—a story told in undistinguished prose. The series in which this volume appears, the production of the book, and the scantiness of its matter have an air of pretentiousness which is ill justified by perusal.

'A Ne'er-Do-Well [*sic*],' By 'Valentine Caryl.' Fisher, Unwin, London.

NEW FICTION

This little volume is a collection of stories dealing chiefly with Indian life. The reader will find the first five stories—the adventures of Prince Aga Mirza—the most entertaining part of the book, if he is to any extent interested in tales of Indian magic. The appeal, however, of such stories is, frankly, sensational, and we are spared the long explanations which the professional occultists use. The stories that treat of camp life are soundly seasoned with that immature brutality which is always so anxious to be mistaken for virility. But the people who regulate the demand for fiction are being day by day so restricted by the civilisation they have helped to build up that they are not unlike the men of Mandeville's[1] time, for whom enchantments, and monsters, and deeds of prowess were so liberally purveyed.

A book written by the author of 'The Increasing Purpose'[2] is sure of a kind hearing from a public which can be thankful to those who serve it well. Mr Allen has not yet written any work of extraordinary merit, but he has written many which are, so far as they go, serious and patient interpretations of his people. Whether it be in the writer or in his theme, one cannot fail to recognise here the quality of self-reliant sanity—the very mettle (to employ the Shakespearian phrase which serves him for the title) of the pasture.[3] The style is nearly always clean and limpid, and is at fault only where it assumes ornateness. The method is psychological, very slightly narrative, and though that epithet has been used to cover a multitude of literary sins, it can be as safely applied to Mr Allen as longo intervallo[4] to Mr Henry James. It is a tragedy of scandal, the story of a love affair, which is abruptly terminated by a man's confession, but which is renewed again years later when it has passed through the trials which the world proposes to such as would renew any association and so offer offence to time and change. This story is surrounded with two or three other love affairs, all more or less conventional. But the characterisation is often very original—as in the case of old Mrs Conyers[5]—and the general current of the book arrests the reader by its suggestion of an eager lively race working out its destiny among other races under the influence of some vague pantheistic spirit which is at times strangely mournful. 'For her', he says somewhere in a passage of great charm, 'for her it was one of the moments when we are reminded that our lives are not in our keeping, and that whatsoever is to befall us originates in sources beyond our power. Our wills may indeed reach the length of our arms, or as far as our voices can penetrate space; but without us and within us moves one universe that saves us or ruins us only for its own purposes; and we are no more free amid its laws than the leaves of the forest are free to decide their own shapes and seasons of unfolding, to order the showers by which they are to be nourished, and the storms which shall scatter them at last.'[6]

'The Adventures of Prince Aga Mirza.' By Aquila Kempster. Fisher Unwin: London. 'The Mettle of the Pasture,' by James Lane Allen. Macmillan and Co., London, 6s.

A PEEP INTO HISTORY

One may have no satirical reference either to the subject of this book, or to its treatment by Mr Pollock, in saying that this account of the Popish Plot[1] is far more diverting than many works of fiction. Mr Pollock, though he seems thoroughly initiated into the mysteries of the historical method, has set forth an account of the 'Plot' which is clear, detailed, and (so far as it is critical) liberal-minded. By far the most interesting part of the book is the story of the murder of Sir Edmund Godfrey[2]—a murder so artistically secret that it evoked the admiration of De Quincey, a murder so little documented, yet so overwhelmed with false testimonies, that Lord Acton declared it an insoluble mystery.[3] But justice was freely dealt out in those days of political and religious rancour, and Green and Berry suffered the last penalty for a crime of which posterity (unanimous in this one thing at least) has acquitted them.[4] As for those who swore against the poor wretches, Prauce [*sic*] and Bedloe cannot be accorded the same condemnation. Prauce [*sic*], after all, was only lying himself out of a very awkward position, but Bedloe was a more enterprising ruffian, second only to his monstrous, moon-faced leader, the horrible Oates.[5] It is bewildering to read all the charges and counter-charges made in connection with the Plot, and it is with a sigh of sympathy that we read of Charles's conduct. 'In the middle of the confusion the King suddenly left for the races at Newmarket, scandalising all by his indecent levity.'[6] Nevertheless he conducted the examination of Oates in a very skilful manner, and he described Oates very succinctly as 'a most lying knave'. Mr Pollock's treatment of those who have been accused as instigators justifies him in citing a concise phrase from Mabillon on his title page,[7] and the reader will know how patient and scholarly this book is if he compares it with the garbled, ridiculous account set down by L'Estrange.[8]

'The Popish Plot.' By John Pollock. Duckworth and Co., London.

A FRENCH RELIGIOUS NOVEL

This novel, reprinted from the pages of one of the leading French reviews, and now very successfully translated into English, seems to have attracted more attention in London than in Paris. It deals with the problem of an uncompromising orthodoxy, beset by a peculiarly modern, or (as the Churchmen would say) morbid scepticism, and sorely tried by that alluring, beautiful, mysterious spirit of the earth, whose voice is for ever breaking in upon, and sometimes tempering, the prayers of the saints. Augustine Chanteprie, the descendant of an old Catholic family, many of whose members have been disciples of Pascal,[1] has been brought up in an atmosphere of rigid, practical belief, and is destined, if not for a clerical life, at least for such a life in the world as may be jealously guarded from the snares of the devil, sacrificing as little as may be of innocence and piety. Among his ancestors, however, there was one who forsook the holy counsel given him in youth, and assumed the excellent foppery of the world.[2] He built, in protest against the gloomy house of his family, a pleasant folly, which afterwards came to be known as 'The House of Sin'. Augustine, unfortunately for himself, inherits the double temperament, and little by little the defences of the spiritual life are weakened, and he is made aware of human love as a subtle, insinuating fire. The intercourse of Augustine and Madame Manole is finely conceived, finely executed, enveloped in a glow of marvellous tenderness. A simple narration has always singular charm when we divine that the lives it offers us are themselves too ample, too complex, to be expressed entirely:–

Augustine and Fanny were now alone. They retraced their steps toward Chene-Pourpre, and suddenly stopping in the middle of the road, they kissed each other . . . There was neither light nor sound. Nothing lived under the vault of heaven but the man and the woman intoxicated by their kiss. From time to time, without disengaging their hands, they drew away and looked at each other.[3]

The last chapters of the book, the chapters in which the tradition of generations overcomes the lover, but so remorselessly that the mortal temple of all those emotions is shattered into fragments, show an admirable adjustment of style and narrative, the prose pausing more and more frequently with every lessening of vitality, and finally expiring (if one may reproduce the impression somewhat fantastically) as it ushers into the unknown, amid a murmur of prayers, the poor trembling soul. The interest in the politico-religious novel is, of course, an interest of the day, and perhaps because Huysmans is daily growing more formless and more obviously comedian in his books that Paris has begun to be wearied by the literary oblate.[4] The writer of 'The House of Sin', again, is without the advantage of a perverted career, and is not to be reckoned among the converts. The complication of an innocent male and a woman of the world is, perhaps, not very new, but the subject receives here very striking treatment, and the story gains much by a comparison with Bourget's 'Mensonges'[5]—a book that is crude, however detailed and cynical. 'Marcelle Tinayre', who seems to have a finer sympathy with Catholicism than most of the neo-Catholics have, is a lover of life and of the fair shows of the world; and though piety and innocence are interwoven with every change of affection and every mood of our manifold nature in these pages, one is conscious that the writer has suspended over her tragedy, as a spectre of sorrow and desolation, the horrible image of the Jansenist Christ.[6]

'The House of Sin.' By Marcelle Tintyre [*sic*] (translated by A. Smith). Maclaren and Co., London.

UNEQUAL VERSE

Mr Langbridge, in his preface to this volume of his verses, has confessed to so great a number of literary discipleships that one is well prepared for the variety of styles and subjects of which the book is full. Mr Langbridge's worst manner is very bad indeed; here the worst vices of Browning are united with a disease of sentiment of which the 'Master' cannot be justly accused; here 'tears splash on ground', blind beggars, mothers' girlies, pathetic clerks, and cripples are huddled together in dire confusion, and the colloquial style, half American half Cockney, is employed to adorn their easily-imagined adventures. Anything more lamentable than the result would be difficult to conceive; and the result is all the more lamentable because the few sonnets which Mr Langbridge has inserted in his volume are evidences of some care and a not inconsiderable technical power. The lines, 'To Maurice Maeterlinck',[1] are, therefore, curiously out of place in this farrago of banal epics, so dignified are they in theme, so reserved in treatment, and one can only hope that Mr Langbridge, when he publishes again, will see fit to sacrifice his taste for 'comédie larmoyante',[2] and attest in serious verse that love which he professes for the muse.

'Ballads and Legends.' By Frederick Langbridge.
George Routledge and Sons, London.

MR ARNOLD GRAVES'S NEW WORK

In the introduction which Dr Tyrrell[1] has written for Mr Graves's tragedy, it is pointed out that 'Clytemnaestra' [*sic*] is not a Greek play in English, like 'Atalanta in Calydon',[2] but rather a Greek story treated from the standpoint of a modern dramatist—in other words it claims to be heard on its own merits merely, and not at all as a literary curio. To leave aside for the moment the subordinate question of language it is not easy to agree with Dr Tyrrell's opinion that the treatment is worthy of the subject. On the contrary there would appear to be some serious flaws in the construction. Mr Graves has chosen to call his play after the faithless wife of Agamemnon, and to make her nominally the cardinal point of interest. Yet from the tenor of the speeches, and inasmuch as the play is almost entirely a drama of the retribution which follows crime, Orestes being the agent of Divine vengeance, it is plain that the criminal nature of the queen has not engaged Mr Graves's sympathies. The play, in fact, is solved according to an ethical idea, and not according to that indifferent sympathy with certain pathological states which is so often anathematised by theologians of the street. Rules of conduct can be found in the books of moral philosophers, but 'experts' alone can find them in Elizabethan comedy. Moreover, the interest is wrongly directed when Clytemnaestra, who is about to imperil everything for the sake of her paramour,[3] is represented as treating him with hardly disguised contempt, and again where Agamemnon, who is about to be murdered in his own palace by his own queen on his night of triumph, is made to behave towards his daughter Electra with a stupid harshness which is suggestive of nothing so much as of gout. Indeed, the feeblest of the five acts is the act which deals with the murder. Nor is the effect even sustained, for its second representation during Orestes' hypnotic trance cannot but mar the effect of the real murder in the third act in the mind of an audience which has just caught Clytemnaestra and Egisthus redhanded. These faults can hardly be called venial, for they occur at vital points of the artistic structure, and Mr Graves, who might have sought to cover all with descriptive writing, has been honest enough to employ such a studiously plain language as throws every deformity into instant relief. However, there are fewer offences in the verse than in most of the verse that is written nowadays, and it is perhaps only an indication of the mental confusion incident upon seership when Tiresias, the prophet, is heard exclaiming:

> Beware! beware!
> The stone you started rolling down the hill
> Will crush you if you do not change your course.

'Clytmnæstra [*sic*]: A Tragedy,' by Arnold F. Graves. Longman, Green and Co: London.

A NEGLECTED POET

Tennyson is reported to have said that if God made the country and man made the city, it must have been the devil that made the country town.[1] The dreary monotonousness, the squalor, the inevitable moral decay—all, in fine, that has been called 'provincial'—is the constant theme of Crabbe's verse. Patronised in his own day by Edmund Burke and Charles James Fox, the friend of Scott, and Rogers, and Bowles, the literary godfather of FitzGerald,[2] Crabbe has so far fallen in our day from his high estate that it is only by a favour that he is accorded mention in some manual of literature. This neglect, though it can be easily explained, is probably not a final judgment. Of course, much of Crabbe's work is dull and undistinguished, and he never had such moments as those which Wordsworth can always plead in answer to his critics. On the contrary, it is his chief quality that he employs the metre of Pope so evenly, and with so little of Pope's brilliancy that he succeeds admirably as narrator of the obscure tragedies of the provinces. His tales are, therefore, his claim to a place in the history of English fiction. At a time when false sentiment and the 'genteel' style were fashionable, and when country life was seized upon for exploitation as eagerly as by any of the modern Kailyard school,[3] Crabbe appeared as the champion of realism. Goldsmith had preceded him in treating rural subjects, treating them with an Arcadian grace, it is true, but with what remoteness and lack of true insight and sympathy a comparison of Auburn with 'The Village', 'The Borough', and 'The Parish Register' will show.[4] These latter are no more than names in the ears of the present generation, and it is the purpose of the present monograph to obtain a hearing, at least, for one of the most neglected of English writers. The name of its author is one of the most honourable and painstaking in contemporary criticism, and amid a multitude of schools and theories perhaps he may succeed in securing a place for one like Crabbe, who, except for a few passages wherein the world of opinion is divided, is an example of sane judgment and sober skill, and who has set forth the lives of villagers with appreciation and fidelity, and with an occasional splendour reminiscent of the Dutchmen.[5]

'George Crabbe,' by Alfred Ainger. Macmillan and Co., London.

MR MASON'S NOVELS

These novels, much as they differ in their subjects and styles, are curiously illustrative of the truth of one of Leonardo's observations. Leonardo, exploring the dark recesses of consciousness in the interests of some semi-pantheistic psychology, has noted the tendency of the mind to impress its own likeness upon that which it creates. It is because of this tendency, he says, that many painters have cast as it were a reflection of themselves over the portraits of others.[1] Mr Mason, perhaps, in like manner, has allowed these stories to fit themselves into what is doubtless one of the 'moulds of his understanding'. Among Mr Mason's 'properties' the reader will not fail to notice the early, effaceable husband. In 'The Courtship of Morrice Buckler' it is Julian Harwood, in 'The Philanderers' it is the outcast Gorley, in 'Miranda of the Balcony' it is Ralph Warriner. In all three books a previously-implicated girl of wayward habits is associated with a young man, who is a type of class common enough in novels— the sturdy, slow-witted Englishman. It is curious to watch this story reproducing itself without the author's assent, one imagines, through scenes and times differing so widely. A minor phenomenon is the appearance of Horace in each story. In 'The Courtship of Morrice Buckler' the plan of the castle in the Tyrol, which is the centre of gravity of the story, is made on a page of a little Elzevir copy of Horace.[2] In 'The Philanderers' Horace is laid under tribute more than once for a simile worthy of the classical beauty of Clarice. And once again in 'Miranda of the Balcony' that interesting figure 'Major' Wilbraham is represented as engaged on a translation of Horace in the intervals of marauding and blackmailing. Mr Mason is much more successful when he is writing of a time or scene somewhat remote from big towns. The Belgravian atmosphere of 'The Philanderers' (a title which Mr Mason has to share with Mr George Bernard Shaw) is not enlivened by much wit or incident, but 'Miranda of the Balcony' has a pleasing sequence of Spanish and Moorish scenes. Mr Mason's best book, however, is certainly 'The Courtship of Morrice Buckler'. The story is of the cape and sword order, and it passes in the years after Sedgemoor.[3] Germany is an excellent place for castles and intrigues; and in the adventurous air of this romance those who have read too many novels of modern life may recreate themselves at will. The writing is often quite pretty, too. Isn't 'Miranda of the Balcony' a pretty name?

'The Courtship of Maurice Buckley [*sic*]', by A. E. W. Mason. 'The Philanderers,' by A. E. W. Mason. 'Miranda of the Balcony,' by A. E. W. Mason. Macmillan and Co., London.

THE BRUNO PHILOSOPHY

Except for a book in the English or Foreign Philosophical Library,[1] a book the interest of which was chiefly biographical, no considerable volume has appeared in England to give an account of the life and philosophy of the heresiarch martyr of Nola.[2] Inasmuch as Bruno was born about the middle of the 16th century, an appreciation of him—and that appreciation the first to appear in England—cannot but seem somewhat belated now. Less than a third of this book is devoted to Bruno's life, and the rest of the book to an exposition and comparative survey of his system. That life reads like a heroic fable in these days of millionaires. A Dominican monk, a gipsy professor, a commentator of old philosophies and a deviser of new ones, a playwright, a polemist, a counsel for his own defence, and, finally, a martyr burned at the stake in the Campo dei Fiori[3]—Bruno, through all these modes and accidents (as he would have called them) of being, remains a consistent spiritual unity. Casting away tradition with the courage of early humanism, Bruno has hardly brought to his philosophical enquiry the philosophical method of a peripatetic. His active brain continually utters hypotheses; his vehement temper continually urges him to recriminate; and though the hypothesis may be validly used by the philosopher in speculation and the counter-check quarrelsome be allowed him upon occasion, hypotheses and recriminations fill so many of Bruno's pages that nothing is easier than to receive from them an inadequate and unjust notion of a great lover of wisdom. Certain parts of his philosophy—for it is many sided—may be put aside. His treatises on memory, commentaries on the art of Raymond Lally [sic], his excursions into that treacherous region from which even ironical Aristotle did not come undiscredited, the science of morality, have an interest only because they are so fantastical and middle aged.[4] As an independent observer, Bruno, however, deserves high honour. More than Bacon or Descartes must he be considered the father of what is called modern philosophy.[5] His system by turns rationalist and mystic, theistic and pantheistic is everywhere impressed with his noble mind and critical intellect, and is full of that ardent sympathy with nature as it is—natura naturata[6]—which is the breath of the Renaissance. In his attempt to

reconcile the matter and form of the Scholastics[7]—formidable
names, which in his system as spirit and body retain little of their
metaphysical character—Bruno has hardly put forward an hypothesis, which is a curious anticipation of Spinoza.[8] Is it not strange,
then, that Coleridge should have set him down a dualist, a later
Heraclitus,[9] and should have represented him as saying in effect:
'Every power in nature or in spirit must evolve an opposite as the
sole condition and means of its manifestation; and every opposition
is, therefore, a tendency to reunion.'?[10] And yet it must be the chief
claim of any system like Bruno's that it endeavours to simplify the
complex. That idea of an ultimate principle, spiritual, indifferent,
universal, related to any soul or to any material thing, as the Materia
Prima[11] of Aquinas is related to any material thing, unwarranted as it
may seem in the view of critical philosophy,[12] has yet a distinct value
for the historian of religious ecstasies. It is not Spinoza, it is Bruno,
that is the god-intoxicated man.[13] Inwards from the material universe, which, however, did not seem to him, as to the Neoplatonists,
the kingdom of the soul's malady, or as to the Christians a place of
probation, but rather his opportunity for spiritual activity, he passes,
and from heroic enthusiasm to enthusiasm to unite himself with
God. His mysticism is little allied to that of Molinos or to that of St
John of the Cross;[14] there is nothing in it of quietism or of the dark
cloister: it is strong, suddenly rapturous, and militant. The death of
the body is for him the cessation of a mode of being, and in virtue of
this belief and of that robust character 'prevaricating yet firm',
which is an evidence of that belief, he becomes of the number of
those who loftily do not fear to die. For us his vindication of the
freedom of intuition must seem an enduring monument, and among
those who waged so honourable a war, his legend must seem the
most honourable, more sanctified, and more ingenuous than that of
Averroes or of Scotus Erigena.[15]

                    'Giordano Bruno.' By J. Lewis McIntyre. Macmillan and Co.,
                                                          London. 1903.

HUMANISM

Barbarism, says Professor Schiller, may show itself in philosophy in two guises, as barbarism of style and as barbarism of temper, and what is opposed to barbarism is Professor Schiller's philosophical creed: Humanism, or, as he sometimes names it, Pragmatism.[1] One, therefore, who has been prepared to expect courteous humanism both in temper and in style, will read with some surprise statements such as—'The *a priori* philosophies[2] have all been found out'; 'Pragmatism . . . has . . . reached the "Strike, but hear me!" stage', 'It [the Dragon of Scholasticism] is a spirit . . . that grovels in muddy technicality, buries itself in the futile burrowings of valueless researches, and conceals itself from human insight [but not from humane insight, Professor Schiller!] by dust-clouds of desiccated rubbish which it raises.'[3] But these are details. Pragmatism is really a very considerable thing. It reforms logic, it shows the absurdity of pure thought, it establishes an ethical basis for metaphysic, makes practical usefulness the criterion of truth, and pensions off the Absolute once and for all. In other words, pragmatism is common-sense. The reader, accordingly, will not be surprised to find that in the post-Platonic dialogue, which is called 'useless knowledge,' a disciple of William James utterly routs and puts to shame the ghostly forms of Plato and Aristotle. Emotional psychology is made the starting-point, and the procedure of the philosopher is to be regulated in accordance. If Professor Schiller had sought to establish rational psychology as a starting-point, his position would have been well-grounded, but rational psychology he has either never heard of or considers unworthy of mention. In his essay on the desire of immortality he establishes one fact—that the majority of human beings are not concerned as to whether or not their life is to end with the dissolution of the body. And yet, after having set up efficiency as the test of truth and the judgment of humanity as the final court of appeal, he concludes by pleading on behalf of the minority, by advocating the claims of the Society for Psychical Research, of which, it seems, he has been for many years a member. Was it so well done, after all, to reform logic so radically? But your pragmatist is nothing if not an optimist, and though he himself denies philosophies by the score, he declares that pessimism is 'der Geist der stets verneint'.[4] The Mephistopheles of Goethe is the subject of one of the most entertaining essays in the book. 'The subtlest of his disguises,' says Prof. Schiller in a characteristic sentence, 'his most habitual mask, is one which deceives all the other characters in Faust, except the Lord, and has, so far as I know, utterly deceived all Goethe's readers except myself.'[5] But surely Professor Schiller can hardly derive much satisfaction from the knowledge that he shares his discovery with the Lord in Goethe's Faust, a being which (to quote the phrase of the English sceptic upon a term of the English sensationalist-theologians) is taken for God because we do not know what the devil it can be,[6] a being, moreover, which is closely allied to such inefficient and pragmatically annihilated entities as the Absolute of Mr Bradley and the Unknowable of Mr Spencer.

'Humanism: Philosophical Essays,' by F. S. C. Schiller.
Macmillan and Co., London. 8s. 6d.

SHAKESPEARE EXPLAINED

In a short prefatory note the writer of this book states that he has not written it for Shakespearian scholars, who are well provided with volumes of research and criticism, but has sought to render the eight plays more interesting and intelligible to the general reader. It is not easy to discover in the book any matter for praise. The book itself is very long—nearly 500 pages of small type—and expensive. The eight divisions of it are long drawn out accounts of some of the plays of Shakespeare—plays chosen, it would seem, at haphazard. There is nowhere an attempt at criticism, and the interpretations are meagre, obvious, and commonplace. The passages 'quoted' fill up perhaps a third of the book, and it must be confessed that the writer's method of treating Shakespeare is (or seems to be) remarkably irreverent. Thus he 'quotes' the speech made by Marcellus [*sic*] in the first act of 'Julius Caesar', and he has contrived to condense the first 16 lines of the original with great success, omitting six of them without any sign of omission. Perhaps it is a jealous care for the literary digestion of the general public that impels Mr Canning to give them no more than ten-sixteenths of the great bard. Perhaps it is the same care which dictates sentences such as the following:– 'His noble comrade fully rivals Achilles in wisdom as in valour. Both are supposed to utter their philosophic speeches during the siege of Troy, which they are conducting with the most energetic ardour. They evidently turn aside from their grand object for a brief space to utter words of profound wisdom . . .'[1] It will be seen that the substance of this book is after the manner of ancient playbills. Here is no psychological complexity, no cross-purpose, no interweaving of motives such as might perplex the base multitude. Such a one is a 'noble character', such a one a 'villain'; such a passage is 'grand', 'eloquent', or 'poetic'. One page in the account of 'Richard the Third' is made up of single lines or couplets and such non-committal remarks as 'York says then', 'Gloucester, apparently surprised, answers', 'and York replies', 'and Gloucester replies', 'and York retorts'. There is something very naif about this book, but (alas!) the general public will hardly pay sixteen shillings for such naivete. And the same

Philistine public will hardly read five hundred pages of 'replies', and 'retorts' illustrated with misquotations. And even the pages are wrongly numbered.

'Shakespeare Studied in Eight Plays.' By Hon. A. S. Canning.
Fisher, Unwin, London.

[BORLASE AND SON]

'Borlase and Son' has the merit, first of all, of 'actuality'. As the preface is dated for May last, one may credit the author with prophetic power, or at least with that special affinity for the actual, the engrossing topic, which is a very necessary quality in the melo-dramatist. The scene of the story is the suburban district about Peckham Rye, where the Armenians have just fought out a quarrel, and, moreover, the epitasis (as Ben Jonson would call it) of the story dates from a fall of stocks incident upon a revolution among the Latin peoples of America.[1] But the author has an interest beyond that derivable from such allusions. He has been called the Zola of Camberwell, and, inappropriate as the epithet is, it is to Zola we must turn for what is, perhaps, the supreme achievement in that class of fiction of which 'Borlase and Son' is a type. In 'Au Bonheur des Dames'[2] Zola has set forth the intimate glories and shames of the great warehouse—has, in fact, written an epic for drapers; and in 'Borlase and Son', a much smaller canvas, our author has drawn very faithfully the picture of the smaller 'emporium', with its sordid avarice, its underpaid labour, its intrigue, its 'customs of trade'. The suburban mind is not invariably beautiful, and its working is here delineated with unsentimental vigour. Perhaps the unctuousness of old Borlase is somewhat overstated, and the landladies may be reminiscent of Dickens. In spite of its 'double-circle' plot, 'Borlase and Son' has much original merit, and the story, a little slender starveling of a story, is told very neatly and often very humorously. For the rest, the binding of the book is as ugly as one could reason-ably expect.[3]

Borlase and Son, by T. Baron Russell, John Murray, London. 6s.

EMPIRE-BUILDING

Empire-building does not appear to be as successful in Northern, as it has been in Southern, Africa. While his cousins are astonishing the Parisian public by excursions in the air M Jacques Lebaudy, the new Emperor of the Sahara, is preparing to venture into the heavier and more hazardous atmosphere of the Palais.[1] He has been summoned to appear today before M André at the suit of two sailors, Jean Marie Bourdiec and Joseph Cambrai, formerly of the *Frosquetta*.[2] They claim 100,000 francs damages on account of the hardships and diseases which they have contracted owing to M Lebaudy's conduct. The new emperor, it would seem, is not over-careful of the bodily welfare of his subjects. He leaves them unprovided-for in a desert, bidding them wait there until he returns. They are made captive by a party of natives and suffer the agonies of hunger and thirst during their captivity. They remain prisoners for nearly two months and are finally rescued by a French man-o'-war under the command of M Jaurès. One of them is subsequently an inmate of a hospital at the Havre and after a month's treatment there is still only convalescent. Their appeals for redress have been all disregarded and now they are having recourse to law. Such is the case of the sailors for the defence of which Maître Aubin and Maître Labori have been retained. The emperor, acting through a certain Benoit, one of his officers, has entered a plea for arbitration. He considers that the case is between the French Republic and the Saharan empire and that in consequence it should be tried before a tribunal of some other nation. He petitions, therefore, that the case should be submitted for judgment to England, Belgium or Holland. However the case goes (and it is plain that the peculiar circumstances attending it render it an extremely difficult one to try) it cannot be that the new empire will gain either materially or in *prestige* by its trial. The dispute, in fact, tends to reduce what was, perhaps, a colonising scheme into a commercial concern but indeed, when one considers how little the colonising spirit appeals to the French people, it is not easy to defend M Lebaudy against the accusation of faddism. The new scheme does not seem to have the State behind it; the new empire does not seem to be entering on its career under any such capable management as reared up the Southern Empire out of the Bechuanaland Commission.[3] But, however this may be, the enterprise is certainly sufficiently novel to excite an international interest in this new candidate for nationhood and the hearing of a case, in which such singular issues are involved, will doubtless divide the attention of the Parisians with such comparatively minor topics as Réjane and *les petits oiseaux*.[4]

(James A. Joyce,
7 S. Peter's Terrace,
Cabra, Dublin)

[AESTHETICS]

[Paris Notebook]¹

. . . . Desire is the feeling which urges us to go to something and loathing is the feeling which urges us to go from something: and that art is improper which aims at exciting these feelings in us whether by comedy or by tragedy.² Of comedy later. Tragedy aims at exciting in us feelings of terror and pity.³ Now terror is the feeling which arrests us before whatever is grave in human fortunes and unites us with its secret cause and pity is the feeling which arrests us before whatever is grave in human fortunes and unites us with the human sufferer.⁴ But loathing, which an improper art aims at exciting in the way of tragedy, differs, it is seen, from the feelings which are proper to tragic art, namely, terror and pity. For loathing urges us from rest because it urges us to go from something, but terror and pity hold us in rest, as it were, by fascination. When tragic art makes my body to shrink terror is not my feeling because I am urged from rest; and moreover this art does not show me what is grave, I mean what is constant and irremediable, in human fortunes nor does it unite me with any secret cause for it shows me only what is unusual and remediable in human fortunes and it unites me with a cause only too manifest . . . . Nor is an art properly tragic which would move me to prevent human suffering any more than an art is properly tragic which would move me in anger against some manifest cause of human suffering . . . Terror and pity, finally, are germane to sorrow—the feeling which the privation of some good excites in us . . . .

. . . . And now of comedy. An improper art aims at exciting in the way of comedy the feeling of desire but the feeling which is proper to comic art is the feeling of joy.⁵ Desire, it has been seen, is the feeling which urges us to go to something but joy is the feeling which the possession of some good excites in us. Desire, the feeling which an improper art seeks to excite in the way of comedy, differs, it is seen, from joy. For desire urges us from rest that we may possess something but joy holds us in rest so long as we possess something. Desire, therefore, can be excited in us only by a work of comic art which is not sufficient in itself in as much as it urges us to seek something beyond itself; but a work of comic art which does not urge us to seek anything beyond itself excites in us the feeling of joy. All art which excites in us the feeling of joy is so far comic and according as this feeling of joy is excited by whatever is substantial or accidental, general or fortuitous, in human fortunes the art is to be judged more or less excellent: and even tragic art may be said to participate in the nature of comic art so far as the possession of a work of tragic art excites in us the feeling of joy. From this it may be seen that tragedy is the imperfect manner, and comedy the perfect manner, in art . . . . All art, again, is static for the feelings of terror and pity on the one hand and the feeling of joy on the other hand are feelings which arrest us. Afterwards it will appear how this rest is necessary for the apprehension of the beautiful—the end of all art, tragic or comic,—for this rest is the only condition under which the images, which are to excite in us terror or pity or joy, can be properly presented to us and properly seen by us. For beauty is a quality of something seen but terror and pity and joy are states of mind . . . . . .

J. A. J. 13/2/03. Paris.

. . . . . . There are three conditions of art: the lyrical, the epical and the dramatic. That art is lyrical whereby the artist sets forth the image in immediate relation to himself; that art is epical whereby the artist sets forth the image in mediate [*sic*] relation to himself and to others: that art is dramatic whereby the artist sets forth the image in immediate relation to others . . . .[6]

J. A. J. 6 March 1903, Paris.

Rhythm seems to be the first or formal relation of part to part in any whole or of a whole to its part or parts, or of any part to the whole of which it is a part . . . Parts constitute a whole as far as they have a common end.[7]

James A. Joyce, 25 March 1903, Paris

ἡ τεχνη μιμειται την Φυσιν[8]—This phrase is falsely rendered as
'Art is an imitation of Nature'. Aristotle does not here define art; he
says only, 'Art imitates Nature' and means that the artistic process is
like the natural process . . . It is false to say that sculpture, for
instance, is an art of repose if by that be meant that sculpture is
unassociated with movement. Sculpture is associated with movement in as much as it is rhythmic; for a work of sculptural art must
be surveyed according to its rhythm and this surveying is an imaginary movement in space. It is not false to say that sculpture is an art of
repose in that a work of sculptural art cannot be presented as itself
moving in space and remain a work of sculptural art.

                                  James A. Joyce, 27 March 1903, Paris

Art is the human disposition of sensible or intelligible matter for an
aesthetic end.[9]

                                  James A. Joyce, 28 March 1903, Paris

Question:[10] *Why are not excrements, children and lice works of art?*
Answer: Excrements, children, and lice are human products—
human dispositions of sensible matter. The process by which they
are produced is natural and non-artistic; their end is not an aesthetic
end: therefore they are not works of art.

Question: *Can a photograph be a work of art?*
Answer: A photograph is a disposition of sensible matter and may be
so disposed for an aesthetic end but it is not a human disposition of
sensible matter. Therefore it is not a work of art.

Question: *If a man hacking in fury at a block of wood make there an
image of a cow (say) has he made a work of art?*
Answer: The image of a cow made by a man hacking in fury at a
block of wood is a human disposition of sensible matter but it is not a
human disposition of sensible matter for an aesthetic end. Therefore
it is not a work of art.

Question: *Are houses, clothes, furniture, etc., works of art?*
Answer: Houses, clothes, furniture, etc., are not necessarily works of

art. They are human dispositions of sensible matter. When they are so disposed for an aesthetic end they are works of art.

[Pola Notebook][11]

Bonum est in quod tendit appetitus
S. Thomas Aquinas[12]

The good is that towards the possession of which an appetite tends: the desirable. The true and the beautiful are the most persistent orders of the desirable. Truth is desired by the intellectual appetite which is appeased by the most satisfying relations of the intelligible; beauty is desired by the esthetic appetite which is appeased by the most satisfying relations of the sensible.[13] The true and the beautiful are spiritually possessed, the true by intellection, the beautiful by apprehension; and the appetites which desire to possess them, the intellectual and esthetic appetites, are therefore spiritual appetites.

Pola. J. A. J. 7. XI. 04

Pulcera [*sic*][14] sunt quae visa placent
S. Thomas Aquinas[15]

Those things are beautiful the apprehension of which pleases. Therefore beauty is that quality of a sensible object in virtue of which its apprehension pleases or satisfies the aesthetic appetite which desires to apprehend the most satisfying relations of the sensible. Now the act of apprehension involves at least two activities, the activity of cognition or simple perception and the activity of[16] recognition. [If] the activity of simple perception is, like every other activity, itself pleasant [,] every sensible object that has been apprehended can be said in the first place to have been and to be[17] in a measure beautiful; and even the most hideous object can be said to have been and to be beautiful in so far as it has been apprehended. In regard then to that part of the act of apprehension which is called the activity of simple perception there is no sensible object which cannot be said to be in a measure beautiful.[18]

With regard to the second part of the act of apprehension which is called the activity of recognition it may further be said that there is no activity of simple perception to which there does not succeed in whatsoever measure the activity of recognition. For by the activity of recognition is meant an activity of decision; and in accordance with this activity in all conceivable cases a sensible object is said to be satisfying or dissatisfying.[19] But the activity of recognition is, like every other activity, itself pleasant and therefore every object that has been apprehended is secondly in whatsoever measure beautiful. Consequently even the most hideous object may be said to be beautiful for this reason as it is *a priori* said to be beautiful in so far as it encounters the activity of simple perception.

Sensible objects, however, are said conventionally to be beautiful or not for neither of the foregoing reasons but rather by reason of the nature, degree and duration of the satisfaction resulting from the apprehension of them and it is in accordance with these latter merely that the words 'beautiful' and 'ugly' are used in practical aesthetic philosophy. It remains then to be said that these words indicate only a greater or less measure of resultant satisfaction and that any sensible object, to which the word 'ugly' is practically applied, an object, that is, the apprehension of which results in a small measure of aesthetic satisfaction, is, in so far as its apprehension results in any measure of satisfaction whatsoever, said to be for the third time beautiful . . .

J. A. J. Pola. 15. XI. 04

The Act of Apprehension[20]

It has been said that the act of apprehension involves at least two activities—the activity of cognition or simple perception and the activity of recognition. The act of apprehension, however, in its most complete form involves three activities—the third being the activity of satisfaction. By reason of the fact that these three activities are all pleasant themselves every sensible object that has been apprehended must be doubly and may be trebly beautiful. In practical aesthetic philosophy the epithets 'beautiful' and 'ugly' are applied with regard chiefly to the third activity, with regard, that is, to the nature, degree and duration of the satisfaction resultant from the apprehension of any sensible object and therefore any sensible object to which in practical aesthetic philosophy the epithet 'beautiful' is applied must

be trebly beautiful, must have encountered, that is, the three
activities which are involved in the act of apprehension in its
most complete form. Practically then the quality of beauty in
itself must involve three constituents to encounter each of these
three activities . . .

J. A. J. Pola. 16. XI. 04

IRELAND: ISLAND OF SAINTS AND SAGES

Nations, like individuals, have their egos.[1] It is not unusual for a race to wish to attribute to itself qualities or glories unknown in other races—from the time when our forefathers called themselves Aryans and nobles to the Greeks who were wont to call anyone barbarian that did not live within the sacrosanct land of Hellas. The Irish, with a pride that is perhaps less explicable, love to refer to their land as the land of saints and sages.[2]

This honorary title was by no means invented yesterday nor the day before. In fact, it dates back to very ancient times, when the island was a true centre of intellectualism and sanctity, that spread its culture and stimulating energy throughout the continent. It would be easy to make a list of Irishmen who, both as pilgrims or hermits and scholars or sorcerers, have carried the torch of know-ledge from country to country. Even today, traces of them can be seen on some deserted altar: in some tradition or legend in which even the hero's name is hardly recognizable; or in some poetic allusion, such as the passage in Dante's *Inferno* where the guide, pointing out one of the Celtic sorcerers tortured by eternal pain, says:

> *Quell'altro che nei fianchi è così poco*
> *Michele Scotto fu che veramente*
> *Delle magiche frodi seppe il giuoco.*[3]

In truth it would take the learning and patience of a leisurely Bollandist[4] to give an account of the deeds of these saints and sages. Let us at least recall the notorious opponent of St Thomas, John Duns Scotus,[5] known as the subtle doctor (to distinguish him from St Thomas, the angelic doctor, and Bonaventura, the seraphic doc-tor), militant champion of the dogma of the immaculate conception and, judging by what chroniclers of the time say, an unbeatable dialectician. It seems unquestionable that Ireland then was an enor-mous seminary where students from different lands used to meet, so great was its reputation as teacher of spiritual matters. Although assertions of this sort ought to be treated with great reserve, it is more than likely (given the religious fervour that still flourishes in

Ireland of which you, fed over the past years on a diet of scepticism, can only form an idea with difficulty) that this glorious past is not a self-glorying invention. Anyway, if you need to be convinced, there are always the dusty archives of the Germans. Ferrero now tells us that the discoveries of these good German professors, as far as concerns the ancient history of the Roman republic and of the Roman empire, are mistaken from beginning to end, or almost.[6] Perhaps so. But, mistaken or not, it cannot be denied that these learned Germans were the first to present Shakespeare as a poet of world-wide significance, before the amazed eyes of his compatriots (who up until then had considered William as a person of secondary importance, a decent devil with a nice bent towards lyric poetry, but perhaps a bit over-fond of English beer). Similarly, it was those very same Germans who troubled themselves with the languages and history of the five Celtic nations.[7]

The only Irish grammars and dictionaries that existed in Europe until a few years ago, when the Gaelic League[8] was founded in Dublin, were works by Germans. The Irish language, although it forms part of the Indo-European family, is as different from English as the language spoken in Rome is different from the one spoken in Teheran. It has its own alphabet and characters, and a history that is almost three thousand years old. Ten years ago it was spoken only by peasants in the western province, on the Atlantic coast, and a little on the small islands that stand like pickets at the advance outpost of Europe facing the western hemisphere. Now the Gaelic League has revived its use. Every Irish newspaper, except the Unionist mouthpieces, has at least one special section published in Irish. Correspondence between the main municipalities is written in Irish, and Irish is taught in the majority of elementary and secondary schools. In the universities, it has been placed at the same level as other modern languages such as French, German, Italian and Spanish. In Dublin, street names are written in both languages. The League organizes festivals, concerts, debates and social gatherings at which the speaker of *Beurla* [sic][9] (that is, English) feels like a fish out of water, lost in the midst of a crowd chatting away in a harsh, guttural tongue. Often on the streets groups of young people may be seen to pass speaking Irish perhaps a little more emphatically than is really necessary. The members of the League correspond in Irish and on many occasions the poor postman, unable to read the address, has had to turn to the head of his section for help in unravelling the problem.

This language is eastern in origin and has been identified by many philologists with the ancient language of the Phoenicians, the discoverers, according to historians, of commerce and navigation. With their monopoly over the sea, this adventurous people established a civilization in Ireland which was in decline and had almost disappeared before the first Greek historian took up his quill. It jealously guarded the secrets of its science, and the first mention of the island of Ireland in foreign literature is to be found in a Greek poem of the fifth century before Christ in which the historian reiterates the Phoenician tradition. The language that the comic dramatist Plautus puts in the mouth of the Phoenicians in his comedy *Poenula* is virtually the same language, according to the critic Vallancey,[10] as that which Irish peasants now speak. The religion and civilization of that ancient people, later known as Druidism, were Egyptian. The druid priests had temples in the open and worshipped the sun and the moon in forests of oak. In the crude sciences of the day, the Irish priests were considered highly learned, and Plutarch, when he mentions Ireland, says that it was the dwelling place of holy men. Festus Avienus in the fourth century was the first to name it the *Insula Sacra*.[11] Later, having suffered invasions by Spanish and Gallic tribes, and having been converted without any bloodshed to Christianity by St Patrick and his followers, Ireland once again became deserving of the name of 'Holy Island'.

I do not propose to give a complete history of the Irish Church from the early centuries of the Christian era. To do so would go beyond the scope of this lecture and, moreover, would not be very interesting. But it is necessary to give you some explanation of the title, 'Island of Saints and Sages', and to show you its historical basis. Leaving aside the countless names of the ecclesiastics whose work was exclusively national, I beg you to follow me for a moment while I show you the traces left behind in almost every country by the many Celtic apostles. It is important to take account of facts such as these, though, nowadays, they might seem trivial to the lay mind,[12] as the century in which they occurred, and in the Middle Ages that followed, not only history itself, but the various arts and sciences were all religious in character and under the tutelage of a church that was more than maternal. Indeed, what were pre-Renaissance Italian artists if not so many handmaids obedient to the lord—learned commentators on holy writings, or illustrators in verse or painting of the Christian fable?

It may seem strange that an island such as Ireland, so remote from the centre of culture, should have become a school for apostles. However, even a superficial review shows us that the Irish nation's desire to create its own civilization is not so much the desire of a young nation wishing to link itself to Europe's concert, but the desire by an ancient nation to renew in a modern form the glories of a past civilization.

Even in the first century of Christianity under the apostolate of St Peter we find the Irishman, Mansuetus, later canonized, as a missionary to Lorraine, where he founded a church and preached for half a century.[13] Cataldus held the chair as a teacher of theology in Geneva and was later made bishop of Tarentum.[14] The great heresiarch Pelagius, an indefatigable traveller and propagandist, if not Irish (as many maintain), was certainly either Irish or Scottish, as was his right-hand man, Celestius.[15] Sedulius travelled through a large part of the world, finally settling down in Rome, where he composed the fair total of almost fifty theological tracts and many sacred hymns which are still used today in the Catholic ritual.[16] Fridolinus Viator, that is, the Traveller, of royal Irish stock, was a missionary to the Germans and died at Seckinge [*sic*][17] in Germany, where he is buried. The fiery Columbanus had the task of reforming the French Church and, after stirring up a civil war in Burgundy with his sermons, he left for Italy where he became the apostle of the Lombards, and founded the monastery of Bobio [*sic*].[18] Frigidianus, son of the king of the north of Ireland, held the bishop's chair in Lucca.[19] St Gallus, first the pupil and then the companion of Columbanus, lived as a hermit among the Grisons in Switzerland, just tending his fields, hunting and fishing. He refused the bishopric of the city of Constance which was offered to him, and died at the age of ninety-five.[20] On the site of his hermitage an abbey was built, and the abbot, by the grace of God, became the prince of the Canton and greatly enriched the Benedictine library, the ruins of which are still displayed to visitors in the ancient town of St Gall.[21] Finian, known as the learned, founded a school of theology on the banks of the river Boyne in Ireland where he taught

Catholic doctrine to thousands of students from Great Britain, France, Armorica and Germany, giving each of them (blessed were the days!) not just lessons and books, but even free bread and board.[22] However, it seems that occasionally he neglected to refill their study lamps. A student, finding himself suddenly without light, was obliged to invoke divine grace which made his fingers shine miraculously so that, by tracing his finger along the pages, he could quench his thirst for knowledge. St Fiacre, to whom there is a commemorative tablet in the church of S. Maturin in Paris, preached to the French and received a sumptuous funeral paid for by the court.[23] Fursey founded monasteries in five countries and his feast day is still celebrated in Péronne in Picardy, the place where he died.[24] Arbogast [*sic*] put up sanctuaries and chapels in Alsace and in Lorraine, governed the bishopric of Strasbourg for five years until, feeling himself to be at the end of his days, and mindful of his exemplar, he went to live in a hovel situated where criminals were executed, and where the great cathedral of the city was later constructed.[25] St Virus made himself champion of the cult of the Virgin Mary, while Disibod, the bishop of Dublin, travelled here and there throughout Germany for over forty years, finally founding a Benedictine monastery which he called Mount Disibod, now changed to Disenberg.[26] Rumold became bishop of Mechlin in France [*sic*] and a martyr.[27] Albinus, with the assistance of Charlemagne, established an institute of learning in Paris and another in ancient Ticinum (now Pavia), which he governed for many years.[28] Kilian, the apostle of Franconia, was consecrated bishop of Wurzburg in Germany, but, wishing to play John the Baptist between the Duke Gosbert and his paramour, was killed by assassins.[29] Sedulius the Younger was chosen by Pope Gregory II for the mission of pacifying the clerical strife in Spain, but when he got there the Spanish priests refused to listen to him, saying that he was a foreigner. To this Sedulius replied that, as he was Irish and of the old Milesian race, he was, in fact, of Spanish origin, an argument his opponents found so persuasive that they let him install himself in the bishop's palace in Oreto. Overall, the period that ended with the invasion of Ireland by Scandinavian tribes is an uninterrupted record of apostles, missions and martyrs. King Alfred, who visited the country, has left us his impressions in verses called 'The Royal Journey'. In the first verse he tells us:

> I found when I was in exile
> In Ireland the beautiful
> Many women, a serious crowd,
> Laymen and priests in abundance.

and it must be said that the picture hasn't changed much in twelve centuries except that, if the good King Alfred who found an abundance of laymen and priests in those days were to go there now, he might find almost more of the latter than the former.

Whoever reads the history of the three centuries that preceded the arrival of the English will need to have a strong stomach, as the internecine strife, the fights against the Danish and Norwegians (the black strangers and the white strangers as they were called), succeeded one another with such regularity and ferocity that they turn this era into a real butcher's mess.

The Danes occupied all the main ports on the hither coast[30] of the island, and established a kingdom at Dublin, now the capital of Ireland and a large city for over twenty centuries. The native kings were busy killing one another at the time, occasionally taking a well-earned break for games of chess. Finally, the victory of the usurper, Brian Boru, over the Nordic hordes on the sand dunes outside the walls of Dublin put an end to the Scandinavian races, which did not, however, abandon the country, but were gradually assimilated into the community, a fact we should keep in mind if we wish to explain the curious character of the modern Irishman.[31] During this period, culture necessarily languished, but Ireland did have the honour of producing three great heresiarchs, John Scotus Erigena, Macarius and Virgilius Solivagus.[32] The last-mentioned was recommended by the king of France to the abbey of Salzburg and was subsequently made bishop of that diocese, where he built a cathedral. He was a philosopher, mathematician and translator of Ptolemy's works. In his tract on geography, he upheld the then-subversive theory that the earth was spherical, and for such audacity he was condemned a heretic by Popes Boniface and Zacharias. Macarius lived in France and the monastery of St Eligius still preserves his tract *De Anima* in which he taught the doctrine that later became known as Averroism, a masterly examination of which has been left to us by Ernest Renan (himself a Breton-Celt).[33] A pantheist mystic also was Scotus Erigena, rector of the University of Paris, who translated from the

Greek books of mystic theology by the pseudo–Dionysius Areopagite, patron saint of the nation of France.[34] The translation was
the first to introduce to Europe the transcendental systems of the
Orient, and had as great an influence on European religious thought
as later, in the days of Pico della Mirandola, the translations of Plato
were to exercise on the development of the profane civilization of
Italy.[35] It goes without saying that this kind of innovation, which was
like a life–giving breath working a bodily resurrection of the dead
bones of orthodox theology heaped up on an inviolable holy ground,
a field of Ardath,[36] did not have the sanction of the Pope, who invited
Charles the Bald to send both the author and his book under escort
to Rome, probably wishing to give him a taste of some of the delights
of papal hospitality. It seems, however, that Scotus had kept some
good sense in his exalted brain, for he turned a deaf ear to the polite
invitation and returned, as fast as he could, to his own country.

There is an interval of almost eight centuries from the date of
the invasion of the English to the present day. I dwelt a little on the
preceding period with the purpose of enabling you to discern the
roots of the Irish temperament, but I do not intend to detain you
with an account of the affairs of Ireland under foreign occupation. I
do this mainly because Ireland then ceased to be an intellectual force
in Europe. The decorative arts, at which the ancient Irish excelled,
were abandoned and the sacred and profane culture fell into disuse.

Two or three names shine out like the last few stars of a radiant
night that are turning pale because dawn has come. John Duns
Scotus, whom I have mentioned above, founder of the Scotist
school; according to legend, he once listened to the arguments of all
the professors of the University of Paris for three whole days and
then, speaking from memory, confuted them one by one. John de
Sacrobosco,[37] who was the last great advocate of Ptolemy's geo-
graphical and astronomic theories, and Petrus Hibernicus,[38] the
theologian who had the supreme task of educating the mind of the
author of the scholastic apology, *Summa contra Gentiles*, St Thomas
Aquinas, perhaps the keenest and clearest mind that human history
has ever seen. But while these last stars were still reminding the
nations of Europe of the past glories of Ireland, there arose a new
Celtic race which was made up of the old Celtic stock and the Scandinavian, Anglo–Saxon and Norman races. On the foundations of its
ancient predecessor, another national temperament grew up, in

which the various elements intermingled and renovated the ancient body. The ancient enemies made a common cause[39] against the aggression of the English. It was Protestants, who had now become *Hibernis Hiberniores*, more Irish than the Irish themselves, that were inciting the Irish Catholics to oppose the Calvinist and Lutheran fanatics from across the water. The descendants of the Danes, the Normans and the Anglo-Saxon colonizers championed the cause of the new Irish nation against British tyranny. Recently, an Irish deputy, while haranguing his electorate on the eve of an election, boasted that he was of the ancient race, and upbraided his opponent for being a descendant of a Cromwellian settler. This caused general amusement in the press because it is true to say that, in the present nation, it would be impossible to exclude all those who are descended from foreign families. To deny the name of patriot to all those not of Irish stock would be to deny it to almost all the heroes of the modern movement: Lord Edward Fitzgerald, Robert Emmet, Theobald Wolfe Tone and Napper Tandy, leaders of the 1798 rebellion; Thomas Davis and John Mitchel, leaders of the Young Ireland movement; many anti-clerical Fenians; Isaac Butt and Joseph Biggar, founders of parliamentary obstructionism; and, finally, Charles Stewart Parnell, perhaps the most formidable man ever to lead the Irish but in whose veins not a single drop of Celtic blood ran.[40] There are two days in the national calendar which, according to the patriots, ought to be marked as ill-starred: they are, the day of the Anglo-Saxon and Norman invasion, and the day, a century ago, of the union of the two parliaments.[41] Now, at this juncture, it is useful to point out two salient and important facts. Ireland prides itself on being in body and soul as faithful to her national traditions as to the Holy See. The majority of Irishmen consider loyalty to these two traditions as their cardinal article of faith. But the fact is that the English came to Ireland following the repeated requests of a native king,[42] without, it seems, much wanting to and without the sanction of their monarch,[43] but provided with a papal bull from Adrian IV and a papal letter from Alexander.[44] They disembarked on the southern coast, numbering 700 men, a gang of adventurers against a people. They were met by certain native tribes and, less than a year later, the English King Henry II noisily celebrated Christmas in the city of Dublin. Moreover, the parliamentary union of the two countries was not passed in Westminster, but in Dublin, by a parliament elected by the people of

Ireland—a corrupted parliament goaded by the huge sums from the English Prime Minister's agent[45]—but an Irish parliament none the less. In my opinion, these two facts must be perfectly explained before the country in which they took place has even the most elementary right to expect one of its sons to change his position from that of detached observer to convinced nationalist.[46]

On the other hand, impartiality can easily be confused with a convenient forgetfulness of the facts. If an observer, thoroughly convinced that Ireland was a body lacerated by ferocious struggles in the days of Henry II, and a filthily corrupt body in the days of William Pitt, were to deduce from this conviction that England, neither now nor in the future, has no debts to render in Ireland, he would be mistaken and greatly so. If a victorious country tyrannizes over another, it cannot logically take it amiss if the latter reacts. Men are made that way: and no one, unless he were blinded by self-interest or ingenuity, can still believe that a colonizing country is prompted by purely Christian motives when it takes over foreign shores, for all that the missionary and the pocket-bible come some months ahead of the arrival of the army and machine-guns. If the Irish have not been able to do what their American brothers did, this does not mean that they will never do so. It is not logical of British historians to salute the memory of George Washington and to profess themselves well pleased by the progress of an autonomous and virtually socialist republic in Australia, while they treat the Irish separatists as madcaps.

A moral separation already exists between the two countries. I never remember the English anthem, 'God Save the King', being sung in public without a storm of whistles, yells and shushes that rendered the solemn and stately music absolutely inaudible. But to be convinced of the existence of this separateness, you would have needed to have been in the streets of Dublin when the late Queen Victoria entered the capital as she did in the year before her death.[47] First of all, it should be noted that when an English monarch wants to go to Ireland for political reasons, there is always a lively uproar demanding that the Lord Mayor receive him at the city gates; and in fact, the last monarch to go there had to content himself with an informal reception by the sheriff, as the Lord Mayor had refused the honour.[48] (I note here for sheer curiosity's sake that the present Lord Mayor of Dublin is an Italian, Signor Nannetti.)[49] Queen Victoria had been in Ireland only once before, half a century previously, after her wedding.[50] Then the Irish, who had not entirely forgotten their loyalty to the unlucky Stuart family nor to the name of Mary Stuart, the Scottish queen, and the legendary fugitive Bonnie Prince Charlie, had the nasty idea of mocking the queen's consort: poking fun at him for being an uprooted German princeling, imitating the way he stammered his English as well as cheerfully greeting him the very moment he set foot on Irish soil with a head of cabbage.[51] The Irish conduct and character were not to the queen's liking. Fed on the imperialist and patrician theories of Benjamin Disraeli, her favourite minister,[52] she took little or no interest in the fate of the Irish people except to make some disdainful comments to which they, naturally, answered back in kind. Once, it is true, when there had been a terrible calamity in County Kerry that left almost the entire county without food or shelter, the queen (who was greatly attached to her millions) sent the help committee, which had already received thousands from all social classes, a royal cheque for the sum of 10 pounds.[53] The committee, not very grateful for such a gift, put the cheque back in an envelope, included a thank-you note, and sent it back by return of post. From these small items of fact, it is clear that there was no love lost between Victoria and her Irish subjects, and if she decided to pay them a visit in the twilight years of her life, the visit was certainly politically motivated. The truth is that she did not come but was, rather, sent by her advisers. At that time the English disasters in South Africa in the Boer War had made England the laughing-stock of the European press, and it was to take the genius of two commanders, Lord Roberts and Lord Kitchener (both of them Irish, born in Ireland)[54] to restore the endangered prestige, just as, in 1815, it took another Irish soldier, the Duke of Wellington, to overturn the renewed might of Napoleon at Waterloo;[55] just as it needed recruits and volunteers from Ireland to demonstrate the now famous valour in the field in whose recognition the English government allowed the Irish regiments to carry the three-leafed emblem of Irish patriotism on St Patrick's Day. In fact, the queen came to win the easy sympathy of the country and to increase the lists of recruiting-sergeants.

I said that to understand the gulf that still separates the two nations, you need to have been present at her entry into Dublin. There were little English soldiers lining the route (because, ever since the Fenian revolt under James Stephens, the government had never sent an Irish regiment to Ireland), and, behind this barrier, stood the crowd of citizens.[56] Officials and their wives, unionist clerks and their wives, tourists and their wives stood on decorated balconies, and when the procession appeared, they began to shout greetings and wave handkerchiefs. The queen's carriage passed by, tightly protected on all sides by an impressive bodyguard with bared sabres, while inside a little woman, almost a dwarf could be seen, hunched and swaying in movement with the carriage, funereally dressed with horn-rimmed glasses on her ashen vacuous face. From time to time she would nod suddenly in response to some isolated cry of greeting, like a student who has learnt a lesson badly. She bowed to the left and right with an unusual mechanical movement. The English soldiers stood respectfully at attention while their queen passed; behind them, the crowd watched the sumptuous procession and its sad central figure with eyes of curiosity, almost pity. When the carriage passed by, they followed its wake with ambiguous glances. This time there were no bombs or cabbages, but the queen of England entered the capital of Ireland in the midst of a silent people.

The reasons for this difference of temperament that has now become a commonplace among the columnists of Fleet Street[57] are partly racial and partly historical. Our civilization is an immense woven fabric in which very different elements are mixed, in which Nordic rapacity is reconciled to Roman law, and new Bourgeois conventions to the remains of a Siriac religion.[58] In such a fabric, it is pointless searching for a thread that has remained pure, virgin and un-influenced by other threads nearby. What race or language (if we except those few which a humorous will seems to have preserved in ice, such as the people of Iceland) can nowadays claim to be pure? No race has less right to make such a boast than the one presently inhabiting Ireland.[59] Nationality (if this is not really a useful fiction like many others which the scalpels of the present-day scientists have put paid to) must find its basic reason for being in something that surpasses, that transcends and that informs changeable entities such as blood or human speech. The mystic theologian who assumed the pseudonym of Dionysius the Areopagite said somewhere that 'God has arranged the limits of the nations according to his angels' and this is probably not purely a mystic concept.[60] In Ireland we can see how the Danes, the Firbolgs, the Milesians from Spain, the Norman invaders, the Anglo-Saxon colonists and the Huguenots came together to form a new entity, under the influence of a local god, one might say. And although the present race in Ireland is second-rate and backward, it merits some consideration as it is the only one in the entire Celtic family that refused to sell its birthright for a plate of lentils.

I find it a bit naïve to heap insults on the Englishman for his misdeeds in Ireland. A conqueror cannot be amateurish, and what England did in Ireland over the centuries is no different from what the Belgians are doing today in the Congo Free State, and what the Nipponese dwarfs will be doing tomorrow in some other lands. She inflamed the factions and took possession of the wealth.

England sowed seed of strife among the various races; by introducing a new system of agriculture, she reduced the power of the native leaders and granted huge estates to her soldiers; she persecuted the Roman Church when it rebelled, and stopped only when it, too, had become an instrument of subjection. Her main concern was to keep the country divided. If a Liberal English government, with the full backing of the English electorate, were to concede a measure of autonomy to Ireland tomorrow, the Conservative press would not hesitate to rouse the province of Ulster against the new executive in Dublin.[61] She was as cruel as she was cunning: her weapons were, and are, the battering-ram, the club and the noose. If Parnell was a thorn in the side of the English, it was because, in his boyhood in Wicklow, he heard the tale of English ferocity from his nurse. A tale, which he himself used to recount, told of a peasant who had infringed against the Penal Laws and who, by order of the colonel, was taken, stripped, tied to a carriage and whipped by the troops. The whipping was, by order of the colonel, administered to his stomach in such a way that the unfortunate man died in atrocious agony, his intestines spilling out on the road.[62]

The English now laugh at the Irish for being Catholic, poor and ignorant; it will seem hard, for some, however, to justify this disdain. Ireland is poor because English laws destroyed the industries of the country, notably the woollen one; because, in the years in which the potato crop failed, the negligence of the English government left the flower of the people to die of hunger;[63] because, while the country is becoming depopulated and, though criminality is almost non-existent, judges under the present administration receive the salaries of a Pasha, and government and public officials pocket huge sums for doing little or nothing. In Dublin alone, by way of example, a lieu-tenant receives half a million francs a year; for every policeman, Dublin citizens fork out 3,500 francs a year (double, I think, what a schoolmaster receives in Italy).[64] The poor devil who performs the duties of chief clerk for the city is forced to get by on the miserable wages of six lira, in English money, a day.

The English critic is right, then. Ireland is poor and, moreover, politically backward. The dates of the Lutheran Reformation and the French Revolution mean nothing to an Irishman. The feudal struggles against the monarch, known in England as the Wars of the Barons, had their counterparts in Ireland. If the English barons knew how to kill their neighbour with aristocratic style, Irish barons could do so just as well. In those days, Ireland had no lack of those ferocious deeds that are contingent on blue blood. The Irish prince, Shane O'Neill, was so generous in nature that it was occasionally necessary to bury him up to his neck in mother earth when he was feeling lustful.[65] But the Irish barons, cunningly divided by the polit-ics of the foreigner, were never able to act according to a common plan. They let off steam in puerile fights between themselves, con-suming the vitality of the country with civil wars, while their brothers across St George's Channel were forcing King John to sign the Magna Carta (the first chapter in modern liberty) on the fields of Runnymede. The wave of democracy that swept through England in the days of Simon de Montfort,[66] the founder of the House of Commons, and later in the Cromwellian period of the Protectorate, arrived washed out on Irish shores. So Ireland (a country destined by God to be an eternal caricature of the serious world) is now an aristocratic country with no aristocracy. The descendants of the ancient kings (who call themselves by their surnames alone, without using a first name) can be seen with their wigs and notarial deeds in the palaces of justice where they go to defend some accused man or other by invoking the very laws that suppressed their royal titles. Poor fallen kings, they are recognizable even in their declined state as impracticable Irishmen, because it never occurred to them to follow the example of their English brothers in a similar position, to go to wonderful America to ask a different sort of king for his daughter's hand—even if he is only a Paint or Sausage King.

Nor is it any easier to understand why the Irish peasant is

reactionary and Catholic, or why, when he curses, he mixes the names of Cromwell and the Satanic pope. As far as he is concerned, the great Protector of civil rights was a savage animal who came to Ireland to propagate his faith by fire and sword. He does not forget the sack of Drogheda and Waterford; nor the ranks of men and women who were hunted down as far as the furthest islands by this Puritan who declared: 'Let them be gone into the ocean or Hell'; nor the false oath that the English made on the broken rock of Limerick.[67] How could he forget? Does the slave's back forget the rod? The truth is that the English government increased the moral value of Catholicism by banning it. Now, thanks partly to the never-ending discussions and in part to Fenian violence, the reign of terror is over. The Penal Laws have been repealed. Today in Ireland, a Catholic can vote, become a government employee, teach in a public school, take his seat in parliament, hold land for a period of over thirty-one years, have a horse in his stable worth over five pounds sterling or attend a Catholic mass without running the risk of being hanged, drawn and quartered by the town executioner. But these laws were repealed so short a time ago that an Irish deputy is still alive today who was once actually sentenced for high treason by an English court to be hanged, drawn and quartered by the town hangman (who is, in England, a mercenary singled out from his fellow mercenaries by the sheriff for his outstanding ability or industry). The Irish population, which is 90 per cent Catholic, no longer contributes towards the maintenance of the Protestant Church, which only exists for the benefit of a few thousand colonists. This means that the English Treasury has suffered a few losses, while the Roman Church has another child. Meanwhile, an education system is allowing some streams of modern thought to filter slowly into the arid earth. Perhaps in time there will be a gradual reawakening of the Irish consciousness and, perhaps, four or five centuries after the Diet of Worms, we shall witness a monk in Ireland throw off his cowl, run off with a nun, and proclaim aloud the end of the coherent absurdity that is Catholicism, and the beginning of the incoherent absurdity that is Protestantism.[68]

But a Protestant Ireland is almost unthinkable. Beyond doubt, Ireland has so far been the Catholic Church's most faithful daughter. It is perhaps the only country to welcome the first Christian missionaries courteously, and to be converted to the new doctrine without the shedding of a single drop of blood (as the bishop of Cashel once had occasion to boast in response to the gibes of Giraldus Cambrensis).[69] For seven or eight centuries it was the spiritual focus of Christianity. It sent its sons to every country in the world to preach the gospel, and its learned men to interpret and renew the holy texts.

Not even once was its faith seriously shaken, if we except a certain tendency towards the doctrine taught by Nestorius in the fifth century regarding the hypostatic union of the two natures of Jesus Christ, some trivial differences in ritual, visible at that time in the style of clerical tonsures and the date of the celebration of Easter, and, lastly, the defection of a few priests at the insistence of the Reformist envoys of Edward VI. But, at the first hint that the Church was in any real danger, veritable swarms of Irish envoys would leave at once for all the courts of Europe, where they would try to muster up strong concerted action against the heretics by the Catholic powers. Well, the Holy See has repaid this fidelity in its own way. First, by means of a papal bull and a ring, it gave Ireland as a present to Henry II. Later, under the pontificate of Gregory XIII, when Protestant heresy raised its head, it repented of having given a faithful island to the heretical English and, to remedy the fault, named a bastard from the papal court as sovereign supreme of Ireland.[70] This latter, naturally, remained a monarch *in partibus infidelium*,[71] but the Pope meant nothing discourteous by this. Anyhow, the Irish are so accommodatingly affable that they would hardly even grumble if, tomorrow, owing to some unforeseen complication in Europe, the Pope, having already given it to an Englishman and an Italian, were to hand their island over to some temporarily unemployed *hidalgo* from the court of Alphonso.[72] The Holy See, however, was more sparing in its ecclesiastic honours. However much Ireland may once have enriched the hagiographic archives in the way we have seen above, the fact was hardly even acknowledged by the Vatican councils. One thousand four hundred years had to pass before it occurred to the holy father to raise an Irish bishop to the rank of cardinal.

So, what has Ireland gained by its fidelity to the papal crown and its infidelity to the British one? It has gained quite a lot, but not for itself. Among Irish writers who adopted the English language in the seventeenth and eighteenth centuries and almost forgot their native country are to be found the names of Berkeley, the idealist philosopher; Oliver Goldsmith, author of *The Vicar of Wakefield*; two famous comic playwrights, Richard Brinsley Sheridan and William Congreve, whose masterpieces are still admired today on the sterile English stage; Jonathan Swift, author of *Gulliver's Travels*, a satire sharing first place with Rabelais in world literature; and Edmund Burke, dubbed by the English themselves as the modern Demosthenes, and considered the most profound orator ever to have spoken in the Chamber of Deputies.[73] Even today, in spite of the obstacles, Ireland is contributing to English art and thought. The idea that the Irish actually are the incapable and unbalanced cretins we read about in the leading articles in the *Standard* and the *Morning Post*[74] is belied by the names of the three greatest translators in English literature: FitzGerald, translator of the *Rubaiyat* by the Persian poet, Omar Khayyam; Burton, translator of Arabic master-pieces; and Carey [*sic*], the classic translator of the *Divine Comedy*.[75] It is also belied by other Irish names: the doyen of modern English music, Arthur Sullivan; the founder of Chartism, Edward [*sic*] O'Connor; the novelist George Moore, an oasis of intelligence in a Sahara of spiritualist, mystic and detective works whose names are legion in England; and two Dubliners, George Bernard Shaw, the paradoxical and iconoclastic comic playwright, and the over-rated Oscar Wilde, son of a revolutionary poetess.[76] Finally, in the field of practical affairs, this uncomplimentary conception is belied by the fact that the Irishman, finding himself in another environment, out-side Ireland, very often knows how to make his worth felt.[77] The economic and intellectual conditions of his homeland do not permit the individual to develop. The spirit of the country has been weak-ened by centuries of useless struggle and broken treaties. Individual initiative has been paralysed by the influence and admonitions of the church, while the body has been shackled by peelers, duty officers and soldiers. No self respecting person wants to stay in Ireland. Instead he will run from it, as if from a country that had been subjected to a visitation by an angry Jove. From the time of the Treaty of Limerick, or rather, from the time it was broken by the Punic faith of the English, millions of Irish have left their homeland for other shores. These fugitives who, centuries ago, were called the Wild Geese, enlisted in all the foreign garrisons of European Powers, mainly France, Holland and Spain, and won many a victor's laurel on the battlefields for their adoptive masters. In America they found another homeland. The ancient Irish tongue could be heard in the ranks of the American rebels, and Lord Mountjoy himself said in 1784: 'We lost America because of the Irish emigrants.'[78]

Today those Irish emigrants in the United States number sixteen million, a rich, powerful and industrious colony. Does this not perhaps prove that the Irish dream of resurgence is not entirely a chimera? If Ireland has been able to provide others with the services of men such as Tyndall, one of the few scientists whose name has crossed the Channel; the Marquess of Dufferin, Governor of Canada and Viceroy of India; Charles Gavan Duffy and Hennessy, colonial governors; the Duke of Tetuan, lately Prime Minister of Spain; Bryan, the presidential candidate in the United States; Marshal MacMahon, President of the Republic of France; Lord Charles Beresford, virtual captain of the English fleet, recently placed in charge of the Channel fleet; and the three most renowned generals of the English army, Lord Wolseley, the commander-in-chief, Lord Kitchener, victor in the Sudan campaign and presently commander of the Indian army, and Lord Roberts, victor in the wars in Afghanistan and South Africa—if Ireland has been able to place all this practical talent at the service of others, there has to be something inimical, ill-fated and despotic about her present condition that her sons cannot lend their skills to their native land.[79]

For, even today, the flight of these Wild Geese continues. Every year, Ireland, decimated as she already is, loses 40,000 of her sons. From 1850 to now, over 5,000,000 emigrants have left for America; and every postal delivery brings letters of invitation from these emigrants to their friends and relations at home in Ireland. The old, the corrupt, the children, and the poor stay at home where the double yoke etches another groove upon their docile necks. Standing around the death-bed where the poor bloodless and almost lifeless body lies are agitating patriots, proscribing governments, and priests administering the last rites.

Is this country destined some day to resume its ancient position as the Hellas of the north?[80] Is the Celtic spirit, like the Slavic one (which it resembles in many respects), destined in the future to enrich the consciousness of civilization with new discoveries and institutions? Or is the Celtic world, the five Celtic nations, pressed by a stronger race to the edge of the continent—to the very last islands of Europe—doomed, after centuries of struggle, finally to fall headlong into the ocean? Alas, we amateur sociologists are only second-rate soothsayers; we look into and rummage around in the intestines of the human animal, and in the end, we confess that we see nothing there! Only our supermen can write the history of the future.

It would be interesting, but beyond the aims I have set myself this evening, to see what the probable consequences would be of a resurgence of this people; to see the economic consequences of the appearance of a rival, bilingual, republican, self-centred and enterprising island next to England, with its own commercial fleet and its ambassadors in every port throughout the world;[81] to see the moral consequences of the appearance in old Europe of Irish artists and thinkers, those strange souls, cold enthusiasts, artistically and sexually uninstructed, full of idealism and incapable of sticking to it, childish spirits, unfaithful, ingenuous and satirical, 'the loveless Irishmen' as they are called. But in the anticipation of such a resurgence, I confess that I do not see what good it does to fulminate against English tyranny while the tyranny of Rome still holds the dwelling place of the soul. Neither do I see the use in bitter invectives against England, the despoiler, or in contempt for the vast Anglo-Saxon civilization—even if it is almost entirely a materialist civilization. It is vain to boast that Irish works such as *The Book of Kells, The Yellow Book of Leccan [sic], The Book of the Dun Cow,* which date back to a time when England was still an uncivilized country, are as old as the Chinese in the art of miniaturization; or that Ireland used to make and export textiles to Europe generations before the first Fleming arrived in London to teach the English how to make cloth. If it were valid to appeal to the past in this fashion, the fellahins of Cairo would have every right in the world proudly to refuse to act as porters for English tourists. Just as ancient Egypt is dead, so is ancient Ireland. Its dirge has been sung and the seal set upon its gravestone. The ancient national spirit that spoke throughout the centuries through the mouths of fabulous seers, wandering minstrels, and Jacobin poets has vanished from the world with the death of James Clarence Mangan. With his death the long tradition of the triple order of the ancient bards also died.[82] Today other bards, inspired by other ideals, have their turn.

One thing alone seems clear to me. It is high time Ireland finished once and for all with failures. If it is truly capable of resurgence, then let it do so or else let it cover its head and decently descend into the grave forever. 'We Irish,' Oscar Wilde said one day to a friend of mine,[83] 'have done nothing, but we're the greatest talkers since the days of the ancient Greeks.' But, though the Irish are eloquent, a revolution is not made from human breath, and Ireland has already had enough of compromises, misunderstandings and misapprehensions. If it wants finally to put on the show for which we have waited so long, this time, let it be complete, full and definitive. But telling these Irish actors to hurry up, as our fathers before us told them not so long ago, is useless. I, for one, am certain not to see the curtain rise, as I shall have already taken the last tram home.

JAMES CLARENCE MANGAN (1907)

There are certain poets who, in addition to their virtue of revealing aspects of the human consciousness to us that were unknown until their age, also possess the more questionable virtue of embodying in themselves the thousand conflicting tendencies of their age, of turning themselves into, so to speak, storage batteries of a new energy.[1] For the most part, it is by this latter aspect rather than the former that they become esteemed by the masses which, as they are by nature incapable of evaluating any work of straightforward self-revelation, hasten to pay homage by some act of munificence to the invaluable support which a poet's individual affirmation lends to a popular movement. In such cases the preferred act of munificence is the statue, because it honours the dead while flattering the living, and has the further supreme advantage of finality, since, to tell the truth, it is the most efficient and courteous way yet discovered of ensuring a lasting oblivion of the deceased. In serious, rational countries, it is usual to have the statue completed in a decent form, and for the sculptor, civic officials, orators and a large crowd of the public to come to its unveiling. But in Ireland, a country destined by God to be the eternal caricature of the serious world, the statue, even when it represents a highly popular man whose character was most amenable to the will of the common people, very rarely advances beyond the laying of the foundation stone. Given this, perhaps I might manage to give some idea of the profound obscurity that envelops the name of James Clarence Mangan when I say that, in despite of the famous generosity of the Emerald Isle, it has so far not entered into the head of any its fiery spirits to placate the unquiet shade of the national poet with the usual stone and wreaths.[2] Perhaps the undisturbed peace in which he lies has become so welcome to him that he will take umbrage (if mortal sounds should penetrate to that world beyond the grave) at hearing his spectral quietude disturbed by an exiled fellow-countryman delivering an unskilled lecture on him in a strange tongue before a group of well-disposed foreigners.

The contribution of Ireland to European literature may be divided into five periods, and two large categories: in other words, literature written in the Irish language, and literature written in the

English language. The first category encompasses the first two periods. The earlier period, remote and almost lost in the obscurity of time, was that in which all the sacred and epic ancient books, legal codes, topographical histories and legends were written. The more recent period lasted long after the Anglo–Saxon Norman invasion under Henry II and King John. It was a period of the wandering minstrels, the symbolic songs continued by the triple order of ancient Celtic bards about which I had occasion to speak to you a few nights ago.[3] The second category, that of Irish literature written in the English language, can be divided into three periods. The first period, the eighteenth century, includes, among numerous other Irishmen, the glorious names of Oliver Goldsmith, author of the renowned novel *The Vicar of Wakefield*; the two famous comic play-wrights, Richard Brinsley Sheridan and William Congreve, whose masterpieces are admired even today on the sterile stage of modern England; the Rabelaisian Dean Jonathan Swift, author of *Gulliver's Travels*; the so-called English Demosthenes, Edmund Burke, considered even by English critics as the most profound orator ever to speak in the Chamber of Deputies, and one of the most learned men of state even among the crafty ranks of the politicians of blonde Albion. The second and third periods belong to the last century: one was the Young Ireland literary movement of 1842 and 1845; the other is the literary movement of the present day about which I propose to speak to you in a later lecture.[4]

The literary movement of 1842, the date of the foundation of the separatist journal, *The Nation*, founded by the three leaders, Thomas Davis, John Blake Dillon (father of the ex-leader of the Irish Parliamentary Party)

[*One page of the manuscript is missing.*]

of the middle class: and, following a childhood spent in the midst of domestic cruelty, misfortunes and anguish, he became a clerk in a third-rate notary's office. He had always been a gloomy and indolent child, given to the furtive study of various languages, misanthropic, silent, preoccupied with religious questions, without friends or acquaintances. When he began to write, he immediately attracted the attention of the enlightened, who recognized in him a winged lyric music and fervid idealism that manifested themselves in his extraordinary rhythms and unstudied beauty, perhaps unencountered elsewhere in English literature, if we except the inspired songs of Shelley. Thanks to the influence of some literary people, he obtained a position as assistant librarian in the huge library of Trinity College Dublin, an invaluable treasure trove of volumes that is three times the size of the Victor Emanuel Library in Rome,[5] and which houses ancient Irish books, such as *The Book of the Dun Cow*, *The Yellow Book of Leccan* [*sic*], the famous legal essay by the learned King Cormac the magnificent, known as the Irish Solomon,[6] and *The Book of Kells*. These books date back to the first centuries of Christianity and are known to be as old as the Chinese in the art of miniature. It was there that Mitchell [*sic*], Mangan's biographer and friend, first saw him. In his preface to the poet's works, he describes the impression made upon him by this skinny little man with a waxen face and colourless hair, sitting cross-legged on the top of a step-ladder intent on deciphering a huge dusty tome in the dusky light.[7] Mangan passed his days studying in this library, becoming a reasonably accomplished linguist. He was well familiar with the Italian, Spanish, French and German languages and literatures, besides those of Ireland and England, and, it would seem, had some knowledge of oriental languages, probably Sanskrit and Arabic. From time to time he would leave this studious peace to contribute some song to the revolutionary journal, but he took little interest in the regular meetings of the party. He passed his nights alone. His dwelling was a small, dark room in the old city, in the quarter of Dublin that still today preserves the significant name of the 'Liberties'. His nights amounted to a way of the cross among the various notorious public houses of the 'Liberties' where he must have appeared a very strange figure in the midst of the prize blooms of the city's underclass, petty thieves, bandits, wanted criminals, pimps and harlots[8] of mild pretensions. Strange to say (though it is the agreed opinion among his compatriots who are always ready to look into such matters,[9] Mangan had nothing but purely formal dealings with this underworld. He drank little, though drinking produced an extraordinary effect on him, so enfeebled was his health. Moreover, the death-mask we have of him shows a refined and almost patrician face in whose delicate lines it is impossible to discover anything other than melancholy and great weariness. I understand that pathologists deny the possibility of combining the delights of alcohol and opium, and it seems that Mangan was soon convinced of this fact, for he dedicated himself unremittingly to filling himself with narcotics. Mitchell tells us how Mangan looked like a living skeleton towards the end of his life. His face was fleshless, barely covered by a translucent skin, like fine porcelain, his body wasted. His eyes, behind which shone rare glimmers which seemed to hide the horrendous, voluptuous memories of his visions, were dreaming, large and staring; his voice was drawling, faint, and sepulchral. He descended the last steps towards the grave with frightening speed. He had become a mute wasted rag of a man, he ate barely enough to keep body and soul together until, one day, he had a sudden bad fall. When he was brought to hospital, they found a few pennies and a dog-eared volume of German poetry in his pocket. When he died, his miserable corpse sent a shudder through the hospital staff and he was given a squalid burial which was paid for by some charitable friends. So lived and died the man whom I consider the most distinguished poet of the modern Celtic world and one of the most inspired poets of any country ever to make use of the lyric form. It is, I believe, too early to affirm that he will have to live for eternity in the colourless fields of oblivion, but I am quite certain that if he is to gain the posthumous glory which is his due, it will not be through the work of one of his fellow countrymen. Mangan will be accepted by the Irish as their national poet the day the conflict between Ireland and the foreign Powers, the Anglo-Saxon and the Roman Catholic, reaches a settlement that will give rise to a new civilization, either indigenous or purely foreign. Until that time, either he will be forgotten or just barely remembered on holidays, like[10] many other poets and heroes, all the more so because, like Parnell, he sinned against that incorruptible chastity that Ireland would demand of any John who would baptize her or of any Joan who would liberate her, as being the first essential and divine test of their worthiness for such lofty offices.[11]

The question that Wagner placed in the mouth of the simpleton Parsifal is occasionally recalled to mind when one reads certain English criticisms due, for the most part, to the influence of the blind and bitter spirit of Calvinism. It is easy to find an explanation for these criticisms when we are dealing with a powerful, innovative genius, because the appearance of one such genius is always the signal for all corrupt and vested interests to rally behind the defence

of the old order. For instance, anyone who understands the destructive and proudly self-centred tendencies of all Henrik Ibsen's works
will not be astonished to hear the most influential critics in London,
the morning after an Ibsen first night, railing against the playwright,
calling him (I quote the precise words of the now deceased *Daily
Telegraph* critic) 'a dirty dog sticking his snout in the mire'.[12] But the
case is less explicable when the poor condemned man is some poet,
more or less innocuous, whose only fault has been not to have
adhered scrupulously to the cult of respectability. And so, when
Mangan is remembered in his country (for he is sometimes spoken
of in literary societies), the Irish lament that such a poetic faculty
was mated with so little rectitude of conduct, and are naïvely surprised to find this faculty in a man whose vices were exotic and who
was little of a patriot. Those who have written of him have been
scrupulous in holding the balance between the drunkard and the
opium-eater, and have sought to discover whether learning or imposture lies behind such phrases as 'from the Ottoman' or 'from the
Coptic'. And, save for this small remembrance, Mangan has been a
stranger in his country, a rare and bizarre figure in the streets, where
he is seen dejectedly going forward like one who does penance for
some ancient sin. Surely life, which Novalis has called a malady of
the spirit, is a heavy penance for Mangan, one who has, perhaps,
forgotten the sin that laid it upon him, an inheritance all the more
sorrowful because of that fine artist in him which reads so truly the
lines of brutality and of weakness in the faces of men who look upon
him with contempt and hatred. In the short biographical hints that
he has left us, he speaks only of his young life, his infancy and
boyhood, and he tells us how as a boy he knew only squalid misery
and coarseness, that his acquaintances bore down upon him with
their venomous hatred, and that his father was a human rattlesnake.[13] In these violent assertions we can recognize the effect of the
oriental drug, but notwithstanding this, those who believe that it is
merely the figment of a disordered brain have never known, or have
forgotten, how keenly a sensitive boy suffers from contact with a
gross nature. His sufferings forced him into becoming a hermit, and,
indeed, for the greater part of his life he lived in a virtual dream in
that sanctuary of the soul where, for many ages, the sad and the wise
have elected to be. When a friend pointed out to him that the account
quoted above was wildly overstated, and partly false, he answered—

'Maybe I dreamed it.' The world had evidently become for him an unreal thing of little worth.

How will it be with those dreams which, for every young and simple heart, take such dear reality upon themselves? One whose nature is so sensitive cannot forget his dreams in a secure, strenuous life. He doubts them, and puts them from him for a time, but when he hears men denying them with an oath he would acknowledge them proudly, and where sensitiveness has induced weakness, or, in Mangan's case, refined upon natural weakness, would even compromise with the world, and win from it in return at least the favour of silence, if no more, as for something too light to bear a violent disdain, for that desire of the heart so cynically mocked, that rudely maltreated idea. His manner is such that none can say if it be pride or humility that looks out of that vague face, which seems to live only because of those light shining eyes and of the fair silken hair, of which he is a little vain. This reserve is not without its dangers, and in the end it is only his excesses that save him from indifference. Something has been mentioned of an affair of the heart between Mangan and a pupil of his, to whom he gave lessons in German, and later, it seems, he was an actor afterwards in a love-comedy of three, but if he is reserved with men, he is shy with women, and he is too self-conscious, too critical, knows too little of the soft parts of conversation for a gallant. In his strange dress—the high, conical hat, the loose trousers many sizes too big for his little legs, and the old umbrella, so like a bagpipes—one may see an almost comic expression of his diffidence. The learning of many lands goes with him always, eastern tales and the memory of curiously printed medieval books which have rapt him out of his time—gathered together day by day and embroidered as in a web. He has acquaintance with a score of languages, of which, upon occasion, he makes a liberal parade, and has read in many literatures, crossing how many seas, and even penetrating into Peristan, which is not to be found in any atlas. He is interested, too, in the life of the priestess of Prevorst, and in all phenomena of the middle nature, and here, where most of all the sweetness and resoluteness of the soul have power, he seems to seek in a fictional world, how different from that in which Watteau (in the felicitous words of Pater) may have sought, both with a certain typical inconstancy, 'what is there in no satisfying measure or not at all'

His writings, which have never been collected in a definitive edition, show no order whatsoever and often very little thought. His prose essays may perhaps be interesting on the first reading, but, in truth, they are but insipid efforts. Their style is conceited, in the worst sense of the word, contorted and banal, their argument crude and inflated, and, finally, their prose belongs to the style in which trivial items of news in a provincial newspaper are published. It must be remembered, however, that Mangan wrote with no native literary tradition, for a public which cared for the matters of the day, and believed that the poet's only task was to illustrate these facts. He could not, unless in exceptional cases, correct his work, but apart from the so-called humorous jokes and his occasional unlimited verses, the better part of what he has written makes its appeal surely, because it was conceived by the imagination which he called, I think, the mother of things, whose dream are we, who imageth us to herself, and to ourselves, and imageth herself in us—the power before whose breath the mind in creation is (to use Shelley's image) as a fading coal. Though even in the best of Mangan the presence of alien emotions is often felt, the presence of an imaginative personality reflecting the light of imaginative beauty is more vividly felt. East and West meet in that personality (we know how); images interweave there like soft, luminous scarfs and words ring like brilliant mail, and whether the song is of Ireland or of Istambol, it has the same refrain, a prayer that peace may come again to her who has lost her peace, the moonwhite pearl of his soul, Ameen.

This figure which he adores recalls the spiritual ambitions and the imaginary loves of the Middle Ages. Mangan has placed his lady in a world filled with melodies, lights, and perfumes, the world that inevitably develops around and lends context to every face which a poet's eyes have looked upon with love. It is a single chivalrous idea, a single masculine devotion that casts light upon the faces of Vittoria Colonna, Laura, and Beatrice, just as the bitter disillusion and self-contempt that close the chapter are one and the same. And yet, the world in which Mangan would have his lady dwell is different from that marble temple raised up by Buonarotti [*sic*], or the peaceful oriflamme of the Florentine theologian.[14] It is a savage world, a world of eastern nights. The mental activity brought about by the opium has strewn this world with marvellous and horrible images: the whole orient, re-created by the poet in his fevered dreams (which are the paradise of the opium-eater) pulsates through these pages in phrases and similes against apocalyptic landscapes. He speaks of the moon fainting in the midst of hordes of stars, of the magic book of the sky burning red with fiery symbols, of the sea that foams over saffron sands, of the lonely cedar on the Balkan peaks, of the barbaric hall shining with moons of gold luxuriously permeated by the breath of roses from the king's gulistan. The most celebrated verses by Mangan, those in which, under a veil of mysticism, he sings of the fallen glory of his country, resemble a mist covering the horizon on a summer's day: fine, impalpable, about to melt away, but suffused with small points of light. Sometimes the music seems to awake from its languor and cry out in the ecstasy of battle. In the final stanza of the lament for the princes of Tir-Owen and Tirconnell, in lengthy lines of tremendous power, Mangan has put all the desperate energy of his race.

> And though frost glaze to-night the clear dew of his eyes,
> And white ice-gauntlets glove his noble fair fine fingers o'er,
> A warm dress is to him that lightning-garb he ever wore,
> The lightning of the soul, not skies.
>
> Hugh marched forth to the fight—I grieved to see him so depart;
> And lo! to-night he wanders frozen, rain-drenched, sad, betrayed—
> *But the memory of the lime-white mansions his right hand hath laid*
> *In ashes warms the hero's heart.*[15]

I know of no other piece of English literature where the spirit of revenge has attained such heights of melody. It is true that the heroic note occasionally becomes hoarse and a troop of unmannerly passions echoes it derisively; but a poet such as Mangan, who subsumes into himself the spirit of an age and country, aims to create not for some dilettante's entertainment, but to convey, in rough blows, the animating idea of his life to his followers. It cannot be denied, however, that Mangan always kept his poet's soul free from any blemish. Although he wrote such admirable English, he refused to work for English magazines or journals; although he was the spiritual focus of his age, lie refused to prostitute himself to the rabble or become a mouthpiece for politicians. He was one of those strange aberrant spirits who believe that the artistic life should be nothing other than the continuous and true revelation of the spiritual life; who believe that the inner life is of such worth as not to depend on any popular support, and so abstain from offering confessions of faith; one who believes, finally, that the poet is sufficient unto himself, inheritor and preserver of a secular heritage, and has therefore, no need to be strident, preachifying, or cloyingly sweet.

So what is this central idea that Mangan wished to communicate to posterity?

All his poetry remembers wrongs and suffering and the aspiration of one who is moved to great cries and gestures when he sees again in his thoughts the hour of his sorrow. This is the theme of much of Irish poetry, but no other Irish song is as full as those of Mangan of nobly suffered misfortunes and such irreparable devastations of the soul. Naomi would change her name to Mara, because she knew too well how bitter is the existence of mortals, and is it not the deep sense of sorrow and bitterness which explains in Mangan these names and titles and this fury of translation in which he has sought to lose himself? For has he not found in himself the faith of the solitary, or the faith which, in the Middle Ages, sent the spires singing up to heaven, like triumphal chants: but he awaits his hour, the hour which will put an end to his sad days of penance. Weaker than Leopardi, for he has not the courage of his own despair but forgets all ills and forgoes his scorn at the showing of some favour, he has, perhaps for this reason, the memorial he would have had, a

[*One page of the manuscript is missing.*]

in a certain sense, against actuality. It speaks of what seems fantastic and unreal to those who have lost the simple intuitions which are the tests of reality. Poetry takes little account of many of the idols of the market-place, the succession of the ages, the spirit of the age, the mission of race. The essential effort of the poet is to liberate himself from the unpropitious influences of such idols which corrupt him from the inside and out, and it would certainly be untrue to assert that Mangan made this effort. The history of his country encloses him so straitly that even in his moments of high passion he can but barely breach its walls. He, too, cries out, in his life and in his mournful verses, against the injustices of despoilers, but never laments a deeper loss than the loss of plaids and ornaments. He inherits the latest and worst part of a tradition upon which no divine hand has drawn out the line of demarcation, a tradition which dissolves and divides against itself as it moves down the cycles. And because this tradition has become an obsession for him, he has accepted it with all its failures and regrets which he would bequeath just as it is: the poet who hurls his anger against tyrants would establish upon the future an intimate and far more cruel tyranny. In the final view the figure which he worships is seen to be an abject queen upon whom, because of the bloody crimes that she has done and of those as bloody that were done to her at the hands of others, madness is come and death is coming, but who will not believe that she is near to die and remembers only the rumours of voices challenging her sacred gardens and her fair flowers that have become *pabulum aprorum*, the food of boars. Love of sorrow, desperation, high-sounding threats, these are the great traditions of James Clarence Mangan's race; and, in that miserable, reedy, and feeble figure, a hysteric nationalism receives its final justification.

In which niche in the temple of glory should we place his figure? If he did not even manage to win the sympathy of his fellow-countrymen, how can he win it from foreigners? Does it not seem that perhaps the oblivion that he would almost have desired now awaits him? Certainly, he did not find the strength in himself to reveal to us the triumphant beauty and splendour of truth that the ancients deified. He is a romantic, a would-be herald, a prototype for a would-be nation; but, for all that, one who expressed the sacred indignation of his soul in a dignified form cannot have written his name in water. In those huge and varied currents of life that surround us, and in that great memory which is greater and more generous than our own, there is probably no life, no moment of exaltation that is ever lost; and all those who have written in noble disdain have not written in vain even if, tired

[*The concluding page(s) of the manuscript is missing.*]

[THE IRISH LITERARY RENAISSANCE]

physical, either open or masked. Since the great rebellion in the last years of the eighteenth century,[1] we find no less than three decisive clashes between the two nationalist tendencies. The first was in 1848 when the Young Ireland Party disdainfully detached itself from O'Connell's ranks.[2] The second came in 1867, when Fenianism reached its apogee, and the 'Republic' was proclaimed in Dublin. The third belongs to the present day, as the youth of Ireland, disillusioned by the ineffectiveness of parliamentary tactics after the moral assassination of Parnell, aligns itself increasingly with a nationalism that is broader and, at the same time, more severe; a nationalism that involves a daily economic battle, a moral and material boycott, the creation and development of independent industries, the propagation of the Irish language, a ban on English culture and a revival in another guise of the ancient civilization of the Celt. Each of these uncompromising political movements has been accompanied by a literary one: sometimes it is the oratory that prevails, sometimes

FENIANISM: THE LAST FENIAN

The death of John O'Leary, which took place in Dublin recently, on St Patrick's Day,[1] the Irish national holiday, perhaps marked the disappearance of the last actor in the turbulent drama that was Fenianism. A traditional name, from the ancient Irish, the word 'Fenian' means the king's bodyguard, and the Irish rebel movement takes its name from this.

Whoever studies the history of the Irish revolution during the nineteenth century will find himself confronted by a dual struggle: the struggle, that is, of the Irish nation against the English government, and the struggle, perhaps no less fierce, between the moderate nationalists and the so-called physical force party. This party, under its various names: the 'Whiteboys', the 'Men of '98', the 'United Irishmen', the 'Invincibles', and the 'Fenians', has always refused to have any dealings with either the English parties or the Nationalist parliamentarians.[2] They say (and history fully supports them in making such a claim) that any concession by England to Ireland has been granted unwillingly, at bayonet-point, as the saying goes. The intransigent press never fails to greet the efforts of the Nationalist deputies in Westminster with sarcastic and virulent articles. And, while recognizing that, owing to the enormous might of England, armed revolt has become an impossible dream, the press has never ceased to instil the dogma of separatism into the minds of the new generation.

Unlike the ridiculous rebellion of Robert Eminet [*sic*][3] or the fervent Young Ireland movement of 1845, the Fenianism of '67 was not one of those usual outbursts of Celtic temperament that burn brightly for a moment in the darkness, leaving a deeper darkness than before in their wake. When Fenianism first arose, the population of the Emerald Isle was over eight million,[4] while the population of England did not exceed seventeen million. Under the command of James Stephens, the country was organized into cells of twenty-five men each, a plan of campaign eminently suited to the Irish character since it minimized the possibility of betrayal.[5] These cells formed a vast intricate network whose strands were brought together in Stephens' hands. At the same time, the American Fenians were organized in similar fashion, and the two movements worked in unison. Many soldiers from the English army, policemen, guards and warders were in the Fenian ranks.

Everything seemed to be going well, and the Republic was about to be established (in fact, it had been openly proclaimed by Stephens), when O'Leary and Luby, the editors of the party news-paper,[6] were arrested. The government placed a ransom on Stephens and announced that it knew all the places where the Fenians prac-tised their night-time military manoeuvres. Stephens was captured and imprisoned, but managed to escape thanks to the loyalty of a Fenian warder. While the agents and spies were lying in wait at every port in the island watching outgoing ships, he left the capital in a gig, disguised (according to legend) as a bridesmaid with a white crepe veil and orange-blossom. He was then conducted on board a small charcoal boat which hastily set sail for France.[7] O'Leary was tried and condemned to twenty years' hard labour, but was later pardoned and exiled from Ireland for fifteen years.

Why this collapse of such a well-organized movement? Simply because in Ireland, just at the crucial moment, an informer appears.[8] Following the disbanding of the Fenians, the traditional doctrine of physical force sporadically reappears in violent acts. The 'Invin-cibles' blew up Clerkenwell prison,[9] snatched their comrades out of the hands of the police in Manchester and killed the escort,[10] and stabbed the English Chief Secretary and Under Secretary, Lord Frederick Covendish [*sic*] and Burke, in broad daylight in Phoenix Park in Dublin.[11]

After each of these crimes, when the general outrage had died down a bit, an English minister would table some motion for reform in Ireland before the Commons, and the Fenians and the parlia-mentarians would strenuously vilify one other, the former attribut-ing the measure to the success of their parliamentary tactics, the latter attributing it to the hidden persuasiveness of the dagger or the bomb. Meanwhile, as a backdrop to this sad comedy, the spectacle unfolded of a population decreasing with mathematical regularity year by year, in an uninterrupted flow to the United States or Europe of Irish people who had found the economic and intellectual condi-tions of their country intolerable.[12] Almost as if to accentuate this depopulation, a long train of churches, cathedrals, convents, colleges and seminaries came into being to help those who had not been able to find the courage or the money to undertake the voyage from Queenstown to New York.

Tormented by numerous obligations, Ireland succeeded in doing what had until then been considered an impossible feat: serving both God and Mammon. The country allowed itself to be exploited by England, while, at the same time, adding to St Peter's pence, perhaps in recognition of Adrian IV who, in a moment of generosity, made a present of the island to Henry II around eight hundred years ago. It is impossible now that an extremist and bloody doctrine such as Fenianism can continue to survive in such an environment. In fact, as violent agrarian crimes are committed less and less frequently, Fenianism has once again changed its name and form. The new Fenians have regrouped in a party called 'ourselves alone'.[13] They aim to make Ireland a bilingual republic, and, to this end, they have established a direct ferry link between Ireland and France. They boycott English goods, they refuse to become soldiers or swear an oath of allegiance to the British crown.[14] They are attempting to develop the industry of the whole country and, rather than fork out one and a quarter millions each year to maintain the eighty deputies in the English parliament, they want to institute a consular service in the principal world ports with the aim of merchandising industrial produce, without the intervention of England. From many points of view, this latest form of Fenianism may be the most formidable.[15] Its influence has certainly once again remoulded the character of the Irish. When its old leader, O'Leary, returned to Ireland after years of studious exile in Paris, he found himself in the midst of a generation inspired by ideals that were quite different from those of '65. He was welcomed by his countrymen with accolades and would appear in public from time to time to preside over some separatist meeting or banquet. But he was a figure from a vanished world. He could often be seen walking along the river, a venerable old man dressed mostly in light clothes, with a flowing head of pure white hair, almost bent double with age and suffering; he would halt before the darkened shops of the antiquarian book sellers and then, having made his purchase, he would return along the river. He had little reason to be happy: his plans had gone up in smoke, his friends were dead, and very few people in his country knew who he was or what he had done. Now that he is dead, his compatriots escort him to his tomb with a great show of pomp, because the Irish, even when they break the hearts of those who sacrifice their lives for their country, never fail to show a great reverence for the dead.[16]

HOME RULE COMES OF AGE

Twenty-one years ago, on the evening of 9 April 1886,[1] the laneway leading to the offices of the nationalist newspaper of Dublin was crammed with people. From time to time a bulletin printed in block letters appeared on the wall and in this way the crowd was able to share in the drama that was unfolding in Westminster, whose public galleries had been packed with people since dawn.[2] The Prime Minister's speech had begun at four o'clock and went on until eight. A few minutes later the last bulletin appeared on the wall: 'Gladstone wound up with a magnificent oration declaring that the English Liberal Party would refuse to legislate for England until she granted Ireland a measure of autonomy.' At this news the crowd in the street burst into cheers of enthusiasm. From every side 'Long live Gladstone', 'Long live Ireland' could be heard; strangers shook hands with one another to ratify the new national deal, and the old people were actually weeping with joy.

Seven years pass by and we are at the second Home Rule Bill. Gladstone, having in the interim effected the moral assassination of Parnell with the help of the Irish bishops, is reading his measure before the House for the third time. His speech is shorter than before, lasting just an hour and a half. Then the Home Rule Bill is passed. The happy news runs over the wires to the Irish capital, where it provokes a new burst of enthusiasm. In the salon of the Catholic Club, people talk it over, argue, laugh, toast, and prophesize.

Another fourteen years pass by and we are in 1907. Twenty-one years have passed since 1886 and so, according to the English custom, Gladstone's measure has come of age.[3] But in the interval, Gladstone himself has died and his measure has not even been born. As he had clearly foreseen after the third reading of the bill, the alarm bells were sounded in the upper House, and all the Lords temporal and spiritual marshalled themselves in ranks to deliver the bill its deathblow. The English Liberals have forgotten their commitments. A fourth-rate politician who between 1881 and 1886 voted in favour of every coercive measure against Ireland now wears Gladstone's mantle.[4] The post of Irish Chief Secretary, a post which the

English themselves have called the tomb of political reputations, is held by a literary jurist who, when he stood before the electors of Bristol two years ago, would probably have been hard-put to name the counties of Ireland.[5] Despite the undertakings and promises, despite its enormous majority which is unprecedented in the parliamentary history of England, the English Liberal cabinet is introducing a devolutionary measure that does not go beyond the proposals made in 1885 by the imperialist Chamberlain, and the seriousness of which the Conservative English press openly refuses to acknowledge.[6] This proposal was passed on its first reading by a majority of almost 300 votes and while the yellow press breaks out in fits of feigned rage the Lords consult among themselves to decide whether this tottering marionette about to enter the lists really merits their sword.

The Lords will probably kill the measure, as this is their job, but, if they are wise, they will hesitate before they alienate Irish sympathies for constitutional agitation, especially now that India and Egypt are in turmoil and the overseas colonies are demanding an imperial federation. From their own point of view, it would be inadvisable to let a stubborn veto provoke a reaction from a people which, poor in everything else, is rich solely in political ideas, has perfected the tactics of obstructionism and has made the word 'Boycott' an international battle-cry.[7]

Anyhow, England has little to lose. The measure (which is not a twentieth of the Home Rule proposal) gives the executive council in Dublin no legislative power, no power to fix or control taxes, no control over thirty-nine of the forty-seven government offices, including those of the constabulary and the police, the supreme court or the agrarian commission. Furthermore, Unionist interests are jealously guarded. The Liberal minister has taken care to put at the forefront of the discussion the fact that, as the price of the measure, the English electorate will have to fork out over half a million pounds a year. Conservative articles and speakers, divining the intentions of their compatriot, have made good use of this assertion by appealing in their hostile commentaries to the most vulnerable part of the English electorate: its pocket. But neither the Liberal ministers nor the opposition newspapers will explain to the English that this expense is not an outlay of English money, but rather a partial repayment of England's debt to Ireland. Neither of them will cite the findings of the English Royal Commission that, compared to its dominant partner, Ireland is overtaxed by 88 million francs.[8] Nor will they recall the fact that the politicians and scientists who investigated the vast central bog of Ireland concluded that the two spectres that sit beside every Irish fireplace, consumption and insanity, are a refutation of all English claims, and that the moral debt of the English government for not having seen to the reforestation of this disease-ridden swamp for over an entire century amounts to over 500 million francs.

Now, even from a cursory study of the history of Home Rule, it seems that we may draw two conclusions. The first is this: the most powerful weapons that England may use against Ireland are no longer those of Conservatism, but of Liberalism and the Vatican. Conservatism, for all that it may be tyrannical, is a frank and openly hostile doctrine. Its position is logical. It does not want a rival island to grow up beside Great Britain, or Irish factories to compete with English ones, or tobacco and wine to be once again exported from Ireland, or the Irish ports to become an enemy naval base, whether under a foreign protectorate or a native government. This position is logical, just as the Irish separatists' position, which contradicts it point by point, is also logical. It takes little intelligence to see that Gladstone inflicted greater damage on Ireland than Disraeli did,[9] and that the fiercest enemy of the Catholic Irish is the leader of English Vaticanism, the Duke of Norfolk.[10]

The second conclusion is even more obvious. It is this: the Irish Parliamentary Party is bankrupt.[11] For twenty-seven years it has been agitating and talking. In that time it has drawn 35 million from its supporters, and the fruits of its agitation are that Irish taxes have increased by 88 million, while the Irish population has decreased by 1 million.[12] The deputies themselves have improved their lot, apart from such small discomforts as a few months in prison or a few lengthy sittings. From being peasants' sons, street traders and clientless lawyers, they have become salaried administrators, factory and company bosses, newspaper owners and large land holders. Only in 1891 did they give proof of their altruism when they sold Parnell, their master, to the pharisaical conscience of the English nonconformists, without exacting the thirty pieces of silver.[13]

IRELAND AT THE BAR

Several years ago a sensational trial took place in Ireland. In the western province, in a remote place called Maamtrasna, a murder was committed.[1] Four or five peasants from the village were arrested, all of them members of the ancient tribe of the Joyces. The eldest of them, a certain Myles Joyce, sixty years of age, was particularly suspected by the police. Public opinion considered him innocent then, and he is now thought of as a martyr. Both the old man and the other accused did not know English. The court had to resort to the services of an interpreter.[2] The interrogation that took place through this man was at times comic and at times tragic. On the one hand there was the officious interpreter, on the other, the patriarch of the miserable tribe who, unused to civic customs, seemed quite bewildered by all the legal ceremonies.

The magistrate said:

'Ask the accused if he saw the woman on the morning in question.'

The question was repeated to him in Irish and the old man broke out into intricate explanations, gesticulating, appealing to the other accused, to heaven. Then, exhausted by the effort, he fell silent; the interpreter, turning to the magistrate, said:

'He says no, your worship.'

'Ask him if he was in the vicinity at the time.'

The old man began speaking once again, protesting, shouting, almost beside himself with the distress of not understanding or making himself understood, weeping with rage and terror. And the interpreter, once again replied drily:

'He says no, your worship.'

When the interrogation was over the poor old man was found guilty and sent before a high court which sentenced him to be hanged. On the day the sentence was to be carried out, the square in front of the prison was packed with people who were kneeling and calling out prayers in Irish for the repose of the soul of Myles Joyce. Legend has it that even the hangman could not make himself understood by the victim and angrily kicked the unhappy man in the head to force him into the noose.[3]

The figure of this bewildered old man, left over from a culture which is not ours, a deaf-mute before his judge, is a symbol of the Irish nation at the bar of public opinion. Like him, Ireland cannot appeal to the modern conscience of England or abroad. The English newspapers act as interpreters between Ireland and the English electorate which, though it lends an ear every so often is finally irritated by the eternal complaints of the Nationalist deputies who, it believes, have come to their House with the aim of upsetting the order and extorting money. Abroad, Ireland is not spoken of except when some trouble breaks out there such as that which has set the telegraph lines jumping in the last few days.[4] The public skims through the dispatches received from London, which, while they may be lacking in acrimony, have some of the laconic aspect of the interpreter mentioned above. So the Irish figure as criminals, with deformed faces, who roam around at night with the aim of doing away with every Unionist. And to the real sovereign of Ireland, the Pope, this news arrives like so many dogs in church; the cries, weakened by so long a journey, have almost died out by the time they reach the bronze door. The envoys of a people that has never renounced the Holy See in the past, the only Catholic people for which the faith also means the practice of that faith, are rejected in favour of the envoys of a monarch, who, descendant of apostates, solemnly apostatized on his coronation day by declaring that the rites of the Roman Catholic Church are 'superstitions and idolatry'.

There arc twenty million Irish scattered throughout the world. The Emerald Isle contains only a small part of them. Considering how England sees the Irish question as pivotal to her own internal politics and yet proceeds with excellent judgement disposing of the most complicated questions of colonial politics, an observer can only wonder whether St George's Channel does not open a greater abyss than the ocean between Ireland and her arrogant mistress. Indeed, the Irish question is still unresolved today, after six centuries of armed occupation and over a hundred years of legislation that reduced the population of the unhappy island from eight to four million, quadrupled the taxes, and further entangled the agrarian problem with many extra knots.

Truly, there is no question more entangled than this. The Irish themselves understand little of it, the English even less, and for other peoples it is complete darkness. But the Irish do know that it is the cause of all their suffering, and this is why they employ extremely violent methods to resolve it. For example, twenty years ago, seeing themselves reduced to poverty by the oppression of the large land owners, they refused to pay their rents and gained provisions and reforms from Gladstone.[5] Today, seeing the pastures full of well-fed cattle while an eighth of the population is registered as being without the means of subsistence, they drive the cattle from the holdings. In anger, the Liberal government then devises to reinstate the coercive tactics of the Conservatives, and the London press dedicates weeks and innumerable articles to the agrarian crisis which, it says, is very serious, and publishes alarming items on the agrarian revolt that are then reprinted by foreign newspapers.

I do not propose to make an exegesis of the Irish agrarian question, nor to recount the background of the two-faced politics of the government, but I think it is useful to rectify matters a little. Whoever has read the telegrams sent out by London will certainly believe that Ireland is going through a stage of exceptional criminality. This is a complete misjudgement. Criminality in Ireland is lower than in any other country in Europe; organized crime does not exist in Ireland. When one of those deeds which the Parisian journalists, with atrocious irony, call 'a red idyll' occurs, the whole country is shocked. There were, it is true, two violent deaths in Ireland in the past months; but both were at the hands of English troops and occurred in Belfast, where the soldiers charged an unarmed crowd without, it seems, having given any warning, and killed a man and a woman. There were attacks on livestock, but these did not even happen in Ireland, where the mob contented itself with opening the stalls and driving the livestock a few miles down the road, but in Great Wyrley[6] in England where barbaric, insane criminals have been rampaging against livestock for six years, to such an extent that English companies will no longer insure them.

Five years ago, in order to quieten public anger, an innocent man, now freed, was condemned. But even when he was in prison the attacks continued. Last week two horses were found dead with the usual cuts to the base of the stomach and their guts spilled out over the grass.

James Joyce

OSCAR WILDE: THE POET OF 'SALOMÉ'

Oscar Fingal O'Flahertie Wills Wilde. Such were the high-sounding titles that with juvenile vanity he wanted to have printed on the title-page of his first collection of poetry.[1] By this vain gesture which he believed would lend him dignity, he sculpted, perhaps symbolically, the marks of his empty pretences and of the fate that awaited him. His name symbolizes him: Oscar, nephew of King Fingal and only-born of Ossian in the amorphous Celtic odyssey, tragically killed by the hand of his host while sitting at table. O'Flahertie, a fierce Irish tribe whose destiny it was to besiege the gates of medieval towns; their name struck terror into peaceful men, and it is still intoned, at the end of the ancient litany of the saints, in the midst of plagues, the wrath of God or the spirit of fornication: 'from the fierce O'Flaherties, *libera nos Domine'*.[2] Like that Oscar, he too was to meet his civil death while sitting crowned with vine leaves at table and discussing Plato. Like that savage tribe he too was to break the lance of his paradoxical eloquence against the ranks of useful conventions and, exiled and dishonoured, to hear the chorus of righteous men recite his name along with that of the unclean spirit.

Wilde was born in the sleepy Irish capital fifty-five years ago. His father was a talented scientist, who has been called the father of modern otology. His mother took part in the revolutionary literary movement of '48, working for the national journal under the pseud-onym of *Speranza*, and, in her poems and articles, she would incite the people to take Dublin Castle. There are certain circumstances regarding the pregnancy of Lady Wilde and the infancy of her child which, in the opinion of some, partly explain the sad mania (if it can so be called)[3] that would later drag him to his ruin, and it is at least certain that the child grew up in an atmosphere of permissiveness and prodigality.

Oscar Wilde's public life began in the University of Oxford where, at the time of his matriculation, a ponderous professor called Ruskin was leading an effeminate band of Anglo-Saxons towards the promised land of the society of the future, behind a wheelbarrow.[4] The susceptible temperament of the mother was passed on to the son; and he resolved to put into practice, beginning with himself, a theory of beauty partly derived from the books of Pater and Ruskin, and partly original. Defying the jibes of the public, he proclaimed and practised the aesthetic reform of his dress and home. He gave a series of lectures in the United States and in the English provinces, and became the spokesman for the aesthetic movement, while the fantastic myth of the apostle of beauty went on forming itself around him. In the public mind his name evoked a vague idea of delicate finesse, a life bedecked with flowers. The cult of the sunflower, his favourite, flourished among the leisured classes; and the little people would hear tales of his famous white ivory cane burnished with turquoise and of his Neronian hairstyle.

The background to this dazzling picture was more miserable than the middle classes imagined. Medals, trophies of his academic youth, would now and again make the journey up to the pawnbroker's shop; and the young wife of the epigrammatist sometimes had to borrow the money for a pair of shoes from a neighbour. Wilde found himself obliged to accept the post of editor in a very trite journal;[5] only with the staging of his light comedies did he enter the short penultimate period of luxury and wealth in his life. *Lady Windermere's Fan* took London by storm. Wilde entered that literary tradition of Irish comic playwrights that stretches from the days of Sheridan and Goldsmith to Bernard Shaw, and became, like them, court jester to the English. He became an arbiter of elegance in the metropolis, and his annual income from his writings reached almost half a million francs. He scattered his gold among a succession of unworthy friends. Every morning he would buy two expensive flowers, one for himself, the other for his coachman. Even on the day of his notorious trial he had himself driven to the courthouse in his two-horsed coach with the coachman dressed up in formal wear and with the groom powdered.

His fall was greeted by a howl of puritanical joy. On hearing of his condemnation, the mob that was gathered in front of the courthouse began to dance a pavane in the muddy street. The newspaper journalists were admitted into the prison and, through the window of his cell, were able to feed on the spectacle of his shame. White bands covered over his name on theatre billboards; his friends abandoned him; his manuscripts were stolen while he underwent his prison sentence of two years' hard labour. His mother died under the shadow of shame; his wife died. He was declared bankrupt, his belongings were auctioned off and his sons were taken away from him. When he came out of prison, thugs under the instructions of the noble Marquess of Queensberry[6] were lying in wait for him. He was driven, like a hare hunted by dogs, from hotel to hotel. Hotelier after hotelier drove him from the door, refusing him bread and board, and at nightfall he finally ended up under his brother's window crying and blubbering like a child.

The epilogue moved rapidly towards its end, and it is not worthwhile following the unhappy man from the slums of Naples to the poor guesthouse in the Latin Quarter, where he died of meningitis in the last month of the last year of the nineteenth century.[7] It is not worthwhile shadowing him as the Parisian spies did. He died a Roman Catholic, adding a denial of his proud doctrine to the collapse of his public life.[8] He who had defied the idols of the marketplace and had been the singer of the divinity of joy bent his knee and was filled with compassion and sadness; he closed the chapter of the rebellion of his spirit with an act of spiritual devotion.

This is not the place to probe into the strange problem of the life of Oscar Wilde nor to determine to what extent heredity and the epileptic cast of his nervous system can exculpate him from that of which he was accused. Whether innocent or guilty of the charges brought against him, he was undoubtedly a scapegoat. His greatest crime was to have caused in England a scandal; it is well known that the English authorities did all they could to persuade him to flee before issuing an arrest warrant against him. In London alone, declared an official of the ministry of the interior during the trial, over twenty thousand people are under police surveillance, but they remain at large until such time as they cause a scandal. Wilde's letters to his friends were read out before the court and their author was denounced as a degenerate, obsessed by exotic perversions. 'Time wars against you; it is jealous of your lilies and roses'; 'I love to see you wandering through violet-filled valleys, with your honey-coloured hair gleaming.' But the truth is that Wilde, far from being a monster of perversion that inexplicably arose in the midst of the modern civilization of England, is the logical and inevitable product of the Anglo-Saxon college and university system, a system of seclusion and secrecy. His condemnation by the people stemmed from many complex causes; but it was not the simple reaction of a pure conscience. Anyone who patiently studies the graffiti, frank drawings and the expressive gestures of people will hesitate to think of them as being pure of heart. Anyone who follows closely the life and language of men, whether in a soldiers' barracks or in a large office of commerce, will hesitate to believe that all those who cast stones at Wilde were themselves without blemish. In fact, everyone feels reluctant in speaking with others on this subject, fearing that his listener might know more about it than himself. Oscar Wilde's self-defence in the *Scots Observer*[9] should be accepted as legitimate by any bench of impartial judges. Each man writes his own sin into *Dorian Gray* (Wilde's most celebrated novel). What Dorian Gray's sin was no one says and no one knows. He who discovers it has committed it.

Here we touch upon the vital centre of Wilde's art: sin. He deceived himself by thinking that he was the harbinger of the good news of neo-paganism to the suffering people. All his characteristic qualities, the qualities (perhaps) of his race: wit, the generous impulse, the asexual intellect were put to the service of a theory of beauty which should, he thought, have brought back the Golden Age and the joy of youth to the world. But deep down, if any truth is to be educed from his subjective interpretation of Aristotle, his restless thought which proceeds by sophisms rather than syllogisms, his assimilation of other natures alien to his own, such as those of the delinquent and the humble, it is the truth inherent in the spirit of Catholicism: that man cannot reach the divine heart except across that sense of separation and loss that is called sin.[10]

In his last book, *De Profundis*, he bows before a gnostic Christ, risen from the apocryphal pages of *A House of Pomegranates*, and then his true soul, trembling, timid and saddened, shines out from behind the mantle of Heliogabalus.[11] His fantastic myth, his work, a polyphonic variation on the relationship of art and nature, rather than a revelation of his psyche, his golden books, splendid with those epigrams which made him, in the eyes of some, the wittiest speaker of the last century, are now divided booty.

A verse from the Book of Job is engraved on his tombstone in the poor cemetery of Bagneux. It praises his eloquence, *eloquium suum*, the great legendary mantle which is now divided booty. The future might engrave another verse there, less haughty and more pious: *partiti sunt sibi vestimenta mea et super vestem meam miserunt sortes.*[12]

THE BATTLE BETWEEN BERNARD SHAW AND THE CENSOR: 'THE SHEWING-UP OF BLANCO POSNET'

Dublin, 31 August

There is a proud week in the Dublin calendar. In the last week of August the famous Horse Show attracts a multi-coloured and polyglot crowd to the Irish capital from the sister island, from the continent and even from as far away as Japan. For a few days the tired and cynical city dresses itself up like a newly wed bride and its senile sleep is broken by an unaccustomed uproar.

This year, however, an artistic event has almost eclipsed the importance of the show, and everywhere the only thing being spoken about is the dispute between Bernard Shaw and the Viceroy. As is already known, Shaw's latest play, *The Shewing-Up of Blanco Posnet*, has been stamped with the mark of notoriety by the English Lord Chamberlain who has banned its performance in the United Kingdom.[1] This decision probably did not surprise Shaw, as the same censor did as much for two other of his theatrical works, *Mrs Warren's Profession* and the very recent *Press Cuttings*. If anything, he felt honoured by the arbitrary ban imposed upon his comedies as upon Ibsen's *Ghosts*, Tolstoy's *The Power of Darkness* and Wilde's *Salomé*.[2]

He did not admit defeat, however, and he found a way of avoiding the censor's timid vigilance. For some strange reason, the city of Dublin is the only place in the United Kingdom where censorship does not apply, and indeed, the ancient law contains the following words: 'except the city of Dublin'. So Shaw offered his work to the Irish national theatre company which accepted it, simply announcing its performance as if it were nothing extraordinary. The censor was seen to be reduced to helplessness and the Viceroy of Ireland then intervened to save the prestige of the Law. There was a lively exchange of letters between the king's representative and the comic playwright: severe and threatening on one side, insolent and contemptuous on the other.[3] Meanwhile Dubliners, who couldn't care less for art but have an immoderate love of arguments, were rubbing their hands in glee. Shaw held out, insisting on his rights, and the theatre booking office was literally besieged to such an extent that the seats were sold out a full seven times over for the first performance.

A dense crowd thronged around the Abbey Theatre that evening and a platoon of hefty guards kept order, but it was evident from the start that there would be no hostile demonstration by the elect public that packed every corner of the small revolutionary theatre. In fact, the newspaper accounts of the evening reported not the slightest murmur of protest. When the curtain fell an uproarious applause called the performers back on stage for encore after encore.

The comedy, which Shaw describes as a sermon in a plain melodrama, is, as you know, only one act long. The action takes place in an uncouth and barbaric town in the Far West. The hero is a horse-thief, and the play deals only with his trial. He has stolen a horse that he thought belonged to his brother in order to retrieve what his brother had unjustly taken from him. While fleeing the town, however, he meets a woman and a sick child. She wants to reach the nearest large town to save her child's life, and he, moved by her appeal, gives her the horse. He is captured and brought back to the town to be hanged. The trial is summary and violent. The sheriff acts as an aggressive judge, shouting at the accused man, thumping the table and threatening the witnesses with revolver in hand. Posnet, the thief, offers a bit of primitive theology. The moment of sentimental weakness when he gave in to the pleas of the unfortunate mother has been the crisis point of his life. The finger of God has touched his brain. He no longer has the strength to continue the cruel and bestial life which he had led before that meeting. He breaks out into long, disconnected speeches (and it is here that the pious English censor blocked his ears). The speeches were theological in that God was the subject, but not very ecclesiastic in their terminology. In the sincerity of his conviction, Posnet has recourse to miners' slang; among other reflections, and in an attempt to explain how God works in mysterious ways in the hearts of men, he even calls God a horse-thief.

The drama ends happily. The child that Posnet wanted to save dies, and the mother is tracked down. She tells her story to the court, and Posnet is acquitted. Nothing imaginable is more innocuous than this and the audience wonders in amazement why on earth the work was intercepted by the censor.

Shaw is right: it is a sermon. Shaw is a born preacher. His loquacious and lively spirit cannot suffer the imposition of the noble, spare style that befits a modern playwright. By giving vent to his feelings in farraginous prefaces and in endless stage-directions, he creates a dramatic form for himself which has much of the dialogue-novel in it. He has a sense of situation rather than of drama logically and ethically brought to its conclusion. In this case he has exhumed the central event from his play *The Devil's Disciple*, and he has transformed it into a sermon.[4] It is a transformation too rapid to be convincing as a sermon, just as its art is too poor to make it convincing as a drama.

Does this play not perhaps coincide with a crisis in the mind of the writer? Already, at the end of *John Bull's Other Island*, the crisis had announced its advent.[5] Shaw, like his latest hero, has also had an irregular and irreverent past. Fabianism, vegetarianism, antialcoholism, music, painting, drama, all the progressive movements in both art and politics have had him as a champion. Now, perhaps some divine finger has touched his brain: and he, too, just like Blanco Posnet, is shewn up.

James Yoyce [*sic*]

THE HOME RULE COMET

The idea of Irish autonomy has been gradually surrounded by a thin and pale mistiness. A few weeks ago, when a royal decree dissolved the English parliament, a weak and tremulous something could be seen dawning towards the east.[1] It was the Home Rule comet, indefinite, remote, but punctual as always. The word of the sovereign, which in an instant brought darkness down upon the demigods of Westminster, called the obedient and unconscious star from the darkness of the void.

This time, however, it could barely be seen because the skies were clouded. The fogginess that usually envelopes the shores of Britain thickened so as to shroud them in a dense and impenetrable cloudiness. Beyond it the orchestral music of the contesting electoral elements could be heard: noble strings agitated and hysterical, the strident bugles of the people and, from time to time, a floating phrase on the Irish flutes.

The uncertainty of the political situation in England is evident from the fact that from morning to night the press agencies send out enigmatic dispatches which contradict one another. Indeed, the tone of the recent discussions in the United Kingdom makes an impartial scrutiny of the matter extremely difficult. Following the departure of the three leaders, Asquith, Balfour and Redmond,[2] who until now had managed to maintain a certain dignity of conduct that does not ill-become vacuous men, the recent election campaign marks a notable lowering of tone in English public life. Has any such speech ever been heard from the lips of the Chancellor of the Exchequer, wonder the Conservatives. But the jibes of the pugnacious Welsh minister pale before the vulgar invective of Conservatives the like of Deputy Smith, the lawyer Carson and the editor of the *National Review*. In the meantime, the two Irish factions, oblivious of their common enemy, have been waging a secret war in an attempt to exhaust the lexicon of contempt.[3]

And yet (another cause of confusion), the English parties no longer answer to their names. It is the Radicals who want the present free trade policies to be continued, while the Conservatives have been urging tax reform until they are blue in the face. It is the

Can anybody find the promised Home Rule Tail.?

Sinn Féin, 11 June 1910 (National Library of Ireland)

Conservatives who aim to strip parliament of its legislative power, entrusting it instead to the entire nation by means of a plebiscite. Finally, it is the clerical and intractable Irish Party that forms the majority within an anticlerical and Liberal government.

This paradoxical situation is accurately reflected in the persons who are the party leaders. To say nothing of Chamberlain or Roseberry [*sic*] who, the one from extreme radicalism and the other from Gladstonian liberalism, have both crossed over to the ranks of imperialism (while the young minister Churchill has made his imaginary journey in the opposite direction), we find the cause of Anglican Protestantism and conciliatory Nationalism under the guidance of a religious renegade and a converted Fenian.[4] Balfour, in fact, is more of a sceptic than a politician. He is a worthy disciple of the Scottish school. Driven more by the nepotism inherent in the Cecil family than by any personal aspiration, he took over the leadership of the Conservative Party following the death of his uncle, the lamented Marquess of Salisbury.[5] No day goes by without some parliamentary reporter remarking upon his absorbed and quibbling manner. His antics make even his followers smile. Even though under his unsteady banner the orthodox army has gone to meet three defeats in succession, each more ponderous than the last, his biographer (who might perhaps be another member of the Cecil family) will be able to say of him that in his philosophical essays he skilfully dissected and stripped bare the secret fibres of the religious and psychological principles whose champion he became by a turn of the parliamentary wheel of fortune. O'Brien, the leader of the Irish dissidents, who calls his handful of ten deputies the All-for-Ireland League, has become what all fanatics become when their fanaticism dies before they do. Now he fights along with Unionist magistrates who, twenty years ago, would probably have issued a warrant for his arrest; nothing remains of his fiery youth apart from those violent outbursts that make him look like an epileptic.

In the midst of such contradictions it is easy to understand how the dispatches affirm then deny in turn, they announce that Home Rule is at the door, then write its obituary six hours later. The layman cannot be dogmatic about comets, but at any rate, the much-awaited passing of the heavenly body has been reported officially. Last week, the Irish leader Redmond announced the happy news to a crowd of fishermen. English democracy, he said, has for once and all broken the power of the Lords and perhaps within a few weeks Ireland would have autonomy. Now, it would take a voracious nationalist to swallow that mouthful. The Liberal cabinet, as soon as it takes up its position on the ministerial bench, will find itself faced by quite a stack of troubles, among which the problem of the double balance will predominate.[6] Whether the affair is resolved well or otherwise, the peers and the commons will declare an armistice for the coronation of George V.[7] So far the road has been smooth, but only prophets could tell us where a government as heterogeneous as the present one will end up. Wanting to stay in power, will it try to appease the Welsh and the Scots with ecclesiastic and agrarian measures? If the Irish demand autonomy as the price of their support, will the cabinet hasten to dust off one of the many Home Rule Bills and present it before the House? The history of Anglo–Saxon Liberalism teaches us very explicitly what the answers to this and other such ingenuous questions are. The Liberal ministers are scrupulous men. Once again the Irish problem will bring about a symptomatic rupture in the heart of the cabinet, following which it will be amply demonstrated that the English electorate had not really authorized its government to legislate to such an end. If the government pursues the Liberal tactic of deliberately and secretly undermining Nationalist feelings, while, by means of partial concessions and with equal deliberation and secrecy, it creates a new greedy dependent social class that is free from any dangerous enthusiasms, if it introduces reform, or some pretence of reform that Ireland will haughtily reject, will that not then be the opportune moment for the Conservative Party to intervene? Faithful to its long tradition of cynical faithlessness, this party will take the opportunity to declare that the Irish dictatorship is intolerable and promote a campaign to reduce the number of Irish seats from eighty to forty on the basis of a depopulation that is unique rather than simply unusual for a civilized country, and is the bitter fruit of its own misgovernment. The link, therefore, between the abolition of the veto of the Lords and Irish autonomy is not as immediate as some might have us believe. In the final reckoning, it is the business of the English themselves. Admitting that the English populace no longer has the same veneration as once for its temporal and spiritual patrons, it will probably proceed with the reform of the upper House as cautiously and slowly as with the reform of its medieval laws, its triumphant and hypocritical literature, and its monstrous judicial system. In expectation of such reforms, it will matter little to the credulous Irish peasant whether Lord Lansdowne or Sir Edward Grey controls the fate of the ministry of foreign affairs.[8]

The fact that Ireland wishes to make common cause with British democracy should be neither surprising nor persuasive. For seven centuries it has never been a faithful subject of England. Nor, on the other hand, has it been faithful to itself. It entered the British dominion without forming an integral part of it. It almost entirely abandoned its language and accepted the language of the conqueror without being able to assimilate its culture or to adapt itself to the mentality of which this language is the vehicle. It always betrayed its heroes in their hour of need without even earning the bounty payment. It has driven its spiritual creators into exile and then boasted of them. It has only ever served one mistress faithfully, the Roman Catholic Church, which is, however, accustomed to paying her faithful in long-term drafts.

What durable alliance could exist between this strange people and the new Anglo-Saxon democracy? The rhetoricians who now speak so warmly about this alliance will soon become aware (if they have not done so already) that there exists a mysterious communion of blood between the English nobles and workers. The aforementioned Marquess of Salisbury, the perfect gentleman, spoke not just for his class, but for his race, when he said: 'Let the Irish stew in their own juice.'

James Joyce

[A CURIOUS HISTORY]

To the Editor
17 August 1911   *Via della Barriera Vecchia 32, III,*
                                         Trieste (Austria)

Sir   May I ask you to publish this letter which throws some light on the present conditions of authorship in England and Ireland?

Nearly six years ago Mr Grant Richards,[1] publisher, of London signed a contract with me for the publication of a book of stories written by me, entitled *Dubliners*. Some ten months later he wrote asking me to omit one of the stories and passages in others which, as he said, his printer refused to set up. I declined to do either and a correspondence began between Mr Grant Richards and myself which lasted more than three months. I went to an international jurist in Rome (where I lived then) and was advised to omit.[2] I declined to do so and the MS was returned to me, the publisher refusing to publish notwithstanding his pledged printed word, the contract remaining in my possession.

Six months afterwards a Mr Hone[3] wrote to me from Marseilles to ask me to submit the MS to Messrs Maunsel, publishers, of Dublin. I did so: and after about a year, in July 1909, Messrs Maunsel signed a contract with me for the publication of the book on or before 1 September 1910. In December 1909 Messrs Maunsel's manager[4] begged me to alter a passage in one of the stories, 'Ivy Day in the Committee Room', wherein some reference was made to Edward VII. I agreed to do so, much against my will, and altered one or two phrases. Messrs Maunsel continually postponed the date of publication and in the end wrote, asking me to omit the passage or to change it radically. I declined to do either, pointing out that Mr Grant Richards of London had raised no objection to the passage when Edward VII was alive and that I could not see why an Irish publisher should raise an objection to it when Edward VII had passed into history. I suggested arbitration or a deletion of the passage with a prefatory note of explanation by me but Messrs Maunsel would agree to neither. As Mr Hone (who had written to me in the first instance) disclaimed all responsibility in the matter and any connection with the firm I took the opinion of a solicitor in Dublin who advised me to omit the passage, informing me that as I had no domicile in the United Kingdom I could not sue Messrs Maunsel for breach of contract unless I paid £100 into court and that, even if I paid £100 into court and sued them, I should have no chance of getting a verdict in my favour from a Dublin jury if the passage in dispute could be taken as offensive in any way to the late king. I wrote then to the present king, George V, enclosing a printed proof of the story with the passage therein marked and begging him to inform me whether in his view the passage (certain allusions made by a person of the story in the idiom of his social class) should be withheld from publication as offensive to the memory of his father. His Majesty's private secretary sent me this reply:

Buckingham Palace

The private secretary is commanded to acknowledge the receipt of Mr James Joyce's letter of the 1 instant and to inform him that it is inconsistent with rule for His Majesty to express his opinion in such cases. The enclosures are returned herewith.

11 August 1911

Here is the passage in dispute:

—But look here, John,—said Mr O'Connor.—Why should we welcome the king of England? Didn't Parnell himself . . .?—

—Parnell,—said Mr Henchy,—is dead. Now, here's the way I look at it. Here's this chap comes to the throne after his old mother keeping him out of it till the man was grey.[5] He's a jolly fine decent fellow, if you ask me, and no damn nonsense about him. He just says to himself—*The old one never went to see these wild Irish. By Christ, I'll go myself and see what they're like.*—And are we going to insult the man when he comes over here on a friendly visit? Eh? Isn't that right, Crofton?—

Mr Crofton nodded his head.

—But after all now,—said Mr Lyons, argumentatively,—King Edward's life, you know, is not the very . . .—

—Let bygones be bygones.—said Mr Henchy—I admire the man personally. He's just an ordinary knockabout like you and me. He's fond of his glass of grog and he's a bit of a rake, perhaps, and he's a good sportsman. Damn it, can't we Irish play fair?—[6]

I wrote this book seven years ago and, as I cannot see in any quarter a chance that my rights will be protected, I hereby give Messrs Maunsel publicly permission to publish this story with what changes or deletions they may please to make and shall hope that what they may publish may resemble that to the writing of which I gave thought and time. Their attitude as an Irish publishing firm may be judged by Irish public opinion. I, as a writer, protest against the systems (legal, social and ceremonious) which have brought me to this pass. Thanking you for your courtesy, I am, Sir, Your obedient servant

James Joyce

REALISM AND IDEALISM IN ENGLISH LITERATURE · (DANIEL DEFOE — WILLIAM BLAKE)

Daniel Defoe[1] (I)

In the year of grace, 1660, the exiled, fugitive, and dispossessed Charles Stuart landed on English soil at Dover and, escorted by the fanfare and torches of a jubilant people, headed towards the capital to assume the crown that his father, the martyr king, had removed eleven years previously when he was executed on the gallows in Whitehall by order of the regicide generals. The corpses of Cromwell and Ireton were disinterred and dragged to Tyburn (the Golgotha, site of the skulls, in English history) where they were hanged on the gibbets and then, putrefied as they were, beheaded by the executioner. Merriment returned to Merry England; the gracefulness, culture, pomp, and luxury of the Stuart courts returned. The young king flung open the doors of his palace to flatterers of both sexes. Holding his lapdog in his arms, he gave audience to his ministers. Leaning against the fireplace of the House of Lords he would listen to the discourses of that elevated assembly, swearing by God's bodikins (his majesty's favourite oath) that his noblemen entertained him more than his comedians.

But this triumph was misleading and, within a short time, the star of the Stuart dynasty had set forever, and Protestant succession, embodied by the person of William of Nassau, had become the cornerstone of the British constitution. Here, according to the textbooks, the chapter of ancient history comes to an end, and that of modern history begins.[2]

And yet, the constitutional crisis that was then resolved by a covenant between the crown, the church and the legislature is not the only, nor the most interesting, feat accomplished by that prince, who is called in remembrance the pious, glorious and immortal.[3] His victory also signifies a crisis of race, an ethnic revenge. From the days of William the Conqueror onwards, no monarch of Germanic stock had wielded the English sceptre. The Normans were succeeded by the Plantagenets, the Plantagenets by the House of Tudor, the Tudors by the Stuarts.

Even Oliver Cromwell himself, the Lord Protector of civil liberties, was of Celtic origin, son of a Welsh father and a Scottish mother. So, over six centuries had passed since the Battle of Hastings before the true successor of the Anglo-Saxon dynasty was to ascend to the throne of England. The people who acclaimed the coming of the awkward and taciturn Dutch commander were acclaiming themselves, and saluting the human symbol of a true rebirth.

For the first time now the true English spirit begins to appear in literature.[4] Consider how minimal the importance of that spirit was in the earlier times. In Chaucer, a court writer with a polished and comely style, the indigenous spirit can just be discerned as the framework for the adventures of respectable people—meaning Norman clerics and foreign heroes. How is the great English public depicted in the variegated dramas of William Shakespeare, who wrote two hundred years after Chaucer? A boorish peasant, a court jester, a half-mad and half-stupid ragamuffin, a gravedigger. Shakespeare's characters all come from abroad and afar: Othello, a Moorish prince; Shylock, a Venetian Jew; Caesar, a Roman; Hamlet, a Danish prince; Macbeth, a Celtic usurper; Romeo and Juliet, citizens of Verona. Of all the rich gallery, perhaps the only one who can be called English is the fat knight with the monstrous paunch, Sir John Falstaff. In the centuries following the French conquest, English literature was schooled by masters such as Boccaccio, Dante, Tasso and Messer Lodovico.[5] Chaucer's *Canterbury Tales* are a version of the *Decameron* or the *Novellino*;[6] Milton's *Paradise Lost* is a puritanical transcript of the *Divine Comedy*. Shakespeare, with his Titianesque palette, his eloquence, his epileptic passion, and his creative fury, is an Italianized Englishman, while the theatre of the Restoration takes its cue from the Spanish stage and the works of Calderon and Lope de Vega.[7] The first English writer to write without copying or adapting foreign works, to create without literary models, to instil a truly national spirit into the creations of his pen, and to manufacture an artistic form for himself that is perhaps without precedent (with the exception of the monographs of Sallust and Plutarch)[8] is Daniel Defoe, the father of the English novel.

Daniel Defoe was born in 1661, a year after the return of Charles

Stuart. His father was a wealthy butcher from Cripplegate who, like a good burgher, intended his son for holy orders. But the son was anything but a saint, and preaching the gospel of Christian peace ill-fitted this bellicose man whose life from the cradle to the grave was a hard, vigorous, and ineffective struggle.

As soon as he had finished his studies, the young man threw himself into the vortex of politics. When the Duke of Monmouth (one of the merry monarch's many bastard sons) raised the banner of revolt, he enlisted in the ranks of the pretender.[9] The revolt failed and Defoe barely managed to escape with his life. A few years later we find him engaged in business as a hosiery merchant. In 1689, he rode in the volunteer light-horse regiment that escorted the new sovereigns William and Mary to a solemn banquet in the Guildhall. Later, he began trading in eastern drugs.[10] He travelled to France, Spain and Portugal, stopping over there for a time. He also went to Holland and Germany on his business travels, but when he returned to England, the first of a long series of disasters awaited him. He was declared bankrupt and, as his creditors pursued him mercilessly, he thought it best to flee to Bristol, where the townspeople attached the nickname of Mr Sunday to him, because he only dared leave his house on a Sunday, a day on which the bailiffs could not legally arrest him. An agreement with his creditors freed him from his forced domicile, and for a full twelve years he worked to pay off the enormous debt of seventeen thousand pounds sterling.[11]

From his liberation until the death of King William, Defoe was a director of a Dutch tile factory and actively involved himself in politics, publishing pamphlets, essays, satires, tracts, all in defence of the foreign king's party, and all, with the exception of *The True-Born Englishman*, of very little literary value. Following the accession of Queen Anne, parliament voted for a coercive law against Protestant Dissenters (that is, those who did not recognize the supremacy of the Anglican church), and Defoe, masquerading as an extremist Anglican, published his famous satire, *The Shortest Way with the Dissenters*, in which he proposed that all those who did not accept the dogmas and rites of the Anglican Church be condemned to the gallows or prison, reserving the honour of crucifixion for the fathers of the Society of Jesus.[12] The satire caused an enormous uproar, at first fooling the very ministers who, having praised its sincerity and wisdom, realized that they were dealing with a solemn hoax. A warrant was issued for the arrest of Defoe and the London *Gazette* published this description of the satirist:

A spare man, middle-aged, about forty years old, of a brown complexion, dark-brown coloured hair, but wears a wig; a hooked nose, a sharp chin, grey eyes, and a large mole near his mouth, born in London, for many years a hose-factor in Cornhill, now owner of a brick and pantile works at Tilbury in Essex County.[13]

The police put a price on his head, and within the month Defoe was imprisoned in Newgate. His book was burnt by the public executioner, and the writer was pilloried for three successive days in front of the Exchange, in Cheapside, at the gates to the City at Temple Bar. He did not lose heart during his punishment. By an act of royal clemency, his ears were not cropped; flower-sellers wreathed the instrument of torture with garlands; copies of his *A Hymn to the Pillory*, which the newsboys were selling for a few pennies, went like hot cakes, while the mob of citizens filled the square reciting the verses and toasting the health of the prisoner and the freedom of speech.[14]

He was then detained in prison, but his literary activity did not cease. While still in prison, he founded and edited one of the first English Journals, *The Review*,[15] and knew so well how to placate the authorities that a little while later he was not only set free, but appointed by the government to go to Edinburgh as a secret envoy.

Another seven years follow in which the figure of the writer is lost in the grey shadows of politics. Then the government levied a heavy tax on newspapers, and the *Review* folded after nine years of existence. Defoe, indefatigable scribbler that he was, launched himself once again into polemic. His pamphlet on the Jacobite succession earned him another trial and, condemned for contempt, he was again imprisoned in Newgate.[16] He owed his release to a violent attack of apoplexy which almost killed him. Had it been fatal, world literature would have one masterpiece less. After the union of Scotland and England and the establishment of the House of Hanover on the English throne, Defoe's political importance quickly ebbed. He then turned (he had passed his sixtieth year) to literature properly speaking in the first years of the reign of George I (the uneven life of Defoe stretches over seven reigns). He wrote and sent the first part of *Robinson Crusoe* to press. The author offered his book to almost all the publishing houses of the capital which, showing immense fore-sight, turned it down. It saw the light in April 1719; by the end of August it was already in its fourth reprinting. Eighty thousand copies were sold, an unprecedented circulation for those times. The public could not get enough of the adventures of Defoe's hero and wanted more. Like Conan Doyle who, bowing to the insistence of the contemporary public, brought his lanky scarecrow Sherlock Holmes back from the dead to set him off once more chasing scroungers and malefactors,[17] the sixty-year-old Defoe also followed up the first part of his novel with a second, in which the hero, nostalgic for his travels, returns to his island home. To this second part there followed a third, the *Serious Reflections of Robinson Cru-soe*.[18] Defoe, bless his soul, realizing a little late that in his prosaic realism he had taken little account of his hero's spiritual side, wrote a collection of serious reflections on man, human destiny, and the Creator as a third part to his novel. These reflections and thoughts adorn the rough figure of the mariner like votive talismans hanging from the neck and outstretched arms of a miracle-working Madonna. The famous book even had the great fortune to be paro-died by a London wit who also made a pile of money through the sales of a whimsical satire entitled *The Life and Surprizing Adventure of a Certain Daniel Defoe, Wool Merchant, Who Lives All Alone in the Uninhabited Island of Great Britain*.[19]

The pedants strove to uncover the small mistakes which the great precursor of the Realist movement had run into. How could Robin-son Crusoe have filled his pockets with biscuits if he had undressed before swimming from the beach to the stranded ship? How could he have seen the eyes of the goat in the pitch blackness of the cave? How could the Spaniards have given Friday's father a written agreement if they had no ink or quill pens? Are there bears or not on the islands of the West Indies?[20] And so forth. The pedants are right: the mis-takes are there; but the wide river of the new realism sweeps them majestically away like bushes and rushes uprooted by the flood.

From 1719 to 1725 the aged writer's pen was never still: he wrote almost a dozen romances (the so-called *lives*), pamphlets, tracts, journals, travelogues, and spiritualistic studies. Gout and old age forced him to lay aside his pen. It is thought that he was in prison for the third time in 1730. A year later we see him as a fugitive in a citadel[21] in Kent. There is an air of mystery shrouding his death.

Perhaps he was on the run, perhaps the quarrel with his son (a downright scoundrel worthy of inclusion in one of his father's books) had forced him to wander about in misery in a way reminiscent of the tragedy of King Lear. Perhaps the travails of his long life, the excessive writing, the intrigues, the disasters, his ever-increasing avarice had produced a sort of senile atrophy of his quick and fertile intelligence. We are and shall remain uncertain. And yet, there is something meaningful in his strange, solitary death in the little boarding-house in Moorfields. The man that immortalized the strange, solitary Crusoe and many others as lost in their great sea of social misery, as Crusoe was lost in a sea of waters, may have felt a longing for solitude as his end drew nigh. The old lion goes to a secluded place when his final hour approaches. He feels loathing for his worn and tired-out body and wishes to die where no eye may see him. And so, sometimes man, born into shame, will also bow before the shame of death, not wishing others to be saddened by the sight of that obscene phenomenon with which brutal and mocking Nature puts an end to the life of a human being.[22]

James Joyce

Daniel Defoe (II)

It is by no means an easy task to make an adequate study of a writer as prolific as Daniel Defoe who set the presses cranking a good two hundred and ten times over. But if we first of all discard the works which are political in character and the reams of journalistic essays, Defoe's works fall naturally around two focal points of interest. On the one hand, we have those writings that are based upon everyday occurrences, and on the other, the biographies[23] which, if not true romance novels as we understand them—owing to their absence of love-plots, psychological examination and studied balance of characters and dispositions[24]—are still literary works in which the soul of the modern realist novel can be glimpsed, like the dormant soul within an imperfect, amorphous organism. *The Storm*,[25] for example, is a book which describes the havoc wreaked by a terrifying hurricane that raged over the British Isles in two stages towards the end of the month of November 1703. Modern meteorologists have been able to compile a highly accurate barometric chart from the details that Defoe furnishes.[26] His method is simplicity itself. The book opens with an investigation into the causes of the winds; it then reviews the storms that have become famous in human history; and finally, the narrative, like a large snake, begins to slide slowly over a tangle of letters and reports. These follow one another endlessly. In all the letters, which come from every corner of the United Kingdom, we read of the same things: numerous trees (apple-trees, willows, oaks) uprooted here, numerous houses unroofed there; numerous ships smashed against the embankments in one place, numerous steeples collapsed in another. Then there is a meticulous enumeration of the losses of livestock and buildings suffered by various townships, of the deaths and the survivors, and an exact measurement of all the lead torn off the church roofs. Needless to say, the book attains a phenomenal level of boredom. The modern reader grumbles a lot before he reaches the end; but at the end the aim of the chronicler has been achieved. By dint of repetition, contradictions, details, figures, and rumours, the storm is made to exist, the destruction is visible.

In *Journal of the Plague*, Defoe spreads his wings further.[27] Sir Walter Scott, in the preface which he contributed to the definitive edition of Defoe's works, writes:

> Had he not written *Robinson Crusoe*, Daniel Defoe would have deserved immortality for the genius which he has displayed in this his journal of the plague.[28]

The black plague devastated the City of London during the earlier years of the reign of Charles II. The toll of victims cannot be established with any certainty, but it probably exceeded a hundred and fifty thousand. Of this horrible slaughter Defoe provides an account which is all the more terrifying for its sobriety and gloominess. The doors of the infected households were marked with a red cross over which was written: *Lord, have mercy on us!* Grass was growing in the streets. A dismal, putrid silence overhung the devastated city like a pall. Funeral wagons passed through the streets by night, driven by veiled carters who kept their mouths covered with disinfected cloths. A crier walked before them ringing a bell intermittently and calling out into the night, *Bring out your dead!* Behind the church in Aldgate an enormous pit was dug. Here the drivers unloaded their carts and threw merciful lime over the blackened corpses.[29] The desperate and the criminal revelled day and night in the taverns. The mortally ill ran to throw themselves in with the dead. Pregnant women cried for help. Large smoky fires were forever burning on the street corners and in the squares. Religious insanity reached its peak. A madman with a brazier of burning coals on his head used to walk stark naked through the streets shouting that he was a prophet and repeating by way of an antiphony: *O the great and dreadful God!*

In Defoe's story the person who narrates these horrors is an unknown London saddler, but the narrative style has something majestic and (if you'll allow the word) orchestral about it that recalls Tolstoy's *Sebastopol* or Hauptmann's *Weavers*.[30] But in these two works we sense a lyrical drift, a self-conscious art, a musical theme that wishes to act as the emotive revolt of modern man against human or superhuman iniquity. In Defoe, there is nothing: no lyricism, nor art for art's sake nor social sentiment. The saddler walks the abandoned streets, he listens to the cries of anguish, he keeps his distance from the sick, he reads the prefect's edicts, he chats with the garlic- and rue-chewing sextons, he argues with a ferry-man in Blackwall, he faithfully compiles his statistics, he takes an interest in the price of bread, he complains about the night watchmen, he climbs to the top of Greenwich Hill and calculates more or less how many people have taken refuge in the ships anchored on the Thames, he praises, he curses, he cries not infrequently and prays now and again: and he rounds off his account with four halting lines of verse, for which he asks, like a good saddler, the reader's indulgence. They are rough and ready, he says, but sincere. They go like this:

> A dreadful plague in London was
> In the year 'sixty-five,
> Which swept an hundred thousand souls
> Away; yet I alive!

In Defoe, as we can see, the star of poesy is, as they say, conspicuous by its absence—though he has a style of admirable clarity quite free of all pretension, that shines forth unexpectedly in a burst of brief, sweet splendour in certain pages of *Robinson Crusoe* and *Duncan Campbell*.[31] This is why his *History of the Devil* has actually seemed quite nauseating to some.[32] Defoe's devil has little in common with the strange son of Chaos who wages eternal war against the plans of the Supreme Being. Instead he rather resembles a dealer in hosiery who has suffered a calamitous financial setback. Defoe puts himself in the devil's shoes with a realism that strikes us, at first, as disconcerting. He has it out roughly with the majestic protagonist of *Paradise Lost*. He wonders how many days it took the devil to fall from Heaven into the Abyss; how many spirits fell with him; when he realized that the world had been created; how he seduced Eve; where he likes to live; why and how he made his wings. This attitude of mind in the presence of the supernatural, a natural consequence of his literary precepts, is the attitude of a reasonable barbarian. Sometimes, as in the awkward and rushed history of the philosopher *Dickory Cronke*,[33] it seems as if a fool is narrating the deeds of a moron; sometimes, as in *Duncan Campbell* (a spiritualistic study, as we would put it, of an interesting case of clairvoyance in Scotland), the writer's attitude is particularly apt for the subject-matter and reminds us of the precision and innocence of a child's questions.

This story, which must have been the result of a sojourn in the Scottish Highlands or islands where, as is well-known, telepathy is in the air, marks the limits of Defoe's method in these impersonal writings. Seated at the bedside of a boy visionary, gazing at his raised eyelids, listening to his breathing, examining the position of his head, noting his fresh complexion, Defoe is the realist in the presence of the unknown; it is the experience of the man who struggles and conquers in the presence of a dream which he fears may fool him; he is, finally, the Anglo-Saxon in the presence of the Celt.

In those works of Defoe which, belonging to the second category, contain more personal interest, we sporadically hear an accompanying intermittent roll of drums or roar of cannons. *The Memoirs of a Cavalier*,[34] which Defoe, in a characteristic preface, pretends to have found among the papers of a secretary of state to William III, are the personal account of an officer who fought under Gustavus Adolphus and then enlisted in the army of Charles I. Although the dubious origins of the book caused a deal of ink to flow, it cannot be of interest today to anyone but a student of that turbid and bloody age. We have read elsewhere the things that the cavalier reports. We reread them here without caring too much about them and the most we remember is some vivid description, some colourful instance.

On the other hand, the Spanish chapters of *Memoirs of Captain Carleton*,[35] crammed full of gallant adventures, bull-fights, and capital executions are, in today's cinematic jargon, realistic 'takes'. If Defoe were alive today, his gifts of precision and imagination, his farraginous experience and his neat, precise style would probably enable him to enjoy great fame as a special correspondent for some huge American or English newspaper.[36]

The first female figure to stand out from this background is Mrs Christian Davies, known as the Mother Ross.[37] This lady, along with the adventuress Roxana and the unforgettable harlot Moll Flanders, forms the third of that trio of female characters that reduce present-day critics to stupefied speechlessness. Indeed, the elegant literary gentleman and bibliophile Sir Leslie Stephen wonders with a respectable writer's curiosity where on earth Defoe found the models for these figures.[38] The latest editor of Defoe, the poet John Masefield, cannot find an explanation for why a writer should have created women with such a cynical, crass, and indecent realism when he lived in the years following the Restoration of the monarchy, happy years, made pleasant by the easy graces of so many consenting ladies, years whose intimate history is studded with female names: Lucy Walters, Nell Gwynne, Martha Blount, the scandalous Susannah Centlivre and the witty Lady Mary Montagu.[39] For the aforementioned gentlemen critics, *The Life of Mrs Christian Davies* will certainly seem like the transcription of the life of Joan of Arc, done by a stable-boy.

Christian, who is a pretty Dublin tavern-girl, gets rid of her demijohns, and, dressed in male clothes, wanders through Europe in search of her husband as a dragoon in the Duke of Marlborough's army. She catches up with him at the battle of Hochstat, but in the meantime he has taken a Dutch lover. The meeting scene between Christian and her unfaithful husband in the room in the inn presents us with the eternal feminine in an unexpected light. Here is Christian herself speaking.

I saw him in the kitchen drinking with the Dutch woman but, pretending not to see him, I went to the landlady and desired to be shown a private room. She went before me into the room and bringing me a pint of beer which I called for, left me alone with my melancholy thoughts. I sat me down, laid my elbow on the table, and leaning my head on my hand, I began to reflect . . . But why is he thus changed? . . . And his fondness for the Dutch woman gave vent to my tears, which flowing in abundance, was some relief to me. I could not stop this flood, which continued a good quarter of an hour. At length it ceased, and, drinking a little of the hou-garde (which is a white beer, in colour like whey), I washed my eyes and face with the rest, to conceal my having wept. Then, calling my landlady, I desired she would bring me another pint.

Somewhat different from Tristan and Isolde![40] Modern musicians, literate or otherwise, would find very little here in the story of this woman who, while still a girl, began her career by rolling down a hill to send the elderly Count of C—— (note the delicacy of the initials) into ecstasies and who dies, aged sixty-two, in the Chelsea military hospital, a retired sutler, crippled, scrofulous and suffering from dropsy. They would find less than nothing in the life of Moll Flanders, the unique, the inimitable woman who (I quote the words of the old title-page) was born in Newgate prison and lived a life of continuing variety during her sixty years: she was a prostitute for twelve of them, a wife five times (once with her own brother), a thief for twelve years, eight years as a prisoner in a penal settlement in Virginia, then she became rich, lived honestly and died repentant. The realism of this writer, in effect, defies and surpasses the magical artifice of music.

Perhaps modern realism is a reaction. The great French nation which venerates the legend of the Maid of Orléans defiles her name through the mouth of Voltaire, lewdly sullies her at the hands of the nineteenth-century engravers, and lacerates and cuts her to pieces in the twentieth century through the incisive style of Anatole France.[41] The very intensity and refinement of French realism betrays its spiritual origins. But you will search in vain for that angry fervour of corruption in Defoe that illuminates Huysmans's sad pages with a blighted phosphorescence. You will search in vain for that studied fervour of lacerating yet soothing indignation and protest in the works of this writer who, two centuries before Gorky or Dostoievsky,[42] introduced the lowest dregs of the populace into European literature: the foundling, the pick-pocket, the crooked dealer, the prostitute, the hag, the robber, the shipwrecked. If anything, you will find an instinct and prophetic sense beneath the rough skin of his characters. His women have the indecency and self-restraint of beasts; his men are strong and silent like trees. English feminism and English imperialism are already lurking in these souls which have but recently emerged from the animal kingdom. The proconsul of Africa, Cecil Rhodes, is a direct descendant of Captain Singleton and the aforementioned Mrs Christian Davies might be presumed to be the notional great–great–grandmother of Mrs Pankhurst.[43]

Defoe's masterpiece, *Robinson Crusoe*, is the finished artistic expression of this instinct and this prophetic sense. In the life of the pirate-explorer *Captain Singleton*, and in the story of *Colonel Jack*, suffused with such broad and sad charity, Defoe introduces us to the studies and rough drafts of that great solitary figure who later obtains, to the applause of the simple hearts of many a man and boy, his citizenship in the world of letters.[44] The account of the shipwrecked sailor who lived for four years on a lonely island reveals, perhaps as no other book in all English literature does, the cautious and heroic instinct of the rational being and the prophecy of the empire.

European criticism has struggled for several generations with a persistence that is not entirely well-meaning to illuminate the mystery of the immense world conquest achieved by that hybrid race[45] which lives a tough life on a small island in the northern sea, gifted with none of the intellect of the Latin, the forbearance of the Jew, the zeal of the German, nor the sensitivity of the Slav. For some years European caricature has amused itself by contemplating (with a pleasure unmixed with discomfort) an overgrown man with an ape's jaw, dressed in checkered clothes that are too short and tight and with huge feet; or else John Bull, the plump bailiff with his vacuous and ruddy moon-shaped face and miniature top hat. Neither of these two comic figures[46] would have conquered an inch of land in a thousand centuries. The true symbol of the British conquest is Robinson Crusoe who, shipwrecked on a lonely island, with a knife and a pipe in his pocket, becomes an architect, carpenter, knife-grinder, astronomer, baker, shipwright, potter, saddler, farmer, tailor, umbrella-maker, and cleric. He is the true prototype of the British colonist just as Friday (the faithful savage who arrives one ill-starred day) is the symbol of the subject race. All the Anglo-Saxon soul is in Crusoe: virile independence, unthinking cruelty, persistence, slow yet effective intelligence, sexual apathy, practical and well-balanced religiosity, calculating dourness. Whoever re-reads this simple and moving book in the light of subsequent history cannot but be taken by its prophetic spell.[47]

Saint John the Evangelist saw on the island of Patmos the apocalyptic collapse of the universe and the raising up of the walls of the eternal city splendid with beryl and emerald, onyx and jasper, sapphires and rubies.[48] Crusoe saw but one marvel in all the fertile creation that surrounded him, a naked footprint in the virgin sand: and who knows if the latter does not matter more than the former?[49]

James Joyce

[William Blake][50]

[*Ten pages of the manuscript are missing.*]

of an ethical and practical interpretation are not moral aphorisms. While looking at St Paul's Cathedral, he heard in the ear of his soul the cry of the little chimney-sweep who, in Blake's strange literary language, represented downtrodden innocence. While looking at Buckingham Palace, in his mind's eye he saw the sigh of the unhappy soldier running down the wall of the palace as a drop of blood.[51] While still young and strong, he could, when he had come round from these visions, engrave the image of them in a hammered verse or in a copper plate; and often engravings such as these in words or metal would assume an entire sociological system. Prison, he writes, is made from the stones of the law; the brothel from the bricks of religion.[52] But the continuous exertion of these journeys into the unknown and the abrupt returns to normal life slowly but infallibly eroded his artistic power. The myriad visions blinded his vision; and, towards the end of his mortal life, the unknown that he had sought covered him under the shadows of its vast wings. The angels with whom he used to speak as an immortal to immortals cloaked him in the silence of their vestments.

If, through his bitter words and violent poetry, I have called up from the shadows the image of some broken-winded, second- or third-rate demagogue, then I have given you the wrong idea of the personality of Blake. From his youth he was a member of the literary-revolutionary coterie that included Miss Wollstonecraft and the celebrated (perhaps I should say notorious) author of the *Rights of Man*, Thomas Paine.[53] In fact, of the members of that circle, Blake was the only one with the courage to wear the red cap in the street, the emblem of the new age. He soon removed it, though, never to wear it again following the massacres that took place in the Paris prisons in 1792.[54] His spiritual rebellion against the powerful of this world was not made of that type of water-soluble gunpowder to which we have more or less accustomed ourselves. In 1799, he was offered a position as drawing master to the royal family. He refused it, fearing that his art would die of inanition in the artificial environment of the court, but, at the same time, so as not to offend the sovereign, he gave up all his other lower-class students who formed the greater part of his income.[55] After his death, Princess Sophia sent his widow a private gift of one hundred pounds. The widow sent it back with courteous thanks, saying that she could manage without and did not want to accept it because, put to other use, the money might perhaps serve to give life and hope back to someone more unfortunate than herself.[56]

There are clearly quite some differences between Blake, the visionary anarchic heresiarch, and those highly orthodox ecclesiastic philosophers, Francisco Suarez, *Europae atque orbis universi magister et oculus populi christiani*, and Don Giovanni Mariana di Talavera who, in the previous century, had written a grim and logical defence of tyrannicide for the amazement of posterity.[57] The same idealism that enraptured and sustained Blake when he let fly his thunderbolts against human evil or misery restrained him from cruelty even against a sinner's body, the fragile curtain of flesh that lies on the marriage bed of our desire, as he put it in his mystic book, *Thel*.[58] There is no lack of instances testifying to his goodness of heart in the story of his life. Although he struggled to live and only spent half a guinea a week to keep the small house where he lived, he lent a needy friend forty pounds. When he saw a poor consumptive art student pass by his window every morning with his portfolio under his arm, he took pity on him and invited him into his house where he gave him some food and tried to cheer up his sad and flagging life.[59] His relationship with his younger brother is reminiscent of the story of David and Jonathan.[60] Blake took him in, maintained him, loved him, and looked after him during his long illness; he would speak to him of the eternal world and give him comfort. He stayed up constantly by his bedside for days on end before his death and, at the last moment, he saw the soul he loved free itself from the lifeless body and rise towards heaven clapping its hands in joy. Then, exhausted and at peace, he lay down in a deep sleep that lasted for seventy-two consecutive hours.[61]

I have referred two or three times to Mrs Blake, and perhaps I
ought to say something about the poet's wife. Blake had been in love
once when he was twenty. The girl, who seems to have been rather
foolish, was called Polly Woods. The influence of this young love
radiates throughout Blake's first works, the *Poetical Sketches* and the
Songs of Innocence.[62] However, the affair closed suddenly and
abruptly. She thought him mad, or little better, while he thought her
a flirt, or something worse.[63] This girl's face appears in some drawings from his prophetic book, *Vala*; a sweet, smiling face, symbol of
feminine cruelty and sensual deception.[64] To recover from this
setback, Blake left London and went to live in the cottage of a
market-gardener called Bouchier [*sic*]. This gardener had a twenty-
four-year-old daughter called Catherine whose heart was filled with
compassion when she heard of the young man's misadventures in
love. The affection that grew out of her pity and his gratitude finally
brought them together.[65] The lines from *Othello:*

> She loved me for the dangers I had passed,
> And I loved her that she did pity them.[66]

come to mind when we read of this chapter in Blake's life. Blake, like
many other men of great genius, was not attracted by cultivated and
refined women. Either he preferred simple women with sensual and
nebulous minds to those (if I may borrow a commonplace of the
theatre) endowed with all the drawing-room graces and a light and
broad education; or else, in his unlimited egoism, he wanted the soul
of his loved one to be entirely a slow and painstaking creation of his
own,[67] liberating and purifying itself daily before his eyes, the demon
(as he himself puts it) hidden in the cloud.[68] Whatever the case may
be, the fact is that Mrs Blake was neither very pretty nor intelligent.
In fact, she was illiterate, and the poet had a hard time of it teaching
her to read and write. He succeeded, however, since within a few
years his wife was helping him with his engravings, retouching his
drawings, and cultivating the visionary faculty in herself. Elementary
beings and the spirits of deceased great men would often enter the
poet's room at night to speak to him about art and the imagination.
Blake would then bounce out of bed and, grabbing his pencil, stay up
through the long hours of the London night drawing the features
and limbs of the visions while his wife crouched next to his armchair,
lovingly holding his hand and staying quiet so as not to disturb the

ecstasy of the seer. When the visions disappeared towards dawn, the wife would get back under the covers while Blake, radiant with joy and benevolence, would hurriedly set about lighting the fire and making breakfast for them both.[69] Ought we to be amazed that the symbolic beings Los, Urizen, Vala, Tiriel, and Enitharmon and the shades of Homer and Milton[70] should come from their ideal world into a poor room in London, or that the incense that greeted their coming was the smell of Indian tea and eggs fried in lard? Would this be the first time in the history of the world that the Eternal One has spoken through the mouth of the humble? That was how the mortal life of William Blake progressed. The ship of his married life set forth under the auspices of pity and gratitude and sailed towards the usual rocks for almost half a century. There were no children. In the first years of their lives together there were some slight disagreements. These misunderstandings are easy to comprehend if we bear in mind the great differences in culture and temperament that separated the young couple, differences so great that Blake, as I said before, almost devised to follow the example of Abraham and give to Hagar what Sarah refused.[71] His wife's vestal innocence was illsuited to the temperament of Blake, for whom, until his dying day, pleasure was the only beauty. In a scene of tears and recriminations that took place between them, his wife fell into a swoon and injured herself in a manner that prevented the possibility of having children.[72] It is a sad irony that this poet of childhood innocence, the only writer to have written songs for children with the soul of a child and who, in his strange poem *The Crystal Cabinet*, illuminated the phenomenon of gestation in such a tender and mystic light, was fated never to see the face of a human child by his fireside.[73] He who had such great compassion for all things, who lived, suffered and rejoiced in the illusion of the vegetable world: for the fly, the hare, the little chimney-sweep, the robin redbreast, even for the flea,[74] was denied any other fatherhood than a spiritual one. And yet it was an intensely natural fatherhood which still lives in the lines from the *Proverbs*,

> He who mocks the Infant's Faith
> Shall be mock'd in Age & Death.
> He who shall teach the Child to Doubt
> The rotting Grave shall ne'er get out.

> He who respects the Infant's faith
> Triumphs over Hell & Death.[75]

The rotting grave and the king of terrors hold no power over Blake, a fearless and immortal spirit. In his old age, when he was finally surrounded by friends, disciples and admirers, he set about, like Cato the Elder, learning a foreign language.[76] That language was the very same one in which this evening, with your forbearance, I am trying, to the best of my ability, to recall Blake's spirit from the twilight of the universal mind and to hold it fast for a moment to investigate it. He set about studying Italian to read the *Divine Comedy* in the original and to illustrate Dante's vision with mystic drawings.[77] Weakened and exhausted by the afflictions of his illness, he propped himself up on a pile of pillows. On his knees he held open a large book of drawings, and he struggled to trace the lines of his final vision on its white pages. It is in this attitude that he lives for us in the portrait by Philips [*sic*] in the National Gallery of London.[78] His brain did not become enfeebled, his hand did not lose its old mastery. Death came to him under the guise of an icy cold, like the shivers of cholera. It took over his limbs and extinguished the light of his intelligence in a moment, just as the cold darkness that we call space cloaks and puts out the light of a star. He died singing in a strong and sonorous voice that made the beams of the ceiling echo. He sang, as always, of the ideal world, of the truth of the intellect, and of the divinity of the imagination. 'My beloved, the songs that I sing are not mine,' he told his wife, 'no, no, I tell you, they are not mine.'[79]

A full study of Blake's personality should be logically divided in three phases: the pathological, the theosophical and the artistic. I think we can dispense with the first one without too much comment. To say that a great genius is half-mad, while recognizing his artistic prowess, is worth as much as saying that he was rheumatic, or that he suffered from diabetes. Madness, in fact, is a medical expression to which a balanced critic should pay no more heed than he would to the accusation of heresy brought by the theologian, or to the accusation of immorality brought by the public prosecutor. If we were to lay a charge of madness against every great genius who does not share the science undergraduate's fatuous belief in headlong materialism now held in such high regard, little would remain of world art and history. Such a slaughter of the innocents would include most of the peripatetic system, all medieval metaphysics, an entire wing in the immense, symmetrical edifice built by the angelic doctor, St Thomas Aquinas, the idealism of Berkeley and (note the coincidence) the very scepticism that leads us to Hume.[80] As far as art is concerned, those highly useful people, the parliamentarian photographers and reporters, might just manage to save their skins. The foreboding of such an art and philosophy flourishing in the not-too-distant future under the gentle union of the two commodities most highly quoted on the stock-exchanges today, woman and the people, will, if nothing else, reconcile every artist and philosopher—even if they think differently—to the brevity of our life down here.

To determine what place Blake should be assigned in the hierarchy of western mystics goes beyond the aims of this lecture. In my opinion, Blake was not a great mystic. The true home of mysticism is the Orient. Now that linguistic studies have enabled us to understand eastern thought (if we can call thought that ideational energy which created the vast cycles of activity and passivity that the *Upanishads* speak of),[81] the mystic books of the west shine, if at all, with a reflected light. Blake is probably less inspired than the Indian mystics; perhaps he is less inspired than Paracelsus, Jacob Behmen [*sic*], or Swedenborg; at any rate, he is less boring.[82] In Blake, the visionary faculty is immediately connected to the artistic faculty. In the first place, one must be gifted with the patience of a fakir to be able to form an idea of what Paracelsus and Behmen mean in their cosmic pronouncements on the involution and evolution of mercury, salt and sulphur, body, soul and spirit. Blake naturally belongs to another category, that of artists; and in this category he holds, in my view, a unique position because he unites intellectual sharpness with mystic sentiment. The former quality is almost completely lacking in mystic art. St John of the Cross, for example, one of the few artists worthy of standing beside Blake, reveals neither an innate sense of form nor the coordinating force of the intellect in his book *The Dark Night of the Soul*, which quakes and swoons in ecstatic passion.[83] The explanation is to be found in the fact that Blake had two spiritual masters, very different from one another, and yet similar in their formal precision: Michelangelo Buonarotti [*sic*] and Emanuel Swedenborg. The first of Blake's mystical drawings that we have, *Joseph of Arimathea Among the Rocks of Albion*, has the words: *Michelangelo pinxit* in one corner.[84] It is modelled on a draft made by Michel-

angelo for his *Last Judgement*, and it symbolizes the poetic imagination in the power of sensual philosophy. Under the drawing Blake
has written: 'This is one of the Gothic Artists who built the cathedrals in what we call the Dark Ages, wandering about in sheepskins
and goatskins, of whom the world was not worthy.'[85] The influence
of Michelangelo can be felt throughout Blake's works, particularly in
those prose pieces, collected in fragments, in which he continually
insists upon the importance of the pure, clear line that evokes and
creates the image against the background of the uncreated void.[86]
The influence of Swedenborg, who died in exile in London when
Blake was beginning to write and to draw, can be seen in the glorified
humanity that marks all Blake's work. Swedenborg, who haunted
all the invisible worlds for many years, saw heaven itself in the image
of a man.[87] For him, Michael, Raphael and Gabriel were not
three angels, but three angelic choirs. Eternity, which appeared to
the beloved disciple and to St Augustine as a celestial city, and to
Alighieri as a celestial rose, appears to the Swedish mystic in the
form of a celestial man whose every limb is animated by a fluid
angelic life that eternally leaves and re-enters: the systole and
diastole of love and wisdom. From this vision he developed that
enormous system of what he called correspondences which pervades
his masterpiece *Arcana Coelestia*, his new gospel which, according to
him, was to be the apparition of the sign of the Son of Man as
foretold by St Matthew.[88]

Armed with this double-edged sword of Michelangelo's art and
Swedenborg's revelations, Blake killed the dragon of natural experience and natural wisdom. By annihilating space and time and denying the existence of memory and the senses, he wanted to paint his
work upon the void of the divine bosom. For him, every time less
than the pulsation of an artery is equal in its period and value to six
thousand years because in that infinitely brief time the poet's work is
conceived and born.[89] For him, each space greater than a red drop of
human blood was visionary, created by the hammer of Los, while in
each space smaller than this we approached eternity of which our
vegetable world was but a shadow. So the soul must not look *with* but
rather *through* the eye because the eye, born in the night while the
soul slept in the rays of light, would also die in the night.[90]

In his book *The Divine Names*, Dionysius the pseudo-Areopagite
arrives at the throne of God by denying and overcoming every moral

and metaphysical attribute; in the final chapter he falls into an ecstasy and prostrates himself before the divine obscurity, the unnameable immensity that antedates and encompasses the highest wisdom and love in the eternal order.[91] The process by which Blake reaches the threshold of the infinite is similar. His soul, flying from the infinitely small to the infinitely big, from a drop of blood to the universe of stars, is consumed by the rapidity of its flight, and finds itself renewed, winged and imperishable on the edge of the dark ocean of God.

And although he based his art upon such idealistic premises, in the conviction that eternity was in love with the products of time,[92] the sons of God of the daughters of

[*The concluding page(s) of the manuscript is missing.*]

THE CENTENARY OF CHARLES DICKENS

The influence which Dickens has exercised on the English language (second perhaps to that of Shakespeare alone) depends to a large extent on the popular character of his work. Examined from the standpoint of literary art or even from that of literary craftmanship he hardly deserves a place among the highest. The form he chose to write in, diffuse, overloaded with minute and often irrelevant observation, carefully relieved at regular intervals by the unfailing humorous note, is not the form of the novel which can carry the greatest conviction. Dickens has suffered not a little from too ardent admirers. Before his centenary there was perhaps a tendency to decry him somewhat. Towards the close of the Victorian period the peace of literary England was disturbed by the inroads of Russian and Scandinavian writers inspired by artistic ideals very different from those according to which the literary works (at least of the last century) of the chief writers of fiction had been shaped. A fierce and headstrong earnestness, a resoluteness to put before the reader the naked, nay, the flayed and bleeding reality, coupled with a rather juvenile desire to shock the prim middle-class sentimentalism of those bred to the Victorian way of thinking and writing—all these startling qualities combined to overthrow or, perhaps it would be better to say, to depose the standard of taste. By comparison with the stern realism of Tolstoy, Zola, Dostoiewsky [*sic*], Bjornson and other novelists of ultra-modern tendency the work of Dickens seemed to have paled, to have lost its freshness. Hence, as I have said, a reaction set in against him and so fickle is popular judgement in literary matters that he was attacked almost as unduly as he had been praised before. It is scarcely necessary to say that his proper place is between these two extremes of criticism; he is neither the great-hearted, great-brained, great-souled writer in whose honour his devotees burn so much incense nor yet the common purveyor of sentimental domestic drama and emotional claptrap as he appears to the jaundiced eye of a critic of the new school.

He has been nicknamed 'the great Cockney': no epithet could describe him more neatly nor more fully. Whenever he went far afield to America (as in *American Notes*) or to Italy (as in *Pictures from*

Italy) his magic seems to have failed him, his hand seems to have lost her ancient cunning. Anything drearier, and therefore less Dickensian, than the American chapters of *Martin Chuzzlewit* it would be hard to imagine.[1] If Dickens is to move you, you must not allow him to stray out of hearing of the chimes of Bow Bells.[2] There he is on his native heath and there are his kingdom and his power. The life of London is the breath of his nostrils: he felt it as no writer since or before his time felt it. The colours, the familiar noises, the very odours of the great metropolis unite in his work as in a mighty symphony wherein humour and pathos, life and death, hope and despair, are inextricably interwoven. We can hardly appreciate this now because we stand too close to the scenery which he described and are too intimate with his amusing and moving characters. And yet it is certainly by his stories of the London of his own day that he must finally stand or fall. Even *Barnaby Rudge*, though the scene is laid chiefly in London and though it contains certain pages not unworthy of being placed beside the *Journal of the Plague* of Defoe (a writer, I may remark incidentally, of much greater importance than is commonly supposed), does not show us Dickens at his best.[3] His realm is not the London of the time of Lord George Gordon but the London of the time of the Reform Bill.[4] The provinces, indeed the English country of 'meadows trim with daisies pied',[5] appear in his work but always as a background or as a preparation. With much greater truth and propriety could Dickens have applied to himself Lord Palmerston's famous *Civis Romanus sum*. The noble lord, to tell the truth, succeeded on that memorable occasion (as Gladstone, unless my memory misleads me, took care to point out) in saying the opposite of what he had in mind to say. Wishing to say that he was an imperialist he said that he was a Little Englander.[6] Dickens, in fact, is a Londoner in the best and fullest sense of the word. The church bells which rang over his dismal, squalid childhood, over his struggling youth, over his active and triumphant manhood, seem to have called him back whenever, with scrip and wallet in his hand, he intended to leave the city and to have bidden him turn again, like another Whittington, promising him (and the promise was to be amply fulfilled) a threefold greatness.[7] For this reason he has a place for ever in the hearts of his fellow-citizens and also for this reason the legitimate affection of the great city for him has coloured to no slight extent the criticisms passed upon his work. To arrive at a just appreciation of Dickens, to estimate more accurately his place in what we may call the national gallery of English literature it would be well to read not only the eulogies of the London-born but also the opinion of representative writers of Scotland, or the Colonies or Ireland. It would be interesting to hear an appreciation of Dickens written, so to speak, at a proper focus from the original by writers of his own class and of a like (if somewhat lesser) stature, near enough to him in aim and in form and in speech to understand, far enough from him in spirit and in blood to criticize. One is curious to know how the great Cockney would fare at the hands of R.L.S. or of Mr Kipling or of Mr George Moore.[8]

Pending such final judgment we can at least assign him a place among the great literary creators. The number and length of his novels prove incontestably that the writer is possessed by a kind of creative fury. As to the nature of the work so created we shall be safe if we say that Dickens is a great caricaturist and a great sentimentalist (using those terms in their strict sense and without any malice)— great caricaturist in the sense that Hogarth is a great caricaturist,[9] a sentimentalist in the sense which Goldsmith would have given to that word. It is enough to point to a row of his personages to see that he has few (if any) equals in the art of presenting a character, fundamentally natural and probable with just one strange, wilful, wayward moral or physical deformity which upsets the equipoise and bears off the character from the world of tiresome reality and as far as the borderland of the fantastic. I should say perhaps the human fantastic, for what figures in literature are more human and warm-blooded than Micawber, Pumblechook, Simon Tappertit, Peggoty [*sic*], Sam Weller (to say nothing of his father), Sara Gamp, Joe Gargery?[10] We do not think of these, and of a host of others in the well-crowded Dickensian gallery, as tragic or comic figures or even as national or local types as we think, for instance, of the characters of Shakespeare. We do not even see them through the eyes of their creator with that quaint spirit of nice and delicate observation with which we see the pilgrims at the Tabard Inn,[11] noting (smiling and indulgent) the finest and most elusive points in dress or speech or gait. No, we see every character of Dickens in the light of one strongly marked or even exaggerated moral or physical quality—sleepiness, whimsical self-assertiveness, monstrous obesity, disorderly recklessness, reptile-like servility, intense round-eyed stupidity, tearful and absurd melancholy. And yet there are some simple people who complain that, though they like Dickens very much and have cried over the fate of Little Nell and over the death of Poor Joe [*sic*], the crossing-sweeper, and laughed over the adventurous caprices of Pickwick and his fellow-musketeers and hated (as all good people should) Uriah Heep and Fagin the Jew, yet he is after all a *little* exaggerated.[12] To say this of him is really to give him what I think they call in that land of strange phrases, America, a billet for immortality. It is precisely this little exaggeration which rivets his work firmly to popular taste, which fixes his characters firmly in popular memory. It is precisely by this little exaggeration that Dickens has influenced the spoken language of the inhabitants of the British Empire as no other writer since Shakespeare's time has influenced it and has won for himself a place deep down in the hearts of his fellow-countrymen, a honour which has been withheld from his great rival Thackeray.[13] And yet is not Thackeray at his finest greater than Dickens? The question is an idle one. English taste has decreed to Dickens a sovereign position and Turk-like will have no brother near his throne.

James Joyce B.A.

THE UNIVERSAL LITERARY INFLUENCE
OF THE RENAISSANCE

The doctrine of evolution in the light of which our civilization basks teaches us that when we were small, we were not yet grown up.[1] Accordingly, if we take the European Renaissance as a point of division, we must conclude that, until that age, humanity only had the soul and body of a child and it was only after this age that it developed physically and morally to the point of deserving the name of adulthood. It is a very drastic and somewhat unconvincing conclusion. In fact (were I not afraid of seeming to be a *laudator temporis acti*),[2] I should like to oppose this conclusion with all my might. The much trumpeted progress of this century consists for the most part of a tangle of machines whose aim is simply to gather fast and furiously the scattered elements of profit and knowledge and to redistribute them to each member of the community who can afford a small fee. I agree that this social system can boast of great mechanical conquests, of great and beneficial discoveries. To be convinced of this, it is enough just to draw up a brief list of what we see on the street of a large modern city: the electric tram, telegraph wires, the humble and necessary postman, newspaper boys, large companies etc. But in the midst of this complex and many-sided civilization the human mind, almost terrorized by material greatness, becomes lost, denies itself and grows weaker. Should we then conclude that present-day materialism, which descends in a direct line from the Renaissance, atrophies the spiritual faculties of man, impedes his development, blunts his keenness? Let us see.

In the age of the Renaissance the human spirit struggled against scholastic absolutism, against that immense (and in many ways admirable) system of philosophy that has its fundamental origins[3] in Aristotelian thought, cold, clear and imperturbable, while its summit stretched upwards towards the vague and mysterious light of Christian ideology. But if the human spirit struggled against this system, it was not because the system in itself was alien to him. The yoke was sweet and light:[4] but it was a yoke. So when the great rebels of the Renaissance proclaimed the Good News to the peoples of Europe, that there was no more tyranny, that human sadness and suffering had dissolved like mist at sunrise, that man was no longer a prisoner, perhaps the human spirit felt the fascination of the unknown, heard the voice of the visual world tangible, inconstant, where one lives and dies, sins and repents, and, abandoning the cloistered peace in which it had been languishing, embraced the new gospel. It abandoned its peace, its true abode because it had tired of it, just as God, tired (if you will permit a rather irreverent term) of his perfections, called forth the creation out of nothing, just as woman, tired of the peace and quiet that were wasting away her heart, turned her gaze towards the life of temptation. Giordano Bruno himself says that all power, whether in nature or the spirit, must create an opposing power without which man cannot fulfil himself, and he adds that in every such separation there is a tendency towards a reunion. The dualism of the great Nolan faithfully reflects the phenomenon of the Renaissance. And if it seems a little arbitrary to quote a witness against himself and to quote the very words of an innovator so as to condemn (or at least to judge) the work of which he was the author, I respond that I am doing no more than following the example of Bruno himself who, in the course of his long, persistent and quibbling self-defence, turned the weapons of the prosecution against his accuser.

It would be easy to fill these pages with the names of the great writers whom the wave of the Renaissance lifted to the clouds (or thereabouts), easy to praise the greatness of their works which, in any case, no one is calling into doubt, and to end with a ritual prayer: and it might be an act of cowardice since reciting a litany is not philosophical inquiry. The crux of the question lies elsewhere. It must be seen what is really meant by the Renaissance as far as literature is concerned, and towards what end, happy or tragic, it leads us. The Renaissance, to put it briefly, has placed the journalist in the monk's chair: in other words, it has deposed a sharp, limited and formal mind in order to hand the sceptre over to a mentality that is facile and wide-ranging (as the saying goes in theatre journals), a mentality that is restless and somewhat amorphous. Shakespeare and Lope de Vega are to a certain extent responsible for modern cinematography. Untiring creative power, heated, strong passion, the intense desire to see and feel, unfettered and prolix curiosity have, after three centuries, degenerated into frenetic sensationalism. Indeed, one might say of modern man that he has an epidermis rather than a soul. The sensory power of his organism has developed enormously, but it has developed to the detriment of his spiritual faculty. We lack moral sense and perhaps also strength of imagination. The most characteristic literary works that we possess are simply amoral: *The Crisis* by Marco Praga, *Pelléas et Mélisande* by Maeterlinck, *Crainquebille* by Anatole France, and *Smoke* by Turgenev.[5] Perhaps I have taken these somewhat at random. No matter: they will do to document the thesis which I uphold. A great modern artist who wishes to set the sentiment of love to music[6] will reproduce, as far as his art allows him to, every pulsation, every tremor, the lightest shiver, the lightest sigh; the chords interweave and wage a secret war among themselves: one loves while acting cruelly, one suffers when and as much as one rejoices, anger and doubt flash in the eyes of lovers whose bodies are the one flesh. Put *Tristan and Isolde* beside the *Inferno* and you will realize how the poet's hate follows its path from abyss to abyss in the wake of an increasingly intense idea, and the more intensely that the poet is consumed in the fire of the idea of hate, the fiercer becomes the art by which the artist communicates his passion to us. One is the art of circumstance, the other is ideational. In the high Middle Ages, the compiler of an atlas would not lose his composure when he found himself at a loss. He would write over the unknown area the words: *Hic sunt leones.*[7] The idea of solitude, the terror of strange beasts, the unknown were enough for him. Our culture has an entirely different goal: we are avid for details. For this reason our literary jargon speaks of nothing else than local colour, atmosphere, atavism: whence the restless search for what is new and strange, the accumulation of details that have been observed or read, the parading of common culture.

In strict terms the Renaissance should mean a rebirth after a death, an unexpected fecundity like that of Sarah after a long period of sterility. In fact, the Renaissance came about when art was dying of formal perfection, and thought was losing itself in vain subtleties. A poem would be reduced to an algebraic problem, put forth and resolved into human symbols in accordance with the rules. A philosopher was a learned sophist who, for all that he preached the word of Jesus to the crowd, would, like Bellarmine or Giovanni Mariana, strive to construct a moral defence of tyrannicide.[8]

The Renaissance arrived like a hurricane in the midst of all this stagnation, and throughout Europe a tumult of voices arose, and, although the singers no longer exist, their works may be heard just as the shells of the sea in which, if we put them up to our ear, we can hear the voice of the sea reverberating.

Listening to it, it sounds like a lament: or at least, so our spirit interprets it. Strange indeed! All modern conquest, of the air, the land, the sea, disease, ignorance, melts, so to speak, in the crucible of the mind and is transformed into a little drop of water, into a tear. If the Renaissance did nothing else, it did much in creating within ourselves and our art a sense of pity for every being that lives and hopes and dies and deludes itself. In this at least we excel the ancients: in this the popular journalist is greater than the theologian.[9]

James Joyce

THE SHADE OF PARNELL

By voting for the bill on Irish autonomy on its second reading, the House of Commons has resolved the Irish question; a question which, like the hen of Mugello, is a hundred years of age but looks a month old.[1]

The century that began with the buying and selling of the Dublin parliament is now closing with a triangular pact between England, Ireland and the United States.[2] It was a century adorned by seven Irish revolutionary movements that, with dynamite, eloquence, boycotts, obstructionism, armed revolt and political assassination, managed to keep awake the slow, apprehensive conscience of English Liberalism.[3]

The present law has been conceded in the full maturity of time under the double pressure of the Nationalist Party in Westminster which, for over half a century, has obstructed the operations of the British legislature, and the Irish Party across the Atlantic, which has blocked the much sought-after Anglo-American alliance. Devised and moulded with masterly cunning artistry, the bill fittingly crowns the tradition handed down to posterity by the pluterperfect[4] Liberal statesman, William Gladstone. Suffice to say that, while reducing the strong ranks of the one hundred and three Irish constituencies, presently represented in Westminster by a handful of forty deputies,[5] the bill automatically pushes these into the embrace of the small Labour Party so that from this incestuous embrace a coalition will probably arise and function as the far left. In other words, until it receives further orders, the coalition will work as an operational base for the Liberals in their campaign against Conservatism. There is no need to go into the intricacies of the financial clauses. At any rate, the future Irish government will have to cover the deficit skilfully created by the British treasury either by re-deploying local and imperial taxes, or by reducing public expenditure, or by increasing direct taxation. One way or the other, it will come up against the disillusioned hostility of the middle and lower classes.[6]

The Irish separatist party would like to reject this Greek gift that makes the Dublin Chancellor of the Exchequer a titular minister who is fully responsible to the tax-payers yet still dependent upon

THE SHADE OF PARNELL—"AND THIS IS HOW THEY
BLOCK THE WAY WHEN I AM GONE."

Sinn Féin, 3 January 1910 (National Library of Ireland)

the British cabinet. He may tax without having control over the proceeds of his ministry; he is like a vending-machine that cannot work unless the London energy source sends a current of the right voltage.[7]

No matter: the appearance of autonomy is there. At the recent national assembly held in Dublin, the denunciations and protests of the nationalists belonging to the bitterly sceptical school of John Mitchel did not greatly disturb the popular jubilation. In their speeches, the deputies, grown old in their constitutional struggle, and worn out by years and years of disappointed hopes, hailed the end of a long period of misunderstandings. A young orator, Gladstone's nephew, amidst fervent applause from the crowd, called up the name of his uncle and saluted the prosperity of the new nation. In two years' time at the latest, with or without the assent of the House of Lords, the doors of the old parliament in Dublin will re-open, and Ireland, freed from her century-long imprisonment, will set out towards the palace like a new bride accompanied by music and nuptial torches. A grand-nephew of Gladstone (if there is one) will scatter flowers beneath the feet of the sovereign, but there will be a shade at the feast: the shade of Charles Parnell.[8]

Recent criticism has attempted to minimize the greatness of this strange spirit by pointing to the different sources of his parliamentary tactics. Even if we concede to the historical critic that obstructionism was invented by Biggar and Ronayne, that the doctrine of independence of the Irish Party was launched by Gavan Duffy, and that the Land League was Michael Davitt's creation, these concessions evince all the more the extraordinary personality of a leader who, with no forensic gift or original political talent, forced the greatest English politicians to follow his orders.[9] He, like another Moses, led a turbulent and volatile people out of the house of shame to the edge of the Promised Land.[10] The influence that Parnell exercised over the Irish people defies the critic's analysis.[11] Lisping, of delicate build, he was ignorant of the history of his country. His short, broken speeches lacked all eloquence, poetry or humour.[12] His cold, polite behaviour divided him from his own colleagues. He was Protestant, a descendant of an aristocratic family, and (to complete the affliction) he spoke with a distinctly English accent. He would often come to committee meetings an hour or an hour and a half late and not excuse himself. He used to neglect his

correspondence for whole weeks. Neither the applause nor the anger
of the crowd, neither the invectives nor the praises of the press,
neither the denunciations nor the defences of the British ministers
ever perturbed the forlorn serenity of his character. It is even said
that he did not know by sight many of those who sat with him in the
Irish benches. When the Irish people presented him, in 1887, the
national tribute of forty thousand pounds, he put the cheque in his
wallet and, during the speech he addressed to the immense crowd, he
made not the slightest mention of the gift that he had received.[13]
When he was shown the copy of *The Times* containing the famous
autographed letter that was supposed to prove his complicity in the
savage assassination in the Phoenix Park, he placed a finger on a
letter in the signature, simply saying: 'I have not made an "S" that
way since '78.'[14] Later the investigations of the royal commission
revealed the plot that had been ordered against him, and the perjurer
and forger Pigott blew his brains out in a hotel in Madrid.[15] The
House of Commons, without regard to party, greeted Parnell's
entrance with an ovation that has remained unprecedented in the
annals of the British parliament. Is there any need to say that Parnell
responded to the ovation with neither a smile, nor a bow, nor a nod?
He walked over to his place across the aisle and sat down. Gladstone
was probably thinking of this incident when he called the Irish leader
an intellectual phenomenon.[16]

Nothing more singular can be imagined than the appearance of
this intellectual phenomenon in the midst of the stifling morals of
Westminster. Now, looking back over the scenes of the drama and
listening again to the speeches that caused his listeners' souls to
tremble, it is useless to deny that all that eloquence and all those
strategic triumphs begin to taste stale. But time is more merciful
towards the 'uncrowned king' than towards the wag and the orator.[17]
The light of his mild, proud, silent and disconsolate sovereignty
makes Disraeli look like an upstart diplomat dining whenever he can
in rich people's houses, and Gladstone like a portly butler who has
gone to night school. How little Disraeli's wit and Gladstone's culture weigh in the balance today! What trifles are Disraeli's studied
witticisms, greasy hair and doltish novels, or Gladstone's high-
sounding sentences, Homeric studies and speeches on Artemis or
marmalade![18]

Although Parnell's tactic was to avail himself of any one of the

English parties, Liberals or Conservatives, according to his pleasure, a set of circumstances involved him in the Liberal movement. Gladstonian Liberalism was an inconstant algebraic symbol whose coefficient was the political pressure of the moment and whose exponent was personal advantage. While, in internal politics, he temporized, retracted and justified himself in turn, he always, in the case of other nations, maintained (in so far as he could) a sincere admiration for liberty. This elastic quality of Gladstone's liberalism must be borne in mind if we are to appreciate the extent and degree of Parnell's task.[19] Gladstone was, in a word, a politician. He shook with rage at the wickedness of O'Connell in 1835, yet he was the English legislator to proclaim the moral and material necessity of Irish autonomy.[20] He thundered against the admission of Jews to public office, and yet he was the minister who, for the first time in English history, raised a Jew to the peerage.[21] He used proud language towards the rebel Boers in 1881, and after the English defeat at Majuba, concluded a pact with Transvaal that the English themselves called a cowardly submission.[22] In his first speech before parliament, he hotly rebutted Earl Grey's charges of cruelty against his father, a rich slave-owner in Demerara, who had earned two million francs by the sale of human flesh, while in his last letter to the Duke of Westminster, 'a childhood friend', he called down all possible curses upon the head of the great murderer of Constantinople.[23]

Parnell, convinced that such a liberalism would only yield to force, united every element of national life behind him, and set out on a march along the borders of insurrection. Six years after entering Westminster, he already held the destiny of the government in his hands. He was imprisoned, but from his cell in Kilmainham he concluded a pact with the ministers who had jailed him.[24] When the attempt at blackmail failed with the confession and suicide of Pigott, the Liberal government offered him a portfolio. Not only did Parnell turn it down, but he ordered all his followers likewise to refuse any ministerial post whatsoever, and forbade the municipalities and public corporations in Ireland from officially receiving any member of the British royal family until a British government restored autonomy to Ireland.[25] The Liberals were forced to accept these humiliating conditions, and Gladstone, in 1886, read the first Home Rule Bill before parliament.

Parnell's fall came in the midst of these events like a bolt from the blue. He fell helplessly in love with a married woman, and when the husband Captain O'Shea requested a divorce, the ministers Glad-Stone and Morley openly refused to legislate in favour of Ireland if the felon stayed on as leader of the Nationalist Party.[26] Parnell did not appear or defend himself at the trial. He denied the right of a minister to exercise a veto over the political affairs of Ireland, and refused to resign. He was deposed by the Nationalists obeying Glad-stone's orders. Of the eighty-three deputies, only eight remained faithful to him.[27] The Irish press poured the phials of their spitefulness over him and the woman he loved. The peasants of Castlecomer threw quicklime in his eyes.[28] He went from county to county, from city to city, 'like a hunted hind', a spectral figure with the signs of death upon his brow.[29] Within a year he died of a broken heart at the age of forty-five.

The shade of the 'uncrowned king' will weigh upon the hearts of those who remember him, when the new Ireland soon enters into the palace *fimbriis aureis circumamicta varietatibus*:[30] but it will not be a vindictive shade. The sadness that devastated his soul was, perhaps, the profound conviction that, in his hour of need, one of the disciples who had dipped his hand into the bowl with him was about to betray him.[31] To have fought until the very end with this desolating certainty in his soul is his first and greatest claim to nobility. In his last proud appeal to his people, he implored his fellow-countrymen not to throw him to the English wolves howling around him. It redounds to the honour of his fellow-countrymen that they did not fail that desperate appeal. They did not throw him to the English wolves: they tore him apart themselves.[32]

James Joyce

THE CITY OF THE TRIBES:
ITALIAN MEMORIES IN AN IRISH PORT

Galway, *August*

The lazy Dubliner who does not travel much and knows his country only by hearsay thinks that the inhabitants of Galway are of Spanish stock, and that it is impossible to walk through the gloomy laneways of the city of the tribes without coming across a true Spanish type with olive features and crow-black hair. The Dubliner is both wrong and right. Nowadays, at least, dark hair and eyes are rare in Galway where, for the most part, a Titian hue of red dominates. The old Spanish houses are in ruins and tufts of weeds are growing in the splays of the bay windows. Outside the town walls rise the suburbs, new, gay and thoughtless of the past. However, it is enough to close one's eyes against this unsettling modernity just for a moment, and the 'Spanish City' can be seen in the shadows of history.

The City, lying over countless little islands, is veined in all directions by small rivers, cataracts, ponds, and canals. It lies on the bottom of a vast inlet on the Atlantic Ocean in which the entire British navy could anchor. At the mouth of the gulf the three Aran islands, lying like sleeping whales on the grey waters,[1] form a natural breakwater that holds back the assault of the Atlantic breakers. The little lighthouse on the northern island casts a weak beam of light westwards, the last greeting of the Old to the New World, vainly and obstinately calling foreign merchants who have not landed here for many years.

Yet, in the Middle Ages, these waters were ploughed by thousands of foreign ships. The signs on the street corners recall the connections of the city with Latin Europe: Madeira Street, Merchant Street, Spaniards Walk, Madeira Island, Lombard Street, Velasquez Palmyra Avenue. Oliver Cromwell's letters testify that Galway was the second port of the United Kingdom, and the first in the whole kingdom for Spanish and Italian trade.[2] In the first decade of the fourteenth century, a Florentine merchant, Andrea Gerardo, was the collector of custom duties for the city; on the list of mayors in the seventeenth century, we find the name of Giovanni Fante.[3] The city

has St Nicholas of Bari as its patron saint, and the corporation seal
bears an image of the saint, patron of sailors and children.[4] During
the trial of the martyr king, the papal envoy, Cardinal Rinuccini,
came to Galway and placed the city under papal edict. The clergy
and laity refused to recognize his authority, and the fiery Cardinal
smashed the bell of the Carmelite church and posted two priests
from his own cohorts at the door of the church to prevent the faithful from entering.[5] The parochial house of St Nicholas still con-
serves a record of another Italian prelate from the Middle Ages: a
signed letter from the notorious Borgia.[6] In the same house there is a
curious document left by an Italian traveller of the sixteenth century,
in which the writer says that, although he had travelled throughout
the world, he never saw in one glance what he saw in Galway: a priest
raising the host, a pack chasing a deer, a vessel entering the harbour
under full sail and a salmon killed by a spear.[7]

Almost all the wine imported into the kingdom from Spain, Portugal, the Canary Islands, and Italy used to pass through this port.
The amount imported annually amounted to one thousand five hundred 'tuns', or, in other words, almost two million litres.[8] Such was
the importance of this trade that the Dutch government proposed
buying a large estate nearby the city and paying for it by covering the
land in silver coins. The corporation, fearful of foreign competition,
replied through an envoy that it agreed on the condition that the
coins would be placed vertically on the ground. The Dutch response
to this very kind counter-offer has not yet been received.[9]

For many centuries all municipal and ecclesiastical administration
was in the hands of the descendants of the fourteen tribes whose
names are recorded in four lame lines of verse.[10] The strangest and
most interesting historical document in the archives of the city is the
descriptive map that was made for the Duke of Lorraine in the
seventeenth century, when his Highness wanted to assure himself of
the wealth of the city on the occasion of a request for a loan from his
English cousin, the merry monarch. The map, which is full of
engravings and symbolic captions, was the work of Henry Joyce,
Dean of the Chapters of the city.[11] The edges of the parchment are
adorned with the heraldic arms of the tribes, and the map itself
resembles more than anything a topographical symphony on the
theme of the number of the tribes. The cartographer lists and draws
fourteen bastions, fourteen wall-towers, fourteen main thorough-

fares, fourteen monasteries, fourteen castles, fourteen laneways and then, sliding into a minor key, he lists and draws seven ascents to the walls, seven gardens, seven altars for the Corpus Christi procession, seven markets and seven other wonders. Among the last of these—in fact, in very last place—the worthy Dean lists the 'old pigeon house located in the southern district of the city'.[12] The most famous of all the tribes was that of the Lynches. In the century and a half that runs from the founding of the city and the devastating raids of Cromwellian soldiers, a member of this family occupied the post of chief magistrate no less than eighty-three times. The most tragic event in the history of the city was in 1493 when the young Walter Lynch, only son of the mayor James Lynch FitzStephen, paid the penalty for a crime he had committed.[13] The mayor, a rich wine merchant, undertook a journey in that year to Spain, where he was guest of a Spanish friend of his, a certain Gomez. This latter's son, while listening to the tales of the traveller every night, became enamoured of faraway Ireland, and asked his father for permission to accompany their guest on his return journey home. His father hesitated: times were dangerous and travellers were wont to make their wills before departing for known or unknown shores. The mayor Lynch, however, made himself guarantor of the youth's safety, and they left together. When he had arrived in Galway, the young Spaniard became friendly with the mayor's son, Walter, a wild young man of impulsive character who was paying court to Agnes Blake, the daughter of another grandee of the city. A love very soon grew up between Agnes and the Spaniard. One evening, while Gomez was leaving the Blake house, Walter Lynch, who had been lying in wait, stuck a dagger in his back and, blind with rage, dragged the corpse along the road and threw it into a pond. The murder was discovered and young Walter was arrested and tried. The judge was his father, mayor of the city. Deaf to the claims of blood and mindful only of the honour of the city and his own pledged word, he condemned the murderer to death. His friends tried in vain to dissuade him. The people, moved by pity for the unhappy youth, besieged the mayor's house, the mournful castle that still darkens the main street.[14] The mayor remained unyielding even when the executioner refused to carry out the sentence. Father and son sat up together in the prison cell on the eve of the execution, praying until dawn. When the hour of the execution arrived, father and son appeared together at the window of the house. They kissed and bade one another farewell, then, before the eyes of the appalled crowd, the father himself hanged his son from the window beam.[15]

The old Spanish houses are in ruins. The castles of the tribes have been demolished. Tufts of weeds grow in the windows and in the wide courtyards. Above the porticoes the heraldic arms cut into the black stone are fading: the wolf of the Capitol with the two twin brothers, the two-headed eagle of the Hapsburgs, the black bull of the Darcy family, descendants of Charlemagne.[16] In the city of Galway, writes an ancient chronicler, reign the passions of pride and lust.[17]

The evening is silent and grey. From afar, from beyond the falling waters, comes a humming sound. It is like the buzzing of bees around their hive. It comes nearer. Seven young men come into sight, bagpipe players, at the head of a train of people. They pass proud and martial, heads uncovered, playing a music that is vague and strange. In the uncertain light the green plaids hanging from their right shoulders and their saffron kilts are just distinguishable. They turn into the road to the Presentation Convent and, while the vague music permeates the twilight, in the windows of the convent appear, one by one, the white wimples of the nuns.[18]

James Joyce

THE MIRAGE OF THE FISHERMAN OF ARAN: ENGLAND'S SAFETY VALVE IN CASE OF WAR

Galway, *2 September*

The steamboat, carrying a small load of day-trippers, pulls away from the quays under the watchful eyes of the Scottish director who is absorbed in a dream of mental arithmetic. It goes out from the small port of Galway and takes to the open sea, leaving behind on its right-hand side the village of the Claddagh, a cluster of cabins outside the city walls. A cluster of cabins, and yet a kingdom. Until a few years ago, the village elected its own king, had its own style of dress, made its own laws and lived apart. The wedding ring of the inhabitants is still adorned with the seal of the king: two hands joined together and holding a crowned heart.[1]

We leave for Aranmor, the holy island which sleeps like a large shark on the grey waters of the Atlantic Ocean which the islanders call the old sea. Under the waters and along the coast of this gulf lies the wreckage of a fleet of ships from the unfortunate Spanish Armada. After their defeat in the Channel, the ships set sail northwards where they were scattered by squalls and ocean storms. The peasants of County Galway, recalling the long friendship between Spain and Ireland, hid the fugitives from the revenge of the English garrison and gave holy burial to the shipwrecked dead, wrapping the corpses in white cloth. The waters have repented. Every year on 14 August, when the herring fishing starts, the waters of the gulf are blessed. The flotilla of fishing boats leaves from the Claddagh preceded by a flagship on whose deck stands a Dominican friar. When it has reached a favourable point, the flotilla comes to a halt, the fishermen kneel and bare their heads, and the friar, murmuring prayers to ward off ill-fortune, shakes his aspergill over the sea, and divides the dark air in the form of a cross.

A lick of white sand on the right marks the place where the new transatlantic port might be destined to rise.[2] My companion unfolds a large map on which planned shipping lanes from Galway to the large Canadian ports branch out, turn and crisscross one another.

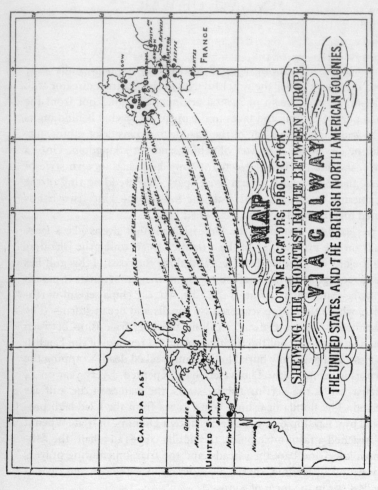

'Planned shipping lanes from Galway to the large Canadian ports branch out, turn and crisscross one another . . . *Quasi lilium germinans germinabit*' (Galway Harbour Commissioners)

According to the figures, the voyage from Europe to America will take less than three days. From Galway, the last European port, to St John's (Newfoundland), the steamboat will take two days and sixteen hours; from Galway to Halifax, the first Canadian port, three days and ten hours. The text of the booklet accompanying the map is bristling with figures, cost estimates, and oceanographic sections. The writer makes a heartfelt appeal to the British admiralty, to the railway company, to the chamber of commerce, and to the Irish populace. The new port would be a safety valve for England in the event of war. From Canada, the grain warehouse of the United Kingdom, the great cargoes of grain would enter into the Irish port, thereby avoiding the dangers of navigation in St George's Channel and enemy fleets. In peacetime the new line would be the shortest path between one continent and the other. A large part of the merchandise and passengers that now land at Liverpool would in future land at Galway, proceeding directly to London via Dublin and Holyhead.[3] The old decaying city would arise once more. Wealth and vital energy from the New World would run through this new artery into blood-drained Ireland. Once again, after ten centuries or so, the mirage that dazzled the poor fisherman of Aran, St Brendan's follower and emulator, appears in the distance, vague and tremulous on the mirror of the ocean.[4]

Christopher Columbus, as everyone knows, is venerated by posterity because he was the last to discover America. A thousand years before the Genoese sailor was laughed at in Salamanca, St Brendan set sail for the New World from the barren strand towards which our boat is headed, and, crossing the ocean, landed on the Florida coast. At that time the island was wooded and fertile.[5] In the shade of the wood lay a hermitage of Irish monks, founded in the fourth century by Enda, a saint of royal stock. Finnian left this hermitage to become bishop of Lucca. Here lived the visionary St Fursa, described in the Irish hagiographic calendar as a precursor to Dante Alighieri.[6] A medieval copy of the visions of St Fursa depicts the journey of the saint from Hell to Heaven, from the grim valleys of the four fires amidst the ranks of the diabolic, up through the universe to the divine light reflected by countless angelic wings. These visions might have served as a model for the poet of *The Divine Comedy*, who (like Columbus) is venerated by posterity because he was the last to visit and describe the three kingdoms of the souls.

Fragile rowing-boats of stretched canvas are drawn up to dry on the shore of the bay. Four islanders descend towards the sea moving nimbly across the rocks covered in the purple and reddish seaweed that can be seen in the shops of the greengrocers of Galway. The fisherman of Aran is sure-footed. He wears a rough, flat sandal of oxhide, open at the shank, without heels and tied with laces of rawhide. He dresses in wool as thick as felt and wears a black, wide-brimmed hat.[7]

We halt, uncertain, in one of the steep laneways. An islander, who speaks an English all of his own, bids us good day, adding that it has been a horrible summer, thanks be to God. The phrase which at first seems to be one of the usual Irish blunders comes, rather, from the inmost heart of human resignation. The man who said it bears a princely name, O'Flaherty, the name which the young Oscar Wilde proudly had printed on the cover of his first book.[8] But time and the wind have razed to the ground the civilization to which he belongs— the sacred oaken groves of the island, the principality of his fore-fathers, his language and perhaps the name of that Aran hermit who used to be called the dove of the church.[9] Around the shrubs grow-ing with difficulty on the hillocks of the island, his imagination has woven legends and fables that reveal the hereditary taint of his psyche. Under his apparent simplicity there is something sceptical, humorous, spectral. He looks away when he has spoken and lets the enthusiastic scholar note down in his pocket-book the amazing fact that it was from yonder whitethorn bush that Joseph of Arimathea cut his walking stick.[10]

A little old woman comes up to us and invites us into her house. She places an enormous teapot on the table, a loaf of bread and some salted butter. The islander, who is her son, sits next to the fireplace and answers my companion's queries with an embarrassed and humble air. He does not know how old he is, but he says that he will be old soon. He does not know why he has not taken a wife: perhaps because there are no women for him. My companion again asks him why there are no women for him, and the islander, taking off his cap, buries his face in the soft wool, confused and smiling. Aran, he says, is the strangest place in the world, a poor place; but however poor it may be, when my companion tries to pay, the old woman rejects his coin almost in anger, asking us if we want to dishonour her house. A delicate thick drizzle is falling from the grey clouds. The rainy mist advances from the west, while the steamboat despairingly calls out to the latecomers. Little by little the island disappears, wrapped in a slow smoky veil.[11] The three Danish sailors, seated impassively on the hill top, also disappear. They were out summer-fishing on the ocean, and stopped off at Aran. Silent and melancholic, they look as if they are thinking of the Danish hordes that burned the city of Galway in the eighth century and of the Irish lands which, as legend has it, are included in the dowries of Danish girls; they look as if they are dreaming of reconquering them. The rain is falling on the islands and on the sea. It is raining as it can rain only in Ireland. Under the forecastle, where a girl is noisily flirting with a deckhand, holding him on her knees, we open up our map once more. In the twilight, we cannot make out the names of the ports, but the lines that start from Galway, branching and extending outwards, recall the symbol placed next to the arms of his native city by the mystic, perhaps even prophetic Dean of the Chapters: *Quasi lilium germinans germinabit et quasi terebinthus extendens ramos suos.*[12]

James Joyce

POLITICS AND CATTLE DISEASE

Though the country has not been deceived by the pitiable endeavours of Unionists and factionists[1] to make political capital out of the national calamity involved in the outbreak of the foot and mouth disease in a few Irish districts, Mr Dillon renders a valuable service by pointing out the injury done by the dishonest clamour in which the mischief-makers have indulged.[2] They have, he points out, played into the hands of English Protectionists like Mr Henry Chaplin and Mr Bathurst, whose object is not the security of English herds, but the prolonged exclusion of Irish cattle from the English markets.[3] By enabling such enemies of the Irish farmer to raise the cry that any relaxation of the restrictions that may be proposed is due, not to Mr Runciman's unbiased opinion that the conditions justify the relaxation,[4] but to 'Irish dictation', they have simply raised fresh obstructions to the fair treatment of the Irish stock-owners and traders' claims. All these stupid threats and calls upon the Irish Party to 'turn out the government' have been ammunition to the English exclusionists. We have seen how the *Globe* has turned them to account.[5] It will have been noticed, too, that none of these Unionist fire-eaters have appealed to their own party for assistance in the matter. According to the London correspondent of the *Irish Times*, 'Irish members of all shades of opinion are asking for the removal of restrictions, but without success.'[6] This will be news to most people. Hitherto Irish members of the Unionist shade of opinion have been only remarkable for their silence on the matter. Not one of the Irish Unionist Party attended the deputation to Mr Runciman. Mr Chaplin and Mr Bathurst have been allowed to rampage without a word of protest from an Irish Unionist member. Yet the Unionist landlords, land agents, and eleven-months' men,[7] and the defeated factionist candidates who have been joining in their cry, have not addressed a word of protest or appeal to the Irish Unionist leaders to put a snaffle on Mr Chaplin. The simple fact is sufficient to explain the motives and purpose of all the Unionist talk upon the matter.

Mr Dillon points out what would be the certain consequence of action of the kind recommended to the Irish Party. Not only would it involve the sacrifice of the Home Rule Bill and the Home Rule movement, but it would defeat the very object alleged by these advisers. After such an incident no British Minister dare open the English ports for months, because his motives would be instantly challenged. Equally bad and dangerous has been the talk about the unimportance of the disease, and the advice given by some foolish people to the farmers to conceal it. Fortunately the Irish farmers have not listened to the advice. They have proved their common-sense by reporting every suspicious case. Their anxiety to assist the public authorities has been proved by the fact that a majority of the cases so reported have proved to be cases of some other ailment. It is obvious that only by such action can the confidence of the trading public be so restored that the English minister will be free to act upon the facts disclosed. The talk that the disease is only 'like measles in children and that all the cattle should be allowed to get it', like the foolish advice to farmers to conceal cases of the disease, is probably the explanation of the extraordinary official suggestion that the healthy areas should be denied their rights 'until the situation disclose itself further'. The situation is fully disclosed, because the Irish stock-owners have been perfectly above-board in the matter. They ought not to be held responsible for the stupidities of irresponsible speakers like those whom we have quoted. But a moment's reflection will convince the stock-owners that stupid people of the kind are worth as much as ten outbreaks of the disease to persons like the Right Hon. Henry Chaplin and Mr Charles Bathurst.

We do not mean to urge that the Irish farmers and traders should relax their efforts or cease their agitation. Quite the contrary. The situation is critical, and they have sound and solid reasons for demanding the reopening of the ports to healthy Irish stock. These sound and solid reasons are only weakened by menaces that defeat themselves, and by declarations that allow slanderers to say that the disease is being concealed in Ireland. The stock-owners can point to the fact that since the original outbreak, when the existence of the disease could scarcely have been suspected, not a single prosecution for concealment has taken place, though the Constabulary and the officials of the Department are actively watching for symptoms of the disease all over the country. A fact of that kind is the most complete justification of the demand for equality of treatment with the English healthy areas, which the Irish stock-owners and traders are pressing. In putting forward that demand they have the full and hearty co-operation of the Irish Party and its leader. The influence of the party will be exercised no less strongly, because it is being used in a legitimate and reasonable way, and in a manner that will leave the exclusionists with no ground for slander. The Irish Department is, we have the strongest grounds for believing, no less active. Mr Russell has not concealed his endorsement of the claim of the Irish stock-owners.[8] On the contrary, he has taken the strong step of publicly proclaiming his agreement. His statement is the best justification for a vigorous agitation against the unreasonable prolongation of the embargo. It is essential to maintain that agitation, but it is no less essential to discountenance the use of silly and mischievous language, which is the only justification the intimidators of Mr Runciman can plead for their attitude.

PROGRAMME NOTES FOR THE ENGLISH PLAYERS

THE TWELVE POUND LOOK

BY J. M. BARRIE[1]

One Sims is about to be knighted: possibly, as the name would sug-gest, for having patented a hairgrower He is discovered rehearsing his part with his wife whose portrait we see on the wall, painted by a Royal Academician, also knighted, presumably for having painted the label for the hairgrower. A typist is announced. This typist is his runaway wife of some fourteen years before. From their conversation we learn that she left him not for another man but to work out her salvation by typewriting. She had saved twelve pounds and bought a typewriter. The twelve pound look, she says, is that look of indepen dence in a wife's eye which every husband should beware of. The new knight's new wife, 'noted for her wit'—chary of it, too—seems likely to acquire the look if given time. Typewriters, however, are rather scarce at present.

RIDERS TO THE SEA

BY JOHN M. SYNGE[2]

Synge's first play, written in Paris in 1902 out of his memories of Aran. The play shows a mother and her dead son, her last, the αναγκη[3] being the inexorable sea which claims all her sons. Seamus and Patch and Stephen and Shaun. Whether a brief tragedy be possible or not (a point on which Aristotle had some doubts) the ear and the heart mislead one gravely if this brief scene from 'poor Aran' be not the work of a tragic poet.[4]

THE DARK LADY OF THE SONNETS
BY G. B. SHAW[5]

Mr Shaw here presents three orthodox figures—a virgin queen, a Shakespeare sober at midnight and a free giver of gold, and the dark-haired maid of honour, Mary Fitton, discovered in the eighties by Thomas Tyler and Mr Harris.[6] Shakespeare comes to Whitehall to meet her and learns from a well-languaged beefeater that Mr W. H.[7] has forestalled him. The poet vents his spleen on the first woman who passes. It is the queen and she seems not loth to be accosted. She orders the maid of honour out of the way. When Shakespeare, however, begs her to endow his theatre she refers him with fine cruelty to her lord treasurer and leaves him. The most regicide of playwrights prays God to save her and goes home weighing against a lightened purse, love's treason, an old queen's leer and the evil eye of a government official, a horror still to come.

THE HEATHER FIELD
BY EDWARD MARTYN[8]

Edward Martyn, the author of the 'Heather Field', has in company with W. B. Yeats inaugurated the Irish National Theatre. He is an accomplished musician and man of letters. As a dramatist he follows the school of Ibsen and therefore occupies a unique position in Ireland, as the dramatists writing for the National Theatre have chiefly devoted their energies to peasant drama. The plot of the 'Heather Field', the best known of Martyn's plays, is as follows:

Carden Tyrrell has made an unhappy marriage early in his youth and is now living on bad terms with his wife, Grace. He is an idealist who has never cared for the ordinary routine of life. Forced to settle down on his estate and finding most of his neighbours uncongenial, he has idealised farming and is engaged at the opening of the play in trying to bring into cultivation a vast tract of heather land. To carry on this work he has had to borrow large sums of money. His friend Barry Ussher and his brother Miles warn him of the danger he is running, but in vain. They urge that he is likely to get little profit from his work, for Ussher knows that it is very hard to reclaim lands on which heather grows, for the wild heather may break out upon them soon again. Grace learns that Carden intends borrowing further large sums of money and fears that he will ruin himself. Carden has admitted to his brother Miles that he hears mysterious voices in the air and that every day life is becoming more and more unreal to him. Convinced that he has lost his reason, Grace confides to her friend, Lady Shrule, that she has arranged for two doctors to come and see Carden; she hopes to have him certified as a lunatic and put under restraint. Lady Shrule sympathises, but neither she nor her husband will do anything to help. The doctors come on an excuse of examining Kit, Carden's son, but the plan is defeated by Barry Ussher who warns them of the danger they are running by falling in with Grace's scheme. However matters go from bad to worse; Carden quarrels with his tenants, thus losing further money and having to have police protection. He is unable to pay the interest on the sums he has borrowed and is threatened with financial ruin. At this crisis Kit comes back from a ride and shows his father some wild heather buds which he has found in the heather field. Carden loses his reason and memory; his mind goes back to happy days before his marriage. As Grace tried to domesticate him, so he has tried to domesticate the heather field, and in each case the old wild nature avenges itself.

FROM A BANNED WRITER
TO A BANNED SINGER

He strides, booted with anger, along the spurs of Monte Rossini, accompanied solely by Fidelion, his mastiff's voice. They quarrel consonantly about the vocality of the wind, calling each and its other clamant names.[1]

*

Just out of kerryosity howlike is a Sullivan? It has the fortefaccia of a Markus Brutas, the wingthud of a spreadeagle, the body uniformed of a metropoliceman with the brass feet of a collared grand. It cresces up in Aquilone but diminuends austrowards. It was last seen and heard of by some macgilliccuddies above a lonely valley of their reeks, duskening the greylight as it flew, its cry echechohoing among the anfractuosities: *pour la dernière fois!* The blackbulled ones, stampeding, drew in their horns, all appailed and much upset, which explaints the guttermilk on their overcoats.[2]

*

A pugilant gang theirs, per Bantry! Don Philip, Jay Hell, Big O'Barry of the Bornstorms, Arthur, siruraganist who loosed that chor. Damnen. And tramp, tramp, tramp. And T. Deum sullivamus.[3]

Faust of all, of curse, damnation. But given Parigot's Trocadéro for his drawingroom with Ballaclavier in charge at the pianone the voice becomes suburban, sweethearted and subdued. The heat today was really too much of a hot thing and even Impressario is glad to walk his garden in the cool of the evening, fanning his furnaceface with his sweltertails. *Merci, doux crépuscule!*[4]

*

Who is this that advances in maresblood caftan, like Hiesous in Finisterre, his eyeholes phyllistained, his jewbones of a crossbacked? A little child shall lead him. Why, it's Strongman Simpson, Timothy Nathan, now of Simpson's on the Grill! Say, Tim Nat, bald winepresser, hast not one air left? But yeth he hath. Regard! Auscult! He upbraces for supremacy to the potence of Mosthigh and calls upon his baiters and their templum: You daggones, be flat![5]

*

What was in that long long note he just delivered? For the laib of me I cannot tell. More twopenny tosh and luxus languor about I singabob you? No such thing, O son of an envelope. Dr to J. S. Just a pennyplain loafletter from Braun and Brotmann and it will take no rebutter. You may bark Mrs Liebfraumich as long as you love but you must not burk the baker. Pay us disday our daily bread. And oblige.[6]

*

On his native heath. Speech! Speech! cry the godlets. We are in land of Dan. But their words of Muskerry are harsh after that song of Othello. *Orateur ne peut, charlatan ne daigne, Sullivan est.*[7]

*

11.59 p.m. *Durch diese hohle Gasse muss er kommen.* Guillaume's shot telled, sure enough. But will that labour member for Melckthal be able to bring off his coo for the odd and twentieth supererogatory time? *Wartemal!* That stagesquall has passed over like water off a Helvetian's back. And there they are, yodelling yokels, none the worse for their ducking and *gewittermassen* as free as you fancy to quit their homeseek *heimat* and leave the ritzprinz of their chyber-schwitzerhoofs all over both worlds, cisalpic and transatlantine. And how confederate of gay old Gioacchino to have composed this finale so that Kamerad Wagner might be saved the annoyance of finding flauts for his *Feuerzauber! Pass auf!* Only four bars more! He draws the breathbow: that arrownote's coming. Aim well, Arnold, and mind puur blind Jemmy in the stalls! But, great Scott, whas is thas for a larm! Half a ton of brass in the band, ten thousand throats from Thalwyl: Libertay. libertay lauded over the land. (Tay!) And pap goes the Calville![8]

*

Saving is believing but can thus be? Is this our model vicar of Saint Wartburgh's, the reverend Mr Townhouser, Mus.Bac., dis-covered flagrant in a *montagne de passe*? She is obvious and is on her three-legged sofa in a half yard of casheselks, Madame de la Pierreuse. How duetonically she hands him his harp that once, bit-ting him, whom caught is willing: do blease to, fickar! She's as only roman as any *puttana madonna* but the trouble is that the reverend T is reformed. She, *simplicissima*, wants her little present from the reverend since she was wirk worklike never so nice with him. But he harps along about Salve Regina Terrace and Liza, mine Liza, and sweet Marie. Till she cries: bilk! And he calls: blak! O.u.t. spells out!⁹

*

Since we are bound for a change of supper, was that really in faith the reverend Townhouser for he seemed so verdamnably like? *Ecco trovato!* Father Lucullus Ballytheacker, the parish priest of Tarbert. He was a songful soul at the keyboard and could achieve his Château Kirwan with cigar thuriferant, without ministrance from platform or pulpit, chase or church. Nor used he to deny his Mary neither. *Nullo modo*. Up to maughty London came a muftimummed P.P. Censored.¹⁰

*

Have you got your knife handy? asks the bellman Saint Andy. Here he is and brandnew, answers Bartholomew. Get ready, get ready, scream the bells of Our Lady. And make sure they're quite killed, adds the gentle Clotilde. Your attention, sirs, please, bawls big Brother Supplice. *Pour la foi! Pour la foi!* booms the great Auxerrois.¹¹

*

Grand spectacular exposition of gorge cutting, mortarfiring and general martyrification, bigleighted up with erst classed instrumental music. *Pardie!* There's more sang in that Sceine than mayer's beer at the Guildhall. Is he a beleaper in Irisk luck? Can he swhipstake his valentine off to Dublin and weave her a frock of true blue poplin to be neat for the time Hugenut Cromwell comes over, gentlest lovejesus as ever slit weasand? Their cause is well sainted and they are centain to won. Still I'll pointe half my crown on Raoul de Nangis, doublet mauve and cuffs of buff. Attagirl! *Ah ah ah ah ah ah viens!* Piffpaff, but he's done it, the bully mastiff again. And woops with him through the window tallyhoed by those friers pecheurs who are selfbarked. Dominie's canes. Can you beat that, you papish yelpers? To howl with the pups!¹²

*

Enrico, Giacomo and Giovanni, three dulcetest of our songsters, in liontamers overcoats, holy communion ties and cliqueclaquehats, are met them at a gaslamp. It is kaputt and throws no light at all on the trio's tussletusculums. Rico is for carousel and Giaco for luring volupy but Nino, the sweetly dulcetest, tuningfork among tenors, for the best of all; after hunger and sex comes dear old *somnium*, brought on by prayer. Their lays, blent of feastings, June roses and ether, link languidly in the unlit air. Arrives a type in readymade, dicky and bowler hat, manufactured by Common Sense and Co. Ltd., carrying a bag of tools. Preludingly he conspews a portugaese into the gutter, recitativing: now then, gents, by your leave! And, to his job. Who is this hardworking guy? No one but Geoge, Geoge who shifts the garbage can, Geoge who stokes in the engine room, Geoge who has something to say to the gas (*tes gueules!*) and mills the wheel go right go round and makes the world grow lighter. *Lux!* The aforesung Henry. James and John stand mouthshut. Wot did I say? Hats off *primi assoluti!* Send him canorious, long to lung over us, high topsea-soarious! Guard safe our Geoge![13]

[ON THE MORAL RIGHT OF AUTHORS]

A particular point in the history of the publication of *Ulysses* in the United States seems to me both interesting and noteworthy: it makes explicit one aspect of an author's right over his work which has not been brought to light until now. The importation of *Ulysses* had been forbidden since 1922, and this ban was not lifted until 1934. In such circumstances it had been impossible to secure copyright for the United States. In 1925 an unscrupulous American publisher circulated a truncated edition of *Ulysses* over which the author, unable to secure copyright, had no control. An international protest signed by 167 writers was published and legal proceedings were begun. The result of these proceedings was the judgement delivered at a sitting of the Supreme Court of New York on 27 December 1928, a judgement which forbade the defendants (the publishers) 'from using the name of the plaintiff (Joyce), first, in any journal, periodical or other publication published by them; second, in relation to any book, piece of writing, manuscript, understood to be the work entitled *Ulysses*' (Joyce against *Two Worlds Monthly* and Samuel Roth, II Dep. Supreme Court New York, 27 December 1928).

It is, I believe, possible to reach a judicial conclusion from this judgement to the effect that, while unprotected by the written law of copyright and even if it is banned, a work belongs to its author by virtue of a natural right and that thus the law can protect an author against the mutilation and the publication of his work just as he is protected against the misuse that can be made of his name.

APPENDIX

The Appendix contains the original Italian and French versions of items which appear above in translation.

The nine articles from *Il Piccolo della Sera* are placed in the order that Joyce proposed for a book to which he gave the title, *L'Irlanda alla sbarra*. The six remaining items are placed in chronological order.

L'IRLANDA ALLA SBARRA

IRELAND AT THE BAR

Parecchi anni or sono si tenne in Irlanda un processo sensazionale. Nella provincia occidentale, in un luogo romito, che si chiama Maamtrasna, era stato commesso un eccidio. Furono arrestati quattro o cinque villici del paese, appartenenti tutti all'antica tribù dei Joyce. Il più anziano di loro, tale Milesio Joyce, vecchio di sessant'anni, era particolarmente sospetto alla gendarmeria. L'opinione pubblica lo giudicava allora innocente ed oggi lo stima un martire. Tanto il vecchio quanto gli altri accusati ignoravano l'inglese. La Corte dovette ricorrere ai servizi di un interprete. L'interrogatorio svoltosi col tramite di costui ebbe a volta del comico e a volta del tragico. Dall'un lato vi era l'interprete formalista e dall'altro il patriarca della misera tribù, il quale, poco avvezzo alle usanze civili, sembrava istupidito da tutte quelle cerimonie giudiziarie.

Il magistrato diceva:

—Chieda all'imputato se vide la donna quella mattina.

La domanda gli era riferita in irlandese e il vecchio prorompeva in spiegazioni intricate, gesticolando, facendo appello agli altri accusati, al cielo. Poi, sfinito dallo sforzo, taceva e l'interprete, volgendosi al magistrato, diceva:

—Afferma di no, 'your worship'.

—Gli chieda se era in quei pressi a quell'ora.

Il vecchio si rimetteva a parlare, a protestare, a gridare, quasi fuori di sé dall'angoscia di non capire e di non farsi capire, piangendo d'ira e di terrore. E l'interprete, di nuovo, secco:

—Dice di no, 'yo[u]r worship'. Ad interrogatorio finito si dichiarò provata la colpabilità del povero vecchio, che fu rinviato al tribunale superiore, il quale lo condannò al capestro. Il giorno dell'esecuzione della sentenza, la piazza davanti al carcere era gremita di gente che, in ginocchio, ululava in irlandese preghiere pel riposo dell'anima di Milesio Joyce. La leggenda vuole che neppure il carnefice potesse farsi comprendere dalla vittima e, indignato, desse un calcio alla testa dell'infelice per cacciarla nel nodo.

La figura di questo vecchio inebetito, avanzo di una civiltà non nostra, sordomuto dianzi il suo giudice, è la figura simbolica della nazione irlandese alla sbarra dell'opinione pubblica. Essa al pari di lui, non può fare appello alla coscienza moderna dell'Inghilterra e dell'estero. I giornali inglesi fanno da interpreti, fra l'Irlanda e la democrazia inglese, la quale pur dando loro di tratto in tratto ascolto, finisce coll'essere seccata dalle eterne lagnanze dei deputati nazionalisti venuti in casa sua, come ella crede, a turbarne l'ordine e a estorcere denari. All'estero non si parla dell'Irlanda se non quando scoppiano colà tumulti come quelli che fecero sussultare il telegrafo in questi ultimi giorni. Il pubblico sfiorando i dispacci giunti da Londra, che pur mancando di acredine, hanno qualche cosa della laconicità dell'interprete suddetto, si figura allora gli irlandesi come malandrini, dai visi asimmetrici, scorazzanti nella notte con lo scopo di fare la pelle ad ogni unionista. E al vero sovrano dell'Irlanda, il papa, tali notizie giungono come tanti cani in chiesa; le grida, infiacchite dal viaggio lungo, sono già quasi spente quando arrivano alla porta di bronzo: i messi del popolo che non rinnegò mai nel passato la Santa Sede, l'unico popolo cattolico pel quale la fede vuol dire anche l'esercizio della fede, vengono respinti in favore dei messi di un monarca, il quale, discendente di apostati, s'apostatizzò solennemente nel giorno della sua consacrazione, dichiarando in presenza dei suoi nobili e comuni che i riti della chiesa romano-cattolica sono 'superstizione ed idolatria'.

Gli irlandesi sparsi in tutto il mondo sono venti milioni. L'isola di smeraldo ne raccoglie solo una piccola parte. Pure l'osservatore, pensando come l'Inghilterra imperni tutta la sua politica interna sulla questione irlandese, mentre procede con ampiezza di criteri nello sbrigare le questioni più complesse della politica coloniale, non può far[e] a meno di chiedersi se il canale di San Giorgio non getti un abisso più profondo dell'Oceano fra l'Irlanda e la superba dominatrice.

La questione irlandese difatti non è risolta ancora oggi, dopo sei secoli di occupazione armata e più di cento anni di quella legislazione inglese che ridusse la popolazione dell'isola infelice da otto a quattro milioni, quadruplicò le imposte, aggrovigliò il problema agrario di molti nodi di più.

Invero, non vi è problema più arruffato di questo. Gli irlandesi stessi ne capiscono poco; gli inglesi ancor meno, per gli altri popoli è buio pesto. Ma gli irlandesi sanno invece come esso sia la causa di tutte le loro sofferenze e perciò adottano sovente metodi di soluzione violentissimi. Per esempio, ventotto anni fa, vedendosi ridotti alla miseria dalle angherie dei latifondisti, ricusarono di pagare gli affitti ed ottennero dal Gladstone provvedimenti e riforme. Oggi, vedendo i pascoli pieni di buoi ben pasciuti, mentre un ottavo della popolazione è registrata come priva di mezzi di sussistenza, scacciano i buoi dai poderi. Il Governo liberale, irritato, divisa di ripristinare la tattica coercitiva dei conservatori e la stampa londinese consacra da parecchie settimane innumerevoli articoli alla crisi agraria che dice gravissima e pubblica notizie allarmanti di rivolte agrarie, riprodotte poi dai giornali dell'estero.

Non mi propongo di fare l'esegesi della questione agraria irlandese né di narrare il retroscena della politica bifronte del Governo, ma credo utile fare una modesta rettifica. Chi abbia letto i telegrammi lanciati da Londra credeva certo che l'Irlanda attraversi un periodo di delinquenza eccezionale. Criterio erroneo, quanto mai. La delinquenza in Irlanda è inferiore a quella di qualsiasi altro paese di Europa; in Irlanda non vi è la malavita organizzata; quando avviene uno di quei fatti che i giornalisti parigini chiamano, con atroce ironia, un idillio rosso, tutto il paese ne è scosso. Ci furono, è vero, in questi ultimi mesi due morti violente in Irlanda: ma per opera delle truppe inglesi: a Belfast, dove i soldati caricarono la folla inerme, senza pare le intimazioni, e uccisero un uomo e una donna. Ci furono attentati contro il bestiame, ma neppur questi in Irlanda, dove la folla si appagò di aprire le stalle e di scacciare il bestiame per qualche miglio di strada: ma a Great Wyrley, in Inghilterra, ove da sei anni delinquenti bestiali e pazzeschi infuriano contro il bestiame, tanto che le società inglesi non vogliono più assicurarlo.

Cinque anni fa un innocente, ora in libertà, fu condannato ai lavori forzati per appagare l'indignazione pubblica. Ma anche quando egli si trovava in carcere i delitti continuavano. E la settimana scorsa due cavalle furono trovate morte con i soliti tagli nel basso ventre e con le budella sparse sull'erba.

James Joyce

HOME RULE MAGGIORENNE
HOME RULE COMES OF AGE

Ventun'anni fa, la sera del 9 aprile 1886, la viuzza che conduce agli uffici del giornale nazionalista a Dublino era rigurgitante di gente. Di tempo in tempo un bollettino stampato in caratteri da scatola appariva sul muro e la folla poteva in questo modo assistere alla scena che si svolgeva a Westminster ove le gallerie erano state gremite sin dall'alba. L'orazione del primo ministro cominciata alle 4 era durata fino alle 8. Pochi minuti dopo l'ultimo bollettino apparve sul muro 'Gladstone ha conchiuso con una magnifica perorazione dichiarando che il partito liberale inglese rifiuterà di far leggi per l'Inghilterra fino a che essa non conceda una misura di autonomia all'Irlanda.' A questa notizia la folla nella strada scoppiò in grida entusiastiche. Da ogni lato si udì 'Evviva Gladstone', 'Evviva l'Irlanda': gente che non si conosceva si strinse la mano per ratificare il nuovo patto nazionale ed i vecchi piansero addirittura di gioia.

Passano sette anni e siamo al secondo atto dell' 'home rule'. Gladstone, avendo nel frattempo coll'aiuto dei vescovi irlandesi compiuto l'assassinio morale di Parnell, legge la sua misura per la terza volta alla Camera. Il discorso è più corto dell'altro, dura appena un'ora e mezzo. Poi l' 'Home Rule Bill' è passato. La lieta notizia corre sui fili fino alla capitale irlandese, ove suscita un nuovo scoppio d'entusiasmo. Nel salotto del club cattolico si discorre, si discute, si ride, si brinda e si profetizza.

Passano altri quattordici anni e siamo nel 1907. Ventun anni sono passati dal 1886 e quindi la misura gladstoniana deve essere diventata maggiorenne secondo l'usanza inglese. Ma nell'intervallo il Gladstone stesso è morto e la sua misura non è neppure nata. Come egli ben prevedeva subito dopo la terza lettura si è suonato nella Camera superiore lo squillo d'allarme e tutti i lords spirituali e temporali si sono radunati a Westminster in falange solida per dare il colpo di grazia al progetto. I liberali inglesi hanno scordato i loro impegni. Un politicante di quarta fila che dal 1881 al 1886 aveva votato in favore di ogni misura coercitiva per l'Irlanda, indossa il manto di Gladstone. Il posto di capo-segretario irlandese, posto che gli inglesi stessi hanno chiamato la tomba delle riputazioni politiche, è occupato da un giurista letterario, il quale probabilmente quando si presentò due anni fa per la prima volta agli elettori di Bristol sapeva appena i nomi delle contee irlandesi: nonostante gli impegni e le promesse, nonostante l'appoggio del voto irlandese durante un quarto di secolo, nonostante la sua maggioranza enorme ch'è senza precedente nella storia parlamentare dell'Inghilterra, il ministero liberale inglese introduce una misura di devoluzione la quale non va oltre le proposte fatte dall'imperialista Chamberlain nel 1885 e della quale la stampa conservatrice londinese ricusa apertamente di riconoscere la serietà. Questo progetto è passato in prima lettura con una maggioranza di quasi 300 voti e mentre la stampa gialla prorompe in ismanie di collera finta, i lords si consultano fra di loro per decidersi se questo fantoccio vacillante che sta per entrare in lizza sia realmente degno della loro spada.

Probabilmente i lords ammazzeranno la misura, essendo questo il loro mestiere, ma se sono savi esiteranno prima di alienare la simpatia degli irlandesi dall'agitazione costituzionale, precipuamente ora che l'India e l'Egitto sono in subbuglio e le colonie d'oltremare rivendicano una federazione imperiale. Dal loro punto di vista non sarebbe consigliabile di provocare con un rifiuto ostinato una reazione di un popolo il quale, povero in ogni altra cosa, è ricco soltanto d'idee politiche, ha perfezionato la tattica dell'ostruzionismo ed ha fatto della parola 'boicottaggio' un grido di guerra internazionale.

Del resto, l'Inghilterra ha poco da perdere. La misura (che non è la ventesima parte della misura di Home Rule) non dà al consiglio esecutivo a Dublino nessun potere legislativo, nessun potere di fissare né di controllare le imposte, nessun controllo su 39 dei 47 uffici governativi, fra i quali quei della gendarmeria, della polizia, della corte suprema di giudicatura e della commissione agraria. Inoltre gli interessi unionisti sono tutelati gelosamente. Il ministro liberale ha badato di mettere in prima linea del suo discorso il fatto che l'elettorato inglese deve sborsare, come prezzo della misura, più di mezzo milione di lire sterline l'anno: e di questa asserzione gli articoli e gli oratori conservatori, indovinando l'intenzione del loro connazionale, hanno fatto buon uso, facendo appello nei loro commenti ostili alla parte più vulnerabile dell'elettorato inglese, la tasca. Ma né i ministri liberali, né i giornalisti dell'opposizione spiegheranno agli elettori inglesi che questa spesa non è uno sborso di denaro inglese ma bensì un saldo parziale del debito dell'Inghilterra verso l'Irlanda. Né gli uni né gli altri citeranno il resoconto della commissione reale inglese constatante il fatto che l'Irlanda, in confronto col socio predominante, è sopratassata di 88 milioni di franchi, né ricorderanno il fatto che gli statisti e gli scienziati i quali esaminarono la vasta palude centrale dell'Irlanda, affermarono che i due spettri che sedono ad ogni focolare irlandese, la tisi e la pazzia, sono una smentita di ogni pretesa inglese e che il debito morale del Governo inglese verso l'Irlanda, per non aver mai durante un secolo intiero preveduto al rimboschimento di questo pantano pestifero, ammonta a 500 milioni di franchi.

Ora, da uno studio anche frettoloso della storia dell'Home Rule, possiamo fare, a quanto pare, due deduzioni. La prima è questa: le armi le più potenti che l'Inghilterra possa adoperare contro l'Irlanda non sono più quelle del conservatorismo, ma quelle del liberalismo e del vaticanismo. Il conservatorismo, per quanto sia tirannico, è una dottrina franca ed apertamente nemica. La sua posizione è logica. Non vuole che un'isola emula sorga accanto alla Gran Bretagna, che le fabbriche irlandesi facciano concorrenza a quelle inglesi, che il tabacco ed il vino s'esportino di nuovo dall'Irlanda e che i grandi porti lungo la costa irlandese diventino, sotto il Governo nativo o sotto un protettorato straniero, una base navale nemica. Questa sua posizione è logica come è logica quella dei separatisti irlandesi che la contradice punto per punto. Ci vuole poca intelligenza per capire

che il Gladstone ha fatto maggior danno all'Irlanda che non facesse il
Disraeli e che il nemico più accanito degli irlandesi cattolici è il capo del
vaticanismo inglese, il duca di Norfolk.

La seconda deduzione è anche più ovvia. Ed è questa: il partito parlamentare irlandese ha fatto bancarotta. Da ventisette anni agita e parla. In
quell'intervallo ha riscosso 35 milioni dai suoi sostenitori, ed il frutto della
sua agitazione è che le imposte irlandesi sono salite di 88 milioni, che la
popolazione irlandese è decresciuta di un milione. I deputati stessi hanno
migliorato la loro sorte, a parte i piccoli disagi come qualche mese di
carcere o qualche seduta lunga. Da figli di contadini, agenti di piazza ed
avvocati senza clienti sono diventati sindaci stipendiati, direttori di fabbriche e di ditte, proprietari di giornali e latifondisti. Diedero prova del
loro altruismo soltanto nel 1891, quando vendettero Parnell, loro maestro,
alla coscienza farisaica di nonconformisti inglesi senza esigere i trenta
scudi.

James Joyce

LA COMETA DELL' 'HOME RULE'
THE HOME RULE COMET

L'idea dell'autonomia irlandese si è circondata a poco a poco di una
materialità tenue e pallida e appunto alcune settimane fa quando un dec-
reto reale sciolse il parlamento inglese si vide un non so che di scialbo e di
tremulo albeggiare verso oriente. Era la cometa dell' Home Rule vaga,
lontana ma puntuale come sempre. La parola sovrana che in un attimo
fece cadere il crepuscolo sui semidei a Westminster aveva chiamato dal
buio e dal vuoto l'ubbidiente ed inconscia stella.

Questa volta, però, se ne distingueva ben poco causa l'annuvolamento
dei cieli. La nebbia che di solito vela i lidi britannici si addensava in tal
modo da ammantarli in una nuvolaglia fitta ed impenetrabile al di là della
quale si udiva la musica orchestrale degli elementi elettorali in lotta, gli
archi nobili agitati ed isterici, le bucine rauche del popolo e di quando in
quando una frase volante sugli ottavini irlandesi.

L'incertezza della posizione politica in Inghilterra è evidente dal fatto
che le agenzie lanciano da mattina a sera dispacci enigmatici che smentiscono se stessi. Difatti, il tenore dei discorsi tenuti ultimamente nel regno
unito rende difficilissima una disamina imparziale della quistione. Tolti i
tre capi Asquith, Balfour e Redmond, che hanno saputo serbare tuttora
quel certo contegno dignitoso che non si disdice a duci fatui, la campagna
elettorale testé terminata segnala un notevole ribasso del tono della vita

pubblica inglese. Si è mai sentito un simile discorso dalle labbra di un cancelliere dello scacchiere? si domandavano i conservatori. Ma i lazzi del battagliero ministro gallese impallidiscono dinanzi ai vituperi da trivio di conservatori dello stampo del deputato Smith, del noto legale Carson e del direttore della 'National Review' mentre le due fazioni irlandesi, immemori del nemico comune, si sono fatte guerra sorda nel tentativo d'esaurire il florilegio del turpiloquio.

Eppoi (altro motivo di confusione) i partiti inglesi non rispondono più ai loro nomi. Sono i radicali che vogliono continuata l'attuale politica doganale del libero scambio, mentre i conservatori propugnano a perdifiato la riforma della tariffa. Sono i conservatori che mirano a togliere al parlamento il potere legislativo, affidandolo invece all'intera nazione mediante un plebiscito. È il partito irlandese, finalmente, clericale ed intransigente che costituisce la maggioranza di un governo anticlericale e liberale.

Questa situazione paradossale è specchiata fedelmente nelle persone dei capigruppo. Per non parlare del Chamberlain né del Roseberry, i quali, l'uno dal radicalismo ad oltranza e l'altro dal liberalismo gladstoniano, sono passati alle schiere dell'imperialismo (mentre il giovine ministro Churchill ha fatto il suo viaggio ideale nel senso inverso) troviamo le cause del protestantesimo anglicano e del nazionalismo conciliatore guidate da un rinnegato religioso e da un feniano convertito. Il Balfour, infatti, anziché politicante è uno scettico, degno discepolo della scuola scozzese, ch'assunse la direttiva del partito conservatore dopo la morte di suo zio, il compianto marchese di Salisbury, spinto più dall'istinto di nepotismo insito nella famiglia Cecil che da predilezione individuale. Non passa giorno in cui gli stenografi non accennino alla sua aria distratta e cavillosa. I suoi raggiri fanno sorridere i suoi stessi seguaci: ed anche se sotto la sua bandiera vacillante l'esercito ortodosso sia andato incontro a tre successive sconfitte, una più solenne dell'altra, il suo biografo (che sarà forse un altro membro della famiglia Cecil) potrà dire di lui che nei suoi saggi filosofici sezionò e mise a nudo con grande arte le intime fibre dei principii religiosi e psicologici di cui un giro della ruota parlamentare lo fece poi il campione. L'O'Brien, il 'leader' dei dissidenti irlandesi e che chiama il suo manipolo di dieci deputati il partito 'All-for-Ireland', è diventato ciò che diventa ogni buon fanatico quando il suo fanatismo gli premuore. Combatte ora in alleanza con magistrati unionisti, i quali forse venti anni fa avrebbero spiccato contro di lui un mandato di cattura, e della sua focosa gioventù nulla gli rimane all'infuori di quelle irruenze violente che lo fanno somigliare a un epilettico.

In mezzo a tali contradizioni è facile capire come i dispacci dicano e disdicano, annunzino che l' 'Home Rule' è alla porta e ne scrivano il necrologio sei ore dopo. Il profano non può essere dommatico in fatto di comete ma ad ogni modo il passaggio del tanto aspettato corpo celeste ci è stato comunicato dall'osservatorio ufficiale.

La scorsa settimana il capo irlandese Redmond proclamò ad una folla di pescatori la lieta novella. La democrazia inglese, disse, ha schiantato una volta e per sempre il potere dei pari ed entro poche settimane forse l'Irlanda avrà l'autonomia. Ora bisogna essere nazionalista vorace per poter ingoiare una tale boccata. Il gabinetto liberale, appena accomodatosi sul banco ministeriale, si troverà di fronte ad una discreta congerie di brighe, fra le quali primeggerà il duplice bilancio. Risolta in bene o in male questa faccenda, pari e comuni dichiareranno una tregua d'armi in omaggio all'incoronazione di Giorgio V. Sin qua la strada è piana ma soltanto i profeti potranno dirci dove un governo così eterogeneo come quello odierno andrà a finire. Volendo restare al potere tenterà di placare i gallesi e gli scozzesi con misure chiesastiche ed agrarie? Se gli irlandesi esigeranno l'autonomia quale prezzo dell'appoggio del loro voto, il gabinetto si affretterà a spolverare uno dei tanti 'Home Rule Bills' ed a presentarlo di nuovo alla Camera?

La storia del liberalisiun anglosassone insegna molto chiaramente le risposte a queste ed a simili domande ingenue. I ministri liberali sono gente scrupolosa: ed ancora una volta il problema irlandese cagionerà delle scissure sintomatiche in seno al gabinetto, in seguito alle quali sarà pienamente provato che l'elettorato inglese veramente non autorizzò il governo a legiferare in quel scuso. E se il governo, proseguendo la tattica liberale che mira a fiaccare lentamente e segretamente il sentimento separatista, mentre crea con uguale lentezza e segretezza mediante concessioni parziali un nuovo ceto sociale avido, dipendente e scevro d'entusiasmi pericolosi, introduce una riforma o un simulacro di riforma che l'Irlanda rifiuti altezzosamente, non sarà allora il momento propizio per l'intervento del partito conservatore? Fedele alla sua lunga tradizione di cinica malafede, non coglierà esso l'occasione per dichiarare intollerabile la dittatura irlandese e promuoverà una campagna per la riduzione del numero dei collegi irlandesi da ottanta a quaranta. In base a quello spopolamento più unico che raro in un paese civile che fu ed è il frutto acerbo del suo malgoverno?

Il nesso, dunque, fra l'abolizione del 'veto' dei pari e la concessione dell'autonomia agli irlandesi non è così immediato come taluno vorrebbe far credere. In fin dei conti quello è affare degli inglesi stessi e ammettendo che il popolo inglese non abbia più il culto d'una volta per i suoi padri temporali e spirituali è probabile che proceda alla riforma della Camera superiore così cautamente e lentamente come procederà alla riforma delle sue leggi medioevali, alla riforma della sua letteratura tronfia ed ipocrita, alla riforma del suo mostruoso sistema giudiziario. Ed in attesa di tali riforme importerà assai poco al credule bifolco in Irlanda se Lord Lansdowne o Sir Edward Grey regga le sorti del ministero degli esteri.

Il fatto che l'Irlanda vuole far causa comune adesso colla democrazia britannica non deve né sorprendere né persuadere. Da sette secoli non è mai stata suddita fedele dell'Inghilterra. Né, d'altro canto, è stata fedele a se stessa. È entrata nel dominio britannico senza formarne una parte integrale. Ha abbandonato la sua lingua quasi interamente accettato la lingua del conquistatore senza poter assimilare la coltura né adattarsi alla mentalita di cui questa lingua è il veicolo. Ha tradito i suoi eroi sempre nell'ora del bisogno e sempre senza guadagnare il taglione. Ha cacciato i suoi creatori spirituali in esilio per poi farsi vanto di loro. Non ha servito bene che una padrona sola, la chiesa romana–cattolica, la quale però usa pagare i suoi fedeli con tratte a lunga scadenza.

Che alleanza duratura potrà sussistere fra questo strano popolo e la nuova democrazia anglosassone? I retori che ne parlano così caldamente oggi si accorgeranno presto (se non se ne accorgono già) che fra i nobili inglesi e gli operai inglesi esiste la misteriosa comunione di sangue e che non parlò per la sua casta soltanto, ma anche per la sua razza il sullodato marchese di Salisbury, squisito gentiluomo, quando disse: 'Lasciate bollire gli irlandesi nel loro proprio sugo'.

LA BATTAGLIA FRA BERNARD SHAW E LA CENSURA: 'BLANCO POSNET SMASCHERATO'

THE BATTLE BETWEEN BERNARD SHAW AND THE CENSOR

Dublino, 31 *agosto*

C'è una settimana orgogliosa ogni anno nel calendario dublinese; l'ultima settimana d'agosto nella quale la rinomata 'Horse show' (Fiera di cavalli) attrae alla capitale irlandese una folla multicolore e poliglotta dall'isola consorella, dal continente e persino dal lontano Giappone. Per pochi giorni la città stanca e scettica si veste da sposa novella; le sue strade brunastre brulicano di vita febbrile; un chiasso inusitato interrompe il suo sonno senile.

Quest'anno, però, un avvenimento artistico ha quasi eclissato l'importanza della fiera e dappertutto non si parla che della vertenza fra Bernard Shaw e il viceré. Com'è già noto l'ultimo dramma di Shaw *The Shewing Up of Blanco Posnet* (Blanco Posnet smascherato) fu bollato del marchio d'infamia dal gran ciambellano inglese che ne vietò la rappresentazione nel

Regno unito. Probabilmente questa decisione del censore non sorprese molto lo Shaw poiché lo stesso censore fece altrettanto per due altri lavori teatrali shaviani, *La professione della Signora Warren* ed il recentissimo *Press Cuttings*: e probabilmente pure lo Shaw si ritenne onorato più che altro dal bando arbitrario che ha colpito le sue commedie assieme cogli *Spettri* d'Ibsen e *La potenza delle tenebre* di Tolstoi e la *Salomè* di Wilde.

Però non si diede per vinto e trovò il modo di eludere la vigilanza paurosa del censore. Per uno strano motivo la città di Dublino è l'unico luogo in tutto il dominio britannico ove la censura non vige, e difatti l'antica legge reca queste parole testuali: 'tranne la città di Dublino'. Lo Shaw, allora. offrì il suo lavoro alla compagnia del teatro nazionale irlandese che l'accettò e ne annunziò la rappresentazione semplicemente come nulla fosse. Il censore si vide ridotto all'impotenza ed allora intervenne il viceré d'Irlanda per salvaguardare il prestigio dell'autorità. Ci fu uno scambio vivace di lettere fra il rappresentante del re ed il commediografo, severe e minacciose da una parte, insolenti e schernitrici dall'altra, mentre i dublinesi, che s'infischiano dell'arte ma amano d'un amore smodato le dispute, si stropicciavano le mani dalla gioia. Lo Shaw tenne duro, insistendo nel suo diritto, ed il camerino del teatro era letteralmente assediato sicché alla prima rappresentazione il teatro era venduto ben sette volte.

Una densa folla si pigiava stasera nei pressi del teatro dell'Abbazia ed un drappello di guardie gigantesche manteneva l'ordine, ma era evidente già a prima vista che nessuna dimostrazione ostile sarebbe stata fatta dal pubblico scelto che gremiva ogni cantuccio del piccolo teatro rivoluzionario. Difatti la cronaca della serata non ha da segnalare neppure il più leggero mormorio di protesta: ed al calar del telone un applauso fragoroso chiamò gli esecutori alla ribalta ripetute volte.

La commedia, che lo Shaw descrive come una predica in melodramma crudo, è, come sapete, in un atto solo e l'azione si svolge in una città rozza e barbara del Far West. Il protagonista è un ladro di cavalli e il dramma non è che il suo processo. Egli ha rubato un cavallo, che credeva fosse di suo fratello per ricompensarsi della sostanza che questo gli ha tolto ingiustamente. Però mentre fugge dalla città si imbatte in una donna con un bambino malato. Essa vuoi raggiungere il capoluogo per salvare la vita della sua creatura ed egli, commosso dall'appello ch'essa gli fa, le dà il cavallo. È ripreso poi e ricondotto alla città per essere impiccato. Il processo è sommario e violento. Lo sceriffo funge da presidente energico, gridando all'imputato, battendo il tavolo e minacciando i testi colla rivoltella in pugno. Posnet, il ladro, fa un po' di teologia primitiva. Il momento di debolezza sentimentale in cui cedette alle preghiere della povera madre è stato per lui la crisi della sua vita. Il dito di Dio gli ha toccato il cervello.

Non ha più la forza di vivere la vita crudele e bestiale che menava prima di quell'incontro. Prorompe in discorsi lunghi e sconnessi (ed è qui che il pio censore inglese si turava le orecchie), discorsi teologici inquantoché Domineddio ne è l'oggetto ma poco chiesastici riguardo alla terminologia. Nella sincerità della sua convinzione Posnet ricorre al gergo dei minatori e, fra altre riflessioni, volendo dire che Dio opera segretamente nei cuori degli uomini, gli dà addirittura del ladro di cavalli.

Il dramma si chiude felicemente. Il bambino che Posnet voleva salvare muore e la madre è ripresa. Essa racconta il suo caso alla corte e Posnet viene assolto. Nulla di più tenue si poteva immaginare: e l'ascoltatore, si chiede meravigliato perché mai il lavoro sia stato intercettato dalla censura.

Lo Shaw ha ragione: è una predica. Lo Shaw è un predicatore nato. Il suo spirito ciarliero e vivace non può soffrire l'imposizione dello stile nobile e parco che conviene al drammaturgo moderno e, sfogandosi in prefazioni farraginose ed in norme sceniche sterminate, crea per sé stesso una forma drammatica che ha molto del romanzo dialogato. Il suo è un senso di situazione piuttosto che di dramma logicamente ed eticamente condotto alla sua fine. In questo caso egli ha esumato l'incidente centrale del suo *Discepolo del Diavolo* e l'ha trasformato in una predica: e la trasformazione è troppo rapida per essere convincente come predica, come pure l'arte è troppo povera per renderlo convincente come dramma.

E questo dramma non coincide forse con una crisi nella mente dello scrittore? Già, nella chiusa dell'*Altra Isola di John Bull*, questa crisi si annunziava. Tanto lui quanto il suo ultimo protagonista hanno avuto un passato sregolato e profano. Il fabianismo, il vegetarianismo, l'anti-alcoolismo, la musica, la pittura, il dramma, tutti i movimenti progressisti sia nell'arte che nella politica l'hanno avuto per campione. Ed ora forse qualche dito divino gli ha toccato il cervello: ed egli pure al par di Blanco Posnet, si smaschera.

LA CITTÀ DELLE TRIBÙ: RICORDI ITALIANI IN UN PORTO IRLANDESE

THE CITY OF THE TRIBES

Galway, *agosto*

Il dublinese ozioso che viaggia poco e conosce la propria patria per sentita dire, crede che gli abitanti di Galway siano oriundi della Spagna e che non si possano fare quattro passi nelle viuzze tetre dell'antica città delle tribù senza incontrare il vero tipo spagnuolo dalla cera olivastra e dalla chioma corvina. Il dublinese ha torto ed ha ragione. Oggi almeno gli occhi ed i

capelli neri scarseggiano a Galway ove predomina per lo più un rosso
tizianesco. Le vecchie case spagnuole rovinano e ciuffi di malerba crescono
negli strombi delle finestre sporgenti. Fuori le mura il suburbio sorge,
nuovo, gaio, inconscio del passato: ma basta chiudere gli occhi un
momento a questa modernità molesta per vedere nella penombra della
storia la 'città spagnuola'.

Giace, sparsa sopra innumerevoli isolette, venata in ogni senso di
fiumicelli, cateratte, gore, canaletti, in fondo ad una vasta insenatura
dell'Oceano Atlantico nella quale l'intera flotta britannica potrebbe
ormeggiarsi. Allo sbocco del golfo le tre isole di Aran, supine sulle
acque grigie a guisa di balene somnolente, formano una diga naturale e
sostengono l'assalto dei marosi atlantici. Il piccolo faro dell'isola set-
tentrionale lancia un debole raggio di luce verso l'ovest, l'ultimo saluto
del vecchio al nuovo mondo, e chiama ostinatamente ed invano il mercante straniero che da molti anni a questa parte non viene più
all'approdo.

Eppure nel medioevo queste acque erano solcate da migliaia di navi straniere. Le targhe alle cantonate delle strade anguste ricordano i rapporti della
città coll'Europa latina: via di Madeira, strada dei mercanti, passeggio
degli spagnuoli, isola di Madeira, via dei lombardi, viale Velasquez de
Palmeira. Il carteggio di Oliviero Cromwell attesta che il porto di Galway
era il secondo porto del regno unito ed il primo emporio di tutto il regno
per il commercio spagnuolo ed italiano. Nel primo decennio del trecento,
un mercante fiorentino, Andrea Gerardo, fu ricevitore doganale del
comune e nell'elenco dei sindaci del seicento si trova il nome di Giovanni
Fante. La città stessa ha come protettore San Nicolò di Bari ed il cosidetto
sigillo del collegio porta l'effige del santo, patrono dei naviganti e dei
bambini. L'inviato papalino, il cardinale Rinuccini, venne a Galway
durante il processo del re martire e mise la città sotto il bando del pontefice. Il clero e gli ordini religiosi rifiutarono di riconoscere la sua autorità
ed il focoso cardinale ruppe la campana nella chiesa dei carmelitani e
stazionò due preti del suo seguito alla porta della chiesa per impedire
l'ingresso dei fedeli. La casa parrocchiale di san Nicolò serba tuttora un
ricordo di un altro prelato italiano del medioevo: una lettera autografa del
famigerato Borgia. Nella medesima casa c'è un curioso documento lasciato
da un viaggiatore italiano del cinquecento nel quale lo scrittore dice che,
quantunque avesse viaggiato per tutto il mondo, non vide in un colpo
d'occhio quello che vide a Galway: un prete che alzava l'ostia, una muta
che inseguiva un cervo, un vascello che entrava nel porto a tutta vela, un
salmone ucciso con un giavellotto.

Quasi tutto il vino importato nel regno dalla Spagna, dal Portogallo, dalle isole Canarie e dall'Italia passava per questo porto. L'importazione annua ammontava a millecinquecento 'tuns', vale a dire, quasi due milioni di litri. Tale fu l'importanza di questo commercio che il governo olandese fece la proposta al comune di comperare un grande fondo vicino alla città e di pagarne il prezzo coprendo il terreno con scudi d'argento. Il comune che temeva la concorrenza straniera fece rispondere mediante il suo inviato che acconsentiva a patto che gli scudi fossero disposti verticalmente sul terreno. La risposta degli olandesi a questa gentilissima controfferta non è ancora giunta.

Per molti secoli l'intera gestione municipale e chiesastica era nelle mani dei discendenti delle quattordici tribù, i cui nomi vengono ricordati in quattro versi zoppicanti. Il più strano ed il più interessante documento storico dell'archivio cittadino è la carta descrittiva della città fatta per il duca di Lorena nel seicento quando Sua Altezza voleva sincerarsi della grandezza della città in occasione di un prestito chiestogli dal suo confratello inglese, l'allegro monarca. La carta, ricca d'incisioni e di diciture simboliche, fu opera di Enrico Joyce, preposito capitolare della città. Il margine della pergamena è tutto fregiato degli stemmi nobiliari delle tribù; e la carta stessa è più che altro una sinfonia topografica sul tema del numero delle tribù. Così, il topografo enumera e disegna quattordici bastioni, quattordici torri sulle mura, quattordici vie principali, quattordici monasteri, quattordici castelli, quattordici vicoli e poi, scivolando nel modo minore, enumera e disegna sette salite alle mura, sette giardini, sette altari per il corteo di Corpus Domini, sette mercati e sette altre cose mirabili. Tra queste ultime, anzi ultima delle ultime, il degno proposito enumera 'la vecchia piccionaia che si trova nel rione meridionale'.

Di tutte le tribù la più famosa era quella dei Lynch. Durante il secolo e mezzo che intercorse fra la fondazione del comune e le scorrerie devastatrici della soldatesca cromwelliana, un membro di questa famiglia coprì la carica di podestà ben ottantatre volte. Il più tragico fatto della storia cittadina fu l'espiazione di un delitto commesso nel 1493 dal giovine Gualtiero Lynch, figlio unico del sindaco Giacomo Lynch Fitz Stephen. Il sindaco, ricco mercante di vino, intraprese in quell'anno un viaggio in Ispagna ove fu ospite di un suo amico spagnuolo, certo Gomez. Il figlio di questo, ascoltando ogni sera i racconti del viaggiatore, s'invaghì dell'Irlanda lontana e chiese al babbo il permesso di accompagnare il loro ospite quando tornava in patria. Il babbo esitò. I tempi erano pericolosi ed i viaggiatori prima di partire per lidi noti od ignoti usavano fare i loro testamenti. Il sindaco Lynch, però, si rese mallevadore per la sicurezza del giovane ed ambedue partirono. Arrivato a Galway il giovine spagnuolo divenne amico del figlio del sindaco, Gualtiero, giovine discolo, di carattere impulsivo, che faceva la corte ad Agnese Blake, figlia di un altro magnate cittadino. Ben presto un amore sorse fra Agnese e lo straniero ed una sera mentre il Gomez esciva dalla casa dei Blake, Gualtiero Lynch, che stava in agguato, gli conficcò un pugnale nella schiena e poi, accecato dall'ira, trascinò il cadavere lungo la via e lo gettò in una gora. Il delitto fu scoperto ed il giovine Gualtiero fu arrestato e processato. Il giudice era il padre, sindaco della città, il quale, sordo all'appello del sangue e memore soltanto dell'onore della città e della propria parola impegnata, condannò a morte l'assassino. Invano gli amici tentarono di dissuaderlo. Il popolo, compreso di pietà per l'infelice giovine, assediò la casa del sindaco, il triste e scuro castello che ancora nereggia nella via principale. Il sindaco fu inesorabile anche quando il boia rifiutò di eseguire la sentenza. La vigilia dell'esecuzione padre e figlio vegliarono insieme nella cella del carcere, pregando fino all'alba. Giunta l'ora dell'esecuzione padre e figlio comparvero alla finestra della casa. Si baciarono e si congedarono: eppoi il padre stesso impiccò il figlio alla trave della finestra dinanzi agli occhi della folla esterrefatta.

Le vecchie case spagnuole rovinano. I castelli delle tribù sono diroccati. Ciuffi di malerba crescono nelle finestre e negli ampi cortili. Sopra i portici gli stemmi gentilizi, incisi nella pietra nerastra, sbiadiscono: la lupa del Campidoglio coi due gemelli, l'aquila bicipite degli Absburgo, il toro nero dei Darcy discendenti di Carlomagno. Nella città di Galway, scrive un vecchio cronista, imperano le passioni di superbia e di lussuria.

La sera è quieta e grigia. Da lontano, da oltre le cascate d'acqua, viene un sussurro. Pare ronzio d'api attorno l'alveare. S'avvicina. Si vedono sette giovanotti, suonatori di cornamusa, alla testa di uno stuolo di gente. Passano superbi e marziali, a capo scoperto, suonando una musica vaga e strana. Nella luce incerta si distinguono appena gli scialli verdi pendenti dalla spalla destra e le sottane, color di zafferano. Imboccano la via del convento della presentazione: e mentre la musica vaga si diffonde nel crepuscolo, alle finestre del convento, ad uno ad uno, spuntano i soggòli bianchi delle monache.

IL MIRAGGIO DEL PESCATORE DI ARAN: LA VALVOLA DELL'INGHILTERRA IN CASO DI GUERRA

THE MIRAGE OF THE FISHERMAN OF ARAN

Galway, *2 settembre*

Il vaporino, che porta un piccolo carico di gitanti, si scosta dalla banchina sotto gli occhi vigili del gerente scozzese, assorto in un sogno di aritmetica mentale. Esce dal porticino di Galway e prende il largo, lasciando a destra il villaggio del Claddagh, una congerie di tuguri fuori le mura della città. Una congerie di tuguri eppure un regno. Fino a pochi anni fa il villaggio eleggeva il proprio re, aveva un costume proprio, legiferava per sé stesso e viveva a parte. L'anello nuziale degli abitanti è ancora fregiato dallo stemma dei re: due mani congiunte che reggono un cuore incoronato.

Partiamo per Aranmor, l'isola santa che dorme come un grande squalo sulle acque grigie dell'Oceano Atlantico che gli isolani chiamano il vecchio mare. Sotto le acque di questo golfo e lungo la costa giacciono i rottami di una squadra dell'infelice armata spagnuola. Dopo la sconfitta nella Manica le navi fecero vela per il nord ove le burrasche e le mareggiate le dispersero. I contadini della contea Galway, memori della lunga amicizia tra la Spagna e l'Irlanda, nascosero i fuggiaschi dalla vendetta del presidio inglese e diedero pia sepoltura ai naufraghi, avvolgendo le salme in pannilini bianchi. Le acque si sono pentite. Ogni anno alla vigilia di ferragosto quando si inizia la pesca delle aringhe le acque del golfo vengono benedette. La flottiglia di barche pescherecce parte dal Claddagh preceduta dall'ammiraglia sulla tolda della quale sta un frate domenicano. Giunta in un luogo propizio la flottiglia si ferma, i pescatori si inginocchiano e si scoprono ed il frate, mormorando preghiere di scongiuro, scuote l'aspersorio sul mare e divide l'aria bruna nella forma della croce.

Un lembo di rena bianca a destra segna il luogo ove il nuovo porto transatlantico è forse destinato a sorgere. Il mio compagno spiega una grande carta geografica sulla quale le linee progettate ramificano, girano e s'incrociano da Galway ai grandi porti canadesi. Il viaggio da Europa all'America si compierà, secondo le cifre, in meno di tre giorni. Da Galway, l'ultimo porto europeo, a Saint John (Terra Nuova) il vapore impiegherà due giorni e sedici ore e da Galway a Halifax, il primo porto canadese, tre giorni e dieci ore. Il testo dell'opuscolo unito alla carta geografica è irto di cifre, stime di spese, quadri oceanografici. Lo scrittore fa caldo appello all'ammiragliato britannico, alle società ferroviarie, alle Camere di commercio, alla popolazione irlandese. Il nuovo porto sarebbe la valvola di sicurezza per l'Inghilterra in caso di guerra. Dal Canadà, granaio e dispensa del Regno Unito, i grandi carichi di grano entrerebbero nel porto irlandese, evitando così i pericoli della navigazione nel canale di San Giorgio e delle squadre nemiche. In tempo di pace la nuova linea sarebbe la via più breve fra un continente e l'altro. Gran parte dei carichi di merci e di passeggeri che ora vengono sbarcati a Liverpool verrebbero in avvenire sbarcati a Galway, proseguendo direttamente a Londra, via Dublino e Holyhead. La vecchia città decaduta risorgerebbe. Dal nuovo mondo la ricchezza ed il vigore vitale scorrerebbero per questa nuova arteria nell'Irlanda dissanguata. Di nuovo, dopo una decina di secoli, il miraggio, che abbacinò il povero pescatore di Aran, seguace ed emulo di San Brendano, appare lontano, vago e tremulo sullo specchio dell'oceano.

Cristoforo Colombo, come ognuno sa, è venerato dai posteri perché fu l'ultimo a scoprire l'America. Mille anni prima che il navigatore genovese fosse dileggiato a Salamanca dalla spiaggia brulla ove il vaporino approda, San Brendano salpò per il mondo ignoto e, attraversando l'oceano, sbarcò sulla costa del Florida. L'isola allora era boscosa e fertile. Nella penombra del bosco trovavasi l'eremo dei monaci irlandesi, fondato da Enda, santo di sangue reale, nel quarto secolo dopo Cristo. Da quest'eremo partì Finniano, poscia vescovo di Lucca. Qui visse e sognò il visionario San Fursa, descritto nel calendario agiografico dell'Irlanda quale precursore di Dante Alighieri. Una copia medioevale delle visioni di Fursa dipinge il viaggio del santo dall'inferno al paradiso, dalla tetra valle dei quattro fuochi fra le schiere diaboliche su per l'universo fino alla luce divina, riflessa da innumerevoli ali angeliche. Queste visioni avrebbero servito da modello al poeta della Divina Commedia venerato, dai posteri, al par di Colombo, perché fu l'ultimo a visitare ed a descrivere i tre regni delle anime.

Sulla spiaggia della baia fragili palischermi di canovaccio teso sono tirati a secco. Quattro isolani scendono lesti verso il mare fra le rocce coperte di quelle alghe violacee ed arruginite che si vedono nelle botteghe delle erbivendole di Galway. Il pescatore di Aran ha il piede sicuro. Calza una rozza pianella di pelle di bue cruda, aperto al fiosso, senza tacchi e legato con stringhe da frusta. Si veste di lana grossa come il feltro e porta un cappellone nero a larghe falde.

Ci fermiamo in una delle viuzze ripide, incerti. Un isolano, che parla un inglese tutto suo, ci dà il buon giorno, aggiungendo ch'è stato un'estate orribile, grazie a Dio. La frase, che pare sulle prime uno dei soliti strafalcioni irlandesi, viene invece dall'imo cuore della rassegnazione umana. L'uomo che l'ha detto porta un nome principesco, quello degli O'Flaherty, un nome che il giovine Oscar Wilde fece stampare orgogliosamente sul frontispizio del suo primo libro. Ma il tempo ed il vento hanno raso al suolo la civiltà decorsa alla quale appartiene, i querceti santi della sua isola, il principato dei suoi antenati, la lingua e forse il nome di quell'eremita di Aran che fu chiamato il colombo della chiesa. Intorno agli arbusti che crescono a stento sui clivi dell'isola la sua immaginazione ha tessuto leggende e fiabe che tradiscono la tara della sua psiche. E sotto l'apparente semplicità serba un che di scetticismo, d'umorismo, spettrale. Guarda dall'altra parte quando ha parlato e lascia che l'entusiasta studioso noti nel taccuino il fatto mirabolante che fu il biancospino, l'alberello dal quale Giuseppe D'Arimatia tagliò il suo bastone da passeggio.

Una vecchietta ci viene incontro e ci invita ad entrare nella sua casa. Depone sulla tavola un enorme teiera, una pagnotta e del burro salato. L'isolano, ch'è suo figlio, si siede vicino al focolare e risponde alle domande del mio compagno con un'aria impacciata ed umile. Non sa quanti anni ha, ma dice che sarà vecchio fra poco. Non sa perché non ha preso moglie: forse perché non ci sono donne per lui. Il mio compagno domanda ancora perché non ci sono donne per lui: e l'isolano, toltosi il berretto dalla testa, affonda il viso nella lana soffice, confuso e sorridente. Aran, dice, è il più strano luogo del mondo, un povero luogo; ma, per quanto povero sia, quando il mio compagno vuol pagare la vecchia respinge la moneta quasi con ira e ci chiede se vogliamo disonorare la sua casa.

Un'acquerugiola fina e fitta scende dalle nuvole bigie. La nebbia piovosa s'avanza da ponente, mentre il vaporino chiama disperatamente i ritardatari. L'isola scompare a poco a poco, avvolta in un velo fumolento. Scompaiono anche i tre marinai danesi seduti impassivi sulla cresta del pendio. Erano fuori nell'oceano per la pesca estiva e fecero sosta ad Aran. Silenziosi e malinconici pare che pensino alle orde danesi che incendiarono la città di Galway nell'ottavo secolo, alle terre irlandesi le quali, secondo la leggenda, vengono contate nelle doti delle ragazze di Danimarca, e che sognino la riconquista. Sulle isole e sul mare cade la pioggia. Piove come sa piovere in Irlanda. Sotto il castello di prora ove una ragazza amoreggia rumorosamente con uno della ciurma, tenendolo sulle ginocchia, apriamo di nuovo la carta geografica. Nella luce crepuscolare non si possono distinguere i nomi dei porti: ma la linea che parte da Galway e si ramifica e si estende, ricorda il simbolo, messo accanto allo stemma della sua città natìa dal preposito capitolare, mistico e fors'anche profeta: 'Quasi lilium germinans germinabit et quasi terebinthus extendens ramos suos'.

OSCAR WILDE: IL POETA DI 'SALOMÈ'

OSCAR WILDE: THE POET OF 'SALOMÉ'

Oscarre Fingal O'Flahertie Wills Wilde. Tali furono i titoli altisonanti ch'egli, con alterigia giovanile, volle far stampare sul frontispizio della sua prima raccolta di versi e con quel medesimo gesto altiero con cui credeva nobilitarsi scolpiva, forse in modo simbolico, i segni delle sue pretese vane e la sorte che già l'attendeva. Il suo nome lo simboleggia: Oscarre, nipote del re Fingal e figlio unigenito di Ossiano nella amorfa odissea celtica, ucciso dolorosamente per mano del suo ospite mentre sedeva a mensa: O'Flahertie, truce tribù irlandese il cui destino era di assalire le porte di città medioevali, ed il cui nome incutendo terrore ai pacifici, si recita tuttora in calce all'antica litania dei santi fra le pesti, l'ira di Dio e lo spirito di fornicazione 'dai feroci O'Flahertie, *libera nos Domine*'. Simile a quell'- Oscarre egli pure, nel fior degli anni, doveva incontrare la sua morte civile, mentre sedeva a mensa coronato di pampini e discorrendo di Platone: simile a quella tribù selvatica doveva egli spezzar le lance della sua facondia paradossale contro la schiera delle convenzioni [in]utili: ed udire, esule e disonorato, il coro dei giusti recitare il suo nome assieme con quello dello spirito immondo.

Il Wilde nacque nella sonnolenta capitale irlandese cinquantacinque anni fa. Suo padre era un valente scienziato, ed è stato chiamato il padre dell'otologia moderna: sua madre partecipò al movimento rivoluzionario letterario del '48, collaborando all'organo nazionale sotto il pseudonimo di *Speranza* con le sue poesie e con articoli incitanti il popolo alla presa del castello di Dublino. Ci sono delle circostanze riguardanti la gravidanza di lady Wilde e l'infanzia di suo figlio che, a parer di alcuni, spiegano in parte la triste mania (se così è lecito chiamarla) che lo trasse più tardi alla sua rovina, ed è certo almeno che il fanciullo crebbe in un ambiente di sregolatezza e di prodigalità.

La vita pubblica di Oscarre Wilde si aperse all'Università di Oxford ove, all'epoca della sua immatricolazione, un solenne professore, di nome Ruskin, conduceva uno stuolo di efèbi anglosassoni verso la tetra promessa della società avvenire, dietro una carriola.

Il temperamento suscettibile di sua madre riviveva nel giovane; ed egli risolse di mettere in pratica, cominciando da sé stesso, una teoria di bellezza in parte derivata dai libri di Pater e di Ruskin ed in parte originale. Sfidando le beffe del pubblico proclamò e praticò la riforma estetica del vestito e della casa. Tenne dei cicli di conferenze negli Stati Uniti e nelle province inglesi e diventò il portavoce della scuola estetica, mentre intorno a lui andava formandosi la leggenda fantastica dell'apostolo del bello. Il suo nome evocava nella mente del pubblico una idea vaga di sfumature delicate, di vita illeggiadrita di fiori: il culto del girasole, il suo fiore prediletto, si propagò tra gli oziosi ed il popolo minuto udì narrare del suo famoso bastone d'avorio candido luccicante di turchesi e dell'acconciatura neroniana dei suoi capelli.

Il fondo di questo quadro smagliante era più misero di ciò che i borghesi maginavano. Medaglie, trofei della gioventù accademica, salivano di quando in quando il sacro monte che ha nome di pietà; e la giovane moglie dell'epigrammatico dovette qualchevolta farsi prestare da una vicina il danaro per un paio di scarpe. Il Wilde si vide costretto ad accettare il posto di direttore di un giornale molto insulso; e solo colla rappresentazione delle sue commedie brillanti egli entrò nella breve fase penultima della sua vita: il lusso e la ricchezza. *Il ventaglio di Lady Windermere* prese Londra d'assalto. Il Wilde, entrando in quella tradizione letteraria di commediografi irlandesi che si stende dai giorni di Sheridan e Goldsmith fino a Bernard Shaw, diventò, al par di loro, giullare di corte per gli inglesi. Diventò un arbitro d'eleganza nella metropoli e la sua rendita annua, provento dei suoi scritti, raggiunse quasi il mezzo milione di franchi. Sparse il suo oro fra una sequela di amici indegni. Ogni mattina acquistò due fiori costosi, uno per sé, l'altro per il stio cocchiere; e persino il giorno del suo processo clamoroso si fece condurre al tribunale nella sua carrozza a due cavalli col cocchiere vestito di gala e collo staffiere incipriato.

La sua caduta fu salutata da un urlo di gioia puritana. Alla notizia della sua condanna la folla popolare, radunata dinanzi al tribunale, si mise a ballare una pavana sulla strada melmosa. I redattori dei giornali furono ammessi all'ispettorato ed, attraverso la finestrina della sua cella, poterono pascersi dello spettacolo della sua vergogna. Strisce bianche coprirono il suo nome sugli albi teatrali; i suoi amici lo abbandonarono; i suoi manoscritti furono rubati mentre egli, in prigione, scontava la pena inflittagli di due anni di lavori forzati. Sua madre morì sotto un nome d'infamia: sua moglie morì. Fu dichiarato in istato di fallimento, i suoi effetti furono venduti all'asta, i suoi figli gli furono tolti. Quando uscì dal carcere i teppisti sobillati dal nobile marchese di Queensberry l'aspettavano in agguato. Fu cacciato, come una lepre dai cani, da albergo in albergo. Un oste dopo l'altro lo respinse dalla porta, rifiutandogli cibo ed alloggio, e al cader della notte giunse finalmente sotto le finestre di suo fratello piangendo e balbettando come un fanciullo.

L'epilogo volse rapidamente alla sua fine e non vale la pena di seguire l'infelice dalla suburra napoletana al povero albergo nel quartiere latino, ove morì di meningite nell'ultimo mese dell'ultimo anno del secolo decimonono. Non vale la pena di pedinarlo come fecero le spie parigine: morì da cattolico romano, aggiungendo allo sfacelo della sua vita civile la propria smentita della sua fiera dottrina. Dopo aver schernito gli idoli del foro, piegò il ginocchio, essendo compassionevole e triste chi fu un giorno cantore della divinità della gioia: e chiuse il capitolo della ribellione del suo spirito con un atto di dedizione spirituale.

Questo non è il luogo di indagare lo strano problema della vita di Oscarre Wilde né di determinare fino a che punto l'atavismo e la forma epilettoide della sua nevrosi possano scagionarlo di ciò che a lui si imputò. Innocente o colpevole che fosse delle accuse mossegli, era indubbiamente un capro espiatorio. La sua maggiore colpa era quella di aver provocato uno scandalo in Inghilterra; ed è ben noto che l'autorità inglese fece il possibile per indurlo a fuggire prima di spiccare contro di lui un mandato di cattura.

A Londra sola, dichiarò un impiegato del ministero dell'interno, durante il processo, più di ventimila persone sono sotto la sorveglianza della polizia, ma rimangono a piede libero fintantoché non provochino uno scandalo. Le lettere di Wilde ai suoi amici furono lette dinanzi alla Corte ed il loro autore venne denunziato come un degenerato, ossessionato da pervertimenti esotici. 'Il tempo guerreggia contro di te; è geloso dei tuoi gigli e delle tue rose.' 'Amo vederti errare per le vallate violacee, fulgido colla tua chioma color di miele'. Ma la verità è che il Wilde, lungi dall'-essere un mostro di pervertimento sorto in modo inesplicabile nel mezzo della civiltà moderna d'Inghilterra, è il prodotto logico e necessario del sistema collegiale ed universitario anglosassone, sistema di reclusione e di segretezza. L'incolpazione del popolo procedeva da molte cause compli-cate; ma non era la reazione semplice di una coscienza pura. Chi studi con pazienza le iscrizioni murali, i disegni franchi, i gesti espressivi del popolo, esiterà a crederlo mondo di cuore. Chi segua dal di presso la vita e la favella degli uomini, sia nello stanzone dei soldati, che nei grandi uffici commerciali, esiterà a credere che tutti coloro che scagliarono pietre contro il Wilde furono essi stessi senza macchia. Difatti ognuno si sente diffidente nel parlare con altri di questo argomento, temendo che forse il suo interlocutore ne sappia più di lui. L'autodifesa di Oscarre Wilde nello *Scots Observer* deve ritenersi valida dinanzi alla sbarra della critica spas-sionata. Ognuno, scrisse, vede il proprio peccato in Doriano Gray (il più celebre romanzo di Wilde). Quale fu il peccato di Donano Gray nessun lo dice e nessun lo sa. Chi lo scopre l'ha commesso.

Qui tocchiamo il centro motore dell'arte di Wilde: il peccato. Si illuse credendosi il portatore della buona novella di un neopaganesimo alle genti travagliate. Mise tutte le sue qualità caratteristiche, le qualità (forse) della sua razza, l'arguzia, l'impulso generoso, l'intelletto asessuale al servizio di una teoria del bello che doveva, secondo lui, riportare l'evo d'oro e la gioia della gioventù del mondo. Ma in fondo in fondo se qualche verità si stacca dalle sue interpretazioni soggettive d'Aristotele, dal suo pensiero irrequieto che procede per sofismi e non per sillogismi, dalle sue assimilazione di altre nature, aliene dalla sua, come quelle del delinquente e dell'umile, è questa verità inerente nell'anima del cattolicismo: che l'uomo non può arrivare al cuor divino se non attraverso quel senso di separazione e di perdita che si chiama il peccato.

Nell'ultimo suo libro *De profundis* si inchina davanti ad un Cristo gnostico, risorto dalle pagine apocrife della *Casa del Melagrani* ed allora la sua vera anima, tremula, timida e rattristata, traluce attraverso il manto di Eliogabalo. La sua leggenda fantastica, l'opera sua, una variazione poli-fonica sui rapporti fra l'arte e la natura anziché una rivelazione della sua psiche, i libri dorati, scintillanti di quelle frasi epigrammatiche che lo resero, agli occhi di alcuno, il più arguto parlatore del secolo scorso, sono ormai un bottino diviso.

Un versetto del libro di Giobbe è inciso sulla sua pietra sepolcrale nel povero cimitero di Bagneux. Loda la sua facondia, *eloquium suum*, il gran manto leggendario che è ormai un bottino diviso. Il futuro potrà forse scolpire là un altro verso, meno altiero, più pietoso: *Partiti sunt sibi vestimenta mea et super vestem meam miserunt sortes.*

IL FENIANISMO: L'ULTIMO FENIANO

FENIANISM: THE LAST FENIAN

Colla morte di John O'Leary, avvenuta testé a Dublino nel giorno di S. Patrizio, la festa nazionale degli irlandesi, sparisce forse l'ultimo attore del dramma torbido ch'era il fenianismo. Nome tradizionale, derivato dalla vecchia lingua irlandese dove la parola feniani significa il corpo di guardia del re e col quale veniva denominato il movimento insurrezionale irlandese.

Chi studi la storia della rivoluzione irlandese durante il secolo decimonono si trova dinanzi ad una duplice lotta, la lotta, cioè, della nazione irlandese contro il Governo inglese, e la lotta, forse non meno acuta, fra i patrioti moderati ed il partito cosidetto della forza fisica. Questo partito, sotto diversi nomi: 'fanciulli bianchi', 'uomini del '98', 'irlandesi uniti', 'invincibili', 'feniani', ha sempre rifiutato ogni contatto, sia coi partiti inglesi come coi parlamentari nazionali. Sostiene (ed in questa sua asserzione la storia gli dà pienamente ragione) che ogni concessione accordata dall'Inghilterra all'irlanda è stata accordata a malincuore, e come si suol dire, colla punta della baionetta. La stampa intransigente non fa che salutare con articoli ironici e virulenti le gesta dei deputati nazionali a Westminster: e, quantunque riconosca che la rivolta armata è oramai, vista la strapotenza dell'Inghilterra, diventata un sogno impossibile, non ha mai smesso di inculcare nelle menti della nuova generazione il domma del separatismo.

Il fenianismo del '67 non fu, come la rivolta ridicola di Roberto Eminet o il movimento ardente della giovane Irlanda nel '45, uno dei soliti scatti del temperamento celtico che folgorano per un momento nelle tenebre e lasciano dietro di sé un buio più fitto di prima. All'epoca in cui sorse, la popolazione dell'isola di smeraldo contava più di otto milioni mentre quella dell'Inghilterra non superava i diciassette milioni. Il paese, sotto la direzione del capo dei feniani Giacomo Stephens, era organizzato in cerchi di venticinque uomini affidati a sergenti, un piano di campagna eminentemente adatto al carattere irlandese perché riduce ad un minimo la possibilità di tradimento. Questi cerchi formavano una vasta rete intricata i fili della quale erano nelle mani dello Stephens. Contemporaneamente i feniani americani furono organizzati nello stesso modo ed i due movimenti lavoravano di concerto. Fra i feniani ci erano molti soldati dell'esercito inglese, poliziotti, guardie e carcerieri.

Tutto pareva andasse bene e la repubblica stava per essere fondata, anzi fu apertamente proclamata dallo Stephens, quando O'Leary e Luby, i direttori dell'organo del partito, vennero arrestati; il Governo pose una taglia sulla testa dello Stephens ed annunziò che conosceva tutti i luoghi dove i feniani facevano di nottetempo i loro esercizi militari. Stephens è catturato ed imprigionato ma riesce ad evadere, grazie alla fedaltà di un carceriere feniano, e mentre gli agenti e le spie stanno in agguato ad ogni porto dell'isola sorvegliando le navi in partenza, esce dalla capitale in biroccino travestito da sposa (secondo la leggenda) col velo di crespo bianco ed i fiori d'arancio. Poscia è condotto a bordo d'una piccola barca di carbone che salpa lestamente per la Francia. O'Leary è processato e condannato a vent'anni di lavori forzati ma è graziato più tardi e sfrattato dall'Irlanda per quindici anni.

E perché questo sfacelo di un movimento così bene organizzato? Semplicemente perché in Irlanda proprio al momento psicologico si presenta sempre il delatore.

Dopo lo sbandamento dei feniani la tradizione della dottrina di forza fisica si manifesta ad intervalli in attentati violenti. Gli 'invincibili' fanno saltare in aria il carcere di Clerkenvell, strappano i loro amici dalle mani della polizia a Manchester ed uccidono la scorta, pugnalano il capo segretario ed il sottosegretario inglesi, Lord Federico Covendish e Burke, di pieno giorno nel Parco della Fenice a Dublino.

Dopo ciascuno di questi delitti, quando l'indignazione generale è un po' calmata, un ministro inglese propone alla Camera qualche misura di riforma per l'Irlanda, ed i feniani ed i nazionalisti si vilipendono di tutto cuore, gli uni attribuendo la misura al successo della loro tattica parlamentare e gli altri attribuendola alla facoltà di persuadere latente nello stiletto o nella bomba; e, come retroscena di questa triste commedia, havvi lo spettacolo della popolazione che diminuisce di anno in anno con regolarità matematica, di una emigrazione ininterrotta agli Stati Uniti o in Europa di irlandesi pei quali le condizioni economiche ed intellettuali della loro patria sono insopportabili, e, quasi per mettere in rilievo questa spopolazione, una lunga teoria di chiese, cattedrali, conventi, collegi, seminari, per soccorrere ai bisogni spirituali di coloro che non hanno potuto trovare o il coraggio od i quattrini per intraprendere il viaggio da Queenstown a Nuova York.

L'Irlanda, travagliata da molteplici doveri, ha compiuto ciocchè sinora era ritenuto un compito impossibile, il servire Dio e Mammone, lasciandosi sfruttare dall'Inghilterra e sempre aumentando l'obolo di San Pietro, forse in riconoscenza al sommo pontefice Adriano IV che, in un momento di generosità, fece regalo dell'isola al re inglese Enrico II circa ottocento anni fa.

Ora è impossibile che una dottrina drastica e sanguinosa come il fenianismo possa continuare a sussistere in un tale ambiente, e, difatti, mentre da una parte i delitti agrari e violenti si sono fatti di più in più rari, il fenianismo ha ancora una volta cambiato nome e figura. È sempre una dottrina separativa ma non adopera più la dinamite. I nuovi feniani si sono riuniti nel partito che si chiama 'noi stessi'. Mirano a fare dell'Irlanda una repubblica bilingue ed a questo scopo hanno stabilito un servizio diretto di vapori fra l'Irlanda e la Francia; praticano il boicottaggio delle merci inglesi, rifiutano di farsi soldati o di prestare il giuramento di fedeltà alla corona britannica, cercano di sviluppare l'industria per tutta l'isola e, invece di sborsare un milione ed un quarto annualmente pel mantenimento degli ottanta deputati al Parlamento inglese, vogliono inaugurare un servizio di consoli presso i principali porti del mondo allo scopo di smerciare i prodotti industriali senzi intervento dell'Inghilterra.

Per molti punti di vista quest'ultima fase del fenianismo è forse la più formidabile. Certamente la sua influenza ha rimodellato a nuovo il carattere degli irlandesi ed il vecchio capo, O'Leary, quando tornò in patria, dopo anni d'esilio studioso a Parigi, si vide tra una generazione animata da ideali ben differenti da quelli del '65. Fu accolto dai suoi compatriotti con onoranze e a quando a quando appariva in pubblico, a presiedere ora qualche conferenza separatista, ora qualche banchetto. Ma era una figura di un mondo scomparso. Si vedeva spesse volte camminare lungo il fiume, un vegliardo vestito per lo più di vestiti chiari, con una chioma spiovente e bianchissima, quasi piegato in due dalla vecchiaia e dalle sofferenze; si fermava dinanzi alle botteghe oscure dei librai antiquari e poi, fatto qualche acquisto, ritornava lungo il fiume. Aveva poca ragione, del resto, di essere allegro. I suoi piani erano sfumati, i suoi amici morti, e nella sua patria ben pochi sapevano chi egli fosse e che avesse fatto. Ora ch'egli è morto i suoi connazionali lo scorteranno alla tomba con gran fasto, perché gli irlandesi, anche quando spezzano il cuore di coloro che sacrificarono la loro vita per la patria, non mancano mai di testimoniare grande riverenza ai defunti.

L'OMBRA DI PARNELL

THE SHADE OF PARNELL

Col votare il progetto d'autonomia parlamentare in seconda lettura, la Camera dei Comuni ha risolto la questione irlandese, questione che, come la gallina mugellese, ha cent'anni e mostra un mese.

Il secolo che si iniziò con la transazione di compravendita del parlamento dublinese e si chiude ora con un patto triangolare fra l'Inghilterra, l'Irlanda e gli Stati Uniti, fu illegiadrito da sette movimenti rivoluzionari irlandesi, i quali con la dinamite, coll'eloquenza, col boicottaggio, coll'ostruzionismo, con la rivolta armata, coll'assassinio politico, sono riusciti a tener desta la tarda ed ansiosa coscienza del liberalismo inglese.

La legge odierna, concessa nella piena maturità del tempo sotto la duplice pressione del partito nazionalista a Westminster, che intralcia da mezzo secolo l'opera dei legislatori britannici, e del partito irlandese d'al di là dell'Atlantico, che ostacola la tanto ambita alleanza anglo-americana, legge ideata e foggiata con arte subdola e magistrale, corona degnamente la tradizione tramandata ai posteri dal più che perfetto statista liberale Guglielmo Gladstone. Basti dire che, mentre riduce la forte falange dei centotré collegi gli irlandesi, attualmente rappresentati a Westminster da un manipolo di quaranta deputati, spinge automaticamente questi ultimi fra le braccia del piccolo partito del lavoro, dimodoché da questo abbraccio incestuoso nascerà probabilmente una coalizione che fungerà da estrema sinistra, vale a dire da base d'operazioni per il partito liberale nella sua campagna contro il conservatorismo fino ad ordini ulteriori. Nel groviglio delle clausole finanziarie non è il caso di entrare. Il nascituro governo irlandese dovrà ad ogni modo coprire uno sbilancio, abilmente creato dal tesoro britannico con manovre di imposte locali ed imperiali, o con la riduzione delle spese amministrative o coll'aumentare le imposte dirette, andando incontro, nell'uno o nell'altro caso, all'ostilità disillusa della borghesia o del popolino.

Il partito separatista irlandese vorrebbe respingere questo dono greco che fa del cancelliere dello scacchiere a Dublino un ministro titolare pienamente responsabile verso i contribuenti e nel medesimo tempo alle dipendenze del gabinetto britannico; che può tassare senza poter controllare gli incassi del suo dicastero; una macchina distributrice che non può funzionare se la dinamo a Londra non le trasmettesse una corrente del voltaggio necessario.

Non monta: la parvenza d'autonomia c'è. Al recente comizio nazionale tenuto a Dublino, i rimproveri e le proteste dei nazionalisti che appartengono alla scuola aspramente scettica di Giovanni Mitchel non turbarono gran che il giubilo popolare. I deputati, invecchiati nella lotta costituzionale e sfibrati da tanti anni di speranze disilluse, salutarono nei loro discorsi la chiusa di una lunga era di malintesi. Un giovine oratore, nipote di Gladstone, evocò fra le acclamazioni frenetiche della folla il nome di suo nonno ed inneggiò alla prosperità della nuova nazione. Fra due anni al più tardi, con o senza l'assenso della Camera dei Pari, le porte dell'antico parlamento di Dublino si riapriranno e l'Irlanda, uscita dalla sua prigionia secolare, s'avvierà come sposa novella, verso la reggia, scortata dai musici e fra le tede di rito. Un pronipote di Gladstone (se ve ne sia) spargerà fiori sotto i piedi della sovrana, ma ci sarà un'ombra alla festa: l'ombra di Carlo Parnell.

La critica più recente ha cercato di menomare la grandezza di questo strano spirito, additando le diverse fonti della sua agile tattica parlamentare. Ma anche se concediamo al critico storico che l'ostruzionismo fu inventato da Biggar e Ronayne, che la dottrina dell'indipendenza del partito irlandese fulanciata da Gavan Duffy, che la lega agraria fu la creazione di Michele Davitt, queste concessioni fanno emergere di più la straordinaria personalità di un duce che senza doti forensi, nè talento politico originale costrinse i più grandi politicanti inglesi ad eseguire i suoi ordini, e condusse, come un altro Mosè, n'i popolo turbolento e mutevole dalla casa di vergogna fino al limite della terra promessa. L'influenza esercitata da Parnell sul popolo irlandese sfida l'analisi del critico. Bleso, di corporatura delicata, ignorava la storia della sua patria; i suoi discorsi brevi e frammentari erano privi d'eloquenza, di poesia o d'umore; il suo comportamento freddo e cortese lo separava dai suoi stessi colleghi; era protestante, discendente d'un casato patrizio e (per colmo di sciagura) parlava con uno spiccato accento inglese. Veniva ai comizi spesse volte un'ora o un'ora e mezzo dopo l'ora fissata e non si scusava. Trascurava la sua corrispondenza per settimane intere. Il plauso e l'ira della folla, i vituperi e le lodi della stampa, le denunzie e le difese dei ministri britannici non turbarono mai la triste serenità del suo carattere. Si dice persino che non conoscesse di vista molti di coloro che sedevano con lui sui banchi irlandesi. Quando il popolo irlandese gli presentò nel 1887 il tributo nazionale (quarantamila lire sterline) mise lo 'chèque' nel suo portafogli e nel discorso che tenne all'immensa moltitudine non fece la minima allusione al dono che aveva ricevuto. Quando gli fu mostrato l'esemplare del *Times* contenente la famosa lettera autografa che doveva comprovare la sua correità nell'efferato assassinio del parco della Fenice, mise un dito su una lettera della firma e disse semplicemente: 'Non ho fatto un'esse in quel modo dal settantotto in poi.' Più tardi le indagini della commissione reale rivelarono il complotto ordito contro di lui, e lo spergiuro e falsario Pigott si fece saltare il cervello in un albergo a Madrid. La Camera dei Comuni, senza distinzione di partiti, salutò l'entrata di Parnell con un'ovazione che rimane senza precedenti negli annali del parlamento britannico. Occorre dire che il Parnell non rispose all'ovazione né con un sorriso, né con un inchino, né con un cenno? Passò al suo posto oltre la corsia e si sedette. Pensava probabilmente a questo incidente il Gladstone quando chiamò il duce irlandese un fenomeno intellettuale.

Niente di più singolare si può immaginare che l'apparenza di questo fenomeno intellettuale in mezzo all'afa morale del palazzo di Westminster. Ora, rivedendo le scene del dramma e riudendo i discorsi che fecero fremere le anime degli ascoltatori, è inutile negare che tutta quell'eloquenza e tutti quei trionfi strategici comincino a sapere di stantio. Ma il tempo è più clemente verso il 're senza corona' che verso il motteggiatore e il retore. La luce di quella sua sovranità mite ed altiera, silenziosa e sconsolata, fa somigliare il Disraeli ed il Gladstone l'uno ad un diplomatico arrivista che pranza quando può in casa dei ricchi e l'altro ad un imponentissimo maggiordomo che ha frequentato le scuole serali. Come pesano leggieri nella bilancia oggi lo spirito disraeliano e la coltura gladstoniana! Che cose lievi sono oggi i lazzi studiati, le cemecchie bisunte, i romanzi melensi del Dismeli, i periodi altisonanti, gli studi omerici, i discorsi su Artemis o sulla marmellata del Gladstone!

Quantunque la tattica di Parnell fosse di servirsi di qualunque partito inglese, liberale o conservatore, a suo piacimento, un nesso di circostanze lo coinvolse nel movimento liberale. Il liberalismo gladstoniano era un incostante simbolo algebrico di cui il coefficiente era la pressione della politica del momento e l'indice il tornaconto personale; e, mentre nella politica interna temporeggiava, si smentiva e si giustificava a vicenda, serbò sempre (per quanto poteva) un'ammirazione sincera della libertà in casa altrui. Bisogna tenere a mente questa qualità elastica del liberalismo di Gladstone per comprendere quanto e quale fosse il compito di Parnell. Il Gladstone, per dirlo in una parola, era un politicante. Fremette alla nequizie irrequieta di O'Connell nel 1835 e fu il legislatore inglese che proclamò la necessità morale e materiale dell'autonomia irlandese; tuonò contro l'ammissione degli ebrei agli uffici pubblici e fu lui il ministro che per la prima volta nella storia inglese innalzò un ebreo al pariato; tenne fiero linguaggio coi boeri insorti nel 1881 e dopo la sconfitta delle truppe inglesi a Majuba conchiuse col Transvaal un patto che fu chiamato dagli stessi inglesi una dedizione vigliacca; nel suo primo discorso parlamentare difese calorosamente dall'accusa di crudeltà mossagli dal conte Grey il proprio padre, ricco padrone di schiavi in Demerara, che aveva ricavato due milioni di franchi dalla vendita di carne umana, mentre nell'ultima sua lettera ad un altro 'amico dell'infanzia' il duca di Westminster, invocò tutti i fulmini disponibili sul capo del grande assassino di Costantinopoli.

Parnell, convinto che un tale liberalismo non si sarebbe arreso che alla forza, riunì dietro di sé ogni elemento della vita nazionale e si mise in marcia camminando sull'orlo dell'insurrezione. Sei anni dopo la sua entrata a Westminster teneva già nelle mani il destino del governo. Fu incarcerato, ma nella sua cella a Kilmainham conchiuse un patto coi ministri che l'avevano incarcerato. Fallito il tentativo di ricatto con la confessione del suicida Pigott, il governo liberale gli offrì un portafoglio. Parnell lo rifiutò non soltanto, ma ordinò a tutti i suoi seguaci di rifiutàre parimenti qualunque carica ministeriale e vietò ai municipi e alle corporazioni pubbliche in Irlanda di ricevere ufficialmente qualunque membro della casa reale britannica finché un governo inglese non avesse ridato l'autonomia all'Irlanda. Fu giocoforza per i liberali accettare queste condizioni umilianti e Gladstone, nel 1886 lesse a Westminster il primo progetto di 'Home Rule'.

La caduta di Parnell venne in mezzo a questi avvenimenti come un fulmine a ciel sereno. S'innamorò perdutamente di una donna maritata e quando il marito, il capitano O'Shea, chiese il divorzio, i ministri Gladstone e Morley rifiutarono apertamente di legiferare in favore dell'Irlanda se il colpevole restasse a capo del partito nazionalista. Al processo, Parnell non comparve né si difese. Negò il diritto di un ministro di esercitare un veto sugli affari politici dell'irlanda e rifiutò di dare le dimissioni. Fu deposto dai nazionalisti in ubbidienza agli ordini di Gladstone. Degli ottantatré deputati, soli otto gli rimasero fedeli. Il clero alto e basso entrò in lizza per dargli il colpo di grazia. La stampa irlandese vuotò sopra di lui e sopra la signora che amava le fiale del suo livore. I contadini a Castlecomer gli gettarono calce viva negli occhi. Passò da contea a contea, da città a città, 'come un cervo cacciato', figura spettrale coi segni della morte sulla fronte. Entro un anno morì di crepacuore all'età di quarantacinque anni.

L'ombra del 're senza corona' coprirà i cuori di coloro che si ricordano di lui quando la nuova Irlanda entrerà fra poco nella reggia 'fimbriis aureis circumamicta varietatibus': ma non sarà un'ombra vendicativa. La tristezza che devastò la sua anima era forse la profonda convinzione che nell'ora del bisogno uno dei discepoli che intingeva la mano con lui nel catino stava per tradirlo. L'aver combattuto fino alla fine con questa desolante certezza nell'anima è il suo primo e il più grande titolo di nobiltà. Nel suo ultimo fiero appello al popolo suo implorò i suoi connazionali di non gettarlo in pasto ai lupi inglesi che gli urlavano attorno. Ridondi ad onore dei suoi connazionali che non mancarono a quel disperato appello. Non lo gettarono ai lupi inglesi: lo dilaniarono essi stessi.

L'IRLANDA: ISOLA DEI SANTI E DEI SAVI
IRELAND: ISLAND OF SAINTS AND SAGES

Le nazioni hanno i loro egoismi come gli individui. Non è mica nuovo nella storia l'esempio di un popolo che si compiace di attribuirsi qualità o glorie ignoti ad altri popoli, dall'epoca dei nostri antenati che si chiamavano ariani o nobili a quella dei greci i quali usavano chiamare barbari tutti coloro che non abitavano la terra sacrosanta d'Ellade. Gli irlandesi, con orgoglio forse meno spiegabile, amano alludere alla loro terra come l'isola dei santi e dei savi.

Questo titolo onorevole non è ne d'ieri nè d'ieri l'altro. Data anzi dai tempi antichissimi quando l'isola era un vero foco d'intellettualità e di santità, diffondendo da per tutto il continente una coltura ed un'energia vivificante. Sarebbe facile compilare un'elenco degli irlandesi i quali, sia come pellegrini od eremiti sia come dotti o magi hanno portato di paese in paese la fiaccola della scienza. Le loro orme vedonsi anche oggidi in qualche ara deserta, in qualche tradizione o leggenda ove persino il nome del protagonista è appena riconoscibile, o in qualche allusione poetico, per esempio, quel passo dell'inferno di Dante in cui il mentore addita uno dei maghi celtici travagliato dalle pene infernali, dicendo:

> Quell'altro che nei fianchi è così poco
> Michele Scotto fu che veramente
> Delle magiche frodi seppe il giuoco

Ci vorrebbero, in verità, l'erudizione e la pazienza di un bollandista ozioso per narrare gli atti di questi santi e savi. Riccordiamo almeno il famigerato opponente di San Tommaso, Giovanni Duns Scotus, nominato il dottore sottile per distinguerlo da S. Tommaso il dottore angelico e da Bonaventura il dottore serafico, campione militante del domma della concezione immacolata ed, a quanto ci dicono le cronache d'allora, dialletico insuperabile. Pare indiscutibile che l'Irlanda fu allora un immenso seminario ove si congregavano alunni dai diversi paesi europei, tanto grande ne era la fama di maestra nelle cose spirituali. Benchè bisogni accogliere con gran riserbo asserzioni di questo genere è più che probabile (veduto il fervore religioso che ancora vige in Irlanda e di cui potete con difficoltà, nutriti come siete del cibo scettico di questi ultimi anni, farvi una guista idea), che questo passato glorioso non sia una finzione dovuta allo spirito di autoglorificazione. Del resto se desiderate convincervi ci sono sempre gli archivi polverosi dei tedeschi. Il Ferrero ci dice adesso che le scoperte di questi buoni professori della Germania, in quanto riguardino la storia antica della repubblica romana e dell'impero romano, sono sbagliate da capo a fondo o quasi. Può darsi. Ma, sia così o no, nessuno può negare che siccome sono stati questi dotti tedeschi i primi a presentare Shakespeare come poeta di significazione mondiale agli occhi stralunati dei suoi compatrioti (i quali sino allora avevano considerato Guglielmino una persona d'importanza secondaria, un buon diavolo dotato di una vena piacevole di poesia lirica ma forse troppo affezionato alla birra inglese), così furono questi stessi tedeschi i soli in Europa ad occuparsi delle lingue celtiche e della storia delle cinque nazioni celtiche.

Le sole grammatiche e vocabolari irlandesi ch'esistevano in Europa fino a pochi anni fa, quando fu fondata a Dublino la lega gaelica, erano opere di tedeschi. La lingua irlandese, benché sia sempre della famiglia indo-europea, differisce dall'inglese quasi quanto la lingua che si parla a Roma differisce da quella che si parla a Teheran. Ha un'alfabeta e caratteri speciali, una letteratura ed una storia vecchie quasi di tremila anni. Dieci anni fa era parlato soltanto dai contadini nella provincia occidentale, sulla costa atlantica, un po' anche nel sud e nelle piccole isole che sono come i picchetti dell'avanguardia dell'Europa di fronte all'emisfera del ponente. Ora la lega celtica ne ha resuscitato l'uso. Ogni giornale irlandese, eccettuati gli organi unionisti, ha almeno una rubrica speciale redatta in irlandese. La corrispondenza dei principali municipi è scritta in irlandese, la lingua irlandese s'insegna nella maggior parte delle scuole elementare e secondarie, e nelle università è stata posta al livello delle altre lingue moderne, come il francese, il tedesco, l'italiano e lo spagnuolo. A Dublino i nomi delle strade sono scritte in ambedue le lingue. La lega organizza feste, concerti, dibattimenti e convegni sociali ai quali il parlatore di *Beurla* (cioè: inglese) si sente un pesce fuor d'acqua, confuso in mezzo una folla che chiacchera in una favella aspra e gutturale. Sovente nella strada si vedono passare dei gruppi di giovani che parlano l'irlandese forse un poco più enfaticamente che non sia necessario. Gli soci della lega corrispondono in irlandese e molte volte il povero postino non sapendo leggere l'indirizzo deve rivolgersi a qualche capo sezione per sgroppare il nodo.

Questa lingua è d'origine orientale ed è stata identificata da molti filologi coll'antica lingua dei fenici, gli scopritori, secondo gli storici, del commercio e della navigazione. Questo popolo avventuriero, avendo il monopolio del mare, stabilì in Irlanda una civiltà ch'era decade ente e quasi scomparsa prima che il primo storico greco prendesse in mano il suo calamo. Conservava gelosamente i segreti delle sue scienze e la prima menzione che c'è in letteratura straniera dell'isola d'Irlanda si trova in un poema greco del quinto secolo avanti Gesù Cristo, ove lo storico ripete la tradizione fenicia. La lingua che il commediografo latino Plauto ha messa in bocca di fenici nella sua commedia *Poenula* è quasi la stessa lingua, secondo il critico Vallancey, che parlano adesso i contadini irlandesi. La religione e la civiltà di quell'antico popolo, più tardi conosciute sotto il nome di druidismo, erano egiziane. I preti druidici avevano i loro tempi nell'aperto e adoravano il sole e la luna in nemori di rovere. Nelle scienze rudi di quei tempi i preti irlandesi erano allora ritenuti dottissimi e Plutarca, quando menziona l'Irlanda, dice ch'era la dimora di nomini santi. Festo Avieno nel quarto secolo fu il primo che le diede il titolo di *Insula Sacra*, e più tardi, dopo aver subito le invasioni di tribù spagnuole e galliche, l'irlanda, convertita al cristianesimo da S. Patrizio ed i suoi seguaci senza spargimento di sangue, meritò di nuovo il titolo di 'isola sacra'.

Non propongo di dare una storia completa della chiesa irlandese nei primi secoli dell'éra cristiana. Il fare così sarebbe oltre lo scopo di questa conferenza e vieppiù, non soverchiamente interessante. Ma è necessario di darvi qualche spiegazione del titolo 'isola dei santi e dei savi' nonchè di dimostrarvene le basi storiche. Lasciando da banda i nomi degli ecclesiastici la cui opera era esclusivamente nazionale, nomi innumerabili, vi pregherò di volermi seguir per qualche momento mentre vi faccio vedere le orme che hanno lasciate dopo di sè i moltissimi apostoli celtici in quasi ogni paese. Ne bisogna tener poco conto di tali fatti, i quali oggidì possono sembrare triviali all'intelligenza laica, visto che nei secoli in cui avvennero ed in tutto il medioevo seguente non soltanto la storia stessa ma anche le scienze e le arti diverse furono tutte e quante di carattere religioso e sotto tutela di una chiesa più che materna. E difatti che cose erano gli scienziati e gli artisti italiani prima del rinascimento sè non tante ancelle ubbedienti del signore, commentatori eruditi di scritti sacri od illustratori in verso od in pittura della favola cristiana.

Parrà strano che un'isola remota come l'Irlanda dal centro di coltura potesse diventare la scuola superiore di apostoli ma anche una rivista superficiale ci dimostra che la pretesa della nazione irlandese di compire la sua civiltà da sè non è tanto la pretesa di una nazione giovane che vuol fare capo al concerto europeo quanto la pretesa di una nazione vecchissima di rinnovare, sotto nuove forme, le glorie di una civiltà decorsa.

Persino nel primo secolo del cristianesimo sotto l'apostolato di San Pietro troviamo l'irlandese Mansueto più tardi canonizzato, missionario nella Lorena ove fondò una chiesa e predicò per mezzo secolo. Cataldo ebbe una cattedra di docente teologo a Ginevra e poi fu creato vescovo di Taranto. Il gran eresiarca Pelagio, viaggiatore e propagandista instancabile, se non era un irlandese (ciocche molti ritengono) era certamente o un'irlandese od uno scozzese: come lo era pure la sua mano destro, Celestio. Sedulio percorse gran parte del mondo e finalmente si stabilì a Roma ove compose la bellezza di quasi cinquanta trattati teologici e molti inni sacri che usansi anche oggi nel rito cattolico. Fridolino Viator cioè il viaggiatore, di ceppo reale irlandese, fu missionario fra i tedeschi e morì a

Seckinge in Germania ove è sepolto. Il focoso Colombano ebbe l'incarico di riformare la Chiesa francese e dopo aver suscitato una guerra civile nella Borgogna colle sue prediche si recò in Italia dove diventò l'apostolo dei Lombardi, fondando il monastero di Bobio. Frigidiano, figlio del re dell'-Irlanda del nord, occupò la sede vescovile di Lucca. San Gallo, prima l'allievo ed il compagno di Columbano, visse fra i Grigioni in Svizzera da eremita, coltivando solo le sue glebe e cacciando e pescando, rifiutò il vescovato della città di Costanza che gli fu offerto e morì all'età di 95 anni. Sul luogo del suo eremitaggio sorse un'abbazia e l'abate, per la grazia di dio, diventò il principe del cantone, ed arrichì di molto la biblioteca bendettina, le rovine della quale sono ancora mostrate a coloro che visitano la vecchia borga di San Gallo. Finiano, detto il dotto, fondò una scuola di teologia sulle sponde del fiume Boyne in Irlanda, dove insegnò la dottrina cattolica a migliaja di studenti dalla Gran Brettagna, dalla Francia, dall'-Armorica e dalla Germania, dando a tutti (o tempo beato!) non solamente l'istruzione ed i libri ma perfino il vitto e l'alloggio gratis. Sennonchè, a quanto pare, trascurava qualche volta di empire bene le lucerne di studio ed uno studente, a cui venne meno ad un tratto la luce, fu costretto d'invocare la grazia divina, la quale fece splendere meravigliosamente le sue dita, dimodochè percorrendo i fogli con le dita luminose potè soddisfare alla sua sete di sapere. San Fiacro, a cui c'è una tabella commemorativa nella chiesa di S. Maturino a Parigi, predicò ai francesi ed ebbe funerali fastosi a spese della corte. Fursey fondò monasteri in cinque paesi e la sua festa è ancora celebrato nel luogo della sua morte, a Peronne, in Picardia. Arbogasto eresse reliquari e cappelle in Alsazia ed in Lorrena, governò per cinque anni la sede vescovile di Strasburgo, fino a che, sentendosi presso alla sua fine in ricordanza del suo esemplare andò ad abitare mi tugurio nel luogo ove venivano giustiziati i malfattori, ed ove più tardi fu costruitta la grande cattedrale della città. San Viro si fece campione del culto della Santa Vergine in Francia e Disibodo, vescovo di Dublino, viaggiò in qua ed in là per tutta la Germania durante più di quaranta anni e fondò finalmente un monastero dell'ordine benedettino che nominò Monte Disibodo ora cambiato in Disenberg. Rumoldo diventò vescovo di Mechlin in Francia e martire. Albino, coll'aiuto di Carlo il Grande, fondò un istituto di scienza a Parigi ed un'altro nell'antico Ticino (ora Pavia), il quale governò per molti anni. Kiliano, l'apostolo di Franconia, era consecrato vescovo di Wurtzburgh in Germania, ma volendo fare la parte di Giovanni Battista fra il duca Gosberto e la sua druda, venne ucciso da sicari. Sedulio il più giovane era scelto da Gregorio II per la missione di pacificare le beghe clericali in Spagna ma quando giunse colà i preti spagnuoli rifiutarono di ascoltarlo, dicendo ch'egli era uno straniero, a quale accusa il Sedulio ripose che, essendo egli un irlandese e della vecchia razza milesiana era difatti oriundo spagnuolo, argomento che convinse talmente i suoi opponenti che gli permisero di installarsi nel palazzo vescovile di Oreto. La perioda, insomma, che si chiude coll'invasione delle tribù scandinave in Irlanda nel secolo ottavo non è che il ricordo ininterrotto di apostolati. di missioni, e di martinii ed il re Alfredo, che visitò il paese e ce ne ha lasciato le sue impressioni, nei versi chiamati 'L' Itinerario Reale' ci dice nella prima strofe:

> Trovai quando fui esule
> In Irlanda la bella
> Donne molte, una folla seria,
> Laici e preti in abbondanza.

e, bisogna amettere che in dodici secoli il quadro non si è cambiato di molto sennonchè se il buon Alfredo che trovò in Irlanda allora grande abbondanza di laici e di preti ci andasse adesso vi troverebbe quasi quasi più di questi che di quei.

Chi legga la storia dei tre secoli che precedettero l'avvento degli inglesi deve aver lo stomaco forte perchè le lotte intestine ed i conflitti contri i danesi ed i norvegesi, gli stranieri neri e bianchi come erano denominati, si succedevano così continui e feroci da rendere tutta quest'epoca un vero macello. I danesi occuparono tutti i porti principali sulla costa citeriore dell'isola, e stabilirono un regno a Dublino, ora capitale dell'Irlanda e da una ventina di secoli grande città. I re indigeni si ammazzavano allora vicendevolmente, prendendo soste meritate da tempo in tempo in partite di scacchi. Finalmente la vittoria sanguinaria dell'usurpatore Brian dei Tributi sulle orde nordiche sulle dune fuori le mura di Dublino mise fine alle razzie degli scandinavi, i quali però non abbandonarono il paese ma furono man mano assimilati nella comunità, fatto che dobbiamo tenere in mente se vogliamo spiegare il curioso carattere dell'irlandese moderno. Durante questo periodo la coltura necessariamente languiva ma l'Irlanda ebbe l'onore di produrre i tre grandi eresiarchi, Giovanni Scotus Erigena, Macario e Virgilio Solivago. L'ultimo nominato fu raccomandato dal re francese all'abbazia di Salzburgo e fu indi creato vescovo di quella diocesi ove costrusse una cattedrale. Era filosofo e matematico e traduttore degli scritti di Ptolemago e sostenne in un suo trattato geografico la teoria allora sovversiva della sfericità della terra e fu per tale audacia dichiarato seminatore di eresie dai papi Bonifazio e Zaccaria. Macario visse in Francia ed il monastero di S. Eligio conseva ancora il suo trattato *De Anima* nella quale insegnò la dottrina più tardi conosciuta sotto il nome di averroismo riguarda alla quale Ernesto Renan (egli stesso un bretone celtico) ci ha lasciato un esame magistrale. Panteista mistico fu pure Scotus Erigena, rettore dell'università di Parigi, che tradusse dal greco i libri di teologia mistica del pseudo-Dionisio l'Areopagita, patrono della nazione francese, traduzione che presentò per la prima volta all'Europa i sistemi trascendentali dell'oriente e che ebbe tanta influenza sul corso del pensiero religioso europeo quanto ebbe più tardi sullo sviluppo della civiltà profana italica le traduzioni platoniche fatte nei tempi di Pico della Mirandola. Va senza dire che una tale innovazione, che pareva il soffio vivificatore concitando al risorgimento corporale le ossa morte della teologia ortodossa ammucchiate in un camposanto inviolabile, un campo di Ardath, non ebbe la sanzione del papa, il quale invitò Carlo il Calvo a mandare a Roma sotto scorta tanto il libra quanto l'autore volendo egli probabilmente far gustare a questi qualche delizia della cortesia papalina. Scotus però pare che abbia conservato nel suo cervello esaltato un granuccio di buon senso perché al gentile invito fece orecchio di mercante e si recò con tutta celerità in patria sua.

Dal tempo dell'invasione inglese sino ai giorni nostri vi è un'intervallo di quasi otto secoli: e se mi sono indugiato un po'a lungo sul periodo precedente allo scopo di farvi realizzare le radici del temperameto irlandese non intendo di trattenervi con un resoconto delle vicende dell'-Irlanda sotto l'occupazione straniera. Anzitutto non lo faccio perchè fu allora che l'Irlanda cessò di essere una forza intelletuale in Europa. Le arti decorative nelle quali gli antichi irlandesi eccellevano erano abbandonate, la coltura sacra e profana caddero in desuetudine.

Due o tre nomi illustri splendono qui come le ultime rare stelle di una notte radiante che impallidisce perchè l'alba è giunta, Giovanni Duns Scotus, di cui vi ho parlato innanzi, fondatore della scuola degli scotisti il quale, secondo la leggenda, ascoltò per tre giorni intieri gli argomenti di tutti i dottori dell'università di Parigi e poi si alzò e, parlando a memoria, li confutò ad uno ad uno, Giovanni a Sacrobosco, ch'era l'ultimo grande sostenitore delle teorie geografiche ed astronomiche di Ptolemago, e Petrus Hibernicus, il teologo ch'ebbe il sommo incarico di educare la mente dell'autore dell'apologia scolastica, *Summa contra Gentiles*, S. Tommaso d'Aquino, forse la mente la più acuta e lucida di cui la storia umana abbia conoscenza. Ma mentre queste ultime stelle ancora rammentava alle nazioni dell'Europa la gloria passata dell'Irlanda, una nuova razza celtica sorgeva, composta dal vecchio ceppo celtico e dalle razze scandinave, anglo-sassone e normanna. Un altro temperamento nazionale sorse a base di quell'antico, i vari elementi interpenetrando e rinnovellando la vecchia corporatura. Gli antichi nemici fecero causa [comune] contro le agressioni inglesi, gli stessi abitatori protestanti diventati *Hibernis Hiberniores*, più irlandesi degli irlandesi stessi incitando i cattolici irlandesi nella loro opposizione ai fanatici calvinisti e luterani d'oltremare, ed i discendenti dei danesi, dei normanni, e dei colonizzatori anglo-sassoni campionando la causa della nuova nazione irlandese contro la tirannide brittanica. Un deputato irlandese recentemente quando arringava gli elettori alla vigilia di un'elezione si vantò di essere della vecchia razza e rimproverò al suo opponente di essere discendente di un colòno cromwelliano. Il rimprovero suscitò generale riso nella stampa perchè a vero dire, l'escludere dalla nazione attuale tutti coloro che discendono da famiglia straniera sarebbe impossibile ed il negare il nome di pattriota a tutti coloro che non sono di ceppo irlandese sarebbe il negarlo a quasi tutti gli eroi del movimento moderno, a lord Edoardo FitzGerald, Roberto Emmet, Teobaldo Wolfe Tone e Napper Tandy, capi dell'insurrezione del 1798, a Tommaso Davis e Giovanni Mitchel capi del movimento della Giovane Irlanda, a molti dei feniani anticierali, a Isacco Butt e Giuseppe Biggar, fondatori dell'ostruzionismo parlamentare, e finalmente a Carlo Stewart Parnell, l'uomo il più temibile forse che abbia mai capitanato gli irlandesi ma nelle cui vene non correva neppure una goccia di sangue celtico.

Nel calendario nazionale due giorni, secondo i pattrioti, devono segnarsi come giorni infausti, quello, cioè, dell'invasione anglo-sassone e normanna e quello, un secolo fa, dell'annessione dei due parlamenti. Ora, in questa giuntura, giova rilevare due fatti piccanti e significativi. L'Irlanda si pregia di essere in corpo ed anima fedele tanto alle sue tradizioni nazionali quanta alla S. Sede. La più gran parte degli irlandesi ritengono fedeltà a queste due tradizioni il loro articolo di fede cardinale. Ma il fatto è che gli inglesi vennero in Irlanda dopo richieste ripetute di un re nativo, senza, a quanto pare, gran voglia e senza la sanzione del loro monarca, ma muniti di una bolla papale di Adriana IV e di una lettera papale di Alessandro. Sbarcarono sulla costa meridionale in numero di 700 uomini, una masnada di avventurieri contro un popolo, furono accolti da certe tribù indigene ed in meno di un anno il re inglese Enrico II celebrò la festa di Natale chiassosamente nella città di Dublino. Vi è di più, l'unione parlamentare dei due paesi non era votato a Westminster ma a Dublino, da un parlamento eletto dai voti del popolo d'Irlanda, un parlamento corrotto e sobillato con somme ingenti dagli agenti del primo ministro inglese ma ciònondimeno un parlamento irlandese. Questi due fatti, secondo me, devono essere perfettamente spiegati prima chè il paese in cui avvennero abbia il diritto il più elementare di pretendere da un suo figlio che cambi la sua posizione d'osservatore spregiudicato in quella di nazionalista convinto.

Dell'altra parte l'imparzialità può facilmente confondersi con una dimenticanza conveniente di fatti: e se un'osservatore, pienamente convinto che l'Irlanda nei tempi di Enrico II era un corpo dilaniato da lotte feroci e nei tempi di Guglielmo Pitt un corpo venale e laide di corrutele, deduce da queste sue convinzioni che l'Inghilterra non abbia tanto ora come in avvenire debiti da scontare in Irlanda, sbaglia e sbaglia di molto. Quando un paese vincitore tiranneggia un altro non può logicamente prenderlo a male se questo reagisce. Gli uomini sono fatti così: e nessuno che non abbia gli occhi abbindolati dall'interesse o dal dabennagine, crederà più a questa ora che un paese colonizzatore è mosso da puri motivi di cristianità impossible quando s'impossessa di lidi stranieri, per quanto il missionano e la bibbia tascabile precedano di consueto di qualche mese l'arrivo del milite e della mitragliatrice. Se gli irlandesi a casa non hanno potuto fare ciocchè i loro fratelli hanno fatto in America non vuol dire che non lo faranno mai nè è logici da parte dei storici inglesi di salutare la memoria di Giorgio Washington e di protestarsi ben contenti del progresso di una repubblica autonoma e quasi socialista in Australia, mentre trattano di mattoide il separatista irlandese.

Una separazione morale già esiste fra i due paesi. Io non ricordo di aver mai inteso l'inno inglese 'God Save the King' suonato in pubblico senza una burrasca di fischi, di grida e di zittii che ne rendeva la musica solenne e maestosa assolutamente inaudibile nia per convincersi dell'esistenza di questa separazione bisogna essere stati nella strada quando entrò nella capitale d'Irlanda (quando vi entrò) la defunta regina Vittoria l'anno che precedette la sua morte. Anzitutto bisogna render noto che quando un monarca inglese vuol andare per iscopi politici in Irlanda c'è sempre un putiferio vivace per indurre il sindaco a riceverlo alle porte della città: e, difatti, l'ultimo monarca che vi entrò ha dovuto accontentarsi del ricevimento informale dello sceriffo, il sindaco avendone rifiutato l'onore. (Rilevo qui a puro titolo di curiosità che il sindaco attuale di Dublino è un italiano, Signor Nannetti.) La regina Vittoria era stato in Irlanda una volta sola mezzo secolo prima dopo le sue nozze. Allora, gli irlandesi, i quali non avevano completamente dimenticato la loro fedeltà alla casa sventurata degli Stuardi nè i nomi di Maria Stuarda regina degli Scotti e del fuggiasco leggendario 'Bonnie Prince Charlie', ebbero la cattiva idea di prendere in giro il consorte della regina, burlandosi di lui come un principotto tedesco spiantato, imitando il modo in cui si diceva che babettasse l'inglese, nonchè salutandolo giulivamente, proprio al momento quando metteva piede su terra irlandese, con un fresco torzolo di cavolo. Il contegno ed il carattere irlandesi erano antipatici alla regina, la quale, nutrita delle teorie imperialistiche e patrizie di Benjamino Disraeli, il suo ministro prescelto, s'interessò per poco o nulla, se non in qualche frase spregiativa, alla sorte del popolo irlandese il quale naturalmente rispondeva per le rime. Una volta, è vero, quando ci fu una catastrofe orrenda nella contéa di Kerry che lasciò senza tetto e pane quasi tutta la contéa la regina che teneva molto ai suoi millioncini mandò al comitato di soccorso, il quale aveva già incassato migliaja di sterline da benefattori di tutti i ceti sociali, l'assegno regio per l'importo di [5] 10 sterline. Il comitato, poco riconoscente dell'invio di tale dono, rimise lo cheque in una busta ed accludendo un suo biglietto di ringraziamento, lo rimandò alla mittente a volta di corriere. Da questi fatterelli apparira che c'era poco amor perduto fra Vittoria ed i suoi sudditi irlandesi e, se essa si decise ad andare a visitarli nel crepuscolo dei suoi giorni, tale visita era ben certamente motivata da cagioni politiche. La verità è ch'essa non venne ma fu mandata dai suoi consiglieri. In quel tempo i disastri inglesi nell'Africa del Sud nella guerra contro i boeri avevano fatto dell'esercito inglese uno zimbello della stampa europea, e se ci voleva allora il genio dei due capi-comandanti Lord Roberts e Lord Kitchener (ambedue irlandesi nati in Irlanda) per redimerne il prestigio pericolante, come ci volle nel 1815 il genio di un'altro soldato irlandese, il duca di Wellington, per sopraffare la strapotenza rinata di Napoleone a Waterloo, ci volevano pure i volontari e le réclute dell'Irlanda per mostrare sul campo di battaglia quel valore ormai famoso, in riconoscenza del quiale, conchiusa la guerra, il governo inglese permise ai reggimenti irlandesi di portare il trifoglio l'emblema pattriotico, nel giorno di S. Patrizio. La regina venne difatti colla missione di catturare la simpatia facile del paese e di aumentare le liste dei sergenti di reclutamento.

Ho detto ehe per capire il golfo che ancora separa le due nazioni uno deve aver assistito alla sua entrata a Dublino. Lungo la rotta erano disposti i piccoli soldati inglesi (perchè dal tempo della rivolta feniana sotto Giacomo Stephens il governo non ha mai mandato i reggimenti irlandesi in Irlanda) e, dietro questa siepe, c'era la folla cittadina. Nei balconi arredati c'erano gli ufficiali e le loro signore, gli impiegati unionisti e le loro signore, i turisti e le loro signore e quando apparve il corteo la gente nei balconi comincia a gridare saluti ed a sventolare fazzoletti. La carrozza della regina passò, protetta da ogni lato strettamente dall'imponente corpo di guardia colla sciabola snudata, e dentro si vedeva una piccina donna, quasi nana, curba [?] e titubante dal movimento della carrozza, vestita lugubremente e portando gli occhiali di corno su una faccia terréa e vacua, la quale a quando a quando s'inchinava di scatto, in risposta a qualche isolato grido di saluto, come una che avesse male imparato la sua lezione. S'inchinava a destra ed a sinistra con una movenza rara e meccanica. I soldati inglesi stettero rispettosamente sugli attenti mentre passava la loro padrona, e, dietro di loro, la folla cittadina guardava il corteo sfarzoso e la figura centrale triste con occhi curiosi e quasi di misericordia e, quando passò la carrozza, volse nella sua scia i suoi sguardi ambigui. Non ci furono questa volta nè bombe nè torzoli di cavolo ma la vecchia regina d'Inghilterra entrò nella capitale irlandese in mezzo ad un popolo muto.

*

Le cagioni di questa differenza di temperamento, ora diventata un luogo comune dei *parafagristi* di Fleet Street, sono in parte di razza ed in parte storiche. La civiltà nostra è un'immensa tessitura nella quale mescolansi gli elementi i più diversi, nella quale sono riconciliati la rapacità nordica, il diritto romano, la nuova convenzione borghese e gli avanzi di una religione siriaca. In tale tessitura inutile cercare un filo che sia rimasto mero e vergine senza aver subito l'influenza di fili vicini. Quale razza o quale lingua, se eccettuiamo quelle poche che una volontà scherzevole pare che abbia conservato in ghiaccio come l'islandese, può oggidì vantarsi di essere pura? E nessuna razza ha meno diritto della razza che ora abita l'Irlanda di proferire un tale vanto. La nazionalità (se essa non è veramente una comoda finzione come tante altre alle quali il bistourì degli scienziati odierni ha dato il colpo di grazia) deve trovare la sua ragione d'essere stabile in qualcosa che supera, che transcende e che informa cose mutabili come il sangue e la parola umana. Il teologo mistico che assunse il pseud-ònimo di Dionisio l'Areopagitico dice qualche parte 'Iddio ha disposto i limiti delle nazioni secondo i suoi angeli' e probabilmente non è questa una concezione puramente mistica. Non vediamo che in Irlanda i danesi, i firbolgiani, i milesiani dalla Spagna, gli invasori normanni, i colòni anglosassoni, gli ugonotti si uniscono per formira un nuovo ente si direbbe sotto l'influenza di un nume locale. E benchè la razza attuale in Irlanda sia una razza inferiore ed attardata è degna di essere presa in considerazione perchè essa è la sola razza dell'intiera famiglia celtica che non abbia voluto vendere il suo diritto di primogenitura per un piatto di lenticchie.

Lo trovo un po' ingenuo di colmare d'ingiurie l'inglese per i suoi mis-fatti in Irlanda. Un conquistatore non può essere dilettante e l'inglese non fece altro in Irlanda durante tanti secoli di quello che fà oggi il belga nello Stato Libero del Congo o di quello che farà domani il nano nipponico in altre terre. Caldeggiava le fazioni e s'impossessava dell'erario.

Seminò la discordia fra le varie razze, coll'introduzione di un nuovo sistema agrario ridusse il potere dei capi nativi e diede grandi fondi ai suoi soldati, perseguitò la chiesa romana quando questa era ribelle e smise quando essa pure diventò uno strumento efficace di soggiogazione. La sua preoccupazione principale era di tener diviso il paese e se domani un governo liberale inglese, in pieno godimento della fiducia dell'elettorato inglese, concedesse una misura d'autonomia all'Irlanda la stampa con-servatrice londinese non metterebbe tempo in mezzo per incitare la pro-vincia di Ulster contro il nuovo esecutivo a Dublino. Fu crudele come furbesca: le sue armi erano e sono l'ariete, la mazza, ed il capestro e sè Parnell era una spina nella costa inglese lo era primariamente perche quando era ragazzo in Wicklow udì dalla sua nutrice le leggende della ferocia inglese. Una leggenda ch'egli stesso narrò era di un contadino ch'aveva agito in contravenzione alle leggi penali e che, per ordine del colonnello, fu preso, snudato, attaccato ad un carro e fustigato dalla truppa. La fustigazione, per ordine del colonnello, gli fu amministrata sul ventre dimodochè lo sventurato spirò fra dolori atroci, i suoi intestini irrompendo sulla via.

L'inglese ora deride l'irlandese perchè questo è cattolico, povero ed ignorante: ma ad alcuni, però, non sembrerà tanto facile di giustificare tale disprezzo. L'Irlanda è povera perchè le leggi inglesi rovinarono la industrie del paese, notabilmente quella della lana, perchè la noncuranza del governo inglese negli anni in cui venne manco la raccolta della patata lasciò morire di fame il fiore della popolazionè, e perchè sotto l'amministrazione attuale mentre l'isola si spopola ed i delitti quasi non esistono i giudici ricevono stipendi da pascia e gli ufficiali governativi o del pubblico servizio percepiscono somme ingenti per fare poco o nulla. A Dublino solo, per prendere un'esempio, il luogotenente riceve un mezzo millione di franchi all'anno, per ogni poliziotto i cittadini dublinesi sborsano 3500 franchi annui (il doppio, suppongo, di ciocchè riceve in Italia un professore di liceo), ed un povero diavolo, il quale disimpegna i doveri di capo scrivano al municipio, è costretto a campare alla meglio collo stipendio miserrimo di 6 lire sterline al giorno.

Ha ragione dunque il critico inglese: l'Irlanda è povera e, vieppiù, è politicamente attardata. Per l'irlandese le date della riformazione luterana e della rivoluzione francese non significano niente. Le lotte feudali della nobiltà contro il monarca conosciute in Inghilterra sotto il nome delle guerre dei baroni ebbero la loro controparte in Irlanda. Se i baroni inglesi seppero ammazzare il prossimo in nobil modo i baroni irlandesi lo seppero pure. Non mancarono allora in Irlanda quelle gesta feroci che sono il frutto di sangue patrizio. Il principe irlandese Shane O' Niàll, era di natura così generosa ch'era d'uopo di seppellirlo periodicamente nella madre terra fino al collo allorquando aveva talento di lussuria. Ma i baroni irlandesi, scaltramente divisi dalla politica straniera, non poterono mai agire in un piano comune, si sfogarono in risse puerili fra di loro e consunsero la vitalità del paese in guerre civili mentre i loro fratelli oltre il canale di S. Giorgio forzarono il re Giovanni a firmare la magna carta (il primo capitolo della libertà moderno) nei campi di Runnimede. L'onda democratica che percorse l'Inghilterra nei tempi di Simone di Montfort, il fondatore della camera dei comuni, e più tardi all'epoca del prottettorato cromwelliano giunse spenta ai lidi irlandesi sicchè adesso l'Irlanda (paese destinato da Dio ad esser l'eterna caricatura del mondo serio) è un paese aristocratico senza un'aristocrazia. I discendenti degli antichi re (ai quali si da il cognome solo senza prefisso) si vedono nelle sale del palazzo di giustizia, colla parruca e gli atti notarili, ove vengono per invocare in favore di qualche imputato le leggi che hanno soppresso i loro titoli reali. Poveri re caduti, riconoscibili persino nella loro caduta come irlandesi poco pratici perchè non hanno mai pensato di seguire l'esempio dei loro fratelli inglesi in simil istato, di andare nella meravigliosa America per chiedere la mano di sua figlia a qualche altro rè, fosse pure il re della vernice o delle salsiccie.

Nè è meno facile il capire perchè il contadino irlandese è reazionario e cattolico o perchè quando bestemmia mescola insieme i nomi di Cromwell e di Papa Satana. Per lui il gran protettore dei diritti civili è una bestia selvatica che venne in Irlanda a propagare la sua fede colla spada e col fuoco. Non dimentica il saccheggiare di Drogheda e di Waterford, nè le schiere di uomini e donne cacciate nelle ultime isole dal puritano che disse 'Che vadano nell'oceano o nell'inferno' nè il giuramento falso che gli inglesi fecero sulla pietra rotta di Limerick. Come potrebbe egli dimenticare? La schiena di uno schiavo dimentica forse la verga? La verità è che il governo inglese innalzò il valore morale del cattolicismo quando lo mise sotto bando. Ora, grazie un po' ai discorsi interminabili e un po' alla violenza feniana, il regno di terrore è cessato. Le leggi penali sono state revocate. Oggi un cattolico in Irlanda può votare, diventare impiegato del governo, esercitare un mestiere od una professione, insegnare in una scuola pubblica, sedere nel parlamento, possedere terre sue per periodi che superino trentun anni, tenere nelle sue stalle un cavallo che valga più di 5 lire sterline, assistere ad una messa cattolica senza correre il rischio di essere impiccato, sbudellato e squartato dal boia comune. Ma queste leggi sono state revocate da tanto poco tempo che un deputato nazionalista che vive ancora era attualmente condannato da un tribunale inglese per il delitto di alto tradimento ad essere impiccato, sbudellato e squartato dal boja comune, il quale è in Inghilterra un mercenario scelto dallo scieriffo fra altri suoi colleghi mercenari per merito perspicuo sia di destrezza o di operosità. La popolazione irlandese ch'è di 90% cattolica nini contribuisce più al mantenimento della chiesa protestante la quale esiste soltanto per il benessere di qualche migliajo di coloni. Vale a dire che l'erario inglese ha sofferto qualche perdita e che la chiesa romana ha una figlia di più. Frattanto un sistema educativo permette ai rivi di pensiero moderno di filtrare lentamente nel suolo arido. Col tempo vi sarà forse un risveglio graduale della coscienza irlandese e forse, quattro o cinque secoli dopo la dieta di Worms, vedremo un frate in Irlanda gettare giù la tonaca, scappar via con qualche suora, e proclamare ad alta voce la fine dell'assurdità coerente ch'era il cattolicismo ed il cominciamento dell'assurdità incoerente che è il protestantesimo.

Ma un'Irlanda protestante è quasi impensabile. Senza alcun dubbio l'Irlanda è stata finora la figlia la più fedele della chiesa cattolica. È forse il solo paese che abbia accolto i primi missionari cristiani con cortesia e che fosse convertita alla nuova dottrina senza lo spargimento di una goccia di sangue e, difatti, nella storia ecclesiastica dell'Irlanda manca affatto il martirologio, come il vescovo di Cashel ebbe occasione di vantare in risposta allo schernitore, Giraldus Cambrensis. Per sette o Otto secoli era il foco spirituale del cristianesimo, mandò i suoi figli in ogni paese del mondo per predicare il vangelo ed i suoi dottori per interpretare e rinnovellare i santi scritti.

Neppure una volta fu seriamente scossa la sua fedeltà se eccettuiamo una certa tendenza alla dottina insegnata da Nestorio nel quinto secolo riguarda all'unione ipostatica delle due nature in Gesù Cristo, qualche differenza di culto nugatoria osservabile alla stessa epoca come il modo di tonsura chierica ed il tempo di celebrare le feste pasquali, e, finalmente, la defezione di alcuni prelati all'insistenza degli emissari riformatori di Edoardo VI. Ma, alla prima intimazione che la chiesa versava in pericoli dei veri sciami d'inviati irlandesi partirono alla volta di tutte le corti europee ove cercarono di fomentare un forte movimento simultaneo fra le potenze cattoliche contro gli eretici. Orbene, la Santa Sede ha ricompensato questa fedeltà in modo suo. Prima, mediante una bolla papale ed un annello, regalò l'Irlanda ad Enrico II d'Inghilterra e più tardi, sotto il pontificato di Gregorio XIII, quando l'eresia protestante alzò la testa, si pentì di aver data un'isola fedele agli inglesi eretici e, per rimediare al fallo, nominò sovrano supremo dell'Irlanda un bastardo della corte papalina. Questi rimase naturalmente un monarca *in partibus infidelium* ma l'intenzione pontificale non era, per questo, meno gentile: e del resto, gli irlandesi sono di un'accondiscendenza così arrendevole ch'appena brontolerebbero sè domani, causa una complicazione impreveduta in Europa, il papa, avendola già regalata ad un inglese e ad un'italiano, desse la loro isola ancora una volta in balia a qualche hidalgo della corte d'Alfonso, trovantesi per il momento senza impiego. Fu più parca, però, degli onori ecclesiastici la Santa Sede; e quantunque l'Irlanda avesse ud passato arrichito gli archivi hagiografici nel modo ch'abbiamo veduto, essa è appena riconosciuta nei concili del Vaticano e passarono più di mille quattrocento anni prima che venisse in mente al santo padre di innalzare al cardinalato un vescovo irlandese.

Ora, che cosa ha guadagnato l'Irlanda colla sua fedeltà al papato e colla sua infedeltà alla corono brittanica? Ha guadagnato abbastanza ma non per sè stessa. Fra gli scrittori irlandesi che adoperarono la lingua inglese nei secoli decimo settimo e decimottavo, e quasi dimenticarono il loro paese natìo, trovansi i nomi di Berkeley, il filosofo idealista, di Oliviero Goldsmith, autore del *Vicario di Wakefield*, dei due famosi commediografi

Riccardo Brinsley Sheridan e Guglielmo Congreve, i capolavori dei quali si ammirano anche oggi sulla scena sterile dell'Inghilterra moderna, di Gionathan Swift, autore dei *Viaggi di Gulliver* il quale condivide con Rabelais il posto di primo satirico nella letteratura mondiale e di Edmondo Burke, che gl'inglesi stessi nominarono il Demostene moderno e ritennero il più profondo oratore che avesse mai parlato alla Camera dei Deputati. Anchè oggi, ad onta che sia talmente inceppata, l'Irlanda da il suo contributo al pensiero ed all'arte inglesi. Che l'irlandese sia veramente il cretino incapace e squilibrato di cui leggiamo negli articoli di fondo dello *Standard* e del *Morning Post* lo smentiscono i nomi dei tre più grandi traduttori nella letteratura inglese, FitzGerald, traduttore del *Rubaiyat* del poeta persiano Omar Khayyam, Burton traduttore dei capolavori arabi, e Carey, traduttore classico della *Divina Commedia*. Lo smentiscono pure i nomi di altri irlandesi, il decano della musica inglese moderna Arturo Sullivan, il fondatore del cartismo Edoardo O'Connor, il romanziere Giorgio Moore, oasi intelligente nella Sahara delle opere spiriste, mistificatori, poliziesche e messianiche di cui il nome è legione in Inghilterra, dei due dublinesi Giorgio Bernard Shaw, il commediografo paradossale ed iconoclasta, e il troppo celebre Oscar Wilde, figlio di una poetessa rivoluzionaria. Finalmente nel campo pratico questa concezione spregiativa è smentita dal fatto che l'irlandese quando si trova fuori d'Irlanda, in un altro ambiente sa molte volte farsi valere. Le condizioni economiche ed intellettuali che vigono in suo paese non permettono lo sviluppo dell'individualità. L'anima del paese è indebolita da secoli di lotta inutile e di trattati rotti, l'iniziativa individuale paralizzata dall'influenza e dalle ammonizioni della chiesa, mentre il corpo è ammanettato dagli sbirri, i doganieri e la guarnigione. Nessun che si rispetta vuol stare in Irlanda ma fugge lontano siccome da un paese ch'abbia subito la visitazione di un Gèova adirato. Dal tempo del trattato della città di Limerick, o piuttosto dal tempo della sua rottura dagli inglesi di fede punica millioni d'irlandesi hanno lasciato la patria per altri lidi. Questi fuggiaschi che furono secoli or sono chiamati le oche selvatiche s'arruolarono in tutte le brigate straniere di potenze europée, la Francia, l'Olanda, la Spagna precipuamente, e vinsero su molti campi di battaglia il lauro vittorioso per i loro maestri adottivi. In America trovarono un'altra patria. Nei ranghi degli insorgenti americani si udiva la vecchia lingua irlandese e lord Mountjoy stesso disse nel 1784 'Abbiamo perduto l'America per opera degli emigranti irlandesi'.

Oggi questi emigranti irlandesi sono negli Stati Uniti in numero di 16 millioni, una colònia ricca, potente, ed industriale. Non prova questo forse che il sogno irlandese di un risorgimento non è tutto una chimera? Se l'Irlanda ha potuto dare al servizio d'altri uomini come il Tyndall, uno dei pochi scienziati il cui nome ha varcato la manica, il marchese di Dufferin governatore del Canada e viceré dell'India, Carlo Gavan Duffy ed Hennessy governatori coloniali, il duca di Tetuan, recentemente 1° ministro della Spagna, il Bryan, candidato presidenziale degli Stati Uniti, il maresciallo MacMahon, presidente della repubblica francese, lord Charles Beresford, il capo virtuale della marina inglese testé messo al commando della flotta del Canale, ed i tre generali più rinomati dell'esercito inglese, lord Wolseley, il capo-comandante, lord Kitchener, vincitore della campagna del Sudan ed attualmente comandante dell'esercito indiano, e lord Roberts, vincitore delle guerre in Afganistan ed in Sud Africa, se l'Irlanda ha potuto dare tutto questo talento pratico al servizio altrui vuol dire che ci deve essere qualcosa di nemico d'infausto e di tirranico nelle sue condizioni attuali se i suoi figli non possono dare l'opera loro alla loro patria.

Perché anche oggi continua la fuga di queste oche selvatiche. Ogni anno l'Irlanda, per quanto decimata che già sia, perde 40,000 dei suoi figli. Dal 1850 fino ad ora più di 5,000,000 d'emigranti sono partiti per l'America: ed ogni posta reca in Irlanda lettere d'invito da questi ai loro amici e parenti a casa. I vecchi, i corrotti, i fanciulli ed i miseri rimangono a casa ove il giogo doppio li rode ancora un solco nel collo domato: ed intorno al capezzale ove giace agonizzante il povero corpo esangue e quasi esanime i patriottardi esortano, i Governi prescrivono ed i preti amministrano l'estrema unzione.

È destinato questo paese a riprendere un giorno la sua antica posizione d'Ellade del nord? L'anima celtica, come quella slava alla quale in molte cose rassomiglia, sono esse destinate nel futuro ad arricchire la coscienza civile di nuove scoperte e di nuove intuizioni? Oppure, il mondo celtico, le cinque nazioni celtiche, spinte da razze più forti fino all'orlo del continente e fino alle ultime isole dell'Europa, devono esse dopo una lotta di secoli precipitarsi finalmente nell'oceano? Ahimè, noi altri sociologhi dilettanti non siamo che aruspici e di second'ordine: guardiamo e frughiamo negli intestini della bestia umana e, dopo tutto, confessiamo che non ci vediamo nulla! Soltanto, i nostri superuomini sanno scrivere la storia del futuro.

Sarebbe interessante ma oltre lo scopo che mi sono proposto stasera di vedere quali sarebbero le conseguenze probabili alla civiltà nostra di un risorgimento di questo popolo, le conseguenze economiche dell'apparizione di un'isola emula accanto all'Inghilterra, un'isola bilingue, repubblicana, egoista ed intraprendente, colla sua propria flotta commerciale ed i suoi consoli in ogni porto del mondo, e le conseguenze morali dell'apparizione nella vecchia Europa dell'artista e del pensatore irlandesi, quegli strani spiriti, entusiasti freddi, artisticamente e sessualmente ineducati, pieni di idealismi ed incapaci di aderirvi, spiriti fanciulleschi, infedeli, ingenui e satirici, 'the loveless Irishmen', come sono chiamati, 'gli irlandesi senza amore'. Ma, nell'attesa di tale risorgimento confesso che non vedo che cosa giova il fulminare contro la tirranide inglese mentre la tirannide romana occupa il palazzo dell'anima. Non vedo che cosa giovano gli invettivi acerbi contro l'Inghilterra spogliatrice, il disprezzo della vasta civiltà anglo-sassone, sebbene questa sia quasi del tutto una civiltà materiale, nè i vani vanti che gli antichi libri irlandesi come il *Libro di Kells*, il *Libro Giallo di Leccan*, il *Libro della Vacca Fulva* che datano dal tempo quando l'Inghilterra era ancora un paese incivile, sono di una vetustà cinese nell'arte della miniatura e che l'Irlanda fabbricava ed esportava in Europa i suoi tessuti per parecchie generazioni innanzicche il primo fiammingo giungesse a Londra per insegnare agli inglesi come si fa il panno. Se fosse lecito di fare appello valido al passato in questo modo i fellahin a Cairo avrebbere tutto il diritto del mondo se rifiutassero orgogliosamente di farsi i facchini dei turisti inglesi. Come è morto l'antico Egitto, così l'antica Irlanda pure è morta. La sua nenia è stata cantata e sulla pietra del suo sepolcro è stato posto il suggello. La vecchia anima nazionale che parlò durante i secoli per la bocca di vati favolosi, di menestrelli erranti, e di poeti giaccobiti, è scomparsa dal mondo colla morte di Giacomo Clarenzio Mangan, con la quale si chiuse la lunga tradizione dell'ordine triplo dei vecchi bardi celtici: ed oggi altri bardi, animati da altri ideali, hanno il grido.

Una cosa sola mi pare chiara. Sara ben tosto tempo per l'Irlanda di finirla una buona volta con gli insuccessi. Sè essa è veramente capace di risorgere, che risorga, oppure, che si copra il capo e scenda decentemente e per sempre nella tomba. 'Noi altri irlandesi' disse Oscar Wilde un giorno ad un mio amico 'non abbiamo fatto nulla ma siamo i più grandi parlatori sin dal tempo dei greci.' Ma, sebbene gli irlandesi siano facondi, una rivoluzione non si fa del fiato umano: e dei compromessi, degli equivoci, e dei malintesi l'Irlanda ha già avuto abbastanza. Se vuol darci finalmente lo spettacolo ch'abbiamo aspettato per tanto tempo che sia, questa volta, completo, integrale e definitivo. Ma abbiamo un bel dire agli impresari irlandesi di affrettarsi, come lo dissero anche i nostri padri or non ha guari. Io, almeno, son sicuro di non veder mai quel sipario alzarsi perchè sarò già tornato a casa coll'ultimo tram.

GIACOMO CLARENZIO MANGAN
JAMES CLARENCE MANGAN

Vi sono certi poeti, i quali, oltre il merito di averci rivelato qualche fase della coscienza umana fino al loro epoca ignota, hanno pure il merito più discutabile di aver riassunto in sè stessi le mille tendenze contrastanti del tempo loro e di essersi fatti, per così dire, gli accumulatori elettrici di forze nuove. Per lo più è sotto quest'ultimo aspetto anzichè sotto quell'altro che vengono poi apprezzati dalla folla, la quale essendo per natura incapace di valutare qualsiasi opera di schietta autorivelazione s'affretta a riconoscere mediante qualche atto di grazia l'appoggio incalcolabile che presta ad un movimento popolare l'affermazione individuale di un vate. L'atto di grazia prediletto in tali casi è il monumento perciocchè onora il morto mentre adula i viventi ed ha pure il vantaggio supremo della finalita', essendo esso, a vero dire, il modo il più efficace e cortese sinora scoperto di assicurare una dimenticanza duratura del trapassato. Nei paesi serii e logici il monumento usa compiersi in forma decente ed allo scoprimento intervengono lo scultore, i poteri civili, i rettorici e gran ressa di pubblico. Ma in Irlanda, paese ch'è destinato da Dio ad essere la caricatura eterna del mondo serio, il monumento, anche quando si tratta degli uomini i più popolari e di fibra la più arrendevole alla volontà delle plebe, ben di rado progredisce oltre il deporre la lapide di fondamento. Premesso ciò forse riuscirò a dare un'idea della notte cimmeriana che involge il nome di Clarenzio Mangan se dico che ad onta della nota generosità dell'isola di smeraldo, non è venuto finora in mente ad alcuno spirito bollentc di colà di placare l'ombra irrequieta del poeta nazionale con la lapide e le ghirlande consuete.

Per lui forse la pace indisturbata in cui giace sarà diventata oramai talmente grata che s'adonterà (se mai in quel mondo d'oltretomba pervengano gli accenti mortali) al sentire turbare la sua quiete spettrale da un connazionale in esiglio, al sentire un inesperto ragionar di lui dinanzi a stranieri benevoli ed in favella strana. Il contributo dell'Irlanda alla letteratura europea può dividersi in cinque epoche ed in due grandi sezioni, vale a dire, letteratura scritta in lingua irlandese e letteratura scritta in lingua inglese. Della prima sezione, che comprende le due prime epoche, quella remota e quasi perduta nella notte dei tempi in cui furono scritti tutti gli antichi libri sacri ed epici, codici legali, storie topografiche e leggende e quella più recente che persistette per molto tempo dopo l'invasione degli anglo-sassoni ed i normanni sotto Enrico II e Re Giovanni, epoca dei menestrelli erranti le canzoni simboliche dei quali continuarono la tradizione dell'ordine triplo dei vecchi bardi celtici, ebbi occasione di parlarvi qualche sera fa. La seconda sezione, quella della letteratura irlandese scritta in lingua inglese, si divide in tre epoche. La prima è quella del secolo decimottavo che numera fra altri irlandesi i nomi gloriosi di Oliviero Goldsmith, autore del rinomato romanzo *Il Vicario di Wakefield*, dei due famosi commediografi Riccardo Brinsley Sheridan e Guglielmo Congreve, i capolavori dei quali si ammirano anehè oggidì sulla scena sterile dell'Inghilterra moderna, il decano rabelaisiano Gionathan Swift, autore dei *Viaggi di Gulliver*, il Demostene cosidetto inglese, Edmondo Burke, il quale persino i critici inglesi ritengono il più profondo oratore che abbia parlato alla Camera dei Deputati ed uno dei più savi uomini di stato anche fra la schiera scaltra dei politicanti della biondo Albione. La seconda e la terza epoca appartengono al secolo scorso, l'una essendo il movimento letterario della Giovane Irlanda nel '42 e 45 e l'altra il movimento letterario odierno sul quale propongo di darvi qualche cenno in una prossima conferenza.

Il movimento letterario del '42 data dalla fondazione del giornale separatista *La Nazione*, fondata dai tre capi Tommaso Davis, Giovanni Blake Dillon (padre dell'ex capo del partito parlamentare irlandese)

[*One page of the manuscript is missing.*]

della borghesia media: e dopo una fanciullezza passata in mezzo a crudeltà domestiche, a sciagure ad angustie, diventò scrivano in un ufficio notarile di terz'ordine. Era sempre stato un ragazzo di carattere cupo ed indolente, dato allo studio furtivo di diverse lingue, misantropo, silenzioso e preoccupato da quistioni religiose, senza conoscenze od amici. Quandò cominciò a scrivere attrasse subito l'attenzione dei colti che riconobbero in lui una musica lirica alata ed un idealismo fervido, rivelantesi in ritmi di straordinaria ed inconscia beltà, introvabili forse in tutta la letteratura inglese se eccettiamo il canto ispirato dello Shelley. Mercè l'influenza di alcuni letterati ottenne un impiego di sottobiblotecario presso la grandissima biblioteca del Collegio della Trinità a Dublino, tesoro ricchissimo di volumi tre volte più grande della biblioteca Vittario Emmanuele a Roma ed ove si conservano i libri antichi irlandesi, come *Il Libro della Vacca Fulva*, il *Libro Giallo di Leccan*, il famoso saggio legale, opera del colto re Cormac il Magnifico, ch'ebbe il nome di Salomone irlandese, ed il *Libro di Kells*, libri che datano dai primi secoli del cristianesimo e sono noti per la loro vestustà addirittura cinese nell'arte della miniatura. Fu ivi che il Mitchell, il suo biografo ed amico, lo vide per la prima volta e ci descrive nella prefazione alle opere del poeta, l'impressione che gli fece un ometto mingherlino, dal volto cerco e dai cappelli pallidi, il quale seduto in cima ad una scaletta colle gambe incrocciate era intento al decifrare nella luce crepuscolare un immenso volume polveroso. In questa biblioteca il Mangan passava i suoi giorni in istudio e diventò linguista discreta. Seppe bene le lingue e le letterature italiane, spagnuole, francesi e tedesche, oltre quelle dell'Inghilterra e dell'Irlanda, ed, a quanto pare, ebbe qualche conoscenza di lingue orientali, probabilmente del sanscritto e dell'arabo. Uscì a quando a quando da quella pace studiosa per dare il contributo di qualche canzone al giornale rivoluzionario ma prese poco interesse ai comizi serali del partito. Passò le sue notti in disparte. La sua dimora era una stanzuccia oscura nella vecchia città, il rione di Dublino che conserva anche oggi il nome significativo delle 'libertà', e le sue notti erano tante vie della croce fra le diverse bettole infami delle 'libertà' ove deve esser apparso una stranissima figura in mezzo ai fiori scelti dei bassifondi della città, ladruncoli, banditi, lattitanti, ruffiane, ed etére di pretese miti. È strano a dirlo (ma è il consenso di opinione fra i suoi connazionali, sempre pronti a spiare in tali quistioni, che il Mangan non ebbe che commercio puramente formale con questo mondo sommerso. Beveva poco, ma il bere gli produceva un effetto straordinario, tanta era indebolita la sua salute. Del resto, la maschera di morte che ci rimane ci mostra una faccia raffinata e quasi patrizia nelle cui linee delicate è impossibile scoprire altro che la malinconia ed la grande stanchezza. Ho inteso che i patologi negano la possibilità di combinare i delizi dell'alcool e dell'oppio e pare che il Mangan si convincesse ben tosto di questa verità perchè si diede accanitamente ad assorbire le droghe narcotiche. Il Mitchell ci dice che verso la fine della sua vita il Mangan sembrava uno scheletro vivente. Il suo volto era scarno, appena coperto da una pelle trasparente come la porcellana fina, il suo corpo dimagrito, l'occhio sognatore grande e fisso, dietro i barlumi rari del quale parevano nascondersi le memorie orrende e voluttuose delle visioni, la voce lenta, fiocca e sepolcrale. Scese gli ultimi gradini verso la tomba con spaventevole rapidità. Era diventato uno straccione muto, mangiava appena ciocchè gli bastava per tener insieme anima e corpo, fino a chè un giorno mentre camminava per la strada stramazzò ad un colpo. Portato all'ospedale gli fu trovato adosso quache soldino ed in una tasca un volume logoro di poesia tedesca. Quando morì il misero cadavere fece rabbrividire gli assistenti ed alcuni amici caritatevoli pagarono le spese della tumulazione sordida. Così visse e morì colui ch'io ritengo il più insigne poeta del mondo celtico moderno ed uno dei più ispirati cantori ch'abbiano mai ed in qualunque paese adoperato la forma lirica. È troppo presto credo, l'asserire ch'egli debba eternamente abitare i pascoli incolori dell'obblìo ma sono ben persuaso che se ne uscirà alfine alla gloria postuma a cui ha diritto, non sarà per opera di un suo compattriota. Il Mangan sarà accettato dagli irlandesi come il loro poeta nazionale in quel giorno in cui sarà deciso il conflitto fra la patria e le potenze straniere, anglo-sassone e romana cattolica, e sorgera una nuova civiltà o indigena puramente straniera. Fino a quell'epoca sarà dimenticato, o ricordato di rado in un giorno di festa, come molti altri poeti ed eroi, tanto più perchè egli, come pure il Parnell, peccò contro quella castità incorrigibile, la quale l'Irlanda pretende da qualunque Giovanni che vorrebbe battezzarla o da qualunque Giovanna che vorrebbe liberarla, come la prima prova essenziale e divina della loro idoneità a cotali alti uffici.

Quella domanda che Wagner ha messo in bocca del semplicione Parsifal deve venirci in mente a volta a volta [quando leggiamo] certe critiche inglesi dovute per lo più all'influenza dello spirito cieco ed acerbo del calvinismo. È facile spiegare queste critiche quando si tratta di un genio potente e novatore perchè l'avvento di un tale genio è sempre il segnale per tutte le forze corrotte ed interessate di schierarsi in difesa del vecchio ordine. Per essempio chiunque abbia capito la tendenza distruggitrice e fieramente egoarca di tutta l'opera di Enrico Ibsen non si stupirà all'udire i più influenti critici di Londra alla dimane della prima serata ibseniana inveire contro il drammaturgo, chiamandolo (cito le parole esatte del defunto critico del *Daily Telegraph*) un canc immondo che ficca il ceffo nel loto. Ma meno spiegabile è il caso ove il povero condannato è qualche poeta più o meno innocuo la cui colpa è quella di non aver potuto aderire scrupolosamente al culto della rispettabilità. E così succede che quando il nome di Mangan è menzionato nella sua patria (e bisogna ammettere che qualche volta si parla di lui nei circoli letterari) gli irlandesi lammentano che una tale facoltà poetica si trovò in lui congiunta a tale scostumatezza: e si meravigliano ingenuamente di scoprire segni della facoltà poetica in un uomo i cui vizi erano esotici ed il cui patriotismo era poco fervente. Coloro che hanno scritto di lui sono stati meticolosi nell'aggiustarc il bilancio fra l'ubbriacone ed il mangiatore d'oppio e si sono dati gran pena ad accertare se fosse erudizione ovvero impostura che si celava dietro frasi come 'tradotto dall'ottomano' o 'tradotto dal copto': ed all'infuorì di questa misera ricordanza il Mangan è stato uno straniero nella sua patria, una figura rara e bizzarra nelle strade, dove è veduto andando mesto e solo come uno che fa penitenza per qualche peccato antico. Certamente la vita, la quale il Novalis ha chiamata una malattia dello spirito, è per Mangan una penitenza grave, per lui che ha, forse, dimenticato il peccato che gliela ha imposto, un retaggio tanto più doloroso, anche, causa l'artista delicato in lui che legge così bene le traccie di brutalità e di debolezza sui volti umani che lo guardano con odio o con isprezzo. Nei brevi cenni biografici ch'egli ci ha lasciati parla soltanto della sua giovane vita, la sua infanzia e la sua fanciullezza, e ci dice che da fanciullo non conobbe altro che miseria gretta e grossolanità, che le sue conoscenze lordarono la sua persona del loro veneno invidioso, e che suo padre era una caudisona umana. In queste asserzioni violente si riconosce l'effetto della droga orientale ma ciononòdimeno coloro che credono che questa sua storia non sia che la finzione di un cervello disordinato non hanno mai saputo od hanno dimenticato quale dolore acuto rechi ad un ragazzo sensitivo il che natura grossolana. Le sue sofferenze l'hanno costretto a farsi eremita e difatti per la maggior parte della sua esistenza visse quasi in un sogno in quel santuario dell'anima ove per secoli e secoli tanto i tristi che i savi hanno eletto di rinchiudersi. Quando un amico gli fece osservare che il resoconto citato sopra era oltremodo esagerato, ed in parte, falso Mangan rispose 'Forse l'avro sognato'. Il mondo evidentemente è diventato per lui qualcosa di irreale e che poco vale.

Che cosa allora diventeranno quei sogni che per ogni cuore giovane e semplice si vestono di una così cara realtà. Uno la cui natura è talmente sensitiva non può dimenticire i suoi sogni in una vita sicura e strenua. Ne dubita per la prima e li respinge ma quando ode qualcuno che li deride e bestemmia, vorrebbe confessarli altieramente, e dove la sensività ha indotto la debolezza oppure, come col Mangan, raffinato una debolezza innata, vorrebbe persino patteggiare col mondo per poter guadagnare almeno il favore del silenzio come per qualcosa troppo fragile per sostenere un disdegno violento, per quel desiderio del cuore sì cinicamente sprezzato, quell'idea, sì brutalmente malmenata. La sua maniera è tale che niuno può dire se sia orgoglio ovvero umiltà che guarda fuori dal suo vago volto, il quale pare che viva soltanto negli occhi chiari e lucenti e nei cappelli biondi e setosi di cui egli si vanta un tantino. Questo riserbo sua non è senza pericoli ed alla fine non sono che i suoi eccessi che lo salvano dall'indifferenza. Si è parlato di un rapporto intimo fra il Mangan ed una sua allieva alla quale diede insegnamento di tedesco e più tardi, a quanto pare, prese parte in una commedia di amore trilaterale ma, sè egli è riserbato cogli uomini, è timido colle donne, ed è troppo conscio di se, troppo critico, conosce troppo poco il florilegio menzognero, per fare mai il galante. Nel suo strano modo di vestirsi, l'alto cappello conico, i calzoni voluminosi tre volte troppo vasti per le sue piccole gambe, ed il vecchio ombrellone foggiato in modo di un ludero, possiamo vedere un'espressione quasi-comica della sua diffidenza. L'erudizione di molti paesi l'accompagna sempre, leggende orientali e la rimembranza di volumi del medioevo curiosamente stampati che l'hanno rapito dal suo secolo, raccolti giorno per giorno e radunati in un tessuto. Conosce più o meno una ventina di lingue e ne fa talvolta una mostra generosa, ed ha letto in moltissime letterature, attraversando tanti mari ed eziandio penetrando nelle terre di Peristan che non si trovano in nessun atlante. S'interessa molto nella vita della sacerdotessa di Prevorst ed in tutti i fenomeni della natura intermedia e qui, dove più di tutto, la dolcezza e la risolutezza dell'anima valgono pare che cerchi in un mondo fittizio, ma tanto differente da quello i in cui il Watteau (secondo la frase felice del Pater) pure abbia cercato, ambedue con una certa incostanza caratterisca, ciocchè si trova li in nessuna misura soddisfacente o non si trova.

I suoi scritti, che non sono stati mai raccolti in un'edizione definitiva, sono completamente privi di ordine qualchessissia e spesse volte anche privi di senso. I suoi saggi in prosa possono interessare forse alla prima lettura ma, in verità, sono sforzi insulsi. Lo stile è concettoso, nel pessimo senso della parola, storto e banale, l'argomento triviale e gonfio, la prosa, insomma, in cui vengono pubblicati fatterelli di cronaca locale in qualche giornaluccio di campagna. Bisogna però tenere in mente che il Mangan scrisse senza una tradizione letteraria nativa e scrisse per un pubblico che s'interessò soltanto nei fatti del giorno, pretendendo ch'era compito unico del vate di illustrare questi fatti. Non potè, se non in casi eccezionali, correggere il suo lavoro ma a parte gli scherzi cosidetti umioristici ed i versi d'occasione ovvi e non limati la migliore parte della sua opera ci fa appello genuino, concepita, com'era, dall'immaginazione ch'egli stesso, credo, ha nominato la madre delle cose, il cui sogno siamo, che c'immagina a sè stessa ed a noi, ed immagina sè stessa in noi, quella potenza dinnanzi al cui soffio la mente in creazione diventa (per adoperare la parola di Shelley) un tizzone morente. Sebbene in ciocchè ha scritto di meglio si sente sovente la presenza di emozioni aliene, si sente pure e più vividamente la presenza di un personalità immaginativa rifiettenute la luce della beltà immaginaria. Levante e poncute incontrannsi in quella personalità (or sappiamo Conte) gli immagini s'intrecciano lì come sciarpe soavi luminose, le parole scintillano e sonagliano comme gli annelli di un cotta d'armi: e sia che canti d'Irlanda o d'Istanbol la sua prece è sempre una, che la pace venga ancora una volta a colei che l'ha perduta, la perla, come la chiama, della sua anima, Amcen. Questa figura ch'adora ricorda gli ambizioni spirituali e gli amori immaginativi del medioevo e Mangan ha posto la sua Donna in un mondo ricolmo di melodia, di luci, e di profumi, quel mondo che cresce fatalmente per incorniciare ogni faccia che gli occhi di un poeta hanno guardato con amore. E una sola idea cavalleresca, una sola devozione maschile, che irradia i volti di Vittoria Colonna, di Laura e di Beatrice come sono una sola e stessa cosa la disillusione amara e lo sprezzo di sè che chiudono il capitolo. Ebbene, il mondo in cui Mangan volle ch'abitasse la sua donna differisce da quel tempio marmóreo eretto dal Buonarotti o dall'oriafiamma pacifica del teologo fiorentino. E un mondo selvatico, un mondo di notte in oriente. L'attività mentale che viene dall'oppio ha sparso questo mondo di immagini mirifiche ed orrende: e tutto l'oriente che il poeta ricreò nel sogno fiammagiante ch'è il paradiso del mangiatore d'oppio, palpita in queste pagine in frasi e similitudini in paesaggi apocalittici. Parla della luna che sviene di languore in mezzo all'orda degli astri, del libro magico del cielo rovente di segni focosi, del mare spumeggiante in sulla rena di zaffarano, del cedro solingo sulle vette dei Balcani, dell'aula barbarica tralucente di crescenti d'oro ove penetra lussuriosamente l'alito di rose dal gulistano del re.

Le canzoni le più celebri del Mangan, quelle in cui sotto un velo di misticismo inneggia alla gloria decaduta del suo paese, rassomigliano alla nebbia che cela l'orizzonte in un giorno d'estate, fina, impalpabile, pronta a sciogliersi ma suffusa da piccoli punti di luce. Qualchevolta la musica pare che si desti dal suo languore e gridi dell'estasi del combattimento. Nell'ultime strofe del lammento per i principe di Tirone e di Tirconnell, Mangan, in versi lunghi e pieni di forza tremenda, ha messo tutta l'energia disperata della sua razza.

> Benchè stanotte il gelo cristallizzi la rugiada limpida dei suoi occhi,
> Benchè manipoli candidi di ghiaccio inguantino le sue dita nobili, fini,
>   sottili e pallide,
> Vestito caldo è per lui quello che portò sempre, vestito di lampo,
> Lampo dell'anima e non dei cieli.
>
> Ugo andò alla battaglia. Piansi al vederlo partir così,
> Ed, ahimè, stanotte erra senza spenie moribondo sotto la pioggia algente,
> Ma la memoria delle magioni nivee che la sua mano mise
> In ceneri del prode affoca il cuor.

Io non conosco mi altro passo nella letteratura inglese ove lo spirito della vendetta abbia raggiunto una tale altezza di melodia. E vero che talvolta questa nota eroica diventa roca ed una frotta di passioni zotiche l'eccheggia derisivamente: ma un poeta, come il Mangan, che riassume in sè stesso l'anima di un'epoca e di un paese, non mira tanto a creare pel sollazzo di qualche dilettante quanto per trasmettere ai suoi posteri, a forza di colpi rudi, l'idea animatrice della sua vita. Del resto è indiscutibile che Mangan ha sempre conservata la sua anima poetica pura da ogni macchia. Benchè scrivesse un inglese così mirabile ricusò di collaborare per le riviste od i giornali inglesi, benchè fosse il foco spirituale dei suoi tempi ricusò di prostituirsi al popolaccio o di farsi il portavoce dei politicanti. Era uno di quegli strani aberrati spiriti i quali credono che la loro vita artistica non deve essere che la continua e vera rivelazione della loro vita spirituale, i quali credono che la loro vita interna vale tanto da non aver bisogno alcuno di appoggio popolare e quindi si astengono di proferire confessioni di fede, i quali credono, insomma, che il poeta è sufficiente a sè stesso, erede e detentore di un retaggio secolare, e quindi non ha alcun bisogno urgente di farsi strillone, predicatore o profumiere.

Ora quale è quest'idea centrale che il Mangan volle tramandare alla posterità.

Tutta la poesia ricorda l'ingiustizia e la tribolazione, e l'aspirazione di uno chi è mosso a grandi gesta ed a grida strazianti quando rivede in pensiero l'ora del suo cordoglio. Questo è il tema di gran parte della poesia irlandese ma nessun altra canzone irlandese è piena, come lo sono quelle di Mangan, di sventura nobilmente patita, di vastazione d'anima così irreparabile. Naomi voleva cambiare il suo nome in Mara, perchè aveva troppo bene conosciuto com'è amara l'esistenza dei mortali, e non è forse un senso profondo di dolore e di amarezza che spiega in Mangan tutti i nomi e titoli ch'egli si diede e la fur[i]a di traduzioni in cui cercò di perdersi. Perchè non trovò in sè stesso la fede del solitario o la fede che nel medioevo mandò le guglie in aria come canti trionfanti: ma aspetta la sua ora, l'ora che finira i suoi tristi giorni di penitenza. Più debole di Leopardi perchè non ha il coraggio della sua disperazione ma scorda ogni malanno e depone ogni disprezzo quando qualcuno gli mostra una piccola grazia, ha, forse per questa stessa ragione, il memoriale che desiderò, una

[*One page of the manuscript is missing.*]

un certo senso, contro l'attualità. Parla di ciocchè possa sembrare irreale e fantastico a quei che hanno perduto le intuizioni semplici che sono le prove della realtà. La poesia fa poco caso di molti degli idoli del foro, la successione dei secoli, lo spirito del secolo la missione di razza. Lo sforzo essenziale del poeta è di liberarsi dall'influenza nefasta di tali idoli che lo corrompono dal di fuori e da dentro, e certamente sarebbe falso di asserire che il Mangan ha sempre fatto questo sforzo. La storia del suo paese lo recinge così strettamente ch'appena appena in qualche ora di soverchia passione individuale puo ridurrne le mura a sfascio. Egli inveisce nella sua vita e nei suoi versi flebili, contro l'ingiustizia dei predatori ha quasi mai lammelita una perdita maggiore di quella e di fibbie e di vesilli. Eredita la parte più recente e peggiore di una tradizione sulla quale nessuna mano divina ha tracciato la linea di demarcazione, una tradizione anche che si scioglie e si divide contro sè stessa a secondo che s'avanza fra i cicli. Ed appunto perchè questa tradizione è diventata per lui un'ossessione egli l'ha accettato con tutti i suoi insuccessi e rammarichi e vorrebbe tramandata tale quale: il poeta che lancia i suoi fulmini contro i tiranni vorrebbe stabilire sul futuro una tirannia più intima e più crudele. La figura ch'egli adora ha la somiglianza di una regina abietta alla quale, causa i delitti cruenti che ha compiuti ed i delitti non meno cruenti fattile da mano altrui, la pazzia è venuta e la morte sta per venire ma che non vuol credere ch'essa sta per morire e rammenta soltanto il rumore delle voci ch'assediano il suo orto sacro ed i suoi fiori avvenenti che sono divenuti *pabulum aprorum*, cibo dei cinghiali. Amore del dolore, disperazione, minnacie altisonanti—queste sono le grandi tradizioni della razza di Giacomo

Clarenzio Mangan: e in quella figura meschina, smilza ed indebolità, una nazionalità isterica riceve un'ultima giustificazione.

In quale niccia del tempio della gloria dobbiamo mettere la sua immagine? Se non ha nemmeno vinto la simpatia dei suoi compattrioti come riuscirà a vincere quella degli stranieri? Non pare forse probabile che gli spetti quella dimenticanza ch'avrebbe quasi bramata? Certamente egli non ha trovato in sè la forza di rivelarci la beltà trionfante, quello splendore della verità, la quale gli antichi deificarono. E un romantico, un araldo mancato, prototipo di una nazione mancata ma con tuttociò uno che ha espresso in forma degna l'indegnazione sacra della sua anima non può aver scritto il suo nome in acqua. In quei immensi corsi di vita molteplice che ci circondano ed in quella vasta memoria, ch'è più grande e più generosa della nostra, probabilmente nessuna vita, nessun momento qual-siasi di esaltazione, è mai perduto: e tutti coloro che hanno scritto in nobil isdegno non hanno scritto invano quantunque, stanci e

[*The concluding page(s) of the manuscript is missing.*]

[IL RINASCIMENTO LETTERARIO IRLANDESE]
THE IRISH LITERARY RENAISSANCE

fisica o aperta o larvata. Sin dal tempo della grande ribellione negli ultimi del secolo decimottavo troviamo ben tre volte un conflitto decisivo tra le due tendenze nazionali: nel 48 quando il partito della Giovane Irlanda si staccò sdegnosamente dalle file di O'Connell, nel 67 quando il fenianismo giunse al suo apogéo e la 'repubblica' fu proclamata a Dublino ed oggi stesso che gran parte della gioventù irlandese disillusionata dall'incapacità della tattica parlamentare dopo l'assassinio morale di Parnell si schiera sempre più dalla parte di un nazionalismo più ampio e, nel medesimo tempo, più severo, un nazionalismo che abbraccia una guerra fiscale gior-naliera, un boicottaggio morale e materiale, lo sviluppo e la creazione d'industrie independenti, la diffusione della lingua irlandese, il bando alla coltura inglese ed il rinascimento sotto altre spoglie dell'antica civiltà del celta. Ognuno di questi movimenti intransigenti è stato accompagnato da un movimento letterario: ora è l'oratoria che prevale, ora

VERISMO ED IDEALISMO NELLA
LETTERATURA INGLESE
(DANIELE DEFOE E WILLIAM BLAKE)

REALISM AND IDEALISM IN ENGLISH LITERATURE

Daniele Defoe (I)

Correva l'anno di grazia 1660 quando Carlo Stuardo, l'esule, il fuggiasco, lo spodestato sbarcò su suolo inglese a Dover e scortato da fanfare e fiaccole in mezzo ad un popolo giubilante s'avviò verso la capitale per cingere quella stessa corona che undici anni prima suo padre, il re martire, aveva deposta pagandone il fio sul patibolo in Whitehall per ordine dei generali regicidi. Furono dissepolti i cadaveri di Cromwell ed Ireton e trascinati fino a Tyburn (il Golgotha, il luogo dei teschi, della storia inglese) ove furono impiccati alla forca e poi decapitati, imputriditi com'erano, dal carnefice. Tornava l'allegria all'allegra Inghilterra, tornavano la grazia, la coltura, il fasto, la lussuria delle corti stuarde. Il giovine re aprì le porte del suo palazzo ad adulatori ed adulatrici. Col cagnolino in braccio, dava udienza ai suoi ministri appoggiato contro il caminetto nella camera dei pari, ascoltava i discorsi di quell'eccelso consesso e giurava per il corpicino di Dio (la bestemmia prediletta di Sua Maestà) che i suoi nobili lo divertivano più che i comici.

Ma fu inganno questo trionfo chè in breve giro di tempo la stella degli stuardi era tramontata per sempre e la successione protestante incarnata nella persona di Guglielmo di Nassau, era diventata la pietra angolare della costituzione brittanica. Qui, secondo i libri di testo, si chiude il capitolo della storia antica e si apre quello della storia moderna.

Eppure la crisi costituzionale che si risolse allora in una tregua duratura fra la corona, la chiesa e la legislatura non è nè l'unico nè il più interessante fatto compiuto da quel principe, detto di niemoria pia, gloriosa ed immortale. La sua vittoria significi inoltre una crisi di razza, una rivincita etnica. Dai giorni di Guglielmo il Conquistatore in poi nessun monarca di sangue germanico aveva impugnato lo scettro inglese. Ai normanni succedettero i plantagenceti, ai plantageneti la casa di Tudor, alla casa di Tudor gli stuardi. Persino Oliviero Cromwell stesso, il signor protettore dei diritti e delle libertà popolari, era di stirpe celta, figlio di padre gallese e di madre scozzese. Erano trascorsi dunque più di sei secoli dalla battaglia di Hastings prima che salisse al trono d'Inghilterra il vero successore della dinastia anglo-sassone: ed il popolo che acclamava alla venuta dell'impacciato e taciturno duce olandese, acclamava a sè stesso, salutava il simbolo personale di un proprio risorgimento.

Ora pure per la prima volta la vera anima inglese comincia a far capolino nella letteratura. Considerate di quale minima importanza era stata quell'anima nei primi secoli. In Chaucer, scrittore cesareo, di stile forbito ed agghindato l'anima indigena si distingue appena quale cornice nella quale sono incastonate le avventure della gente per bene, vale a dire, i chierici normanni e gli eroi stranieri. In che modo è rispecchiato nei drammi variopinti di Guglielmo Shakespeare, che scrisse duecento anni dopo Chaucer, il grande popolo inglese? Uno zotico contadino, un giullare di corte, uno sbrindellone fra il pazzo e lo scemo, un beccaniorto. I personaggi shakespeariani vengono tutti da oltremare e da oltremonti: Otello, un duce moresco, Shylock, un ebreo veneziano, Cesare, un romano, Amleto, un principe di Danimarca, Macbeth, un usurpatore celta, Giulietta e Romeo, veronesi. L'unico grande ritratto, forse, di tutta la ricca galleria che possa chiamarsi inglese è quello del grasso cavaliere dall'epa mostruosa, sir John Falstaff. La letteratura inglese durante i secoli che seguirono la conquista francese andava a scuola ed i suoi maestri erano Boccaccio, Dante, Tasso e messer Lodovico. *I racconti di Canterbury* di Chaucer sono una versione del Decamerone o del Novellino; Il *Paradiso Perduto* di Milton è una trascrizione puritana della Divina Commedia. Shakespeare, colla sua tavolozza tizianesca, la sua facondia, la sua passionalità epilettica e la sua furia creatrice è un'inglese italianizzato mentre il teatro dell'epoca del ristauro della monarchia prende le mosse dal teatro spagnuolo, dalle opere di Calderon e di Lope de Vega. Il primo scrittore inglese il quale scrive senza copiare nè adattare le opere straniere, il quale crea senza modelli letterari ed infonde alle creature della sua penna uno spirito veramente nazionale, il quale fabbrica per sè stesso una forma artistica ch'è forse scuza precedenti, eccezione fatta per le sommarie monografie di Sallustio e di Plutarca è Daniele Defoe, il padre del romanzo inglese.

Daniele Defoe nacque nel 1661 un anno dopo la rientrata di Carlo Stuardo. Suo padre era un ricco macellajo di Cripplegate che, da buon borghese, destinava suo figlio agli ordini sacri. Ma il figlio era tutt'altro che uno stinco di santo ed il predicare il vangelo della pace cristiana mal s'addiceva ad un uomo battagliero, la cui vita dalla culla alla tomba era una lotta dura gagliarda ed inefficace.

Compiuti gli studi il giovine si gettò nella voragine della politica e quando il duca di Monmouth (uno dei numerosi bastardi dell'allegro monarca) innalzò il vessillo della rivolta s'arruolò nelle schiere del pretendente. La rivolta abortì e poco mancò che il Defoe non ci rimettesse la vita. Lo troviamo qualche anno più tardi che esercita il conmmercio di mediatore in maglierie: e nel 1689 cavalcò nel reggimento di cavallegeri volontari che scortò i nuovi sovrani Guglielmo e Maria ad un solenne banchetto nel Guildhall. Poscia si occupò del commercio di droghe orientali. Viaggiò in

Francia, in Ispagna ed in Portogallo, fermandovisi anche qualche tempo. Nei suoi viaggi commerciali si recò perfino in Olanda ed in Germania ma quando ritornò in Inghilterra l'aspettava il primo di una lunga serie di disastri. Era dichiarato in fallimento e siccome i suoi creditori incrudelivano contro di lui pensò bene di rifugiarsi a Bristol dove i cittadini gli affibbiarono il nomignolo del *signore domenicale* perché non osava escire di casa che la domenica giorno in cui, secondo la legge, i cursori del tribunale non potevano arrestarlo. Un accordo coi suoi creditori lo liberò da questo domicilio coatto e per ben dodici anni lavorò ininterrottamente per amortizzare l'ingente somma dei suoi debiti, diciasettemila lire sterline.

Dalla sua liberazione fino alla morte di re Guglielmo il Defoe era gerente di una fabbrica di tegole olandesi e si occupò attivamente di politica, pubblicando opuscoli, saggi, satire, trattatelli, tutti in difesa del partito del re straniero e tutti, ad eccezione del poema *The Trueborn Englishman*, di scarsissimo valore letterario. Dopo l'accessione della regina Anna il parlamento votò una legge coercitiva contro i protestanti dissidenti (quei, cioè, che non riconoscevano la supremazia della chiesa anglicana) ed il Defoe, mascherandosi quale anglicano a tutt'oltranza, pubblicò la famosa satira *La Via piu breve coi dissidenti* nella quale propone che tutti coloro che non accettino i dommi ed i riti della chiesa anglicana siano condannati alla forca o alla galera, riservando l'onore della crocifissione ai padri della compagnia di Gesù. La satira destò immenso scalpore, ingannando sulle prime gli stessi ministri i quali, dopo averne lodato la sincerità e la saviezza, s'accorsero che si trattava di una solenne montatura. Fu spiccato contro il Defoe mandato di cattura e la gazzetta londinese pubblicò la descrizione del satirico. Eccola:

Un uomo magro, attempato, forse quarantenne, di carnagione scura, capelli castagni ma porta la parrucca, naso adunco, mento acuto, occhi grigi con un grande neo presso la bocca, nato a Londra, per molti anni mediatore in maglieric in Cornhill, ora proprietario d'una fabbrica di mattoni ed embrici a Tilbury nella Contea di Essex.

Gli sbirri misero una taglia sulla sua testa ed entro il mese il Defoe era incarcerato in Newgate. Il suo libro fu bruciato dal boja e lo scrittore fu messo alla gogna per tre giorni successivi dinanzi la Borsa, nella via di Cheapside ed alle porte della città a Temple Bar. Non si perdette d'animo durante il supplizio. Per un atto di clemenza sovrana le orecchic non gli furono tagliate: le fioraje addobbarono lo strummento di tortura con festoni di fiori: esemplari del suo *Inno alla Gogna*, che gli strilloni vendevano per pochi soldi, andarono a ruba mentre la plebaglia cittadina, assiepata nella piazza, recitava i versi e brindava alla salute del prigioniero ed alla libertà del discorso.

Tratto poscia in prigione la sua attività letteraria non accennò a cessare. Fondò e diresse (sempre in carcere) uno dei primi giornali inglesi *The Review* e seppe in tal modo placare le autorità che poco dopo fu messo a piede libero non soltanto ma ebbe dal governo l'incarico di recarsi ad Edimburgo quale inviato segreto.

Seguono altri sette anni durante i quali la figura dello scrittore si perde nella grigia penombra della politica. Poi il governo mise una forte imposta sui giornali e la *Review* morì dopo nove anni d'esistenza. Il Defoe, scribacchino indefesso com'era, si tuffò di nuovo nella polemica. Un suo opuscolo sulla successione giacobita gli valse un nuovo processo e, condannato in contumacia, fu incarcerato in Newgate una seconda volta. Dovette la sua liberazione ad un violento accesso d'appoplessia che per poco non l'uccise. La letteratura mondiale avrebbe un capolavoro di meno se il colpo fosse stato mortale. Compiuta l'unione dell'Inghilterra colla Scozia e dopo stabilita sul trono inglese la casa di Annover l'importanza politica del Defoe diminuisce rapidamente. Si rivolse allora (aveva sessant'anni suonati) alla letteratura propriamente detta e nei primi anni del regno di Giorgio I (la vita accidentata del Defoe si estende attraverso sette regni) scrisse e diede alle stampe la prima parte di Robinson Crusoe. Questo libro era stato offerto dall'autore a quasi tutte le case editrici della capitale le quali, con grande perspicacia, lo avevano rifiutato. Vide la luce nell'aprile del 1719; nello scorcio d'agosto se ne vendeva già la quarta edizione. Furono venduti ottantamila copie, tirature senza precedenti per quei tempi. Il pubblico non si saziava delle avventure dell'eroe di Defoe, ne voleva ancora. E come il Conan Doyle, ottemperando alle'insistenze del pubblico odierno, risuscitò il suo fantoccio allampanato Sherlock Holmes per lanciarlo nuovamente alla caccia di scrocconi e malfattori così pure il sessantenne Defoe fece seguire alla prima parte del suo romanzo una seconda nella quale il protagonista sente la nostalgia del viaggiare e torna al suo 'island home'. A questa seconda parte seguì una terza *Serious Reflections of Robinson Crusoe*. Il Defoe, buon'anima, accorgendosi un poco tardi che nel suo verismo prosaico aveva tenuto poco conto del lato spirituale del suo eroe fece raccolta nella terza parte di riflessioni serie sull'uomo, sul destino umano, sul creatore, riflessioni e pensieri che fregiano la figura del rude marinaio nè più nè meno che i talismani votivi che pendono attorno al collo e dalle mani protese di una madonna taumaturga. Il famoso libro ebbe persino la somma fortuna di essere parodiato da un bell'umore londinese che fece, anche lui, il suo gruzzolo colla vendita di una satira bislacca intitolata *La Vita e le Avventure sorprendenti e strane di certo Daniele Defoe, mercante lanaiolo, il quale visse solo soletto sull'isola disabitata della Granbrettagna*.

I pedanti si affaticavano a scoprire i minuscoli sbagli in cui il grande battistrada del movimento verista era incorso. Come poteva Crusoe riempirsi le tasche di biscotti se si era spogliato prima di nuotare dalla spiaggia alla nave arenata? Come poteva vedere gli occhi del caprone nel bujo pesto della caverna? Come potevano gli spagnuoli dare al padre di Venerdì un patto in iscritto se non avevano nè inchiostro nè penne d'oca? Ci sono o non ci sono orsi nelle isole delle indie occidentali? E via dicendo. Hanno ragione i pedanti: gli sbagli ci sono; ma l'ampio fiume del nuovo verismo li asporta maestosamente come fiasche e giunchi divelti dalla piena.

Dal 1719 al 1725 la penna del vecchio scrittore non ristette mai: scrisse quasi una dozzina di romanzi, le cosiddette *rite*, opuscoli, trattati, giornali, racconti di viaggi, studi medianici. La gotta e la vecchiaja lo costrinsero a deporre la penna. Nel 1730 si crede che sia stato per la terza volta in prigione. Un anno dopo lo vediamo un fuggiasco in una cittadella di Kent. Un che di misterioso vela la sua morte. Forse era latitante, forse il dissidio con suo figlio (una birba matricolata degna di essere stata ospitata nelle pagine di suo padre) l'aveva costretto ad un misero vagabondaggio che ci richiama un poco la tragedia di re Lear. Forse i travagli della sua lunga vita, il troppo scrivere, i brogli, i disastri, la sempre crescente avarizia avevano prodotto in lui come un marasma senile di quell'agile e feconda intelligenza. Stiamo e staremo nell'incerto. Eppure nella sua morte solitaria e strana nell'alberguccio di Moorfields vi è qualcosa di significativo. Egli che immortalò lo strano solitario Crusoe e tanti altri solitari perduti nel mare magno della miseria sociale come Crusoe nel mare delle acque sentiva forse coll'avvicinarsi della sua fine la nostalgia della solitudine. Il vecchio leone va in un luogo appartato quando viene la sua ora suprema. Sente il ribrezzo del suo corpo sfiancato e stanco e vuole morire dove nessun occhio possa vederlo. E così talvolta l'uomo che nasce nel pudore si piega anche lui al pudore della morte e non vuole ch'altri si rattristino allo spettacolo di quel fenomeno osceno col quale la natura brutale e beffarda pone fine alla vita di un essere umano.

Daniele Defoe (II)

È un compito tutt'altro che facile il fare uno studio adeguato di uno scrittore voluminoso come fu appunto Daniele Defoe che fece gemere i torchi ben duecentodieci volte. Ma se scartiamo anzitutto le opere d'indole politica e le risme di saggi giornalistici le opere del Defoe si raggruppano naturalmente attorno due foci d'interesse. Dall'una parte abbiamo quegli scritti che s'imperniano attorno un qualsiasi avvenimento del giorno e dall'altra le biografie che, se non sono veri romanzi nel senso ch'intendiamo noi perché vi fanno difetto la trama amorosa, l'esame psicologico e l'equilibrio studiato di caratteri e tendenze, sono documenti letterari dentro i quali l'anima del romanzo verista moderno s'intravede come anima che sonnecchia in un organismo imperfetto ed amorfo. *La Burrasca* per esempio è un libro che descrive lo scempio fatto da uno spaventoso uragano che infuriò sopra le isole brittanche a due riprese verso la fine del mese di novembre 1703. I meteorologi moderni hanno potuto compilare una carta barometrica accuratissima dai dettagli precisi forniti loro dal Defoe. Il suo metodo è la semplicità stessa. Il libro s'apre con un'inchiesta sulle cause dei venti, poi riepiloga le burrasche rimaste famose nella storia umana e finalmente la narrazione, a guisa di un grosso serpente, si mette a strisciare lentamente attraverso un groviglio di lettere e resoconti. Questi si succedono interminabilmente. In tutte le lettere, che vengono da ogni parte del regno unito, leggiamo le stesse cose: tanti alberi (pomi, salici, querce) diverli qua, tante case scoperchiate là, tanti navigli sconquassati contro gli argini in questo luogo, tante guglie crollate in quello: e poi un'enumerazione meticolosa delle perdite sofferte dalle diverse borgate in bestiami e stabili, dei morti e dei salvati ed un esatto metraggio di tutto il piombo strappato dai tetti delle chiese. Il libro riesce, manco a dirlo, d'una noja fenomenale. Il lettore moderno brontola parecchio prima di venirne in capo: ma alla fin fine lo scopo del cronista è stato raggiunto. A furia di ripetizioni, contraddizioni, dettagli, cifre, rumori la burrasca c'è stata, la rovina si vede.

Nel *Giornale della Peste* il Defoe spiega più ampio volo. Sir Walter Scott nella nota di prefazione che contribuì all'edizione definitiva delle opere di Defoe scrive:

> Se non avesse scritto il *Robinson Crusoe* Daniele Defoe avrebbe meritato l'immortalità col genio che dimostra in questo suo giornale della peste.

La peste nera devastò la città di Londra nei primi anni del regno di Carlo II. Il numero delle vittime non si può stabilire con certezza ma probabilmente oltrepassava centocinquantamila. Di questa orrenda strage di Defoe da una narrazione tanto più terrificante perchè sobria e mesta. Le porte delle case infette erano segnate con una croce rossa con sopra scritto: *Signore, abbi pietà di noi!* L'erba cresceva nelle pubbliche vie. Un cupo silenzio ammorbante copriva la città devastata come un baldacchino. Di nottetempo i furgoni funebri traversavano le strade guidati da vetturali velati che si turavano la bocca con dei pannilini disinfettati. Uno strillone li precedeva suonando un campanello ad intervalli e gridando nella notte: *Portateci fuori i vostri morti!* Dietro la chiesa in Aldgate fu scavata un'immensa cavità. Qui i vetturali scaricavano i furgoni e gettavano sui mucchi di cadaveri anneriti la calce pietosa. I disperati ed i delinquenti gozzovigliavano giorno e notte nelle bettole, I moribondi correvano a buttarsi giù fra i morti. Le donne incinte urlavano al soccorso. Grandi fuochi fumosi ardevano sempre alle cantonate e nelle piazze. La pazzia religiosa raggiunse il colmo. Un pazzo con sulla testa un braciere di carboni ardenti, ignudo bruco, camminava nella strada gridando ch'era un profeta e ripetendo a mo' d'antifono: *O il grande e terribile Dio!*

La persona che narra questi orrori nella finzione del Defoe è un ignoto sellajo londinese ma lo stile della narrazione ha qualcosa di magistrale e (mi si passi la parola) d'orchestrale che ci ricorda il *Sevastopulo* di Tolstoy od *I Tessitori* dell'Hauptmann. Ma sentiamo in queste due opere un'ondati di lirismo, un'arte conscia di se stessa, un tema musicale che vorrebbe essere la rivolta emotiva dell'uomo moderno contro la nequizia umana o sovrumana. Nel Defoe nulla: nè lirismo nè l'arte per l'arte nè sentimento sociale. Il sellajo cammina nella strada abbandonata, ascolta le grida d'angoscia, si discosta dai malati, legge gli editti del prefetto, confabula coi santesi che masticano l'aglio e la ruta, discute con un barcajolo a Blackwall, compila fedelmente la sua statistica, s'interessa al prezzo del pane, si lagna delle guardie notturne, sale sulla vetta della collina di Greenwich e calcola a un dipresso quante persone si sono rifugiate sulle navi ancorate nel Tamigi, lodu, biagima, piange non di rado, prega qualchevolta: e termina il suo racconto con quattro versi zoppicanti, per i quali chiede, da buon sellajo, l'indulgenza del lettore. Sono rozzi, dice, ma sinceri. Suonano così:

> C'era in Londra una terribile peste
> Nell'anno sessantacinque
> Spazzò via centomila anime
> Eppur io vivo.

Nel Defoe, come si vede, l'astro della poesia brilla, come si suol dire, per la sua assenza quantunque il suo sia uno stile d'una chiarezza ammirevole senza leziosaggine di sorta, e che in certe pagine di *Robinson Crosoe* e di *Duncan Campbell* s'irradia tutt'ad un tratto d'un breve e dolce splendore. Ecco perchè la sua *Storia del Diavolo* è parsa a taluni addirittura nauseante. Il diavolo del Defoe ha pochi punti di contatto collo strano figlio del Caos che rompe guerra eterna contro gli scopi dell'Altissimo. Rassomiglia piuttosto ad un mediatore in maglierie che ha sofferto un calamitoso dissesto finanziario. Il Defoe si mette nei panni del diavolo con un verismo che ci pare di primo acchito sconcertante. Se la prende gagliardamente col maestoso protagonista del *Paradiso Perduto*. Si domanda quanti giorni mise il diavolo a cadere dal cielo nell'abisso, quanti spiriti caddero con lui, quando s'accorse della creazione del mondo, in che modo sedusse Eva, dove abita di preferenza, perchè e come si fece le ali. Questo atteggiamento mentale in presenza del sovranaturale che segue come corollario logico i suoi principi letterari è l'atteggiamento di un barbaro rinsavito. Talvolta, come nella goffia frettolosa storia del filosofo *Dickory Cronke*, pare che un ebete narri le gesta di un mentecatto: tal'altra, come in *Duncan Campbell*, studio medianico come noi si direbbe, d'un interessante caso di chiaroveggenza in iScozia, l'atteggiamento dello scrittore s'adatta singolarmente al caso che narra e ci rammenta la precisione e l'innocenza delle domande di un fanciullo.

Questo racconto che dev'essere il frutto di un soggiorno negli altipiani o nelle isole della Scozia dove, come è risaputo, la telepatia è nell'aria, segna il limite del metodo del Defoe in questi scritti impersonali. Il Defoe, seduto al capezzale del ragazzo visionario, di cui fissa le palpebre alzate, ascolta il respiro, esamina la posizione della testa, nota la carnagione fresca, è il verista in presenza dell'ignoto, è l'esperienza dell'uomo che travaglia e conquide in presenza del sogno di cui teme l'inganno, è l'anglosassone, insomma, in presenza del celta.

In quelle opere del Defoe che appartengono alla seconda categoria e che hanno un interesse più personale sentiamo or si or no come un accompagnamento intermittente, il rullìo dei tamburi ed il fragore dei pezzi da campo. *I Ricordi di un cavaliere*, i quali il Defoe, in una prefazione caratteristica finge di avere scoperti fra le carte di uno segretario di stato di Guglielmo III, sono la narrazione personale di un ufficiale che combattè sotto Gustavo Adolfo e poi s'arruolò nell'esercito di Carlo I. Benchè questo libro abbia fatto scorrere non poco inchiostro causa la sua dubbiosa provenienza non può interessare oggi che lo studioso di quell'epoca torbida e sanguinaria. Le cose che il cavaliere ci narra le abbiamo lette altrove. Le rileggiamo qui senza curarcene gran che e ricordiamo tutt'al più qualche descrizione vivace, qualche punto di colore.

I capitoli spagnuoli dei *Ricordi del Capitano Carleton*, invece, rimpinzati di avventure galanti, di combattimenti di tori e di esecuzioni capitali sono, come si direbbe oggi nel gergo cinematografico, presi dal vero. Se vivesse tuttora il Defoe per le sue doti d'esattezza e di fantasia, per la sua esperienza farraginosa e per il suo stile lindo e preciso godrebbe probabilmente gran fama quale corrispondente speciale di qualche mastodontico giornale americano o inglese.

La prima figura femminile che si stacca da questo sfondo è quella della signora Cristiana Davies, detta la madre Ross. Codesta signora, assieme coll'avventuriera Roxana e l'indimenticabile meretrice Moll Flanders, forma il terzetto di personaggi femminili che riduce all'impotenza stupefatta la critica odierna. Difatti l'elegante letterato e bibliofilo sir Leslie Stephen si domanda con una curiosità da scrittore per bene dove mai il Defoe abbia trovato le modelle per queste figure: e l'ultimo editore del

Defoe, il poeta John Masefield, non sa spiegarsi come uno scrittore che visse negli anni che seguirono il ristauro della monarchia, anni giocondi, illeggiadriti dalle grazie libere di tante dame accondiscendenti, anni la cui storia intima è tutto uno stellato, di nomi femminili, Lucia Walters e Nell Gwynne e Marta Blount e la scandalosa Susanna Centlivre e la spiritosa Lady Mary Montagu, abbia creato delle donne di un verismo così cinico, crasso ed impudico. *La Vita della Signora Cristiana Davies* sembrerà, certo, ai signori critici surricordati come la trascrizione della vita di Giovanna d'Arco fatta da uno stalliere.

Cristiana, ch'è una belloccia ostessa dublinese, pianta in asso le sue damigiane ed indossando gli abiti maschili erra per tutta l'Europa come dragone nell'esercito del duca di Marlborough in cerca di suo marito. Lo ritrova alla battaglia di Hochstat ma nel frattempo egli si è preso un'amante olandese. La scena dell'incontro di Cristiana col marito fedifrago nella stanza della locanda ci presenta l'eterno feminino sotto una luce inaspettata. Eccola: Cristiana stessa parla:

Lo vidi nella cucina che beveva coll'olandese ma fingendo di non vederlo andai dalla padrona e la pregai di farmi condurre in una camera privata. Essa mi precedette nella camera e dopo avermi portato un pinto di birra che avevo ordinato mi lasciò sola coi miei tristi pensieri. Mi sedetti, misi il gomito sul tavolo ed appoggiando la testa sulla mano mi misi a riflettere... Ma perchè si è così cambiato lui?... E la sua tenerezza verso l'olandese sciolse le mie lagrime dimodochè, scorrendo abbondantemente, mi portarono qualche sollievo. Non potevo trattenere questo fiotto che durò un buon quarto d'ora. Finalmente cessò: e dopo aver bevuto un poco dell'bougarde (ch'è una birra bianca del colore di latte acido) mi lavai gli occhi ed il viso colla birra che avanzava per nascondere il mio pianto. Poi, chiamando la padrona, ordinai ancora un pinto.

Altro che Tristano e Isotta! Offrirebbe pen boco ai musicisti odierni, analfabeti o letterati che siano, la storia di questa donna che inizia la sua carriera, ancora ragazza, rotolandosi giù per un pendio per mandare in visibilio l'attempato Conte di C—— (notate la delicatezza delle iniziali) e muore a sessantadue anni nell'ospedale militare di Chelsea, vivandiera pensionata, storpia, scrofolosa e sofferente d'idropisia: ed offrirebbe meno che meno la vita di Moll Flanders, l'unica, l'impareggiabile, la quale (cito le parole del vecchio frontispizio) nacque nelle carceri di Newgate e visse durante sessant'anni una vita di varietà continua, era dodici anni meretrice, cinque volte moglie (di cui una volta col proprio fratello), dodici anni ladra, otto anni ergastolana al bagno in Virginia, poi diventò ricca, visse onesta e morì penitente. Il verismo, insomma, di questo scrittore sfida e trascende le magiche frodi della musica.

Il verismo moderno è forse una reazione. La grande nazione francese che venera la leggenda della vergine d'Orleans, la deturpa poi per bocca di Voltaire, l'insudicia lubricamente per mano degli incisori dell'ottocento, la foracchia e la sminuzza nel secolo ventesimo collo stile tagliente d'Anatole France. L'intensità stessa, la raffinatezza stessa del verismo francese tradiscono le sue origini spirituali. Ma cercherete invano nelle opere del Defoe quell'iroso ardore della corruzione che illumina d'una fosforescenza pestifera le tristi pagine dell'Huysmans. Cercherete invano nelle opere d'uno scrittore che, due secoli prima del Gorki o del Dostoievski, portò nella letteratura europea l'infima racca della popolazione, il trovatello, il borsaiolo, il manutengolo, la prostituta, la megera, il predatore, il naufrago, quell'ardore studiato d'indegnazione e di protesta che lacera ed accarezza. Troverete, se mai, sotto la scorza rude dei suoi personaggi un istinto ed una profezia. Le sue donne hanno l'indecenza e la continenza delle bestie; i suoi uomoni sono nerboruti e silenziosi come gli alberi. Il feminismo inglese e l'imperialismo inglese covano già in queste anime che appena emergono dal regno animale. Il proconsole africano Cecil Rhodes discende in linea diretta dal capitano Singleton e la signora Cristiana Davies sullodata è la trisnonna presuntiva della signora Pankhurst.

Il capolavoro del *Robinson Crusoe* è la completa espressione artistica di questo istinto e di questa profezia. Nella vita del pirata ed esploratore *Captain Singleton* e nel racconto del *Colonel Jack*, soffuso d'una cosi larga e triste carità, il Defoe ci presenta studi ed abbozzi per quella grande figura solitaria che ottenne più tardi, col plauso di tanti cuori semplici di uomini e di ragazzi, la cittadinanza del mondo delle lettere. Il racconto del marinajo naufragato che abitò quattro anni l'isola solitaria ci rivela, come nessun altro libro forse in tutta la lunga letteratura inglese, l'istinto cauto ed eroico dell'animale ragionevole e la profezia dell'impero.

La critica europea s'arrabatta da parecchie generazioni e con un'insistenza non del tutto amichevole a delucidare il mistero dell'immensa conquista mondiale compiuta da quella razza ibrida che vive a stento su un isolotto del mare nordico e non è stata dotata dalla natura dell'intelletto del latino nè della longanimità del semita nè dello zelo germanico nè della sensibilità dello slavo. La caricatura europea si diverte da parecchi lustri nel contemplare con allegria non scevra di sconforto un uomo sperticato dalle mascelle da bertuccia, dai vestiti a scacchiera troppo corti e troppo stretti, dai piedi enormi oppure il tradizionale John Bull, il pingue fattore, dal viso fatuo e rubicondo come la luna in quintadecima e dal minuscolo cappello a staio. Nessuno di questi due fantocci avrebbe conquistato in mille secoli un palmo di terra. Il vero simbolo della conquista brittannica è Robinson Crusoe il quale, naufragato su un'isola solitaria, con in tasca un coltello ed una pipa diventa architetto, falegname, arrotino, astronomo, prestinajo, costruttore navale, figulo, bastajo, agricoltore, sarto, ombrellajo e chierico. Egli è il vero prototipo del colonizzatore brittanico come Venerdì (il fedele selvatico che vi giunge in un giorno infausto) è il simbolo delle razze assoggettate. Tutta l'anima anglosassone è in Crusoe: l'indipendenza virile, la crudeltà inconscia, la persistenza, l'intelligenza tardiva eppur efficace, l'apatia sessuale, la religiosità pratica e ben librata, la taciturnità calcolatrice. Chi rilegga questo semplice e commovente libro alla luce della storia susseguente non può non subirne l'incanto fatidico.

San Giovanni Evangelista vide nell'isola di Patmo il crollo apocalittico dell'universo e l'ergersi delle mura della città eterna rutilanti di berillo e di smeraldo, d'onice e di diaspro, di zaffiro e di rubino. Crusoe non vide che una meraviglia sola in tutto il creato ubertoso che lo circondava, l'impronta di un piede nudo sulla rena vergine: e chi sa se questa non pesi più di quella?

[*Draft version conclusion. See p. 332, n. 49.*]

La narrazione che s'impernia attorno questa semplice meraviglia è tutta una lunga ed armoniosa e consistente epopea nazionale, una musica solenne e trionfatrice alla quale il flebile canto dell'anima selvatica ed ingenua tiene bordone. Il nostro secolo che ama risalire alle origini dei fenomeni attuali per convincersi ancora una volta della verità della sua dottrina evoluzionista la quale insegna che quando eravamo piccoli non eravamo grandi potrebbe rileggere la storia di Robinson Crusoe e del suo servitore Venerd con gran profitto. Vi troverebbe molti appunti utilissimi per quell'industria internazionale dei nostri giorni che è la fabbricazione economica del tipo imperialista inglese e la vendita del medesimo a prezzi di stralcio.

[WILLIAM BLAKE]

(*Ten pages of the manuscript are missing.*)

d'un'interpretazione etica e pratica non sono aforismi morali. Guardando il duomo di San Paolo Blake udì coll'udita dell'anima il grido del piccolo spazzacammino che, nel suo strano linguaggio letterario, simboleggia l'innocenza calpestata, guardando il palazzo di Buckingham vide coll'occhio della mente il sospiro del soldato infelice che cola giù dal muro della reggia nella forma d'una goccia di sangue. Mentre era ancora vigoroso e giovane sapeva e poteva, riavendosi da queste visioni, inciderne l'immagine in un verso martellato o nella lastra di rame: e tali incisioni in parole o in metallo riassumono spesso un intero sistema sociologico. La carcere, scrive, si fabbrica colle pietre della legge, il lupanare coi mattoni della religione. Ma lo sforzo continuo di questi viaggi nell'ignoto e di questi ritorni bruschi alla vita naturale corrode lentamente ma infallibilmente il potere artistico. Le visioni moltiplicandosi acciecano la visione: e verso la fine della sua vita mortale l'ignoto a cui bramava lo coperse delle tenebre di vaste ali e gli angeli con cui favellava da immortale con immortali lo velarono nel silenzio delle loro vesti.

Vi avrò dato una falsa idea della personalità di Blake se ho evocato dalle ombre con parole aspre e con versi violenti la figura d'un bolso tribuno di secondo o di terz'ordine. Da giovane faceva parte del cenacolo letterario-rivoluzionario che comprendeva la signorina Wollestonecraft ed il celebre (dovrei forse dire) il notorio autore dei *Diritti dell'Uomo*, Tommaso Paine. Anzi fra i soci di quel circolo Blake era l'unico ch'avesse il coraggio di portare nella strada il berretto rosso, emblèma della nuova era. Se lo tolse presto, però, per non mettterselo più dopo i massàcri nelle carceri parigine avvenute nel settembre del 1792. La sua ribellione spirituale contro i potenti di questo mondo non era quella polvere pirica solubile in acqua, alla quale siamo più o meno avvezzi. Gli fu offerto nel '99 il posto di maestro di disegno per la famiglia reale: lo rifiutò, temendo che nell'-ambiente artificioso della corte la sua arte non avesse a perire d'inanizione, ma in pari tempo, per non offendere il sovrano, rinunziò a tutti gli altri allievi plebei che formavano il suo maggiore cespite di rendita. Dopo la sua morte la principessa Sofia mandò alla vedova un dono privato di cento sterline. La signora lo rimandò, ringraziando cortesemente, dicendo che poteva farne a meno e che non voleva accettarlo perchè il denaro, altrimelti impiegato, avrebbe giovato forse a ridare la vita e la speranza a qualcono più sventurato di lei. Evidentemente ci passa una disereta differenza fra questo eresiarca anarcoide e visionario e quegli ortodossissimi filosofi chiesastici, Francesco Suarez *Europae atque orbis universi magister et oculus populi christiani* e don Giovanni Mariana di Talavera che, nel secolo precedente, avevano scritto per lo sbalordimento dei posteri la truce e logica difesa del tirannicidio. Lo stesso idealismo che rapiva e sosteneva il Blake quando lanciava i suoi fulmini contro la malizia e la tristezza umane lo tratteneva dall'incrudelire contro il corpo foss'anche del peccatore, la fragile tenda della carne, come lo chiama nel libro mistico di *Thel*, che giace sul talamo del nostro desiderio. Gli episodi che dimostrano la bontà primitiva del suo cuore non mancano nella storia della sua vita. Quantunque vivesse a stento e non sborsasse che mezza ghinea ogni settimana per il mantenimento della piccola casa che abitava prestò quaranta sterline ad un amico bisognoso. Avendo visto un povero e tisico studente d'arte passare la sua finestra ogni mattina col portafoglio sotto il braccio n'ebbe pietà e l'invitò in casa sua dove gli dava da mangiare e cercava di allietargli la triste e languente vita. I suoi rapporti col suo fratello minore Roberto ci richiamano la storia di Davide e Gionatan. Blake l'ospitava, lo manteneva, l'amava, lo curava durante la sua lunga malattia, gli parlava del mondo eterno e lo confortava. Vegliò al suo capezzale ininterrottamente per molti giorni prima della sua morte e, al momento supremo, vide l'anima amata sprigionarsi dal corpo inerte e salire verso cielo battendo le mani dalla gioja. Poi, spossato e tranquillo, si coricò e dormì di un sonno letargico per settantadue ore consecutive.

Ho accennato due o tre volte già alla signora Blake e forse devo dire qualcosa della vita coniugale del poeta. Il Blake amò una volta quando aveva vent'anni. La ragazza, alquanto scioccherella (pare), si chiamava Polly Wood. L'influenza di questo amore giovanile irradia le prime opere di Blake *Gli Schizzi Poetici* ed i *Canti dell'Innocenza*. Ma l'incidente si chiuse subito e bruscamente. Lei lo credeva pazzo o poco meglio e lui la credeva civettuola o qualcosa di peggio. Il viso di questa ragazza riappare in certi disegni del libro profetico di Vala, un viso soave e sorridente, simbolo della dolce crudeltà femminina e dell'illusione sensuale. Per riaversi di questo sconfitto, Blake partì da Londra ed andò ad abitare il villino di un ortolano, di nome Bouchier. Quest'ortolano aveva una figlia ventiquattrenne, Caterina, il cui cuore si riempì di compassione all'udire le sventure amorose del giovane. L'affezione che nacque da questa pietà e della sua riconoscenza li unì finalmente. I versi d'*Otello*:

> E tu m'amavi per le mie sventure
> Ed io t'amavo per la tua pietà

ci vengono alla memoria quando leggiamo questo capitolo della vita di Blake. Blake, al pari di molti altri uomini di grande ingegno, non si sentiva attratto dalla donna colta e raffinata sia che preferisse alle grazie da salotto ed alla coltura facile ed estesa (se mi è permesso di prendere a prestito un luogo comune del gergo teatrale) la donna semplice, di mentalità sensuale e nuvolosa, o che, nel suo egoismo illimitato volesse che l'anima dell'-amata fosse tutta nua lenta e penosa creazione sua, liberantesi e purificantesi giornalmente sotto i suoi occhi, il demonio (come egli stesso dice) nascosto nella nube. Comunque sia fatto sta che la signora Blake non era nè molto bella nè molto intelligente. Era infatti analfabeta ed il poeta durò fatica ad insegnarle a leggere ed a scrivere. Ci riuscì però sicchè fra pochi anni la moglie l'aiutava nei suoi lavori d'incisione, ritoccava i disegni e coltivò in se stessa la facoltà visionario. Gli esseri elementari e gli spiriti dei grandi morti venivano spesso nella camera del poeta di notte per parlare con lui dell'arte e dell'immaginazione. Allora il Blake sbalzava dal letto ed, afferrando la matita, rimaneva per delle lunghe ore nella fredda notte londinese a disegnare i lineamentie le membra delle visioni mentre la moglie acovacciata accanto alla sua poltrona gli teneva la mano amorevolmente e stava zitta per non turbare l'estasi del veggente. Sparita la visione verso lo spuntare dell'alba la moglie rientrava fra le coperte ed il Blake, raggiante di gioja e di benevolezza, si accingeva lestamente ad accendere il fuoco ed a preparare la colazione per tutt'e due. Dobbiamo meravigliarci perché gli esseri simbolici Los e Urizen e Vala e Tiriel ed Enitharmon e le ombre di Milton e d'Omero venissero dal loro mondo ideale in una povera camera londinese e che altro incenso non salutasse la loro venuta che l'odore di te indiano e di uova fritte nello strutto? È forse la prima volta nella storia del mondo che l'Eterno parla per la bocca dell'umile?

Così si svolse la vita mortale di Guglielmo Blake. La nave della sua vita coniugale salpata sotto gli auspici della pietà e della gratitudine navigò per le solite scogliere per quasi mezzo secolo. Non c'erano figli. Nei primi anni della loro vita unita c'erano stati dei dissapori, dei malintesi facili a comprendersi se poniamo mente alla grande differenza di coltura e di temperamento che divideva i giovani sposi. Tant'è vero che il Blake, come ho detto innanzi, divisava quasi di seguire l'esempio di Abramo e di dare ad Agar quello che Sara ricusava. L'ingenuità vestale della moglie s'accordava male col temperamento di Blake per cui, sino all'ultimo giorno della sua vita, l'esuberanza era la sola bellezza. In una scenata di lagrime e di rimproveri che accadde fra i due la moglie cadde in deliquio e si fece male in tal modo da impedire la possibilità di prole. È una triste ironia il pensare che questo poeta dell'innocenza infantile, l'unico scrittore che abbia scritto dei canti per fanciulli coll'anima di un fanciullo, e che, nello strano poema *Il Gabinetto di Cristallo*, ha illuminato il fenomeno della gestazione d'una luce così tenera e mistica, era destinato a non vedere mai accanto al suo focolare il viso umano di un fanciullo umano. A lui che aveva tale immensa pietà per ogni cosa che vive e soffre e gode nell'illusione del mendo vegetale, per la mosca, per la lepre, per il piccolo spazzacamino, per il pettirosso, persino per la pulce, era negata altra paternità che la paternità spirituale, eppure intensamente naturale, che vive ancora nei versi dei *Proverbi*.

> Chiunque si beffa della fede del bambino
> Sarà beffato nella vecchiaia e nella morte.
> Chiunque insegna al bambino il dubbio
> Non escirà mai dalla putrida fossa.
> Chiunque rispetta la fede del bambino
> Trionferà sull'inferno e sulla morte.

discepoli ed ammiratori, si mise, come Catone il vecchio, a studiare una lingua straniera. Quella lingua era la medesima nella quale io stasera, per la vostra cortesia, cerco, per quanto possa, di richiamare dal crepuscolo della mente universale il suo spirito, di trattenerlo per un istante e d'interrogarlo. Si mise a studiare l'italiano per leggere nell'originale la *Divina Commedia* e per illustrare la visione di Dante con disegni mistici. Indebolito e stremato dagli acciacchi della sua malattia si reggeva su un mucchio di guanciali. Teneva spiegato sulle ginocchia un grande libro di disegno sforzandosi di tracciare sulla pagina bianca le linee dell'ultima visione: È l'atteggiamento nel quale vive per noi nel ritratto di Philips nella Galleria nazionale di Londra. Il suo cervello non s'infrollì, la sua mano non perdette l'antica maestria. La morte gli venne sotto la guisa d'un freddo glaciale, simile ai brividi del colèra, che s'impadronì delle sue membra ed estinse la luce della sua intelligenza in un momento come la fredda oscurità che chiamiamo lo spazio ammanta e spegne la luce d'una stella. Morì cantando con voce potente e sonora che faceva eccheggiare le travi del soffitto. Cantò, come sempre, del mondo ideale, della verità dell'intelletto e della divinità dell'immaginazione. 'Non sono mie, cara' disse a sua moglie 'le canzoni che canto. No, no, ti dico, non sono mie.'

Uno studio integrale sulla personalità di Blake dovrebbe logicamente svolgersi in tre fasi, la patologica, la teosofica e l'artistica. Questa prima credo che possiamo scartare senza troppi rammarichi. Il dire di un grande ingegno che è mattoide, pur riconoscendo la sua valentia artistica, vale tanto quanto il dire ch'era reumatico o che soffriva di diabete. La pazzia, insomma, è un'espressione medica che non può pretendere dalla critica serena maggior riguardo di quello che si tributa all'accusa d'eresia elevata dal teologo o all'accusa d'immoralità elevata dalla questura. Se si deve tacciare di pazzo ogni grande ingegno che non crede nel materialismo frettoloso ch'è adesso in onore, con la beata fatuità di un laureando in scienze esatte, poco ci rimarrà dell'arte e della filosofia mondiali. Una tale strage degli innocenti coinvolgerebbe gran parte del sistema peripatetico, tutta la metafisica medioevale, un'ala intera dell'immenso edificio simmetrico costrutto dal dottore angelico, San Tommaso d'Aquino, l'idealismo di Berkeley e (vedete combinazione) quello stesso scetticismo che fa capo a Hume. In quanto all'arte, poi, tutt'al più riescerebbero a salvar la pelle quelle persone utilissime che sono il fotografo e lo stenografo parlamentare. Il presentimento d'una tale arte e d'una filosofia, fiorenti in un avvenire più o meno lontano sotto il blando connnbio delle due forze sociali più quotate in borsa oggigiorno, la donna e la plebe, riconcilierà, se non altro, ogni artista e filosofo che la pensi diversamente alla brevità della vita di quaggiù

L'indagare, anche, quale posto si deve assegnare al Blake nella gerachia dei mistici occidentali esce dallo scopo di questa conferenza. Mi pare che il

Blake non è un gran mistico. La casa paterna del misticismo è l'oriente ed ora che gli studi linguistici ci mettono in grado di capire il pensiero orientale (se pensiero si può chiamare l'energia ideativa che creò i vasti cicli d'attività e di passività spirituali di cui parlano gli *Upanishads*) i libri mistici dell'occidente splendono, se mai, d'una luce riflessa. Blake, probabilmente, è meno ispirato degli mistici indiani forse, è meno ispirato di Paracelso, di Jacob Behmen, e di Swedenborg: ad ogni modo è meno noioso. In lui la facoltà di visione è immediatamente connessa con la facoltà artistica. Bisogna essere in primo luogo predisposto al misticismo e poi dotato d'una pazienza da fachiro per poter formarsi un'idea di quello che intendano Paracelso e Behmen colle loro esposizioni cosmiche dell'involuzione e dell'evoluzione di mercurio, sale e zolfo, corpo, anima e spirito. Blake, naturalmente, appartiene ad un'altra categoria, quella degli artisti: ed in questa categoria occupa, mi pare, una posizione singolare perché unisce l'acutezza dell'intelletto col sentimento mistico. Questa prima qualità difetta quasi completamente nell'arte mistica. San Giovanni della Croce, per esempio, uno del pochi artisti idealisti ch'è degno di stare accanto al Blake non rivela mai nel suo libro *La Notte Oscura dell'Anima* che freme e sviene d'una passione così estatica nè il senso innato della forma nè la forza coordinatrice dell'intelletto. La spiegazione si trova nel fatto che il Blake ebbe due maestri spirituali, molto differenti l'uno dall'altro eppure simili nella loro precisione formale: Michelangelo Buonarotti ed Emanuele Swedenborg. Il primo disegno mistico che possediamo del Blake *Giuseppe d'Arimatea fra le Rupi d'Albione* ha in un angolo le parole: *Michelangelo pinxit*. È modellato su uno schizzo preparato da Michelangelo per il suo *Giudizio Universale* e simboleggia l'immaginazione poetica in balìa della filosofia sensuale. Sotto il disegno Blake ha scritto: Questo è uno degli artisti gotici che costrussero le cattedrali nei secoli che si chiamano oscuri, errando qua e là vestiti di pelli di capre e di pecore e di cui il mondo non era degno. L'influenza di Michelangelo si sente in tutti l'opera del Blake e massime in quei brani di prosa, raccolti nei frammenti, in cui insiste sempre sull'importanza della linea pura e chiara che evoca e crea la figura sullo sfondo del vuoto mercato. L'influenza dello Swedenborg, che moriva in esilio a Londra, quando il Blake cominciava a scrivere e a disegnare si vede nell'umanità glorificata alla quale tutta l'opera di Blake è improntata. Swedenborg, che bazzicò per parecchi anni tutti i mondi invisibili, vide sotto l'immagine di un uomo il cielo stesso e Michele e Raffaello e Gabriele, che sono, secondo lui, non tre angeli ma tre cori angelici. L'eternità, ch'era parsa al discepolo amato ed a Sant'Agostino una città celeste e all'Alighieri una rosa celeste, appare al mistico svedese nella somiglianza di un uomo celeste, animato in tutte le membra di una fluida vita angelica, eternamente uscente e rientrante, sistole e diastole d'amore e di saviezza. Da questa visione sviluppò quell'-immenso sistema, detto di corrispondenze, che percorre il suo capolavoro *Arcana Celestia*, il nuovo vangelo il quale, secondo lui, doveva essere l'apparizione nei cieli del segno del Figliolo dell'Uomo predetta da San Mattéo.

Armato di questa spada bitagliente, l'arte michelangiolesca e la rivelazione swedenborgiana, Blake uccise il drago dell'esperienza e della saviezza naturali ed, annientando lo spazio ed il tempo e negando l'esistenza della memoria e dei sensi, volle campare la sua opera nel vuoto del seno divino. Per lui ogni tempo più breve di un battito d'arteria equivaleva nel suo periodo e nella sua durata a seimila anni perché in un tale istante, infinitamente breve, l'opera del poeta si concepiva e nasceva. Per lui ogni spazio più grande d'una gocciola rossa di sangue umano era visionario e creato dal martello di Los mentre da ogni spazio più piccolo d'una gocciola di sangue si accedeva all'eternità di cui il nostro mondo vegetale non era che un'ombra. Non *coll'occhio*, dunque, ma *oltre* l'occhio l'anima doveva guardare perché l'occhio che nacque in una notte, mentre l'anima dormiva fra raggi di luce, morirebbe pure in una notte.

Il pseudo-Dionigi l'Areopago nel suo libro *I Nomi Divini* arriva al trono di Dio negando e superando ogni attributo morale e metafisico e s'estasia e si prostra nell'ultimo capitolo dinanzi l'oscurità divina, dinanzi quell'immensità innominabile che precede e abbraccia nell'ordine eterno la somma sapienza ed il sommo amore. Il processo mentale per il quale Blake giunge al soglio dell'infinito è un processo simile. La sua anima, volando dal infinitamente piccolo all'infinitamente grande, dalla goccia di sangue all'universo di stelle, si consuma nella rapidità del volo e si trova rinnovata ed alata ed imperitura sul margine del fosco oceano di Dio.

E quantunque basasse la sua arte su delle premesse così idealiste convinto che l'eternità era innamorata dei prodotti del tempo, i figli di Dio delle figlie degli

[*The concluding page(s) of the manuscript is missing.*]

L'INFLUENZA LETTERARIA UNIVERSALE
DEL RINASCIMENTO
THE UNIVERSAL LITERARY INFLUENCE OF THE RENAISSANCE

Li dottrina evoluzionista, nella loce della quale la nostra società si bea, c'insegna che quando eravamo pieeoli non eravamo ancora grandi: quindi, se poniamo il rinascimento européo quale punto di divisione, dobbiamo arrivare a questa conclusione, che l'umanità fino a quell'epoca, non

possedeva che l'anima ed il corpo di un fanciullo e, soltanto dopo quell'-
epoca, si sviluppò fisicamente e moralmente a tal segno da meritare il nome
di adulto. È una conclusione molto drastica e poco convincente. Anzi (se
non avessi paura di sembrare *laudator temporis acti*) vorrei combatterla a
spada tratta. Il progresso tanto strombazzato di questo secolo consiste in
gran parte in un groviglio di macchine il cui scopo è appunto quello di
raccogliere in fretta e furia gli elementi sparpagliati dell'utile e dello scibile
e di ridistribuirli ad ogni membro della collettività che sia in grado di
pagare una tenue tassa. Convengo che questo sistema sociale possa vantarsi
di grandi conquiste meccaniche, di grandi e benefiche scoperte. Basta, per
convincersene, fare un elenco sommario di quello che si vede nella strada di
una grande città moderna: il tram elettrico, i fili telegrafici, l'umile e necessario postino, gli strilloni, le grandi aziende commerciali ecc. Ma in mezzo a
questa civiltà complessa e multilaterale la mente umana terrorizzata quasi
dalla grandezza materiale si perde, rinnega sè stessa e s'infrollisce. O
dunque bisogna arrivare a questa conclusione che il materialismo odierno,
che discende in linea retta dal rinascimento, atrofizza le facoltà spirituali
dell'uomo, ne impedisce lo sviluppo, ne smussa la finezza? Vediamo.

All'epoca del rinascimento lo spirito umano lottava contro l'assolutismo
scolastico, contro quell'immenso (ed in molti riguardi mirabile) sistema
filosofico che ha le sue ime fondamenta nel pensiero aristotelico, freddo,
chiaro ed imperterrito mentre la sua cima sorge alla luce vaga e misteriosa
dell'ideologia cristiana. Ma se lo spirito umano lottava contro questo sistema non era perche il sistema in se stesso gli era alieno. Il giogo era dolce
e lieve: ma era un giogo. E così quando i grandi ribelli del rinascimento
proclamarono la buona novella alle genti europée che la tirannide non
c'era più, che la tristezza e la sofferenza umane s'erano dileguate come
nebbia al sorgere del sole, che l'uomo non era più un prigioniero, lo spirito
umano sentì forse il fascino dell'ignoto, udì la voce del mondo visuale,
tangibile, incostante, ove si vive e si muore, si pecca e si pente, ed,
abbandonando la pace claustrale nella quale languiva, abbracciò il nuovo
vangelo. Abbandonò la sua pace, la ma vera dimora, perchè n'era stanco,
come Dio stanco (mi si passi la parola alquanto irriverente delle sue per-
fezioni divine chiama il creato fuori del nulla, come la donna stanca della
pace e della quiete che struggono il suo cuore volge lo sguardo verso la vita
tentatrice. Giordano Bruno stesso dice che ogni potere, sia nella natura che
nello spirito, deve creare un potere opposto, senza il quale non può realiz-
zarsi ed aggiunge che in ogni tale separazione c'è una tendenza alla riun-
ione. Il dualismo del sommo nolano rispecchia fedelmente il fenomeno del
rinascimento. E se sembra un poco arbitrario il citare un testimonio contro
sè stesso, citare le stesse parole di un novatore per condannare (o almeno
per giudicare) l'opera di cui fu l'artefice rispondo che non faccio altro che

seguire l'esempio del Bruno stesso, il quale nella sua lunga e persistente e cavillosa autodifesa rivolge le armi dell'accusa contro l'accusatore.

Sarebbe facile riempire queste pagine coi nomi dei grandi scrittori che l'ondata del rinascimento portò alle nuvole (o giù di lì), lodare la grandezza delle loro opere, che, del resto, nessuno pone in dubbio, e terminare con la preghiera rituale: e sarebbe forse una viltà poichè il recitare una litania non è un'indagine filosofica. Il perno del problema è altrove. Bisogna vedere che cosa veramente significhi il rinascimento in quanto riguarda la letteratura e verso quale fine, lieta o tragica, ci conduca. Il rinascimento, per dirla in poche parole, ha messo il giornalista nella cattedra del monaco: vale a dire, ha deposto una mentalità acuta, limitata e formale per dare lo scettro ad una mentalità facile ed estesa (come si suol dire nei giornali teatrali), una mentalità irrequieta ed alquanto amorfa. Shakespeare e Lope de Vega sono responsabili, fino ad un certo punto, per il cinematografo. L'instancabile forza creatrice, la calda e viva passionalità, il desiderio intenso di vedere e di sentire, la curiosità sregolata e diffusa degenerano dopo tre secoli in un sensazionalismo frettoloso. Si potrebbe dire infatti dell'uomo moderno che ha un'epidermide invece di un'anima. Il potere sensorio del suo organismo si è enormemente sviluppato ma si è sviluppato a pregiudizio della facoltà spirituale. Il senso morale e forse anche la forza d'immaginazione ci mancano. Le opere letterarie più caratteristiche che possediamo sono semplicemente amorali: *La Crisi* di Marco Praga, *Pelléas et Melisande* di Maeterlinck, *Crainquebille* d'Anatole France, *Fumée* di Turgenev. Forse le avrò prese piuttosto a vanvera. Non monta: bastano per documentare la tesi che sostengo. Un grande artista moderno volendo musicare il sentimento dell'amore riproduce, per quanto la sua arte glielo permetta, ogni pulsazione, ogni tremito, il più lieve brivido, il più lieve sospiro; gli accordi s'intrecciano e si fanno guerra sorda: si ama mentre s'incrudelisce, si soffre quando e quanto si gode, l'ira ed il dubbio lampeggiano negli occhi degli amanti i cui corpi sono una carne sola. Mettete *Tristano ed Isotta* accanto all'*Inferno* e v'accorgerete come l'odio del poeta segue la sua strada d'abisso in abisso nella scia di un idea che s'intensifica e più intensamente il poeta si consuma nel fuoco dell'idea dell'odio più truce diventa l'arte colla quale l'artista ci comunica la sua passione. L'una è un'arte di circostanze, l'altra è ideativa. Il compilatore d'atlanti nel alto medioevo non si scomponeva quando si trovava in imbarazzo. Scriveva sulla tratta dubbiosa le parole: Hic sunt leones. Gli bastava l'idea della solitudine, il terrore delle strane bestie, l'ignoto. La nostra coltura ha tutt'un altro scopo: siamo avidi di dettagli. Il nostro gergo letterario, per questo motivo, non parla che di colore locale, dell'ambiente, dell'atavismo: onde la ricerca febbrile del nuovo e dello strano, l'accumulazione di dettagli osservati o letti, l'ostentazione della coltura generale.

Il rinascimento a rigor di termini dovrebbe significare una nascita dopo una morte, una fecondità improvisa come quella di Sara dopo un lungo periodo di sterilità. Difatti, il rinascimento venne quando l'arte periva di perfezione formale ed il pensiero si perdeva in sottigliezze oziose. Un poema s'era ridotto un problema algebraico, posto e risolto secondo i regolamenti in simboli umani. Un filosofo era un sofista erudito come il Bellarmino o come Giovanni Mariana che, pur predicando al volgo la parola di Gesù, s'arrabbattava a costruire la difesa morale del tirannicidio.

In mezzo a quest'afa il rinascimento entra come un uragano ed in tutta Europa sorge un tumulto di voci e quantunque i cantori non ci siano più le loro opere sono come le conchiglie marine nelle quali, se porgiamo l'orecchio, udiamo riverberare la voce del mare.

COMMUNICATION DE M. JAMES JOYCE SUR LE DROIT MORAL DES ÉCRIVAINS

ON THE MORAL RIGHT OF AUTHORS

Il me paraît intéressante et curieux de signaler un point particulier de l'histoire de la publication d'*Ulysse* aux Etats-Unis qui précise un aspect de droit de l'auteur sur son oeuvre qui n'avait pas été jusqu'ici mis en lumière. L'importation d'*Ulysse* aux Etats-Unis fut interdite dès 1922 et cette interdiction ne fut levée qu'en 1934. Dans ces conditions, impossible de prendre un copyright pour les Etats-Unis. Or en 1925, un éditeur américain sans scrupules mit en circulation une édition tronquée d'*Ulysse*, dont l'auteur n'était pas maître, n'ayant pu prendre le copyright. Une protestation internationale signée par 167 écrivains fut publiée et des poursuites engagées. Le résultat de ces poursuites fut l'arrêt rendu par une Chambre de la Cour Suprême de New-York le 27 décembre 1928, arrêt qui interdisait aux défenseurs (les éditeurs) 'd'utiliser le nom du demandeur (Joyce)1°, dans aucune revue, périodique ou autre publication publiée par eux: 2°, au sujet d'aucun livre, écrit, manuscrit, y compris l'ouvrage intitulé *Ulysse*.' (Joyce contre *Two Worlds Monthly* and Samuel Roth, II Dep. Supreme Court New York, 27 dec. 1928).

Il est, je crois, possible de tirer une conclusion juridique de cet arrêt dans le sens que, sans être protégée par la loi écrite du copyright et même si elle est interdite, une oeuvre appartient à son auteur en vertu d'un droit naturel et qu'ainsi les tribunaux peuvent protéger un auteur contre la mutilation et la publication de son ouvrage comme il est protégé contre le mauvais usage qu'on pourrait faire de son nom. (*Vifs applaudissements.*)

EXPLANATORY NOTES

The following abbreviations are used:

CW   *The Critical Writings of James Joyce*, ed. Ellsworth Mason and Richard Ellmann (London: Faber, 1959).

D   *Dubliners*, ed. Jeri Johnson (Oxford: Oxford University Press, 2000).

FW   *Finnegans Wake* (London: Faber, New York: Viking, 1939).

JJ   *James Joyce*, by Richard Ellmann, revised edition (New York and London: Oxford University Press, 1982).

JJA   *The James Joyce Archive*, eds. Michael Groden and others, 63 volumes (New York and London: Garland, 1977–80).

Letters   *The Letters of James Joyce*, vol. i ed. Stuart Gilbert (London: Faber, New York: Viking, 1957, revised 1966); vols. ii and iii ed. Richard Ellmann (London: Faber, New York: Viking, 1966).

My Brother's Keeper   Stanislaus Joyce, *My Brother's Keeper*, ed. Richard Ellmann (London: Faber, 1958).

Poems and Exiles   *Poems and Exiles*, ed. J. C. C. Mays (Harmondsworth: Penguin Books, 1992).

Portrait   *A Portrait of the Artist as a Young Man*, ed. Jeri Johnson (Oxford: Oxford Univeristy Press, 2000).

SH   *Stephen Hero*, ed. with Introduction by Theodore Spencer, revised edition with additional material and Foreword by John J. Slocum and Herbert Cahoon (London: Cape, 1956).

U   *Ulysses*, ed. Hans Walter Gabler and others (Harmondsworth: Penguin Books, 1986).

TRUST NOT APPEARANCES

MS Cornell, *JJA* 2.1–3. This essay, a holograph surviving Joyce's papers, dates from his years at Belvedere College, 1893–8. In both 1897 and 1898 Joyce won the prize for the best English composition in the national Intermediate Examinations, prizes of £3 and £4 respectively.

1. *Ad Majorem Dei Gloriam*: 'To the greater glory of God', the Jesuit motto conventionally placed at the beginning of a pupil's essay, along with LDS, *Laus Deo Semper*: 'Praise to God forever', at its end. See *Portrait* 58–9.

2. 'O, how wretched | Is that poor man that hangs on princes' favours', Shakespeare, *Henry VIII*, III. ii.

[SUBJUGATION]

MS Cornell, *JJA* 2.5–14. This fragment, a holograph, survives among manuscripts of which Stanislaus Joyce used the blank versos for his Dublin Journal, 'My Crucible'. The title is lost but its date, 27 September 1898, and corrections in another hand indicate that it is a part of Joyce's matriculation course at university. The title 'Force' supplied in *CW* has been altered here to 'Subjugation' in order to correspond more accurately to the essay's keyword and its theme.

1. Percy Bysshe Shelley, 'Queen Mab; a philosophical poem', III, line 111.
2. John Milton, 'Il Penseroso', line 50.
3. See Frederick Tennyson, *The Isles of Greece: Sappho and Alcaeus*, London: Macmillan (1890), 'The Armoury', IX, lines 157–66.
4. Percy Bysshe Shelley (1792–1822). See *Portrait* 80 for Stephen's reflections on Shelley's ineffectualness.
5. *Hamlet*, III. i. This paragraph may be indebted to Hegel's idea of symbolic, in contrast to classic, art; see *The Introduction to Hegel's Philosophy of Fine Art*, trans. Bernard Bosanquet, London: Kegan Paul, Trench & Co. (1886), 145.
6. John Milton, 'L'Allegro', line 119.
7. Sir Thomas Henry Hall Caine (1853–1931), British novelist and writer of melodramas.
8. Thor and Ospakar feature as heroic figures in Norse sagas and Jason in Greek myth. Daniel Mylrea features in Hall Caine's novel, *The Deemster* (1887).
9. Thomas Carlyle (1795–1881), Scottish author and historian.
10. James 3: 17.
11. Peter Abelard (1079–1142), French scholastic philosopher, lover of Héloïse.

THE STUDY OF LANGUAGES

MS Cornell, *JJA* 2.32–41. This fragment, a holograph, survives among manuscripts of which Stanislaus Joyce used the blank versos for his Dublin Journal 'My Crucible'. Its likely date is 1899 and corrections in another hand place it with the previous essay as part of Joyce's matriculation course at university.

1. See John Ruskin, *Mornings in Florence*, Orpington, Kent: George Allen, 1875–7, 'The Fifth Morning', p. 125. Joyce owned an 1894 edition of this work. The frescoes are in the Spanish Chapel of the church of Santa Maria Novella in Florence. The chapel is dedicated to the honour of St Thomas Aquinas and the series of the Seven Liberal Arts faces that of the Seven Divine Arts. The work is not that of Memmi, i.e. Simone Martini (1283–1344), but of Andrea Di Buonaiuti (*c*.1338–77).
2. Matthew Arnold (1822–88), 'Literature and Science' (Rede Lecture delivered at Cambridge University, 1881): see *The Works of Matthew Arnold*, 15 volumes, London: Macmillan & Co. (1903–04), iv. 279, 317–48.

3. See Bernard Bosanquet, *A History of Aesthetic*, London: Swann Son-nenschein & Co., New York: Macmillan & Co. (1892), 33.
4. Shakespeare, *Henry V*, prologue.
5. *The Christian Year* (1827), a volume of sacred verse by the Anglican John Keble (1792–1866), Professor of Poetry at Oxford (1831–41) and a leading figure in the Oxford Movement.
6. In the novel, *Heart and Science* (1882), by Wilkie Collins (1824–89).
7. *Heart and Science*, chap. 62.

ROYAL HIBERNIAN ACADEMY 'ECCE HOMO'

MS Cornell, *JJA* 2.42–55. This essay, a holograph, survives among manu-scripts of which Stanislaus Joyce used the blank versos for his Dublin Journal, 'My Crucible'. Its date, September 1899, suggests that it is part of Joyce's work at University College Dublin. 'Jesus came out, wearing the crown of thorns and the purple cloak. "Behold the Man!" said Pilate', John 19: 5.

1. Mihály Munkácsy, pseudonym of Mihály (Miska) Leo Lieb (1844–1900), Hungarian painter. The exhibition of his work at the Royal Hibernian Academy, which included his *Ecce Homo* (1896) and other paintings of Christ's Passion, caused some controversy: see Sarah Purser's comments in *The Leader*, 24 November 1900. Munkácsy's Christ trilogy can be found at the Déri Museum, Debrecen, Hungary. Joyce may also have in mind a controversy which had continued to surround an essay, first pub-lished anonymously, by John Robert Seeley, *Ecce Homo: A Survey of the Life and Work of Jesus Christ*, London: Macmillan & Co. (1866).
2. In French, to address familiarly as *tu* (instead of the more formal *vous*).
3. Maurice, Count Maeterlinck (1862–1949), Belgian poet and dramatist whose fame began in 1892 with his play *Pelléas et Mélisande*.
4. The muscular protestant is an ideal espoused by Charles Kingsley (1819–75); see, for example, his *Discipline and other Sermons* (1872).
5. Horace Van Ruith (1839–1923), English painter of figurative and Italianate subjects.
6. Richard Wagner, in 'The Art-Work of the Future', contrasts the mentality of the folk with the mentality of the town. See *Richard Wagner's Prose Works*, translated by William Ashton Ellis, 8 volumes, London: Kegan, Paul, Trench, Trübner & Co. (1892–9), 73 ff., 82–8, 145.

DRAMA AND LIFE

MS Cornell, *JJA* 2.56–73. This essay, a holograph, the author's fair copy, is textually complete and survives among manuscripts of which Stanislaus Joyce used the blank versos for his Dublin Journal, 'My Crucible'. Its date, 10 January 1900, allows for the probability that the essay was read, and disap-proved of, by the President of University College Dublin, Fr. William De-laney, before Joyce delivered it on 20 January at a meeting of the college's Literary and Historical Society. Joyce celebrates these events in chapters 16,

18, 19, and 20 of *Stephen Hero*, where he moves the date forward to the end of March in order that Stephen represent his performance as an Easter sacrifice after his 'forty days' of Lenten preparation. For the circumstances of Joyce's giving this paper see *JJ* 70–3.

1. See Bosanquet, *History of Aesthetic*, 162: 'Shakespeare in every way marks not the opening but the close of a period. Since him there has been no national drama. To-day in England the drama, in the sense of stage-plays which are poetic literature, does not exist.' For the distinction between literature and drama, see also Richard Wagner, 'Art-Work of the Future', 144–5. Joyce's essay, in its title, its ideas and its tone, is deeply indebted to Wagner's essay: see, for example, Wagner's assertion that 'The dramatic Action is thus the *bough from the Tree of Life*' ('Art-Work of the Future', 197.

2. *Macbeth*, I, iii.

3. Pierre Corneille (1606–84), French dramatist; Metastasio, pseudonym of Pietro Trapassi (1698–1782), Italian poet and the creator of *opera seria*; Pumblechook, a fawning character in Dickens's *Great Expectations*; Pedro Calderón de la Barca (1600–81), Spanish dramatist and poet.

4. Charles Haddon Chambers (1860–1921), author of comedies and melodramas; Douglas William Jerrold (1803–57), man of letters and author of comedies and melodrama; Hermann Sudermann (1857–1928), German novelist and dramatist; Gotthold Ephraim Lessing (1729–81), German dramatist and critic. For Joyce's response to Sudermann see *My Brother's Keeper*, 102.

5. Vincenzo Bellini (1801–35), Italian composer whose opera *I Puritani* (1835) provides the music for George Linley's lyric, 'Arrayed for the Bridal', in Joyce's 'The Dead'.

6. What follows in this paragraph re-uses a passage in 'Royal Hibernian Academy "Ecce Homo" ', pp. 17–18 above.

7. From the death-speech of the Countess in W. B. Yeats, *The Countess Cathleen* (1892): 'Do not weep | Too great a while, for there is many a candle | On the High Altar though one fall.' This speech is also quoted in *Portrait* 190. See 'The Day of the Rabblement', pp. 50–1, where the context would suggest that Joyce is here deliberately baiting his audience with a quotation from a play which they, but not he, had condemned.

8. See 'James Clarence Mangan', p. 54: 'Literature is the wide domain which lies between ephemeral writing and poetry (with which is philosophy).' Some confusion has arisen here, especially in Ellmann's suggestion that Joyce gives up this idea when he comes to write *Portrait*. In *SH* 82, the distinction is made between 'the literary form of art as the most excellent' (in contrast with music, painting etc.) and in *Portrait* the same contrast is intended when Stephen contrasts sculpture with 'literature, the highest and most spiritual art' (*Portrait* 180). Such a hierarchy of the arts, in which the art of language is pre-eminent, is no more than a post-Enlightenment cliché. Such a concept is only in apparent conflict with the idea that 'The term "literature" now seemed to him a term of contempt

and he used it to designate the vast middle region which lies between apex and base, between poetry and the chaos of unremembered writing' (*SH* 82). Compare Paul Verlaine (1844–96), *Art Poétique: 'Et tout le reste est littérature'* (which, according to the French idiom Verlaine is playing with, means 'everything else is literature' or 'everything else is irrelevant').

9. See *What To Do? Thought Evoked by the Census of Moscow* by Leo Nikolaevich Tolstoy (1828–1910), Russian novelist and dramatist, translated by I. F. Hapgood (1887).

10. 'My dear friend, clear your mind of cant' (James Boswell, *Life of Samuel Johnson*, 15 May 1783).

11. Wagner, 'Art-Work of the Future', 73 ff., 145.

12. 'Untroubled, the world judges', St Augustine of Hippo (354–430), *Contra Litteras Parmeniani*, iii. 24. Joyce found the sentence in *Apologia pro vita sua* (1864) by John Henry Newman (1801–90), founder of the Catholic University which became University College Dublin. See also, 'Securest jubilends albas Temoram' (*FW* 593.13).

13. '*Littérateurs*': 'men of letters'.

14. *The Master Builder* (1892), one of the later plays of Henrik Ibsen (1828–1906), Norwegian dramatist. Joyce is here answering a previous paper delivered to the Literary and Historical Society on 11 February 1899, 'The Theatre, Its Educational Value', reproduced by its author Arthur Clery in *Dublin Essays* (1919). Clery had championed Greek drama along with *Macbeth* and asserted that 'The effect of Henrik Ibsen is evil.'

15. 'A common impulse toward dramatic art-work can only be at hand in those who actually enact the work of art in common.' Wagner, 'Art-Work of the Future', 140; and see p. 136 where Wagner identifies tragedy as a *communal* art.

16. Ibsen's *The Wild Duck* (1884). See *SH* 91: 'But the play which she [Stephen's mother] preferred to all others was the *Wild Duck* . . . It's so sad: it's terrible to read it even . . . I quite agree with you that Ibsen is a wonderful writer.'

17. Wagner, 'Art-Work of the Future', 198–201.

18. 'In the dramatic Action, therefore, the Necessity of the art-work displays itself. [. . .] The first and truest fount of Art reveals itself in the impulse that urges from *Life* into the work of art; for it is the impulse to bring the unconscious, instinctive principle of Life to understanding (*verständniss*) and acknowledgement as Necessity' (Wagner, 'Art-Work of the Future', 197).

19. Wagner's last work, *Parsifal*, was produced in 1882.

20. 'At the end of each stanza I score a hit', *Cyrano de Bergerac* (1897) by Edmond Rostand (1869–1918), French dramatist.

21. Monsieur Coupeau in *L'Assommoir* (1877), a grisly depiction of alcoholism, by Émile Zola (1840–1902); surplices and dalmatics are ecclesiastical vestments; Mr Beoerly remains untraced.

22. In Hinduism an earthly paradise on Mount Meru.

23. 'The House Beautiful' is the title of a poem by Robert Louis Stevenson

and also of a popular interior-decoration magazine, ed. Clarence Cook, New York: Scribner (1881).

24. Herbert Beerbohm Tree (1853–1917), British actor-manager and founder of the Royal Academy of Dramatic Art. See his *Some Interesting Fallacies of the Modern Stage* (1892).

25. Rembrandt Harmensz van Rijn (1606–69), Dutch painter; Anthony van Dyck (1599–1641), Flemish painter.

26. Alfred de Musset, *Rolla*: 'Je suis venu trop tard dans un siècle trop vieux.'

27. 'Who would fardels bear?' (*Hamlet*, III. i).

28. For a comparable attack on fashion see Wagner, 'Art-Work of the Future', 82–8.

29. A city mentioned in the Old Testament: 'Jehoshaphat made ships of Tarshish to go to Ophir for gold' (1 Kings 22: 48).

30. The gardens of the voluptuous sorceress in *Gerusalemme Liberata* (1574) by Torquato Tasso (1544–95), Italian poet.

31. Richard Wagner, *Lohengrin* (1847).

32. Henrik Ibsen, *Ghosts* (1881).

33. Yggdrasil, the great tree of Scandinavian mythology: its branches extend through, and its roots support, the universe.

34. Alexander Pope, *The Rape of the Lock*, Canto IV, line 124.

35. From Act I of Henrik Ibsen, *Pillars of Society* (1877).

IBSEN'S NEW DRAMA

Fortnightly Review NS, 67 (London, 1 Apr. 1900), 575–90. Joyce had proposed to the *Fortnightly*'s editor, W. L. Courtney, a general essay on Ibsen's work. Courtney's reply, that he would consider a review of Ibsen's new play, *When We Dead Awaken* (1899), arrived on the day that Joyce delivered his paper, 'Drama and Life'. Joyce would later learn that Ibsen had read the article and judged it 'very benevolent'. Joyce wrote to Ibsen in March 1901, described this article as 'immature and hasty' and indicated that he had defended Ibsen 'in debating societies' at the University. 'But we always keep the dearest things to ourselves,' Joyce continued. 'I did not tell them what bound me closest to you . . . how your wilful resolution to wrest the secret from life gave me heart and how in your absolute indifference to public canons of art, friends and shibboleths you walked in the light of your inward heroism. And this is what I write to you of now' (*Letters* i. 51–2). For the circumstances of Joyce's publishing this essay see *JJ* 73–4.

1. George Bernard Shaw, *Quintessence of Ibsenism* (1891, 2nd edn., 1913), 89, had cited this phrase under the heading 'Descriptions of Ibsen's Admirers'. The original phrase, 'Educated and muck-ferreting dogs', had appeared anonymously in a journal called *Truth* and was reprinted with a note of protest in the *Pall Mall Gazette*.

2. Joyce does not include Ibsen's dramas of the 1850s, the satirical *Love's Comedy* (1862), the verse dramas, *Brand* (1866) and *Peer Gynt* (1867), nor *Emperor and Galilean* (1873).

3. A play with close narrative parallels with *Portrait*.
4. The German version of Lohengrin (knight of the swan), who is guided by the swan to discover his wife, is based on two motifs: that of the metamorphosis of humans into swans and that of the wife whose question brings disaster
5. '*fjaell*': 'mountain'.
6. *The Master Builder* (1892).
7. Yégof and Herne of the myth of the Wild Huntsman.
8. Thomas Hardy (1840–1928), English poet and novelist; Ivan Sergeievich Turgenev (1818–83), Russian writer; George Meredith (1828–1909), English novelist and poet.
9. In *The Wild Duck* (1884).
10. Compare Matthew Arnold, 'To a Friend' on Sophocles who 'saw life steadily, and saw it whole', *Works*, i. 4.
11. In *A Doll's House* (1879).
12. In, respectively, *A Doll's House* and *Hedda Gabler* (1890).
13. In *Hedda Gabler*.
14. That is, *Ghosts* (1881) and *An Enemy of the People* (1882).
15. See 'Drama and Life' p. 26.
16. In *The Wild Duck*.

THE DAY OF THE RABBLEMENT·

Published 1901. A copy marked up for some of the many typographical errors and subsequently acknowledged by Joyce's signature in 1930 is in the Slocum Collection at Yale, *JJA* 2.76–9. I have allowed uncorrected errors to stand. Written 15 October 1901 and, according to Stanislaus Joyce, 'written rapidly in one morning', this essay was submitted by Joyce to Hugh Kennedy, editor of the new literary magazine of the University, *St Stephen's*. The essay was refused by the magazine on the advice of a Fr. Henry Browne, who objected to its mentioning Gabriele D'Annunzio's *Il Fuoco* (1900), a novel about the city of Venice, which Joyce, according to Stanislaus, 'considered the highest achievement of the novel to date' but which had been placed on the Vatican Index of Prohibited Books. *St Stephen's* also refused at this time an essay by a friend of Joyce, Francis Skeffington, later Sheehy-Skeffington (1878–1916), 'A Forgotten Aspect of the University Question', which advocates equal status for women as students of the University. Joyce and Skeffington, therefore, had the essays printed at their own expense. Eighty-five copies were printed for £2. 5s. 0d. on 21 October 1901. 'In the end,' commented Stanislaus, 'Jim's article . . . got more publicity than if it had not been censored . . . for he and I distributed it to the newspapers and people of Dublin that my brother wished to see it. A mention of it appeared in the *United Irishman*, and I remember handing it in at Ely Place to George Moore's pretty servant.' See *My Brother's Keeper*, 151–3. Skeffington and Joyce prefaced their essays with the following note: 'These two Essays were commissioned by the Editor of *St Stephen's* for that paper, but were subsequently refused insertion by the Censor. The writers are now publishing them in their original form, and each writer is responsible only for what appears under his own name. F.J.C.S. J.A.J.' The subsequent issue of *St Stephen's* (Dec. 1901) replied to Joyce's essay. For the circumstances of Joyce's publishing this essay see *JJ* 88-9.

1. Giordano Bruno (*c.*1548–1600), Italian philosopher, born near Nola. According to Stanislaus, Joyce 'intended that the readers of his article should have at first a false impression that he was quoting some little-known Irish writer—the definite article before some old family names being a courtesy title in Ireland—so that when they discovered their error, the name of Giordano Bruno might perhaps awaken some interest in his life and work' (*My Brother's Keeper*, 153). For the quotation from Bruno see I. Frith, *Life of Giordano Bruno, the Nolan* (1887), 165: 'No man truly loves goodness and truth who is not incensed with the multitude.'

2. The Irish Literary Theatre was founded at the end of 1898 by W. B. Yeats (1865–1939), Augusta, Lady Gregory (1852–1932), and Edward Martyn (1859–1924). Yeats's intention had been to produce the work of European as well as Irish dramatists. The theatre encountered some resistance from the Irish-Ireland movement led by D. P. Moran (1872–1936) and from the Catholic Church. Joyce had supported the ILT's first play, Yeats's *The Countess Cathleen* (1892), when it was premièred amid hisses and booes on 8 May 1899. Cardinal Michael Logue (1840–1924) had accused it of heresy and Edward Martyn, a devout Catholic, had responded by almost withdrawing his financial support from the ILT. Skeffington and other students composed a letter of protest against this play on the grounds that it 'offers as a type of our people a loathsome brood of apostates'. Joyce refused to sign it. The ILT's second play, Edward Martyn's *The Heather Field*, was liked so well by Joyce that he would produce it in 1919 in Zurich with the English Players and would then write of Martyn that 'as a dramatist he follows the school of Ibsen and therefore occupies a unique position in Ireland, as the dramatists writing for the National Theatre have chiefly devoted their energies to peasant drama.' (See 'Programme Notes for the English Players', p. 210.) As late as February 1900 Joyce had enjoyed at the ILT *The Bending of the Bough*, a play co-written by Edward Martyn and George Moore (1852–1933), the Irish novelist and dramatist who had returned from England in 1901 as a 'convert', in Joyce's phrase, to the literary revival and as a director of the ILT. However, the decision by the ILT in October 1901 to produce *Casadh an tSúgáin* (*The Twisting of the Rope*) by the Gaelic scholar Douglas Hyde (1860–1949) and *Diarmuid and Gráinne* by Moore and Yeats, indicated to Joyce that the ILT had betrayed itself and become narrowly nationalist in its policies.

3. *Bealtaine* was the 'official organ' of the ILT. Both Ibsen's *Ghosts* and Tolstoy's *The Power of Darkness* (1888) had been banned by the Lord Chamberlain of England, but his censorship did not apply to theatres in Ireland. See 'The Battle between Bernard Shaw and the Censor', p. 152, where Joyce celebrates the decision of the Abbey Theatre to perform a play banned on the English stage.

4. Gerhart Hauptmann (1862–1946), German dramatist, novelist and poet. It is probable that Joyce, who during the summer of 1901 had translated Hauptmann's *Vor Sonnenaufgang* (1889), under the title *Before Sunrise*, and *Michael Kramer* (1900), intended to submit these to the ILT. However, he waited three years and submitted them to W. B. Yeats for the Abbey Theatre in 1904. Yeats, in a letter of 2 October 1904, rejected both translations with the explanation, 'We must get the ear of our public with Irish work.' See also 'A Painful Case', *D* 82.

5. That is, Hermann Sudermann (1857–1928), German novelist and playwright; Bjørnstjerne Bjørnson (1832–1910), Norwegian novelist, playwright, poet, and journalist; Giovanni Giacosa (1847–1906), Italian dramatist and librettist, whom Joyce would later angrily describe as 'a paunchy vulgarian whose highest ideal in life is a bellyfull of *pasta asciutta*' (*My Brother's Keeper*, 252).

6. That is, 'the triumphant beast' from Giordano Bruno, *Spaccio della Bestia Trionfante* (1583); José Echegaray (1832–1916), Spanish mathematician, statesman, and dramatist; Maurice Maeterlinck, *Pelléas et Mélisande* (1892).

7. *Esther Waters* (1894) is generally considered to be one of Moore's most distinguished works whereas *Vain Fortune* (1891) is not.

8. Jens Peter Jacobsen (1847–1885), Danish novelist.

9. That is, George Moore, *Celibates* (1895).

10. George Moore's island is in Lough Cara, Co. Mayo, near the family house, Moore Hall. Joyce, with his phrase 'George Moore and his island', is punning on a title of one of Moore's books, *Parnell and his Island* (1887).

11. Joyce places himself in the line of succession from Ibsen and Hauptmann. He is quoting from the first act of Ibsen's *The Master Builder*: 'I tell you the younger generation will one day come and thunder at my door.' See also Epiphany 17, *JJA* 7.

JAMES CLARENCE MANGAN (1902)

St Stephen's, 1/6 (May 1902), 116–18. This essay was first read by Joyce to the Literary and Historical Society of University College Dublin on 15 February 1902. In chapter 19 of *Stephen Hero*, Joyce gives Stephen a version of this essay, omitting any mention of Mangan, under the title 'Drama and Life': 'a careful exposition of a carefully meditated theory of esthetic. When he had finished he found it necessary to change the title from "Drama and Life" to "Art and Life" . . .' (*SH* 85). According to Stanislaus, the essay on Mangan 'bore witness to a determined struggle to impose an elegance of thought on the hopeless distortion of the life that surrounded him' (*My Brother's Keeper*, 168), a comment which may refer, among other things, to their brother George's dying of peritonitis at that time. For the circumstances of Joyce's presentation of this paper see *JJ* 93–6.

James 'Clarence' Mangan (1803–49), Irish poet, a contributor to *The Comet*, an anti-tithes newspaper of the 1830s, to the *Dublin University Magazine*, the journal of Tory unionism, and to the Young Ireland journals, *The Nation*, which was co-founded in 1842 by Charles Gavan Duffy (1816–1903), John Blake Dillon (1816–66) and Thomas Davis (1814–45), and the *United Irishman*, which was founded in 1847 by John Mitchel (1815–75).

1. This quotation remains untraced.

2. According to Stanislaus, a deliberately enigmatic reference to William Blake (1757–1827) (*My Brother's Keeper*, 171).

3. See *SH* 84.

4. The question recurs in Act 1 of Richard Wagner, *Parsifal*.

5. According to Stanislaus, a deliberately enigmatic reference to Robert Browning (1812–89) (*My Brother's Keeper*, 171).

6. Joyce would seem to have in mind various perpetrators of the inconsistent myth of Mangan as *poète maudit*: C. P. Meehan represents Mangan's weakness to be for alcohol, 'the poppy of the West', in his edition of *The Poets and Poetry of Munster: A Selection of Irish Songs by the Poets of the Last Century*, trans. James Clarence Mangan, 3rd [*sic*] edn. (Dublin: James Duffy, n.d. [1884]), p. x. D. J. O'Donoghue, *The Life and Writings of James Clarence Mangan* (Dublin: M. H. Gill, 1897), represents it as opium; Charles Gavan Duffy, *Young Ireland: A Fragment of Irish History, 1840–1850* (London: Cassell, Petter, Calpin, 1880), asserts that Mangan 'cared nothing for political projects'; John Mitchel, however, represents Mangan as a nationalist rebel, 'a rebel with his whole heart and soul against the whole British spirit of the age' and also as one who 'sought at times to escape from consciousness by taking for bread, opium, and for water, brandy' (biographical introduction to John Mitchel (ed.), *Poems by James Clarence Mangan*, New York: Haverty (1859), 8, 12–13).

7. Both Mitchel and O'Donoghue classify Mangan's problematic translations as 'Apocrypha' and 'Perversions'.

8. Novalis, pseudonym of Friedrich Leopold, Freiherr von Hardenberg (1772–1801), German philosopher and poet, *Fragmente*, Vermischten Inhalts, p. 135.

9. Joyce is quoting here from Mangan's 'Fragment of an Unpublished Autobiography', *Irish Monthly*, 10 (1882), 678. This autobiographical fragment was also available to Joyce in Meehan ([1884]), pp. xxi–lvi. See also David Lloyd, *Nationalism and Irish Literature: James Clarence Mangan and the Emergence of Irish Cultural Nationalism* (Berkeley and Los Angeles: University of California Press, 1987), 162, 167 ff., 178. Joyce's misapprehension that Mangan's sentences are about one's 'associates' and not, as they were in fact for Mangan, about 'serpents and scorpions' makes it clear that Joyce here identifies both with Mangan's paranoia and with his idea of the father. Compare Shem, 'Mynfadher was a boer constructor' (*FW* 180. 35).

10. Meehan, p. xli.

11. 'The artist, he imagined, standing in the position of mediator between the world of his experience and the world of his dreams' (*SH* 82). Such a

principle opposes that of W. B. Yeats, 'Poetry is the utterance of desires that can be satisfied only in dreams.' See *My Brother's Keeper*, 169.

12. See Mangan on the strategy of dandyism in his 'An Extraordinary Adventure in the Shades', *Comet* (27 Jan. 1833), 319: 'You shall tramp the earth in vain for a more pitiable object than a man with genius, with nothing else to back it with. He was born to amalgamate with the mud we walk upon, and will, whenever he appears in public, be trodden over like that. Transfuse into this man a due portion of mannerism; the metamorphosis is marvellous. Erect he stands and blows his trumpet, the sounds whereof echo into the uttermost confines of our magnificent world . . . Mannerism! destitute of which we are, so to speak, walking humbugs . . .' It was Charles Gavan Duffy who remembered Mangan's hair 'as fine and silky as a woman's', according to D. J. O'Donoghue, in *Poems of James Clarence Mangan*, with biographical introduction by John Mitchel (Dublin: O'Donoghue, M. H. Gill, 1903), p. xxv.

13. Mangan's poem 'On the Death of a Beloved Friend' (1833) is written on the death of his pupil, Catherine Hayes.

14. D. J. O'Donoghue (1897) adds this supposition to Mangan's celebrated *grande passion*, for which the *locus classicus* is Mitchel: 'It is a vacuum and obscure gulf which no eyes fathomed or measured; into which he entered a bright haired youth and emerged a withered and stricken man . . . he had loved, and was deceived' (Mitchel (1859), 11).

15. Meehan, pp. xv–xvi.

16. Frédérique Hauffe, an early nineteenth-century victim of psychosomatic hallucination. See Mangan's poem, 'To the Spirit-Seeress of Prevorst, as She Lay on Her Death-Bed'.

17. Antoine Watteau (1736–1819), French painter.

18. This is the final sentence of 'A Prince of Court Poets' in Walter Pater, *Imaginary Portraits* (1887).

19. Joyce exaggerates Mangan's obscurity. The editions to which he refers are John Mitchel's (see note 6 above); Louise Imogen Guiney (ed.), *James Clarence Mangan, His Selected Poems* (Boston: Lamson, Wolffe, 1897); C. P. Meehan (ed.), *Essays in Prose and Verse* (Dublin: James Duffy, 1884).

20. Thomas Moore (1779–1852), Irish poet; Edward Walsh (1805–90), Irish poet and folklorist.

21. Percy Bysshe Shelley, *A Defence of Poetry* (composed 1821, published 1840). See *Portrait* 179 and *U* 9. 381–2.

22. Mangan, 'The Last Words of Al-Hassan', in Mitchel (1859), 322.

23. The idealized beloveds of Michelangelo, Petrarch, and Dante.

24. Compare Walter Pater's description of this painting in his essay 'Leonardo da Vinci' (1869).

25. The *Gulistan* (1258), or *Rosegarden*, of the Persian poet S'adi (*c*.1184–*c*.1291).

26. Guiney, 263.

27. Walt Whitman (1819–92), American poet.

28. See John Mitchel, 'Mangan's pathos was all genuine, his laughter hollow

and painful. In several poems he breaks out into a sort of humour, not hearty and merry fun, but rather grotesque, bitter, fescennine buffoonery; which leaves an unpleasant impression, as if he were grimly sneering at himself and at all the world' (Mitchel (1859), 23).

29. Conrad Wetzel, 'Good Night', in Mitchel (1859), 333–4.

30. William Blake, *The Marriage of Heaven and Hell* (1793), plate 9, line 56.

31. John Dowland (1563–1626), English composer and poet. Joyce's 'favourite poem in Dowland's *Songs* was "Weep you no more, sad fountains"' (*My Brother's Keeper*, 166).

32. Edgar Allan Poe (1809–49), American author.

33. Emmanuel Swedenborg (1688–1772), Swedish philosopher; the phrase 'vastation of soul' is used in an essay on Swedenborg by Ralph Waldo Emerson, *Representative Men* (London: Bohn, 1847), 328.

34. Naomi, Hebrew for 'pleasant'; Mara, Hebrew for 'bitterness'. After famine and the death of her menfolk Naomi returned to Bethlehem: 'and the women said, "Can this be Naomi?" But she said to them, "Do not call me Naomi, call me Mara"' (Ruth 1: 19–20).

35. Giacomo, Count Leopardi (1798–1837), Italian poet and philosopher.

36. John Keats, 'for many a time | I have been half in love with easeful Death', 'Ode to a Nightingale' (1819).

37. In Islam, the angel of death, from which Mangan's poem 'The Angel of Death' takes its title.

38. Dante, *Inferno*, v.

39. 'Vision or Imagination is a Representation of what Eternally Exists, Really & Unchangeably. Fable or Allegory is Form'd by the daughters of Memory' (William Blake, *A Vision of the Last Judgment* (1810), plate 68).

40. 'Every time less than a pulsation of the artery | Is equal in its period & value to six thousand years; | For in this period the poet's work is done' (William Blake, *Milton* (1809), plate 28, lines 62–4; *U* 9. 86–8).

41. 'his history and fate were indeed a type and shadow of the land he loved so well' (Mitchel (1859), 15).

42. See the description of Davin (*Portrait* 152), whom the students thought of 'as a young fenian. His nurse had taught him Irish and shaped his rude imagination by the broken lights of Irish myth. He stood towards this myth upon which no individual mind had ever drawn out a line of beauty and to its unwieldy tales that divided themselves as they moved down the cycles in the same attitude as towards the Roman catholic religion, the attitude of a dull witted loyal serf. Whatsoever of thought or feeling came to him from England or by way of English culture his mind stood armed against . . .' Compare Mitchel (1859): 'throughout his whole literary life of twenty years he [Mangan] never deigned to attorn to English criticism, never published a line in any English periodical, or through any English bookseller.'

43. See 'An Irish Poet' p. 62.

44. Novalis, *Fragmente*, Fortsetzung, p. 452.

45. Compare Mitchel on Mangan as the epitome of the Irish 'national

character': 'More than in any other mood of song he seemed to revel in the expression of passionate sorrow'; 'This character of extravagant but impotent passion greatly prevails throughout the Irish ballads at all times, expressing not only that misery produced by ages of torture and humiliation, but the excessively impressible temperament of the Gael, ever ready to sink into blackest despondency and blind rage, or to rise into rapturous triumph' (Mitchel (1859), 20, 22–3). See also Guiney: 'It may be unjust to lend him the epitaph of defeat, for he never strove at all' (Guiney, 5).

46. See *SH* 85.

47. 'This beautiful, marvellous life of earth, this inscrutable life of earth' (Ibsen, *When We Dead Awaken*, Act III).

48. See *SH* 85 and *Portrait* 174, where the definition (a translation of the Latin phrase *splendor veri*) is attributed to Plato, as it is by Flaubert in a letter to Mlle Leroyer de Chantepie, 18 March 1857.

49. Joyce is in this paragraph translating from the final speech of the father in Hauptmann's *Michael Kramer*. See also 'Death is the highest form of life. Ba!' (*U* 15. 2099).

50. Joyce is citing a concept borrowed by Yeats from the *anima mundi* of the Cambridge Platonist, Henry More (1614–87), and from the Theosophists.

51. 'Thus the spirit of man makes a continual affirmation' (*SH* 85). 'Bloom dissented tacitly from Stephen's views on the eternal affirmation of man in literature' (*U* 17. 29–30).

AN IRISH POET

Daily Express (Dublin, 11 Dec. 1902). Written 4 December 1902. The editor of the Dublin *Daily Express*, E. V. Longworth, had agreed (on Lady Gregory's recommendation) to send books for review to Joyce in Paris. The *Daily Express* claimed to seek to reconcile 'the rights and impulses of Irish nationality with the demands and obligations of imperial dominions'. See Gabriel's exchange with Miss Ivors about his reviewing for the *Daily Express* in 'The Dead', *D* 187–8.

Joyce is here reviewing *Poems and Ballads* (n.d. [1902]) by William Rooney (1873–1901), with an introduction by Arthur Griffith (1871–1922) and a biographical sketch by Patrick Bradley. Rooney had been a journalist and Irish language teacher. He had worked with Arthur Griffith in the founding of the *United Irishman*. That newspaper ('headquarters' in Joyce's phrase) had published this posthumous collection of Rooney's verse and, on 20 December 1902, responded to Joyce by quoting his unsympathetic review as part of an advertisement for the book and inserting one word in order to make explicit an alternative value: 'And yet he might have written well if he had not suffered from one of those big words [Patriotism] which make us so unhappy.' See *U* 2.264: 'I fear those big words, Stephen said, which make us so unhappy.'

1. Thomas Osborne Davis (1814–45), poet, Young Irelander, journalist, and co-founder of *The Nation*.

2. Thomas D'Arcy MacGee (1825–68), poet, Young Irelander, journalist, and contributor to *The Nation*, who entered Canadian politics in 1857, became a minister in the government of the federal union in 1867 when Canada acquired Dominion Home Rule status, denounced raids on Canada by the Fenians and was assassinated by them in Ottawa on 7 April 1868.

3. Denis Florence McCarthy (1817–82), poet and scholar, contributor to *The Nation* and to the *Dublin University Magazine*; Sir Samuel Ferguson (1810–86), poet and scholar, contributor to the *Dublin University Magazine* and, on one occasion, to *The Nation*; Timothy Daniel Sullivan (1827–1914), poet, Young Irelander, contributor to, and editor of, *The Nation*, one of the first Irish Members of Parliament to repudiate Parnell, leader of the 'Bantry gang' (see p. 346, n. 3), author of the ballad 'God Save Ireland'; Thomas Rolleston (1857–1920), scholar, poet, and leader-writer on the Dublin *Daily Express*.

4. 'Roilig na Ríogh' is by Rooney and can be found in *Poems and Ballads*, 16; 'The Dead at Clonmacnoise' is by Rolleston and can be found in his *Sea Spray: Verses and Translations* (1909), 47.

5. For Stanislaus's commentary on this apparent confusion see *My Brother's Keeper*, 203–4.

6. 'Aquinas says: *ad pulchritudinem tria requiruntur, integritas, consonantia, claritas.* I translate it so: *Three things are needed for beauty, wholeness, harmony and radiance*' (*Portrait* 178; *SH* 101).

7. Douglas Hyde (1860–1949), scholar and politician, founder-president of the Gaelic League (1893–1915). His works include *Love Songs of Connacht* (1894).

GEORGE MEREDITH

Daily Express (Dublin, 11 Dec. 1902). Written 4 December 1902. Joyce is here reviewing *George Meredith: An Essay towards Appreciation* (1902) by Walter Jerrold (1865–1929). This is one of the series English Writers of Today and not, as Joyce states below, 'the English men of letters series'. For Joyce's attitudes to Meredith see *My Brother's Keeper*, 95, 204–5.

1. Arthur Wing Pinero (1855–1934), British playwright.

2. 'There was a spice of malice in the phrase,' according to Stanislaus. 'It was exactly what my brother was striving heroically not to be' (*My Brother's Keeper*, 204–5). Also W. B. Yeats recalled Joyce's accusation at their first meeting: 'You do not talk like a poet, you talk like a man of letters . . .' *JJ* 101 n.).

3. Meredith, *Modern Love, and Poems of the English Roadside, with Poems and Ballads* (1862); Dante Alighieri, *Vita Nuova* (*c*.1295). Joyce satirizes this levelling in 'Catilina'. 'For every true-born mysticist | A Dante is, unprejudiced' ('The Holy Office' (1904) lines 15–16).

4. George Meredith, 'The Appeasement of Demeter'.

5. *King Lear*, I. ii.

TODAY AND TOMORROW IN IRELAND

Daily Express (Dublin, 29 Jan. 1903). Joyce is here reviewing *Today and Tomorrow in Ireland: Essays on Irish Subjects* (1903) by Stephen Gwynn (1864–1950), scholar, poet, and a Nationalist MP from 1906 to 1918.

1. See *SH* 66, where it is stated that Arthur Griffith, who is 'the editor of the weekly journal of the irreconcilable party [Sinn Féin] reported any signs of Philocelticism which he had observed in the Paris newspapers.' Canada had expressed its imperial preference in its support for Britain during the Boer War (1899–1902), a war which turned much moderate Irish opinion towards anti-imperialism. The issue of the Boer War recurs: 'Colonial Verses', p. 70, and 'Ireland: Island of Saints and Sages', p. 117.

2. 'By the way I wrote nothing in my review . . . about the printing and the binding. My little editor must have added that' (*Letters*, ii. 27, to Stanislaus, 8 Feb. 1903). The 'Dublin firm' was Hodges, Figgis & Company.

A SUAVE PHILOSOPHY

Daily Express (Dublin, 6 Feb. 1903). Joyce is here reviewing *The Soul of a People* (1898, 4th edn. 1902) by Harold Fielding-Hall (1859–1917).

1. Joyce substitutes 'flower' twice for 'blossom' and 'has' for 'hath'

AN EFFORT AT PRECISION IN THINKING

Daily Express (Dublin, 6 Feb. 1903). Joyce is here reviewing *Colloquies of Common People* (1902) by James Anstie.

COLONIAL VERSES

Daily Express (Dublin, 6 Feb. 1903). Joyce is here reviewing *Songs of an English Esau* (1902) by Sir Clive Phillipps Wolley (1854–1918).

1. Phillipps Wolley has altered the biblical story (Genesis 25: 23–34). Esau is the son of Isaac and Rebecca and elder twin brother of Jacob. Yahweh had spoken to the pregnant Rebecca: 'There are two nations in your womb, your issue will be two rival peoples. One nation shall have the mastery of the other, and the elder shall serve the younger.' Jacob is the quiet one, Esau the hunter. When Esau returns exhausted and hungry Jacob secures his elder brother's birthright in exchange for pottage, that is for a bowl of soup. Esau and Jacob continue their conflict in *FW*.

CATILINA

The Speaker (London: NS, 7, 21 Mar. 1903), 615. W. B. Yeats had approached the editor of *The Speaker* on Joyce's behalf (*Letters*, ii. 19). See also Joyce's letter to Stanislaus, 8 February 1903: 'I am feeling very intellectual these times and up to my eyes in Aristotle's psychology [that is *De Anima*]. If the editor of the "Speaker" puts in my review of "Catilina" you will see some of the fruits thereof' (*Letters*, ii. 28).

Joyce is here reviewing *Catilina: drame en 3 actes et en vers* by Henrik Ibsen, translated into French by de Coleville and de Zepelin (Paris: [1903]). Ibsen's *Catilina* first appeared in 1850.

1. Lucius Sergius Catilina (*c.*108–62 BC), son of an impoverished patrician family of Rome. His conspiracy against the city is condemned in speeches by Marcus Tullius Cicero (106–43 BC) and in the history by Gaius Sallustius Crispus (86–34 BC).
2. See 'Ibsen's New Drama', p. 30.
3. This quotation remains untraced.
4. A slip for Furia in Ibsen's play.
5. 'CURIUS. Did you love them both at once? I do not understand it at all. CATILINA. Indeed it is strange and I do not understand it myself.'
6. Honoré de Balzac (1799–1850), French novelist.
7. Boötes is a constellation of the northern hemisphere. The quotation is from Thomas Carlyle, *Sartor Resartus* (1836), Book 1, chap. 3.

THE SOUL OF IRELAND

Daily Express (Dublin, 26 Mar. 1903). This review alone appears over Joyce's initials: Longworth 'the editor wishing by this signature to disclaim any personal responsibility for the article' (*My Brother's Keeper*, 218). Longworth delayed printing the review and urged Joyce in future to write more favourably. In 'The Dead' it is Gabriel Conroy's initials which betray to Miss Ivors that he is a reviewer with the *Daily Express* (*D* 147).

Joyce is here reviewing *Poets and Dreamers: Studies and Translations from the Irish* (1903) by Lady Gregory. Longworth may have sent this book to Joyce because it was Lady Gregory who had recommended him. Joyce wrote to his mother on 20 March 1903: 'I sent in my review of Lady Gregory's book a week ago. I do not know if Longworth put it in as I sent it: the review was very severe. I shall write to Lady Gregory one of these days' (*Letters*, ii. 37–8). See also Mulligan's exclamations to Stephen: 'Longworth is awfully sick . . . after what you wrote about that old hake Gregory. O you inquisitional drunken jew jesuit! She gets you a job on the paper and then you go and slate her drivel to Jaysus. Couldn't you do the Yeats touch?' (*U* 9. 1158–60).

1. Aristotle, *Metaphysics*, I. ii. 9.
2. Contrast Joyce's later estimate of peasant intelligence and dignity in 'The Mirage of the Fisherman of Aran', p. 204.
3. Ben Jonson (1572–1637), *Epicoene, or the Silent Woman* (1609), II. ii.
4. W. B. Yeats, *The Celtic Twilight* (1893).
5. Antoine O Reachtabhra, or Raftery (*c.*1784–1835), Irish poet and musician. In the same year as this article Douglas Hyde edited Raftery's verse, *Abhráin atá Leagtha ar an Reachtúire* (1903).
6. James Abbott McNeill Whistler (1834–1903), American painter whose *Nocturnes* (1877) derive their title from a term in music ('night piece');

Stéphane Mallarmé (1842–98), French poet; 'Recapitulation' is by
Catulle Mendès (1841–1909), French poet. The link between these in
Joyce's mind appears to be an assumption that the art of each aspires
to the condition of music.

7. See notes to 'The Day of the Rabblement', pp. 295–7.

8. Joyce is contrasting different attitudes (both dramatized in 'The Dead') of
two pieces from Walt Whitman, the first chosen as an epigraph by Lady
Gregory, the second suggested by Joyce himself. Both pieces are from
Leaves of Grass (1855). The first is from 'A Song for Occupations', 6:

> Will you seek afar off? you surely come back at last,
> In things best known to you finding the best, or as good as the best,
> In folks nearest to you finding the sweetest, strongest, lovingest,
> Happiness, knowledge, not in another place but this place, not for
>   another hour but this hour

and the second is from 'Song of Myself', 18:

> With music strong I come, with my cornets and my drums,
> I play not marches for accepted victors only, I play marches for
>   conquer'd and slain persons.
>
> Have you heard that it was good to gain the day?
> I also say it is good to fall, battles are lost in the same spirit in
>   which they are won.
>
> I beat and pound for the dead,
> I blow through my embouchures my loudest and gayest for them.
>
> Vivas to those who have fail'd!

THE MOTOR DERBY

Irish Times (Dublin, 7 Apr. 1903). Joyce had hoped to become the French
correspondent of this newspaper, but without success. He sent two pieces
from Paris to the *Irish Times*, but the second piece, about a Paris carnival, was
not accepted.

The motor derby, the Gordon Bennett race, took its name from James
Gordon Bennett, US newspaper proprietor, who gave the trophy that bore his
name for a series of international motor races. The fourth race in the series
would take place in Ireland on 2 July 1903. It forms the basis of the story
'After the Race', in *Dubliners*.

1. A rule of the Gordon Bennett race was that a country might enter a team
of three cars every part of which had to be made in that country.

2. The Paris–Madrid race which, after many fatalities, was stopped at
Bordeaux.

3. The 370 mile Irish course was completed in 6 hours, 36 minutes, 9 sec-
onds. The winner, Camille Jenatzy, a Belgian, drove a Mercedes. The
French came second and third.

ARISTOTLE ON EDUCATION

Daily Express (Dublin, 3 Sept. 1903). Joyce is here reviewing *Aristotle on Education, being Extracts from the Ethics and Politics* (1903), trans. and ed. John Burnet (1863–1928), Scottish classical scholar.

1. Burnet twice refers to Aristotle as 'first and foremost a biologist' (*Aristotle on Education*, 2, 129).
2. A reference to Émile Combes (1835–1921), French politician who initiated a definite separation of church and state. See *Aristotle on Education*, 106: 'The sort of question that Aristotle raises here is really the same as that which divides France at the present moment. The objection of the French government to the teaching of the religious orders is just that it does not produce a "Republican spirit" in the pupils, that it is not, in Aristotle's phrase, an education in conformity with the constitution.'
3. '*Maestro di color che sanno*' translates as 'master of those who know' (Dante, *Inferno*, iv. 131). See also *U* 3. 6–7.

[A NE'ER DO WEEL]

Daily Express (Dublin, 3 Sept. 1903). The review has no title; it appears as *A Ne'er Do Well* in *CW* III. Joyce is here reviewing *A Ne'er Do Weel* (Pseudonym Library, 1903) by Valentine Caryl, pseudonym for Valentina Hawtrey.

1. 'In dismissing this novel cursorily, my brother condemns pseudonyms; however, when a year later his own first stories were published [in the *Irish Homestead*], he yielded to the suggestion (not mine) and used a pseudonym, "Stephen Daedalus", but then bitterly regretted the self-concealment' (Stanislaus Joyce in *The Early Joyce: The Book Reviews, 1902–1903*, ed. Stanislaus Joyce and Ellsworth Mason, Colorado Springs (1955), 25).

NEW FICTION

Daily Express (Dublin, 17 Sept. 1903). Joyce is here reviewing *The Adventures of Prince Aga Mirza* (1903) by James Aquila Kempster and *The Mettle of the Pasture* (1903) by James Lane Allen (1849–1925), American novelist and essayist.

1. 'Sir John Mandeville', supposed author of the *Travels* (English version *c*.1375), a fantastic guide for pilgrims to the Holy Land.
2. James Lane Allen, *The Increasing Purpose* (1900).
3. *Henry V*, III. i.
4. '*longo intervallo*': 'at a great distance'.
5. A character in *The Mettle of the Pasture*.
6. Joyce is remembering *The Mettle of the Pasture*, 125.

A PEEP INTO HISTORY

Daily Express (Dublin, 17 Sept. 1903). Joyce is here reviewing *The Popish Plot: A Study in the Reign of Charles II* (1903) by John Pollock.

1. A supposed plot to murder Charles II of England and to re-establish Catholicism. The evidence of Titus Oates (1649–1705) secured the execution of many innocent Roman Catholics during 1678–1680.
2. Sir Edmund Berry Godfrey (1621–78), English magistrate and politician, before whom, in September 1678, Titus Oates and others had sworn the truth of their information and whose murder the following October appeared to confirm the evidence of a 'plot'.
3. Joyce is paraphrasing *The Popish Plot*, pp. vii, 3, 83. One of Thomas De Quincey's (1785–1859) most famous essays is titled 'On Murder Considered as One of the Fine Arts'; Lord Acton (1834–1902) discussed the murder in 'The Rise of the Whigs' in *Lectures on Modern History* (London, 1930), 213–14.
4. Robert Green, Henry Berry, and Laurence Hill were hanged for the murder in 1679 on the evidence both of Miles Prance, who subsequently pleaded guilty to perjury, and of William Bedloe.
5. Bedloe was merely following Oates's footsteps.
6. A misquotation from *The Popish Plot*, 80.
7. John Mabillon (1632–1707), French Benedictine monk and palaeographer: '*Donner pour certain ce qui est certain, pour faux ce qui est faux, pour douteux ce qui est douteux*': 'To claim as certain that which is certain, as false that which is false, as doubtful that which is doubtful.'
8. Sir Roger L'Estrange (1616–1704), Royalist pamphleteer attacked the Whigs and Titus Oates in his periodical *The Observer* (1681–7).

A FRENCH RELIGIOUS NOVEL

Daily Express (Dublin, 1 Oct. 1903). Joyce is here reviewing *The House of Sin* (1903), a translation by A. Smyth of *La Maison du péché* (1899) by Marcelle Tinayre (1872–1948), French woman of letters. The novel had been serialized in *La Revue de Paris* from May to August 1902.

1. Blaise Pascal (1623–62), French philosopher, mathematician, and defender of Jansenism.
2. *King Lear*, I. ii.
3. Joyce abbreviates a passage in *The House of Sin*, 163.
4. Joris-Karl Huysmans (1848–1907), French novelist, whose quintet of 'politico-religious' novels *À Rebours* (1884), *Là-bas* (1891), *En Route* (1895), *La Cathédrale* (1898), and *L'Oblat* (1903) were highly influential.
5. Joseph Bourget (1852–1935), *Mensonges* (1887).
6. Jansenism, founded by Cornelius Jansen (1585–1638), opponent of scholastic philosophy, emphasized predestination and 'conversion' at God's pleasure, and discovered in Pascal a defender against the Jesuits.

UNEQUAL VERSE

Daily Express (Dublin, 1 Oct. 1903). Joyce is here reviewing *Ballads and Legends* (1903), by Frederick Langbridge (1849–1922).
1. *Ballads and Legends*, 3.
2. That is, maudlin drama.

MR ARNOLD GRAVES'S NEW WORK

Daily Express (Dublin, 1 Oct. 1903). Joyce is here reviewing *Clytæmnestra: A Tragedy* (1903) by Arnold F. Graves (1844–1914), Irish playwright.
1. Robert Yelverton Tyrrell (1844–1914), Irish classical scholar at Trinity College, Dublin.
2. *Atalanta in Calydon* (1865) by Algernon Charles Swinburne (1837–1909), English poet and playwright.
3. That is, Egisthus.

A NEGLECTED POET

Daily Express (Dublin, 15 Oct. 1903). Joyce is here reviewing *George Crabbe* (1903) by Alfred Ainger (1837–1904), chaplain-in-ordinary to Queen Victoria and man of letters.
1. See *George Crabbe*, 118.
2. Edmund Burke (1729–97), Irish politician and political philosopher; Charles James Fox (1749–1806), English Whig politician; Walter Scott (1771–1832), Scottish novelist; Samuel Rogers (1763–1855), English poet; William Lisle Bowles (1762–1850), English poet; Edward Fitzgerald (1809–83), English poet and translator, editor of a selection of Crabbe's verse.
3. The Kailyard school of Scottish writing was one of parochial sentimentality. Among its main exponents was J. M. Barrie (1860–1937), author of *A Window in Thrums* (1889) and *Peter Pan* (1904); see 'Programme Notes for the English Players', p. 209.
4. Auburn is the name of *The Deserted Village* (1770) by Oliver Goldsmith (1728–74), Irish author; *The Village* (1783), *The Borough* (1810), and *The Parish Register* (1807) are by Crabbe.
5. Dutch landscape painters from Adriaen van Ostade (1610–84) to Meindert Hobbema (1638–1709).

MR MASON'S NOVELS

Daily Express (Dublin, 15 Oct. 1903). Joyce is here reviewing three novels, *The Courtship of Morrice Buckler* (1896), *The Philanderers* (1897), *Miranda of the Balcony* (1899), by Alfred Edward Woodley Mason (1865–1948).
1. 'You may readily deceive yourself by selecting such faces as bear a resemblance to your own, since it would often seem that such similarities please

us; and if you were ugly you would not select beautiful faces, but would be creating ugly faces' (Leonardo da Vinci, *Notebooks*, ed. Edward McCurdy, 1938).

2. The Elzevir family of printers, at Leyden in the seventeenth century, produced books of unsurpassed beauty, perhaps about 1,600 in all, including a series of Latin authors such as Horace.

3. Belgravia is a wealthy London suburb; George Bernard Shaw, *The Philanderer* (1893), a play on Ibsenism and the 'new woman'; the battle of Sedgemoor took place in 1685.

THE BRUNO PHILOSOPHY

Daily Express (Dublin, 30 Oct. 1903). Joyce is here reviewing *Giordano Bruno* (1903) by J. Lewis MacIntyre.

1. I. Frith, *Life of Giordano Bruno* (1887).

2. 'Ghezzi ... said Bruno was a terrible heretic. I said he was terribly burned' (*Portrait* 210).

3. The Campo dei Fiori is in Rome.

4. Giordano Bruno, *Ars Memoriae* and *De compendiosa architectura et complemento artis Lullii*, from his earlier, Paris period, along with *Spaccio della Bestia Trionfante*, appear to be the works to which Joyce refers. These can only be 'middle-aged' in the sense of 'medieval' as opposed to 'modern'. Raymond Lully (*c*.1235–1315), Catalan author and mystic.

5. Francis Bacon (1561–1626), English statesman and philosopher; René Descartes (1596–1650), French philosopher. For this comparative estimate of Bruno see *Giordano Bruno*, 324.

6. That is, one half of the opposition between *natura naturans* and *natura naturata*: 'nature naturing' or in process, and 'nature natured' or as it is.

7. The Scholastics are the professors of the theological and philosophical system of Christian Europe in the medieval period. The 'formidable names' in this context are the terms 'matter and form'.

8. Benedict Spinoza (1632–77), Dutch pantheist philosopher. Joyce is paraphrasing *Giordano Bruno*, 338.

9. Heraclitus (*c*.544–483 BC), Greek philosopher.

10. Samuel Taylor Coleridge (1772–1834), *The Friend* (1818), Essay xiii, explicitly derives this argument from Heraclitus and from Giordano Bruno.

11. That is, fundamental matter.

12. That is, the philosophy of Immanuel Kant (1724–1804) and of his successors.

13. This remark is found in *Giordano Bruno*, 110.

14. Miguel de Molinos (1640–97) and St John of the Cross (1542–91), Spanish mystics.

15. Ibn Roshd (1126–98), known as Averroës, philosopher of Córdova, Spain; John Scotus Erigena (*c*.815–77), Irish philosopher.

HUMANISM

Daily Express (Dublin, 12 Nov. 1903). Joyce is here reviewing *Philosophical Essays* (1903) by Ferdinand Canning Scott Schiller (1864–1937).

1. The philosophy founded by Charles S. Peirce (1839–1914) and developed by William James (1842–1910), of whom Schiller remains the leading European disciple.
2. That is, philosophies which argue 'from what comes before', or from given causes to supposed effects.
3. These quotations are from the preface to Schiller's *Philosophical Essays*.
4. '*der Geist der stets verneint*': 'the Spirit always says no' (Goethe, *Faust*, 1808, 1. i). See Joyce's explanation of Molly Bloom, '*Ich bin der [sic] Fleisch der stets bejaht*': 'I am the Flesh that always says yes' (*Letters* i. 170).
5. *Philosophical Essays*, 168.
6. Francis Herbert Bradley (1846–1924), English Hegelian philosopher, uses this phrase to dismiss the concept of the ultimate in Herbert Spencer (1820–1903), English Darwinian philosopher, and the remark is quoted from *Philosophical Essays*, 191.

SHAKESPEARE EXPLAINED

Daily Express (Dublin, 12 Nov. 1903). Joyce is here reviewing *Shakespeare Studied in Eight Plays* (1903) by Albert Stratford Canning (1832–1916).

1. *Shakespeare Studied in Eight Plays*, 6.

[BORLASE AND SON]

Daily Express (Dublin, 19 Nov. 1903). The review has no title. Joyce is here reviewing *Borlase and Son* (1903) by T. Baron Russell.

1. On 26 October, the president of the Armenian Revolutionary Society was assassinated at Peckham Rye; on 3 November, Panama declared its independence from Colombia and a revolution began; on 13 November, the USA recognized Panama's independence. For 'epitasis', or 'that part of a play where the plot thickens', see the epilogue to Act I of Ben Jonson, *The Magnetic Lady* (1632).
2. Émile Zola, *Au bonheur des dames* (1883).
3. This comment appears to be a jibe by Joyce at Longworth, the editor of the *Daily Express*; see 'Today and Tomorrow in Ireland', p. 66. At any rate this was to be Joyce's last book review and the story goes that Longworth threatened to kick Joyce downstairs if ever he came to the newspaper's offices again.

EMPIRE-BUILDING

MS Cornell, *JJA* 2.80–3. This fragment, a holograph, survives among manuscripts of which Stanislaus Joyce used the blank versos for his Dublin Journal, 'My Crucible'. It has neither title nor date, but on internal evidence can be dated to November 1903. It may have been intended by Joyce for publication in a Dublin newspaper. Jacques Lebaudy, an adventurer and self-styled emperor of the Sahara, had seized territory in order to build a colony in North Africa. Five sailors were captured by the native population and the French government sent a ship to secure their release. The sailors sued for compensation and the episode was widely reported in the French newspapers from August 1903 to January 1904.

1. Paul and Pierre Lebaudy were experimental fliers. The Palais is an abbreviated reference to the Palais de Justice.

2. The summons was reported issued on 6 November. Jacques Lebaudy's yacht was, in fact, the *Frasquita*.

3. In 1895, British Bechuanaland (properly Botswana) was annexed to the Cape Colony to become part of the Cape Province of the Union of South Africa.

4. Gabrielle Réjane, pseudonym of Gabrielle Réju (1857–1920), a French actress whose divorce had been announced in October 1903; *Les petits oiseaux*, 'the little birds': Jacques Aubert cites a paragraph in *Le Figaro* (1 Oct. 1903) which describes how a number of aviaries containing brightly feathered birds were delivered to the Savoy Hotel, London, where Lebaudy had installed himself. The phrase has, perhaps, an ironic edge here from its proverbial use which derives from Racine, *Athalie*, II. vii; '*Aux petits des oiseaux il [Dieu] donne leur pâture*': 'God feeds the little birds'.

[AESTHETICS]

1. The first two items below survive on a single sheet in Joyce's hand; MS Yale, *JJA* 7.106–7. The subsequent items from the Paris Notebook are transcripts by Herbert Gorman, *James Joyce* (1940), 98–9. See also Joyce's letter from Paris to his mother, 20 March 1903: 'My book of songs will be published in the spring of 1907. My first comedy about five years later. My "Esthetic" about five years later again. (This *must* interest you!)' (*Letters* ii. 38).

2. See *Portrait* 172–4, where also Stephen identifies 'improper' arts as the pornographic and didactic. Joyce is adapting a Thomist definition of beauty: '*Ad rationem pulchri pertinet quod in ejus aspectu seu cognitione quietetur appetitus*': 'It appertains to the nature of beauty that, when it is seen or known, desire ceases' (*Summa Theologica*, 1 2ae, 1).

3. Aristotle, *Poetics*, 1449[b].

4. See *Portrait* 171–2. Joyce, in order to coincide with a quasi-Thomist aesthetic of stasis, revises Aristotle both in defining catharsis as *arresting*, that is bringing to a condition of stasis, the spectator. Stephen claims that 'Aristotle has not defined pity and terror. I have' (*Portrait* 171). However, Aristotle describes pity and terror as follows: 'terror is a sorrow or a trouble produced by the imagining of an evil, that could arrive, bringing pain and destruction' (*Rhetoric*, 1382[a]); 'pity is a sorrow caused by a destructive and painful evil happening to an unmeriting person and that

ourselves or somebody linked to us could expect to suffer' (*Rhetoric*, 1385ᵇ). Joyce's own definitions derive more appropriately from the implications of Aristotle's insistence that 'since the pleasure the poet is to provide is that which comes from pity and fear through an imitation, clearly the effect must be embodied in the events of the plot' (*Poetics*, 1453ᵇ).

5. This diverges entirely from Aristotle's brief definition of comedy as 'an imitation of persons worse than the average' (*Poetics*, 1449ᵃ).

6. *SH* 81–2; *Portrait* 180. See Bosanquet, *History of Aesthetic*, 55: 'He [Plato] gave a *raison d'être* to the distinction of epic, lyric, and dramatic poetry, not in itself new, by analysis turning on their respective degrees of dramatic personification.' Victor Hugo, in the preface to his drama *Cromwell* (1827), had enunciated the progress of poetry from the primitive to the modern as lyrical, epic, and dramatic. See also the adaptation of this historical model to Irish literature in an anonymous article, 'Recent English Poets, No. 1: Alfred Tennyson and E. B. Browning', *The Nation* (15 Feb. 1845), 314: the author, lamenting that 'the healthy growth of an Irish literature' has been 'thwarted and impeded' by English domination, asserts that 'The different stages of social development have their distinct characters written in the development of mind. First there is the ballad, simple, direct, and unadorned; then lyric poetry, the epic, the drama, history, philosophy, each growing naturally out of the other. So are all great national literatures built; . . . so must it be here, if we are ever to have a literature of our own.'

7. *Portrait* 173.

8. Aristotle, *Physics*, 194ᵃ21–2.

9. *Portrait* 174. This statement condenses chapter 3, 'The Conception of Artistic Beauty', in *Introduction to Hegel's Philosophy of Fine Art*, trans. Bernard Bosanquet, 43–106.

10. On this method of argument see *Portrait* 180: 'That's a lovely one, said Lynch, laughing again. That has the true scholastic stink.'

11. The first item below survives as a note in Joyce's hand: MS Yale, *JJA* 7.108. The subsequent items are transcripts by Herbert Gorman, *James Joyce* (1940), 133–5. The manuscript available to Gorman has been lost. See Joyce's letter from Pola, Austria, to Stanislaus, 19 November 1904: 'I have not written much of the novel—only the end of the 11th [*sic*] chapter in Zürich. I have written about half of "Xmas Eve" and about five long pages of "Esthetic Philosophy" ' (*Letters*, ii. 71).

12. '*Bonum est in quod tendit appetitus*': 'The good is that towards which desire moves' (*Summa Theologica*, Ia 5,4). Joyce, here and in the subsequent paragraphs, is commenting on the following section in Aquinas: 'Beauty and goodness in a thing are identical fundamentally; for they are based upon the same thing, namely the form; and consequently goodness is praised as beauty. But they differ logically, for goodness properly relates to the appetite (goodness being what all things desire); and therefore it has the aspect of an end (the appetite being a kind of movement towards a

thing). On the other hand, beauty relates to the cognitive faculty; for beautiful things are those which please when seen. Hence beauty consists in due proportion; for the senses delight in things duly proportioned, as in what is after their own kind—because every sense is a sort of reason, just as is every cognitive faculty' (*Summa Theologica*, Ia 5, 4). See *Portrait* 156, 174–5; *SH* 100.

13. *Portrait* 211.
14. 'Such things are beautiful as, when seen, give pleasure'; '*Pulcra sunt quae visa placent*' (*Portrait* 156, 174; *SH* 100).
15. '*pulchra enim dicuntur ea quae visa placent*': beautiful things are those which please when seen (*Summa Theologica*, Ia 5, 4). The threefold act of apprehension outlined here derives from the three requirements for beauty defined by Aquinas: *integritas*, *consonantia*, *claritas* (*Summa Theologica*, Ia 39, 8).
16. 'consequent satisfaction', crossed out.
17. 'beautiful', crossed out.
18. 'there is nothing which does not partake in the beautiful and the good' (Dionysius the pseudo-Areopagite, *The Divine Names*, 704b).
19. *Portrait* 176.
20. *Portrait* 178–81.

IRELAND: ISLAND OF SAINTS AND SAGES

MS Yale. Translated from the Italian, 'L'Irlanda: Isola dei Santi e dei Savi', a holograph of forty-six pages, numbered from 1 to 44 with successive insertions of pages 15a and 27a, heavily corrected by Joyce, in the Slocum Collection at Yale University, *JJA* 2. 85–130. There are also corrections in another hand, perhaps by Joyce's friend Alessandro Francini Bruni. Another friend, Attilio Tamaro, invited Joyce to deliver three lectures at the Università Popolare, Trieste, in April and May 1907. This, the first, is in two sections and was given on 27 April. The second and third lectures were 'Giacomo Clarenzio Mangan' and ['The Irish Literary Renaissance'].

Joyce's title derives from the Latin tag, *Insula sanctorum et doctorum*, which is usually translated as 'Island of Saints and Scholars'.

1. 'Patriotism is nationally that which egoism is individually' (Herbert Spencer, *The Study of Sociology*, London (1888); Michigan (1961), 186–7).
2. A popular survey of this early Christian period, from which much of Joyce's material may derive, is P. W. Joyce, *A Short History of Gaelic Ireland* (1893). Almost all the saints and scholars mentioned below by Joyce are described in the *Short History*, 162–89. Such retrievals of Ireland's medieval 'golden age' are commonplace in the late nineteenth and earlier twentieth centuries. Many of these saints, scholars and heroes reappear in the mock invocations of *U* 12. 173–99 and 12. 1676–1739.
3. 'That other there, who looks so lean and small | In the flanks was Michael Scott, who verily | Knew every trick of the art magical' (*Inferno*, xx. 115–17 (trans. Dorothy Sayers).

4. The Bollandists—Belgian Jesuits—performed from the seventeenth century the huge task of compiling and editing the *Acta Sanctorum* which, with the *Analecta Bollandiana*, instituted historiographical standards for the study of hagiography.

5. John Duns Scotus (*c.*1265–1308), philosopher and theologian, nicknamed *Doctor Subtilis*, was not Irish. Joyce confuses John Scotus Erigena (*fl.* 850), Irish philosopher at the court of Charles the Bald, celebrated commentator on the writings of Dionysius the pseudo-Areopagite, with this John Duns Scotus, who was 'regent' of Paris University.

6. Guglielmo Ferrero, *Grandezza e decadenza di Roma* (1902–7).

7. Joyce has in mind such scholars as Johann K. Zeuss (1806–56), who in his *Grammatica Celtica* (1853), according to P. W. Joyce, provides 'a complete grammar of the four ancient Celtic dialects . . . In this work he proves that the Celtic people of the British Islands are the same with the Celtae of the Continent' (*Short History*, 3).

8. The Gaelic League, dedicated to the de-anglicization of Ireland through the revival and preservation of the Irish language, was founded in 1893.

9. *Béarla*, the Irish word for English.

10. Charles Vallancey (1721–1812), *An Essay on the Antiquity of the Irish Language. Being a collation of the Irish with the Punic Language* (1772), 29 ff.

11. Rufus Festus Avienus (*fl.* 366), Roman poet whose *Descriptio Orbis Terrarum* paraphrases the Περιήγησις of Dionysius.

12. Joyce's Italian is so bad here that, perhaps by omitting a single accent, he has succeeded in making his sentence completely ambiguous. If we read '*Ne*' with an accent, it means 'Neither' and has a negative force on the following '*bisogna tener poco conto di tali fatti*', and I have chosen this as being the most likely interpretation. On the other hand, it may be the particle '*Ne*', used pleonastically with '*di tali fatti*', in which case the sentence should mean: 'Such facts should not be considered . . .' '*Triviale*' does not, of course, mean 'trivial', but 'vulgar'. I have translated it as 'trivial', ignoring what I take to be a very basic error. (Translator's note.)

13. St Mansuetus (*fl.* 350), first bishop of Toul in Lorraine; legend also identifies him as a disciple of St Peter and the earliest Irish saint.

14. St Cataldus (*fl.* 650), bishop of Tarentum.

15. Pelagius (*fl.* 400) is described also by P. W. Joyce as 'the great heresiarch' (*Short History*, 11).

16. There is no evidence that the early Christian poet Sedulius was Irish, but he is perhaps confused with Sedulius Scotus of Liège (*fl.* 850).

17. St Fridolin the Traveller (*fl.* 510), patron of Glarus in Switzerland, is credited with founding a double monastery on the island of Seckingen in the Rhine.

18. St Columbanus (*c.*543–615), after a life of controversies about the date of the celebration of Easter in the Celtic and Roman churches, about monastic discipline, and about the morality of bishops and kings in Merovingian Gaul, founded the monastery of Bobbio, which became his resting place. 'You were going to do wonders, what? Missionary to

Europe after fiery Columbanus. Fiacre and Scotus on their creepy-stools . . .' (*U* 3. 192–3).

19. St Frigidianus, or Frediano, was made bishop of Lucca *c.*560. He is often identified in Irish hagiography (and in 'The Mirage of the Fisherman of Aran', p. 203) with St Finnian of Moville, who studied on Aran under St Enda.

20. St Gall (*fl.* 600), hermit of Lake Constance, patron of the monastery later built in his name.

21. St Gozbert, abbot of the monastery of St Gall from 816 to 837.

22. St Finian of Clonard (*fl.* 525), whom legend describes as the 'tutor of the saints of Ireland'.

23. St Fiacre (*fl.* 630), patron saint of the French province of Brie and of French cab drivers either because the Hôtel de St Fiacre in Paris, in 1650, was the first to let coaches on hire or because, as P. W. Joyce claims, he gave his 'name to a kind of vehicle called in French a *fiacre*, from the custom, in after ages, of using it in pilgrimages to his tomb' (*Short History*, 188).

24. St Fursa, or Fursey (*fl.* 640), a member of the Irish colony at Péronne and author of a celebrated *Vision*, recalled below, p. 203.

25. St Argobast (*fl.* 670), bishop of Strasbourg.

26. St Disibod (*fl.* 660), an anchorite who, according to tradition, settled at Mount Disibod or Dysenberg.

27. St Rumold, or Rombaut (*fl.* 750), apostle of Malines (Mechlin), Belgium.

28. St Albinus (*fl.* 780), whom, according to P. W. Joyce, Charlemagne placed 'at the head of two great seminaries' (*Short History*, 188).

29. St Kilian (*fl.* 675), bishop of Würzburg, who was killed at the instigation of Geilana, Duke Gosbert's wife, whom he had urged the duke to dismiss.

30. '*Citeriore*' meaning 'hither' denotes the side nearest the speaker and is, like much of Joyce's phrasing, more Latin than Italian. (Translator's note.)

31. 'After the arrival of the Danes the national character seems to have deteriorated. Chiefs and people, forced continually to fight and kill for their very existence, came to love war for its own sake—to regard it as the chief business of life. Much of the native gentleness and of the respect for peaceful avocations disappeared; and as the people retaliated cruelty for cruelty on their savage invaders, they learned at last to be cruel and relentless to each other. They lost in a great measure the old veneration for schools and monasteries' (*Short History*, 193). In *Finnegans Wake* Joyce emphasizes the Scandinavian origins of his hero Earwicker.

32. St Virgilius (*fl.* 750), geometer, bishop of Salzburg. Joyce writes '*re francese*', 'the king of France', but Virgilius had been patronized by Pippin, the king of the Franks (an error made also by P. W. Joyce, *Short History*, 187).

33. Macarius (*fl.* 800) taught the doctrine of monopsychism, that each person's mind is only a part of a single universal mind. Joyce's allusion is to *Averroès et l'averroïsme* (1852) by Ernest Renan (1823–92).

34. Joyce again confuses John Scotus Erigena (*fl.* 850), Irish philosopher and

commentator on the writings of Dionysius the pseudo–Areopagite, with
John Duns Scotus, 'regent' of Paris University. Joyce also repeats here a
common confusion of Dionysius the pseudo–Areopagite with St Denis,
the patron saint of France.

35. Pico della Mirandola (1463–94), neo-platonist philosopher of the Italian
Renaissance.

36. Where the prophet Ezra ate flowers and experienced visions (2 Esdras 9:
26).

37. John Holywood, or Halifax, in Latin Johannes de Sacro Bosco (*fl.* 1230),
mathematician and astronomer.

38. Peter Hibernicus (*fl.* 1224), Professor of Law at the University of Naples.

39. MS reads '*fecero causa*' and Joyce may have intended the idiomatic
expression '*far causa commune*'. (Translator's note.)

40. Lord Edward Fitzgerald (1763–98); Robert Emmet (1778–1803); Theobald Wolfe Tone (1763–98); James Napper Tandy (1740–1803); Thomas
Davis (1814–45); John Mitchel (1815–75); Isaac Butt (1813–79); Joseph
Biggar (1828–90); Charles Stewart Parnell (1846–91). Parnell's family
tree is given in Richard Barry O'Brien, *The Life of Charles Stewart Parnell, 1846–1891* (1898, 3rd edn., 2 volumes, 1899), i. 31. Contrast D. P.
Moran's attack on the anglicization of Irish culture by Molyneux, Swift
('who had not a drop of Irish blood in his veins') and Grattan: 'No one
wants to fall out with [Thomas] Davis's comprehensive idea of the Irish
people as a composite race drawn from various sources, and professing
any creed they like, nor would an attempt to rake up racial prejudice be
tolerated by anyone. We are proud of Grattan, Flood, Tone, Emmett, and
all the rest who dreamt and worked for an independent country, even
though they had no conception of an Irish nation; but it is necessary that
they should be put in their place . . . The foundation of Ireland is the Gael
. . . The '98 and '48 movements, the Fenians and the Parnellite agitation,
were Pale [that is, of Dublin and its environs] movements in their essence,
even when they were most fiercely rebellious' (*The Philosophy of Irish
Ireland*, Dublin: James Duffy & Co., n.d. [1905], 34, 36–7).

41. The Norman–Welsh invasion by Richard Strongbow took place in 1168.
The Act of Union, 1800, abolished the Irish parliament and allowed for
Irish representation in the House of Commons and in the House of Lords
at Westminster.

42. Dermot MacMurrough (*c.*1110–71), king of Leinster and abductor of the
wife of the prince of Breffni. See Mr Deasy's confusion on this matter (*U*
2. 392–4): 'A faithless wife first brought the strangers to our shore here,
McMurrogh's wife and her leman, O'Rourke, prince of Breffni'. See also
U 5. 1156–8: 'The strangers, says the citizen. Our own fault. We let them
come in. We brought them in. The adulteress and her paramour brought
the Saxon robbers here.' See p. 118, where Joyce correlates the idea of
racial purity with that of virginal purity, and rejects both.

43. Henry II (1133–89), king of England.

44. The papal bull *Laudabiliter* (1155) of Pope Adrian IV (Nicholas

Breakspear) conferred the sovereignty of Ireland on Henry II. See also *U* 14. 578–91. Three letters and a papal franchise of Pope Alexander III confirmed English sovereignty over Ireland.

45. Joyce could intend either Robert Stewart, Viscount Castlereagh (1769–1822), Chief Secretary of Ireland, or Charles, first Marquess and second Earl Cornwallis (1738–1805), Viceroy and commander-in-chief in Ireland, who together secured the Act of Union for the Prime Minister, William Pitt (1759–1806). It is something of an anachronism for Joyce to describe the Protestant Irish parliament before 1800 as 'elected by the Irish people'.

46. 'My ancestors . . . allowed a handful of foreigners to subject them. Do you fancy I am going to pay in my own life and person debts they made?' (*Portrait* 170); 'The programme of the patriots filled him with very reasonable doubts; its articles could obtain no intellectual assent from him' (*SH* 81).

47. Queen Victoria visited Ireland from 4 to 26 April 1900. In spite of Nationalist protests she was given an address of welcome by Dublin Corporation. Parnell, in 1890, had forbidden municipalities from officially receiving royalty, as Joyce recalls, p. 195.

48. Dublin Corporation refused the customary address of welcome to King Edward VII and Queen Alexandra during their visit from 21 July to 1 August 1903. The king's advisers had postponed an earlier visit in 1902 for fear of an unfavourable reception. See 'Ivy Day in the Committee Room' (*D* 94 and 101–2).

49. Joseph Patrick Nannetti became Lord Mayor of Dublin in 1906 and is a subject of discussion in Barney Kiernan's public house (*U* 12. 825–59).

50. Queen Victoria first visited Ireland in June 1849, nine years after her marriage.

51. Albert (1819–61), the Prince-Consort, was the son of Ernest, Duke of Saxe-Coburg-Gotha, and of Louise, daughter of Augustus, Duke of Saxe-Gotha-Altenburg. See *U* 12. 1390–92: 'And as for the Prooshians and the Hanoverians, says Joe, haven't we had enough of those sausage eating bastards on the throne from George the elector down to the German lad and the flatulent old bitch that's dead.'

52. Benjamin Disraeli (1804–81), Conservative politician and man of letters, British Prime Minister, 1868, 1874–80, supported Queen Victoria's opposition to Gladstone's Irish policies.

53. Contrary to popular rumour Queen Victoria donated £500 to the charity fund during the famine of 1878–80. The story that she sent £5 towards the relief of the Great Famine of 1848–9 was part of Irish folklore. In the manuscript, the figure 10 in the text is underlined and substituted by a 5, written in the margin by another hand.

54. Sir Frederick Sleigh, Lord Roberts (1832–1914), soldier, was not born in Ireland but in Cawnpore, India. He was commander of the English army in Ireland. See *U* 14. 1331–2: 'darling little Bobsy (called after our famous

hero of the South African war, lord Bobs of Waterford and Candahar)';
see also *U* 15. 796 and 18. 378. Horatio Herbert, first Earl Kitchener
(1850–1916), born in County Kerry, commander-in-chief at the conclusion of the South African war.

55. Arthur Wellesley, first Duke of Wellington (1769-1852), was born at Dan-
gan Castle, Dublin. See also *U* 12. 1459–60.

56. There is a note in English in the margin by, perhaps, Stanislaus Joyce:
'Explain why the soldiers were English.' The explanation in parentheses
is given in Joyce's hand also in the margin. James Stephens (1824–1901),
Fenian, a leader of the 1867 rebellion, founder of the Irish Republican
Brotherhood and of the newspaper *The Irish People*.

57. The street in London in which most newspaper offices were situated.

58. Joyce is arguing against the exceptionalism asserted about Ireland by
Ernest Renan: 'Ireland in particular (and herein we perhaps have the
secret of her irremediable weakness) is the only country in Europe where
the native can produce the titles of his descent.' Renan (and to some
extent his assumptions are similar to those of Joyce) took the view that a
'noble' nation is a mingling of elements: 'Racial considerations have then
been for nothing in the constitution of modern nations . . . The truth is
that there is no pure race . . . The most noble countries, England, France,
Italy, are those where blood is most mingled.' See *The Poetry of the Celtic
Races, and Other Studies*, trans. William G. Hutchinson (1896), New York
and London: Kennikat Press (1970), 5, 72.

59. Contrast D. P. Moran, who urges 'a separation of national personality, the
keeping distinct and clear cut as many things as possible that may mark us
off from our neighbours . . . We must retrace our steps, and take as much
of our inspiration from our own country and its history. We must be
original Irish, and not imitation English. Above all, we must relearn our
language, and become a bi-lingual people' (*Philosophy of Irish Ireland*, 26).
Joyce is also rebutting the claims of Oliver St John Gogarty's series of
articles under the title 'Ugly England' in *Sinn Féin*, 15 September, 24
November, and 1 December 1906. Gogarty had complained of England's
'venereal excess' and of the 'Jew mastery of England'. Joyce's letters to
Stanislaus reject Gogarty's 'stupid drivel' and wish that 'some kind person would publish a book about the venereal condition of the Irish; since
they pride themselves so much on their immunity. It must be rather worse
than England, I think' (*Letters* ii. 164, 170–1, 189–92, 200). See also *U* 5.
71–2; 12. 1197.

60. Dionysius the pseudo-Areopagite, *The Celestial Hierarchy*, 261a, also
cited by Yeats, 'The Theatre' (1900) in *Ideas of Good and Evil*.

61. This was to happen in 1912 during the crisis of the third Home Rule Bill.

62. Barry O'Brien records such a tale in his *Life of Charles Stewart Parnell*
(1899), i. 53–4.

63. Compare the Citizen, 'Where are our missing twenty millions of Irish
should be here today instead of four, our lost tribes? And our potteries and
textiles, the finest in the whole world! And our wool that was sold in

Rome' (*U* 12. 1240–3). See also D. P. Moran: 'We are ever laying contribution on poor history to explain away our shortcomings ... you will meet men every day who will ask you how in the world could Ireland be prosperous considering that England stole our woollen industry from us some hundreds of years ago. Heaven knows we have overdone that sort of nonsense ... I look in vain for that fiery hate of subjection we hear so much of from the political platforms' (*Philosophy of Irish Ireland*, 2–3).

64. Compare the editorial 'Finance and Devolution', *Sinn Féin*, 22 Sept. 1906.

65. Shane O'Neill, 2nd Earl of Tyrone (*c*.1530–67).

66. Simon de Montfort, Earl of Leicester (*c*.1208–65).

67. Oliver Cromwell (1599–1658) was sent to Ireland as commander-in-chief and Lord Lieutenant in 1649; the storming and massacre of Drogheda took place on 2 September, the attempt on Waterford from 2 November to 2 December. The Treaty of Limerick (1691), which ended the Williamite wars in Ireland, guaranteed Irish Catholics religious toleration. The Protestant Irish parliament broke this clause and passed a system of penal laws which disabled Catholics both economically and politically throughout the eighteenth century.

68. Martin Luther, summoned to the city of Worms by Charles V in 1521, refused to renounce his Protestant teachings. Also compare Stephen, 'What kind of liberation would that be to forsake an absurdity which is logical and coherent and to embrace one which is illogical and incoherent?' (*Portrait* 205).

69. Giraldus Cambrensis, Gerald of Wales (*c*.1146–1223), *The History and Topography of Ireland*, ed. John O'Meara (Penguin, 1982), Third Part, 107, pp. 115 16.

70. It may be that Joyce is referring to Giacomo Boncompagni, the illegitimate son of Pope Gregory XIII (1502–85), who availed of Ireland in his counter-reformation attack upon Queen Elizabeth I.

71. That is, 'in the regions of the infidels'.

72. Alphonso XIII (1886–1941) acceded to the Spanish throne in 1902. '*Hidalgo*' is Spanish for a 'nobleman'.

73. Oliver Goldsmith (1728–74), Richard Brinsley Sheridan (1751–1816), dramatist, William Congreve (1670–1729), dramatist, Jonathan Swift (1667–1745) and Edmund Burke (1729–97), all Irish writers who spent some or all of their professional lives in metropolitan London.

74. Both of these newspapers were published from London.

75. Edward Fitzgerald (1809–83) published a version of the *Rubaiyat of Omar Khayyám*; Sir Richard Burton (1821–90) translated *A Thousand and One Nights*; Henry Francis Cary (1772–1844) translated the *Divine Comedy*.

76. Sir Arthur Seymour Sullivan (1842–1900), composer of comic operas with the librettist W. S. Gilbert; Feargus O'Connor (1794–1855), Chartist leader and editor of *The Northern Star*; Oscar Wilde was the son of Jane

Francesca Wilde (1826–96), who contributed poems to *The Nation* under the pseudonym Speranza.

77. Compare D. P. Moran: 'The Irishman of modern times has succeeded in every land but his own. For at home is the only place he cannot make up his mind . . . he will not be English or Irish' (*Philosophy of Irish Ireland*, 113).

78. Luke Gardiner, Viscount Mountjoy (1745–98), MP for County Dublin and Irish Privy Councillor, killed at the battle of New Ross.

79. John Tyndall (1820–93), natural philosopher and pioneer of popular scientific writing; Frederick Temple Blackwood, Marquess of Dufferin and Ava (1826–1902); Sir Charles Gavan Duffy (1816–1903), Young Irelander and co-founder of *The Nation* who emigrated to Australia in 1856 and became Governor-General of Victoria; John Bobanau Nickerlieu Hennessey (1829–1910), Deputy Surveyor-General of India; Leopold O'Donnell, Duke of Tetuan (1809–67), Spanish general and statesman; William Jennings Bryan (1860–1925), political orator, Secretary of State, Democratic candidate for the presidency of the USA, 1896, 1900, 1907/1908; Marie Edmé Patrice, Comte de MacMahon (1808–93), Marshal of France, President of the French Republic from 1873 to 1879; Lord Charles William de la Poer, Baron Beresford (1846–1919), commander-in-chief of the Channel fleet; Garnet Joseph, first Viscount Wolseley (1833–1913), field marshal and military reformer.

80. 'God, Kinch, if you and I could only work together we might do something for the island. Hellenise it' (*U* 1.157–8).

81. Compare *Sinn Féin*, 15 September 1906, and see p. 140. See also *U* 12. 1572–6, where it is proposed that Bloom suggested some of these ideas to Griffith to put in his newspaper, *Sinn Féin*.

82. It used to be common, on a supposed Greek and Latin model, to distinguish a triple order of the learned professions in the Celtic world: *druidh*, *filidh*, and *baird*.

83. That is, W. B. Yeats.

JAMES CLARENCE MANGAN (1907)

MS Yale and Cornell. Translated from the Italian, *Giacomo Clarenzio Mangan*, an incomplete and heavily corrected holograph of twenty-four pages numbered 1–4, 6–10, 12–22, 24–6 in the Slocum Collection at Yale University, plus one unnumbered holograph leaf preserved among Stanislaus Joyce's papers (Cornell 42), *JJA* 2. 131–54. This leaf constitutes the conclusion to the first section and, for the first time in English translation, is inserted below. This lecture, the second intended to be given by Joyce at the Università Popolare, Trieste, is in two sections. It is an expanded and modified version, with much of the original retained especially in its second section, of the Mangan essay of 1902 printed above, with also some repetitions from 'Ireland: Island of Saints and Sages'. Only such notes as are additional to the 1902 essay are supplied below.

1. 'The poet is the intense centre of the life of his age to which he stands in a relation than which none can be more vital. He alone is capable of absorbing in himself the life that surrounds him' (*SH* 85).

2. Joyce is exaggerating Mangan's obscure reputation, as he had done before in 1902. Since that date celebrations of the centenary of Mangan's birth included two editions by D. J. O'Donoghue, *Poems of James Clarence Mangan*, with biographical introduction by John Mitchel (Dublin: O'Donoghue, M. H. Gill, 1903) and *The Prose Writings of James Clarence Mangan*, with an essay by Lionel Johnson (Dublin: O'Donoghue, M. H. Gill, 1904).

3. That is, 'Ireland: Island of Saints and Sages', from which many of these sentences are borrowed.

4. That is, 'The Irish Literary Renaissance'.

5. The National Library of Italy.

6. Cormac MacArt, to whom, as High King of Ireland, *The Book of Aicill* (which Joyce confuses with *The Yellow Book of Lecan*) is attributed.

7. Mitchel (1859), 13.

8. A rather humdrum translation of Joyce's '*etére*'. I chose 'harlot' as it has the advantage of being English rather than Greek. (Translator's note.)

9. Joyce forgets to close his parentheses here. He uses the word '*quistioni*' for what I take to have been '*questioni*'. The classical influence is obviously very strong here, though, despite appearances, 'quistioni' is not a Latin word either. (Translator's note.)

10. From here to the end of the paragraph the text is that of MS Cornell 42.

11. The allusions are to Joan of Arc and to John the Baptist, to Mangan's narcotic addictions and to Parnell's relationship with Katherine O'Shea.

12. See p. 30 and p. 294, n. 1.

13. Joyce makes an odd substitution here for Mangan's boa-constrictor: '*Caudisona*' is not Italian, but Latin for 'rattlesnake'. (Translator's note.)

14. *U* 7. 721–2. The Florentine theologian is Dante (*Paradiso*, xxxi. 127).

15. The lines are taken in fact from Mangan's 'O'Hussey's Ode to the Maguire'.

[THE IRISH LITERARY RENAISSANCE]

MS Yale, *JJA* 2. 156. Translated from the Italian, a single unnumbered holograph leaf from a notebook, in the Slocum collection at Yale University, and at one time appended to the 1907 Mangan lecture by John J. Slocum. It is likely that this page is the only surviving fragment of the third lecture in the series which Joyce intended to deliver at the Università Popolare, Trieste, in May 1907.

1. The rebellion of the United Irishmen in 1798.

2. The Young Irelanders split with Daniel O'Connell on the issue of physical force and proceeded with an insurrection, triggered by the onset of famine and European events, in 1848.

FENIANISM: THE LAST FENIAN

Translated from the Italian 'Il Fenianismo: L'ultimo Feniano', *Il Piccolo della Sera* (Trieste, 22 March 1907). This newspaper, nationalist in character, 'kept its readers up to date on events in Italy, included reports on international politics, fashion, culture, gossip, serialised versions of popular novels, and cartoons. *Il Piccolo della Sera* rarely missed an opportunity to write about countries which suffered under foreign domination and so the Irish question received a lot of coverage—even if it was usually through the filter of English news agencies. So when Joyce wrote his leading articles he knew he was writing for a readership already reasonably acquainted with matters Irish.' (John McCourt, 'Joyce on National Deliverance: The View from 1907 Trieste,' *Prospero: Rivista di Culture Anglo-Germaniche*, 5, (1998), 34). Roberto Prezioso, a student of Joyce, was familiar with Joyce's views on Ireland and invited these articles. In an exchange of letters with his brother, Stanislaus, in 1912, Charles Joyce recalls that in reply to a charge that *Dubliners* is not a book which betters his country or people, Joyce invoked these articles: 'Jim replied that he was probably the only Irishman who wrote leading articles for the Italian press and that all his articles in "Il Piccolo" were about Ireland and the Irish people' (*Letters*, ii. 316). In a letter to the Italian publisher Angelo Fortunato Formiggini, 25 March 1914, Joyce made the following proposal: 'This year the Irish problem has reached an acute phase, and indeed, according to the latest news, England, owing to the Home Rule question, is on the brink of civil war. The publication of a volume of Irish essays would be of interest to the Italian public. These essays (nine) which I wrote, were published during the last seven years as signed editorials in the *Piccolo della Sera* of Trieste.' See Giorgio Melchiori, 'The Language of Politics and the Politics of Language', *James Joyce Broadsheet*, 4 (Feb. 1981), 1. Transcriptions and unsigned typescript translations of these articles can be found in *JJA* 2. 653–703.

1. John O'Leary (1830–1907), died at 5.20 p.m. on 16 March, the day before St Patrick's Day.

2. The Whiteboys were a secret agrarian society of the eighteenth century; the Invincibles were founded in 1881 as an extremist breakaway group from the Irish Republican Brotherhood. Joyce, here and below, uses the terms with little historical exactness.

3. Robert Emmet, whose rebellion took place in 1803. There is a parodic version of this rebellion and of Emmet's execution in *U* 12. 525–678.

4. This is an exaggeration by Joyce: the Irish population which stood at just over eight million in 1841 had, as a result of famine, reduced to under six million in the 1860s.

5. James Stephens (1824–1901), Fenian leader and founder of the Irish Republican Brotherhood. 'James Stephens' idea was the best. He knew them. Circles of ten so that a fellow couldn't round on more than his own ring' (*U* 8. 457–8).

6. James Stephens established the newspaper *Irish People* in 1863 with O'Leary and Thomas Clarke Luby (1821–1901).

7. 'How the head centre got away, authentic version. Got up as a young bride, man, veil, orangeblossoms' (*U* 3. 241–2). Desmond Ryan tells the story of how a Mrs Washington Downey, the popular poetess 'Christabel', returning to her house in London, aided Stephens's escape and gave rise to this version of events: 'Mrs Washington Downey went on board the Sabania accompanied by Stephens, who in the character of her personal servant, carried her little boy. This led to the legend that Stephens escaped disguised as a lady's maid, a plan which was in fact proposed, because, as the *Kilkenny Moderator*, 21 September 1865, explained with malicious delight in circulating this myth, "being low in stature, and of slight build, effeminate in appearance and without a beard, the idea of dressing him as a female naturally occurred to those aiding his flight; and in the character of a rather respectable female on board a vessel at Cork, and in the same capacity passed from the Dover Steamer safely into France"' (*The Fenian Chief* (1967), 42). Stephens was vehemently to deny this story. For an alternative version which includes a collier or 'charcoal boat', see *The Fenian Chief*, 229, and John Devoy's more reliable account in *Recollections of an Irish Rebel* (1929), chap. 13. Stanislaus Joyce suggests that his father knew the anti-Parnellite captain of this boat and tells the story with much the same relish as Joyce does (*My Brother's Keeper*, 77–8, 93). The expression 'There's the man that got away James Stephens' was a catchphrase in Dublin and recurs in *U* 4. 491–2, 12. 880–81, 15. 15–33.

8. Compare Stephens's comments on 'the indispensable informer' (*Portrait* 169). In the case of the Fenians other factors contributed to their failure, not least the open avowal by Stephens and the other leaders, through *Irish People*, that 1865 would be the year of insurrection.

9. The attempt to rescue Colonel Richard O'Sullivan Burke from Clerkenwell House of Detention in London, which caused twelve deaths, took place on 13 December 1867. See *U* 3. 245–50.

10. The rescue of three Fenians from custody in Manchester on 18 September 1867 resulted in the killing of Sergeant Charles Brett, for which three men, the 'Manchester Martyrs', were executed on 23 November 1867.

11. Lord Frederick Cavendish and Thomas Henry Burke were assassinated outside the Vice-Regal Lodge in Dublin's Phoenix Park on 6 May 1882.

12. The Irish population had reduced to below four and a half million by 1907.

13. The Sinn Féin (literally, 'ourselves') movement developed, from 1905 to 1908 under Arthur Griffith, out of Cumann na nGaedheal, which he had founded in 1900 with William Rooney.

14. *Sinn Féin*, 26 May, 9 June, 16 June, 15 September 1906.

15. Joyce's opposition to physical force places him alongside Arthur Griffith's Sinn Féin policy of non-violence which had been opposed by Bulmer Hobson (1883–1969) and others in Sinn Féin through Hobson's weekly paper, *The Republic*, a paper Joyce was reading while in Rome and which appeared from 13 December 1906 to 16 May 1907. See *Letters* ii. 205.

16. John O'Leary had himself made such an observation, to the effect that the

great funeral is the only recognition allowed to an Irish leader; see Denis Gwynn, *Edward Martyn and the Irish Revival*, London: Jonathan Cape (1930), 297. Joyce exaggerates O'Leary's isolation. From his arrival back in Ireland in 1885 O'Leary had, while cultivating a detachment from the new generation, been active in literary culture and the Young Ireland Society. He actively supported Parnell after the divorce case. He was President of the National Literary Society on its foundation by W. B. Yeats and others in 1892. During the 1898 celebrations of the United Irishmen and 1798 O'Leary laid the foundation stone for the Wolfe Tone monument at Stephen's Green, a ceremony Stephen, with little enthusiasm, remembers attending with his father (*Portrait* 154). O'Leary became President of Arthur Griffith's Cumann na nGaedheal in 1900. An accurate characteristic in Joyce's sketch is the purchase at the antiquarian book stall by O'Leary, whose library Yeats described in 1889 as 'the best I know'.

HOME RULE COMES OF AGE

Translated from the Italian 'Home Rule maggiorenne', *Il Piccolo della Sera* (19 May 1907). The title of this essay is borrowed by Joyce from a leading article in *Sinn Féin* (13 Apr. 1907). Also Joyce's rhetorical device of beginning his first paragraphs with 'Twenty-one years . . . Seven years . . .' derives from Arthur Griffith's article 'Devolution' in *Sinn Féin*, 11 May 1907.

1. The first Home Rule Bill was introduced in the House of Commons on 8 April 1886, by the Liberal Prime Minister, W. E. Gladstone. The second Home Rule Bill was introduced in the Commons, also by Gladstone, in January 1893. Both of these Bills were defeated.

2. 'Scene in House of Commons Today (by telegraph). At half-past five this morning before the doors of the House of Commons were opened or even the servants astir, members began to present themselves for admission' (*Dublin Evening Mail*, Thursday 8 Apr. 1886).

3. 'The infant born on the morrow of its publication has come of age. He is a man—he demands his birthright' (*Sinn Féin*, 13 Apr.1907).

4. Archibald Philip, fifth Earl of Rosebery (1847–1929), succeeded Gladstone as leader of the Liberals.

5. Augustine Birrell (1850–1933), lawyer, politician, and man of letters, Chief Secretary of Ireland, 1907–16.

6. On 7 May 1907 Augustine Birrell introduced in the House of Commons the Irish Council Bill which the National Convention would reject on 21 May. Joseph Chamberlain (1836–1914), leader of the Liberal Unionists against the Gladstonian Liberals, had presented in 1885 a plan for a 'Central Board' or national council in Ireland with very limited powers.

7. The term 'boycott' derives from Captain Charles Boycott (1832–97), land agent for Lord Erne's estate at Lough Mask in Co. Mayo during the Land League agitation of 1873.

8. *Sinn Féin*, 17 May, 14 July, 22 September 1906.

9. 'In Ireland the Tory is regarded as an open enemy; the Whig as a treach-

erous friend. It is the Whigs, not the Tories, who have habitually sapped the integrity of Irish representation' (O'Brien, *Life of Charles Stewart Parnell* (1899), i. 90).

10. 'At present what takes place is this: the Duke of Norfolk visits the Vatican three times each year as the representative of the Catholics of the "United Kingdom". Of course this mean-souled man whose hatred of Ireland and the Irish is perhaps the most intense part of his nature does not "represent" the Irish Catholics . . . Every slander this man pours out on Irish Nationalism is accepted at the Vatican as the views of an accredited representative' (*Sinn Féin*, 15 Dec. 1906).

11. *Sinn Féin*, 11 August, 25 August 1906. See also Arthur Griffith, *How Ireland Is Taxed*, Dublin: National Council Pamphlets, No. 6 (1907), 3.

12. *Sinn Féin*, 6 June, 25 August, 29 September 1906.

13. 'Then one of the Twelve, the man called Judas Iscariot, went to the chief priests and said, "What are you prepared to give me if I hand him over to you?" They paid him thirty pieces of silver and from that moment he looked for an opportunity to betray him' (Matthew 26: 14–16). Parnell was stripped of his leadership of the Irish Parliamentary Party in December 1890. Joyce's version of the 'selling' of Parnell in response to Gladstone's demands derives from the story of how Parnell insisted that the Irish Parliamentary Party should demand from Gladstone as the price for dismissing him nothing less than Home Rule: 'Mr Redmond: "When we are asked to sell our leader to preserve the English alliance, it seems to me that we are bound to inquire what we are getting for the price we are paying." "Don't sell me for nothing," interrupted Parnell. "If you get my value you may change me tomorrow"' (O'Brien (1899), ii. 278). An instance of English, nonconformist outrage at Parnell's relationship with Katherine O'Shea is given in O'Brien, ii. 275.

IRELAND AT THE BAR

Translated from the Italian, 'L'Irlanda alla sbarra', *Il Piccolo della Sera* (16 Sept. 1907). The title presents the image of Ireland in the dock and unable to defend itself against the charges of the international press and popular opinion. When Joyce in 1914 planned to gather together his articles from *Il Piccolo* into a volume of essays about Ireland for Italian readers his intention was to place this article first and to give the book its title. See Giorgio Melchiori, 'The Language of Politics and the Politics of Language', *James Joyce Broadsheet*, 4 (Feb. 1981), 1.

1. On the night of 17 August 1882 John Joyce, his wife, mother, and children were murdered in their house at Maamtrasna, an isolated townland on the shore of Lough Mask in Connemara. The crime was thought to be an agrarian outrage committed by a secret society. Ten men, Joyces and Caseys from neighbouring townlands, were accused of the crime and trials took place in November. On 15 December three of the accused were hanged in Galway jail. One of these three, Myles Joyce, was subsequently

thought to be innocent. An account of Joyce's interest in these events and their probable use in *FW* is given by John Garvin, *James Joyce's Disunited Kingdom* (Dublin: Gill and Macmillan, 1976), 159–69.

2. For a transcript of the trial, which Joyce knew inaccurately and by hearsay, see T. Harrington, *The Maamtrasna Massacres* (Dublin, 1884). However, the role of the interpreter for the Gaelic-speaking defendants was as Joyce describes it.

3. At his execution Myles Joyce continued to proclaim his innocence. The hangman, Marwood, failed to place the noose correctly and Myles Joyce was strangled with Marwood kicking down at him through the open trapdoor in an attempt to correct the rope and hurry his death.

4. Joyce is referring to the riots in Belfast, which had begun on 4 August and continued into September, and also to various incidents in an anti-cattle-grazing agitation during July, August, and September 1907. These 'outrages' dominated the reporting from Ireland by *The Times* during these months. A state of emergency was declared in the counties of Clare, Galway, Leitrim, Roscommon.

5. Joyce's reference is to the Land League and its policies during the last quarter of the nineteenth century.

6. The 'Maiming Outrages' at Great Wyrley are reported in *The Times* from 28 August to 16 September 1907.

OSCAR WILDE: THE POET OF 'SALOMÉ'

Translated from the Italian, 'Oscar Wilde: il poeta di "Salomé"', *Il Piccolo della Sera* (24 Mar. 1909). The article was published on the occasion of a performance in Trieste of the opera *Salomé* (1905) by Richard Strauss (1864–1949), which is based on the play of the same title written in French by Wilde in 1892.

1. Oscar Wilde, *Poems* (1881).

2. 'From the fierce O'Flaherties, deliver us, Lord', an inscription on one of the medieval gates of the city of Galway.

3. 'Wilde's love that dare not speak its name' (*U* 3. 451). Lady Wilde is reported to have wished for this, her second child, to have been a girl.

4. John Ruskin (1819–1900), art critic and socialist, organized his students to work at mending country roadways around Oxford.

5. Oscar Wilde edited a magazine, *The Woman's World*, in November 1887.

6. The eighth Marquess of Queensberry, whom Wilde sued for libel with disastrous consequences, was the father of Lord Alfred Douglas (1870–1945), English poet, lover of Wilde, and the translator into English in 1894 of Wilde's *Salomé*.

7. Wilde died in Paris on 30 November 1900.

8. See W. B. Yeats's report of Joyce's comment to him in 1902 about Wilde's deathbed conversion: 'He said that he hoped his conversion was not sincere. He did not like to think that he had been untrue to himself at the end' (*JJ* 102).

9. In reply to a negative review of *The Picture of Dorian Gray* (1891), Wilde wrote 'Each man sees his own sin in Dorian Gray. What Dorian Gray's sins are no one knows. He who finds them has brought them' ('Mr Wilde's Rejoinder', *Scots Observer*, 4/86 (12 July 1890), 279).

10. 'and in my misery it was revealed to me that man can only come to that Heart through the sense of separation from it which we call sin' (W. B. Yeats, *The Tables of the Law*).

11. Oscar Wilde, *De Profundis* (1905) and *A House of Pomegranates* (1891). Varius Avitus (203–22), Roman Emperor, adopted the name of a Syrian god, Heliogabalus, whom he proclaimed god of Rome and to whom, until slain with his mother by the offended citizens, he offered profligate worship.

12. 'They divide my garments among them and cast lots for my clothes' (Psalms 22: 18–19). The inscription on Wilde's gravestone at Bagneux (from where his remains were removed to Père Lachaise in 1909) read: '*Verbis meis addere nihil audebant et super illos stillebat eloquium suum*': 'To my words they durst add nothing and my speech dropped upon them' (Job 29: 22).

THE BATTLE BETWEEN BERNARD SHAW AND THE CENSOR

Translated from the Italian 'La battaglia fra Bernard Shaw e la censura: "Blanco Posnet smascherato"', *Il Piccolo della Sera* (5 Sept. 1909). This piece was sent from Dublin by Joyce, who had returned to the city in the hope of finalizing the publication of *Dubliners*.

1. Bernard Shaw's *The Shewing-Up of Blanco Posnet* had been banned in England. W. B. Yeats and Lady Gregory availed of the technicality by which the Lord Chamberlain's authority did not extend to Ireland and, having overcome the objections of the Viceroy, produced the play from 25 August at the Abbey Theatre. There is a report on Joyce's article in Dublin's *Evening Telegraph*, 8 September 1909 (*Letters* ii. 238, 252).

2. Bernard Shaw, *Mrs Warren's Profession* (1898) and *Press Cuttings* (1909); Leo Tolstoy, *The Power of Darkness* (1888); Oscar Wilde's *Salomé* was staged first in Paris in 1896 and in London in 1905.

3. A typewritten copy of this article in the Slocum Collection in the University of Yale Library has a handwritten note by Shaw: 'There was no exchange of letters between myself and Dublin Castle. The campaign was conducted by Lady Gregory and W. B. Yeats. I did not interfere. G. Bernard Shaw, 21 July 1949.' Joyce attributes the correspondence to Shaw.

4. Bernard Shaw, *The Devil's Disciple* (1901).

5. Bernard Shaw, *John Bull's Other Island* (1904).

THE HOME RULE COMET

Translated from the Italian, 'La Cometa dell' "Home Rule"', *Il Piccolo della Sera* (22 Dec. 1910). There is an authorial fair copy of this article in the

Slocum Collection at Yale University. However, this manuscript did not serve as printer's copy. See *JJA* 2. xxvii–xxviii. The title of the article is taken by Joyce from that of a cartoon in *Sinn Féin*, 11 June 1910.

1. The dissolution of parliament had been brought on by the refusal of the House of Lords to accept the 'people's budget' of David Lloyd George (1863–1945), Welsh Liberal politician, and Chancellor of the Exchequer 1908–15.

2. Herbert Asquith (1852–1928), Prime Minister and leader of the Liberal Party, needed the support of John Redmond (1856–1918), leader of the reunited Irish Parliamentary Party, in his struggle against the right of the House of Lords to veto legislation. During the election campaigns of 1910 Asquith made a public commitment to Home Rule for Ireland. The Parliament Act of 1911 restricted the power of the House of Lords and asserted the legislative supremacy of the House of Commons. In return Redmond got the Home Rule Bill of 1912. Arthur James Balfour (1848–1930), Scottish politician, was leader of the Conservative Party, 1902–11.

3. Frederick Edwin Smith, Earl of Birkenhead (1872–1930) and Sir Edward Carson (1854–1935) were both leaders of unionist opinion; the editor of the *National Review* was Leopold James Maxse (1864–1932). The two Irish factions were the nationalist and unionist interests.

4. Joyce refers to Winston Churchill (1874–1965), who became Home Secretary in 1910; to Arthur Balfour, who had published *A Defence of Philosophic Doubt* (1879); and to William O'Brien (1852–1928), land agitator, nationalist politician, and journalist who re-entered parliament in 1910 after founding, in the interests of 'conciliation' and 'conference' with unionists, a new party, the All-for-Ireland League.

5. Robert Arthur Talbot Gascoyne-Cecil, third Marquess of Salisbury (1830–1903), Conservative politician and Prime Minister.

6. The double balance between the Liberal Party and the Conservative and Unionist Party, each of which won 272 seats in the election, rested on the Labour Party, with 47 votes, and the Irish Party, with 84 votes.

7. George V (1865–1936), king of Great Britain, acceded to the throne in 1910.

8. Henry Petty-Fitzmaurice, fifth Marquess of Lansdowne (1845–1927), served as Foreign Secretary, 1900–1905, and was succeeded by Edward Grey, first Viscount Grey of Fallodon (1862–1933), who held the position 1905–16.

[A CURIOUS HISTORY]

MS Cornell. Joyce sent copies of this letter about the fate of *Dubliners* at the hands of various publishers to several newspapers; it was published in full in *Sinn Féin* on 2 September 1911 and, with the controversial passage omitted, in the *Northern Whig* (Belfast) on 26 August 1911. Ezra Pound published an article which included this account by Joyce under the title 'A Curious History' in the *New Freewoman*, 15 January 1914.

1. Grant Richards, the publisher to whom Joyce first sent the manuscript of *Dubliners* on 3 December 1905 and who, after many reversals, finally published the collection of stories on 15 June 1914.
2. See *JJ* 231 for Joyce's visit to the lawyer St Lo Malet in Rome.
3. Joseph Maunsel Hone (1882–1959), Irish literary historian and biographer.
4. George Roberts, managing director of Maunsel and Co.; see 'Gas from a Burner' (1912), *Poems and Exiles*, 107–10.
5. In the later published version of the story, another sentence was introduced here: 'He's a man of the world, and he means well by us.' See *D* 102.
6. This whole quotation from the story is pasted in *printed* form on the second page of Joyce's letter.

REALISM AND IDEALISM IN ENGLISH LITERATURE

Joyce returned to deliver two lectures in March 1912 at the Università Popolare, Trieste, under the announced title, 'Verismo ed idealismo nella letteratura inglese (Daniele De Foe—William Blake)'.

1. MS Buffalo, *JJA* 2. 170–213. Translated from the Italian, 'Daniele Defoe', a complete author's fair copy of forty pages (Buffalo VII, A. 1–2) in two parts, the first numbered 1 to 17 and the second 1 to 22, with two pages numbered 8. A second holograph of four pages (Buffalo VII. A. 3), numbered 33 to 36, which appears to be a fragment of a draft version of the lecture, also survives. This second MS provides a copy of an earlier conclusion to the lecture: see note 49 below. Joyce's main sources of information about Defoe appear to be William Minto, *Daniel Defoe* (London: Macmillan, 1879), and John Masefield (ed.) *Defoe* (London, 1909).
2. William III (1650–1702), Prince of Orange, born at The Hague, declared King of England by declaration of right, thereby establishing the Protestant succession after the 'Glorious Revolution' of 1688.
3. See the Orange toast to William III of 'Glorious, pious and immortal memory' (*U* 2. 273).
4. Joyce is elaborating on the theme of Defoe's *The True-Born Englishman: A Satyr* (1701), in which Defoe ironically undermined English objections to the 'foreign' King William III. 'What were the English, he demanded, that they should make a mock of foreigners? They were the most mongrel race that ever lived upon the face of the earth; there was no such thing as a true-born Englishman; they were all the offspring of foreigners; what was more, of the scum of foreigners' (Minto, 26).
5. Ludovico Ariosto (1474–1533), Italian poet.
6. Giovanni Boccaccio (1313–75), Italian poet and author of the *Decameron* (1348–58); Tommaso Guardati, pseudonym Masuccio (*c.*1420–80), Italian author of *Il Novellino* (1476).
7. Felix Lope de Vega (1562–1635), Spanish poet and dramatist.
8. Plutarch (*c.*46–120), Greek biographer; Gaius Sallustius Crispus (86–34 BC), Roman historian.

9. James Scott, Duke of Monmouth and Buccleuch (1649–85), natural son of Charles II, whom he plotted to murder, executed in the Tower of London.
10. Masefield, p. xi.
11. Masefield, pp. xi–xii.
12. Daniel Defoe, *The Shortest Way with the Dissenters* (1702).
13. Minto, 39.
14. Daniel Defoe, *A Hymn to the Pillory* (1703). 'His ears were not cropped ... The author of the *True-Born Englishman* was a popular favourite, and his exhibition in the pillory was an occasion of triumph and not of ignominy to him. A ring of admirers was formed round the place of punishment, and bunches of flowers instead of handfuls of garbage were thrown at the criminal. Tankards of ale and stoups of wine were drunk in his honour by the multitude whom he had delighted with his racy verse and charmed by his bold defiance of the authorities' (Minto, 41–2).
15. Defoe edited the *Review* from 1704 until its suppression in 1713.
16. Defoe's anti-Jacobite pamphlets appeared during 1712 and 1713.
17. Arthur Conan Doyle (1859–1930), British author and creator of Sherlock Holmes in *A Study in Scarlet* (1887).
18. Daniel Defoe, *Serious Reflections during the Life and Surprizing Adventures of Robinson Crusoe: with his Visions of the Angelick World* (1720).
19. [Charles Gildon (1665–1724)], *The Life and Strange Surprizing Adventures of Mr D—— De F——, of London, Hosier, Who Has liv'd above fifty Years by himself, in the Kingdoms of North and South Britain* ([1719]), is the correct title and Joyce's error derives from Minto, 151–2.
20. 'He did not mind the sneers of hostile critics. They made merry over the trifling inconsistencies in the tale. How for example, they asked, could Crusoe have stuffed his pockets with biscuits when he had taken off all his clothes before swimming to the wreck? How could he have been at such a loss for clothes after those he had put off were washed away by the rising tide, when he had the ship's stores to choose from? How could he have seen the goat's eyes in the cave when it was pitch dark? How could the Spaniards give Friday's father an agreement in writing, when they had neither paper nor ink? How did Friday come to know so intimately the habits of bears, the bear not being a denizen of the West Indian islands?' (Minto, 146, summarizing Gildon's parodic life of Defoe).
21. Joyce may use this unusual term because, according to Minto's final chapter, 'The Mysterious End', Defoe 'at a distance from London in Kent' writes that his circumstances 'make it impossible that he could receive a visit from anybody' (Minto, 164).
22. Joyce rehearses the facts in much the same order as Minto, 168–9, but Joyce gives to Defoe's wandering and lonely death a mythical quality which Minto does not. See also *U* 6. 837–8.
23. This is the term used also by Minto, 134–5.
24. Joyce appears to derive these objections from Leslie Stephen (1832–

1904), 'De Foe's Novels', *Hours in a Library*, 3 volumes (London, 1874–9), i. 1–58. especially pp. 24–5, 47, 56–8.

25. Daniel Defoe, *The Storm: or, a Collection of the Most Dreadful Casualties and Disasters Which Happened in the Late Dreadful Tempest* (1704).

26. *The Storm* 'enables the modern meteorologist to construct a complete chart of the tempest's progress' (Masefield, p. xvi).

27. Daniel Defoe, *Journal of the Plague Year* (1722).

28. Sir Walter Scott, 'Advertisement' in *The Novels and Miscellaneous Works of Daniel De Foe* (London, 1855), p. [vii].

29. 'Time of the plague. Quicklime feverpits to eat them' (*U* 6. 985–6).

30. Gerhart Hauptmann (1862–1946), German dramatist, novelist and poet. 'He has written two or three masterpieces—"a little immortal thing" like *The Weavers*, for example' (*Letters* ii. 173). Leo Tolstoy made his name with *Tales from Sebastopol* (1856); see Stanislaus's comments to Joyce about this work and the writing of internal monologue such as Bloom's (*Letters* iii. 106).

31. Daniel Defoe, *The History of the Life and Adventures of Mr Duncan Campbell* (1720).

32. Daniel Defoe, *The Political History of the Devil, as well Ancient as Modern* (1726). 'His *Political History of the Devil* is nauseating' (Masefield, p. xx).

33. Daniel Defoe, *The Dumb Philosopher: or, Great Britain's Wonder* (1719), the story of Dickory Cronke.

34. Daniel Defoe, *Memoirs of a Cavalier: or, a Military Journal of the Wars in Germany, and the Wars in England* (1720).

35. *The Military Memoirs of Captain George Carleton* (1728) is generally considered not to be a work by Defoe.

36. 'Defoe was essentially a journalist' (Minto, 134).

37. *The Life and Adventures of Mrs Christian Davies commonly called Mother Ross* (1740) cannot be by Defoe, who died nine years before its publication and eight years before the death of its heroine, Christian Davies (1667–1739).

38. Leslie Stephen, in his essay 'De Foe's Novels', does not make this charge against Defoe's heroines.

39. Masefield, p. xxvii. Lucy Walter (1630–58), mistress of Charles II and mother of James, Duke of Monmouth; Eleanor (Nell) Gwynne (1650–87), actress, fruit-seller, mistress of Charles II and mother of the Duke of St Albans; Martha Blount (1690–1762), woman of letters to whom Alexander Pope dedicated his 'Epistle of Women'; Susannah Centlivre (1667–1723), actress and dramatist; Lady Mary Wortley Montagu (1689–1762), woman of letters and wife of the ambassador to Constantinople.

40. The allusion here seems to be to Richard Wagner, *Tristan und Isolde* (1865).

41. St Joan of Arc (1412–31), heroine of France who raised the siege of Orléans and had Charles VII crowned at Reims. She had been canonized in 1909. For Voltaire's ridicule of Joan see his *La Pucelle*; for iconography from the nineteenth century see A. Marby, *L'Histoire de Jeanne D'Arc*

(1907); Anatole France, pen-name of Jacques Anatole Thibault (1844–1924), French author of *Vie de Jeanne D'Arc* (1908).

42. Maxim Gorky, pen-name of Alexei Peshkov (1868–1936), Russian writer; Fyodor Dostoievsky (1821–81), Russian novelist.

43. Defoe's Captain Singleton soldiered in Africa; Cecil Rhodes (1853–1902), English imperialist in Africa, head of De Beers, founder of the British South African Company which annexed the territories which became Rhodesia, now Zimbabwe; Emmeline Pankhurst (1858–1928), British suffragette activist, founder of the Women's Social and Political Union.

44. Joyce ignores the fact that *Robinson Crusoe* (1719) antedates both *Captain Singleton* (1720) and *Colonel Jack* (1722).

45. From this point there survives a second holograph of four pages (Buffalo VII. A. 3), a fragment of an earlier draft version. Joyce's revisions to the draft Italian text are not significant.

46. Both of these caricatures conventionally are found under the name of John Bull.

47. Contrast Leslie Stephen on Crusoe: his morality is that of 'sturdy Englishmen in their passage through the world, and has enabled them to do excellent service to mankind' ('De Foe's Novels', *Hours in a Library*, i. 43–4).

48. Revelation 1: 9–20.

49. The draft version (Buffalo VII. A. 3) continues beyond this point at which Joyce decided to conclude the delivery of his lecture. 'The narrative that pivots upon this simple marvel is a whole, harmonious and consistent national epic, a solemn and triumphant music which the mournful chant of the savage and innocent soul accompanies. Our century which loves to trace present phenomena back to their origins to convince itself once more of the truth of the theory of evolution, which teaches us that when we were little we were not big, might profitably re-read the tale of Robinson Crusoe and his servant Friday. It would find therein many extremely useful tips for that international industry of our times—the cheap manufacture of the English imperialist type and its sale at knock-down prices.'

50. MS Cornell, *JJA* 2. 214–35. Translated from the Italian, a fragment of a lecture on William Blake, a holograph of twenty-two pages, numbered 11 to 30 plus two unnumbered pages on the reverse of 28 and 29. This lecture was given, with the lecture on Daniel Defoe, at the Università Popolare, Trieste, in March 1912.

51. William Blake, 'London', *Songs of Innocence and Experience* (1794).

52. William Blake, 'Proverbs of Hell', *The Marriage of Heaven and Hell* (1793).

53. Mary Wollstonecraft (1759–97), British feminist, author of *Vindication of the Rights of Woman* (1792); Tom Paine (1737–1809), British radical, author of *The Rights of Man* (1792).

54. Edwin Ellis, *The Real Blake* (1907), 164–5.

55. Ellis, 184, describes this loss to Blake of his pupils, an account to which Joyce adds little more than the epithet 'lower-class'.

56. Ellis, 437.

57. Francisco Suarez (1548–1617), Jesuit theologian, 'the teacher of Europe and of the universal world, the eye of the people of Christ'; Juan Mariana de Talavera (1771–1861), Jesuit historian and author of *De Rege et Regis Institutione* (1599), which includes a justification of tyrannicide. See *Portrait* 207.

58. 'Why a little curtain of flesh on the bed of our desire' (William Blake, *The Book of Thel*, (1789), plate 6, line 20).

59. These charities are recounted in Ellis, 185.

60. 'Jonathan's soul became closely bound to David's and Jonathan came to love him as his own soul' (1 Samuel 18: 1–2).

61. 'He saw the soul spring from the suddenly still, blind body, and ascend upwards, clapping its hands for joy. Then taking this sight with him Blake went to bed, and slept continuously for three days and nights' (Ellis, 100).

62. William Blake, *Poetical Sketches* (1783); *Songs of Innocence* (1789).

63. Ellis, 37–8.

64. William Blake, *Vala, or the Four Zoas* (1797–1810).

65. Catherine Boucher: Joyce repeats the error in spelling her surname from Ellis, 38–9, which recounts this courtship in these same terms.

66. William Shakespeare, *Othello*, I. iii.

67. Compare the argument about Bertha between Robert Hand and Richard Rowan in Act II of *Exiles* (*Poems and Exiles*, 189).

68. 'Like a fiend hid in a cloud' (William Blake, 'Infant Sorrow' in *Songs of Innocence and Experience*).

69. Ellis, 435.

70. Each of these figures in Blake's prophetic books after 1789.

71. 'He claimed the right of Abraham to give to Hagar what Sarah refused' (Ellis, 90). 'Abraham's wife Sarah had borne him no child, but she had an Egyptian maidservant named Hagar. So Sarah said to Abraham, "Listen, now! Since Yahweh has kept me from having children, go to my slave-girl. Perhaps I shall get children through her." Abraham agreed to what Sarah had said' (Genesis 16: 1–2).

72. Ellis, 91.

73. William Blake, 'The Crystal Cabinet' (*c*.1803).

74. This list of animals, with the insertion of a flea for a gnat, derives from *Auguries of Innocence* (*c*.1803), lines 13–46.

75. William Blake, *Auguries of Innocence*, lines 85–90.

76. Marcus Porcius Cato (234–149 BC), Roman statesman.

77. Ellis, 402–3.

78. The portrait is by Thomas Phillips (1770–1845).

79. Ellis, 436.

80. George Berkeley (1685–1753), Irish philosopher; David Hume (1711–76), Scottish philosopher and historian.

81. *Upanishads* (800–200 BC), one of a collection of Hindu sacred treatises, monistic, pantheistic, and developing the theory of the transmigration of souls.

82. Theophrastus Bombastus von Hohenheim (1493–1541), known as Paracelsus, Swiss physician; Jakob Boehme (1575–1624), German author of the mystic text *Aurora* (1612).

83. Juan de Yepes y Alvarez (1542–91), known as St John of the Cross, author of *En una nocha oscura* (*c*.1578), *The Dark Night*, one of the greatest of all mystical poems.

84. That is, 'painted by Michelangelo'.

85. This is a detail from Michelangelo's *Crucifixion of St Peter* in the Pauline chapel. Joyce's mistaken account derives from Ellis, 222–3.

86. William Blake, *A Descriptive Catalogue of Pictures* (1809).

87. Swedenborg populated heaven only with the spirits of the dead and his anthropocentric mysticism imagines all men to be figures in a *maximus homo*.

88. Joyce refers to the apostle John and his vision of the new Jerusalem; to St Augustine of Hippo, author of the *City of God*; to Dante's *Paradiso*; to Swedenborg's human form divine as defined in his *Arcana Coelestia* (1749–56); and to Matthew 24: 26–44.

89. See 'James Clarence Mangan (1902)', p. 59.

90. For every space larger than a red globule of man's blood
    Is visionary & is created by the hammer of Los;
    And every space smaller than a globule of man's blood opens
    Into Eternity, of which this vegetable world is but a shadow.

    Milton (1809), plate 29, lines 19–22

    We are led to believe a lie
    When we see not through the eye
    Which was born in a night to perish in a night,
    When the soul slept in beams of light.

    Auguries of Innocence, lines 125–8.

91. 'But the real truth of these matters is in fact far beyond us. That is why their preference is for the way up through negations, since this stands the soul outside everything which is correlative with its own finite nature. Such a way guides the soul through all the divine notions, notions which are themselves transcended by that which is far beyond every name, all reason and all knowledge. Beyond the outermost boundaries of the world, the soul is brought into union with God himself to the extent that every one of us is capable of it' (Dionysius the pseudo-Areopagite, *The Divine Names* 981b).

92. 'Eternity is in love with the productions of Time' (*The Marriage of Heaven and Hell*, plate 7, line 10).

THE CENTENARY OF CHARLES DICKENS

MS Padua. This is the text of an examination essay submitted by Joyce at the Università degli Studi di Padua in late April 1912. The manuscript on eight numbered sheets of official university paper is reproduced in *JJA* 2. 249–67.

The centenary of Charles Dickens's birth occurred on 7 February 1912.

1. Charles Dickens, *American Notes* (1842), *Pictures from Italy* (1846), and *Martin Chuzzlewit* (1843–4).
2. To be within sound of the bells of St Mary-le-Bow church in Cheapside is to be at the centre of the City of London, and to be born within hearing of their chimes is the definition of a Cockney.
3. Charles Dickens, *Barnaby Rudge* (1841).
4. Lord George Gordon (1751–93) led the so-called Gordon Riots of 1780 in protest against the Catholic Relief Act of that year. The Reform Bill of 1832 extended the franchise to include the rich middle class.
5. John Milton, 'L' Allegro', line 75.
6. Henry John Temple, third Viscount Palmerston (1784–1865), Foreign Secretary, who delivered his 'I am a Roman citizen' speech in the House of Commons, 24 June 1850. For Gladstone's reply see G. Barnett Smith, *The Life of the Right Honourable William Ewart Gladstone* (1881), 115. 'Little Englander' was a phrase applied to those writers opposed to imperial adventurism in the early decades of the twentieth century.
7. Richard 'Dick' Whittington (c.1358–1423) heard, according to the old tale, Bow Bells calling, 'Turn again, Whittington, thrice Lord Mayor of London.'
8. Robert Louis Stevenson (1850–94), Scottish author; Rudyard Kipling (1865–1936), born in Bombay and a writer on imperial themes; George Moore (1852–1933), Joyce's compatriot and older contemporary.
9. William Hogarth (1696–1764), English satirical painter and engraver.
10. Characters, respectively, in the following novels by Dickens: *David Copperfield*, *Great Expectations*, *Barnaby Rudge*, *David Copperfield*, *The Pickwick Papers*, *Martin Chuzzlewit*, *Great Expectations*.
11. The Tabard is the inn at Southwark where Geoffrey Chaucer imagines his pilgrims to have assembled for their pilgrimage in *The Canterbury Tales*.
12. Characters, respectively, in the following novels by Dickens: *The Old Curiosity Shop*, *Bleak House*, *The Pickwick Papers*, *David Copperfield*, *Oliver Twist*.
13. William Makepeace Thackeray (1811–63), novelist and author of *Vanity Fair* (1847–8).

THE UNIVERSAL LITERARY INFLUENCE OF THE RENAISSANCE

MS Padua. Translated from the Italian, 'L'influenza letteraria universale del rinascimento', an examination essay submitted by Joyce at the Università degli Studi di Padua in late April 1912. The manuscript on six numbered sheets of official university paper is reproduced in *JJA* 2. 237–47.

1. A repetition from the Defoe essay, p. 332, n. 49.
2. That is, 'Praiser of times past' (Horace, *De Arte Poetica*, line 173).

3. Joyce uses the Latin word *ima* here. (Translator's note.)
4. 'For my yoke is easy and my burden is light' (Matthew 11: 30).
5. Marco Praga (1862–1929), Italian novelist and playwright, *La Crisi: commedia in tre atti* (1907); Anatole France, *L'Affaire Crainquebille* (1901); Ivan Turgenev, *Smoke* (1867).
6. The allusion, as in the lecture on Defoe, is to Richard Wagner's *Tristan und Isolde*.
7. 'The ancient map-makers wrote across unexplored regions, "Here are lions"' (W. B. Yeats, 'Village Ghosts' in *The Celtic Twilight*, 1893).
8. St Robert Bellarmine (1542–1621), Jesuit commentator on Aquinas, graduate of the University of Padua; for Giovanni Mariana Talavera see the essay on Blake, p. 176.
9. A contrast which recalls that of John the Evangelist with Robinson Crusoe in the essay on Defoe, p. 174.

THE SHADE OF PARNELL

Translated from the Italian, 'L'ombra di Parnell', *Il Piccolo della Sera* (16 May 1912). The title of this article is taken by Joyce from that of a cartoon in *Sinn Féin* (8 Jan. 1910).

1. The third Home Rule Bill was introduced in the House of Commons in April 1912. It was January 1913 before it passed its third reading. The House of Lords delayed it until it was signed into law in September 1914. Suspended for the duration of the Great War it was finally superseded by the Government of Ireland Act 1920. *Gallina ... un mese*, Tuscan proverb: 'The hen of Mugello: twenty years old, looks a month'.
2. Joyce refers to the Act of Union of 1800 and to the Arbitration Treaty between England and the United States signed in August 1911. There is no foundation for his view that the Home Rule Bill of 1912 was linked to this treaty, although it is true that the issue of the Arbitration Treaty had aroused the opposition of Irish-Americans to any hint of an alliance of England and the USA at least since 1904.
3. These movements would include O'Connell's campaign for Catholic emancipation; his later campaign for repeal of the Act of Union; the Tithe War of 1834; the Young Ireland movement and the insurrection of 1848; the Fenian organization and the insurrection of 1867; the Invincibles' outrages of 1882; the Land War of the 1880s; and the obstructionism of the Irish Parliamentary Party under Parnell.
4. The original Italian is '*Più che perfetto*' (most perfect) and is a pun by Joyce on *piucchepefetto* (pluperfect). The translation of the phrase as 'pluterperfect' derives from Mr Deasy's neologism, 'The pluterperfect imperturbability of the department of agriculture' (*U* 2. 328–9). See Giorgio Melchiori, 'Two Notes on "Nestor"', *James Joyce Quarterly*, 22/4 (1985), 416–17.
5. This appears to be a confused version of an explanation of how 'The Bill reduces the number of Irish members in the British Parliament from 103

to 42' (Arthur Griffith, *The Home Rule Bill Examined*, Dublin: The National Council (1912), 15).

6. 'The Committee on Irish Finance proposed a surplus, the Government a deficit'; 'Some optimists look to an increasingly prosperous Ireland under Home Rule yielding in income-tax and Custom and Excise duties the required amount without any increase of taxation. Others think the problem will be solved by effecting economies'; if a Home Rule government in Ireland increases taxes it will 'face the hostility of the Orange North with an economic footing for its bigoted opposition. It must face an industrial antagonism in the urban South and a general dissatisfaction among all classes. In short, no Irish Government can vindicate the finance of the proposed measure in practice without committing political suicide' (Arthur Griffith, *The Finance of the Home Rule Bill*, Dublin: The National Council (1912), 5–6, 7, 9). In his perception that England was running Ireland at a gain and not at a loss to itself, Griffith is arguing against Thomas Kettle's *Home Rule Finance: An Experiment in Justice* (1911), a copy of which Joyce had sent to him in Trieste (*Letters*, ii. 287).

7. Arthur Griffith, leader of the 'separatist party' Sinn Féin, argued against the British parliament's continuing right to impose taxes on Ireland and 'the acceptance of an enormous reduction in Irish representation at Westminster whilst Westminster holds Irish services and Irish revenues in its hands' (*Home Rule Bill Examined*, 3, 15).

8. Arthur Griffith similarly appeals to the memory of Parnell as a caution against the new Home Rule Bill: 'But it is to be remembered that Mr Parnell who held the view that Ireland, after Home Rule, should not send members to the British Parliament, held at the same time that so long as any Irish service was retained in English control the Irish representatives in the English Parliament should not be diminished' (*Home Rule Bill Examined*, 15). The 'nephew' of Gladstone referred to here was in fact his son, Herbert John (Viscount) Gladstone (1854–1930).

9. See Michael Davitt, *The Fall of Feudalism in Ireland* (1904), 653, for such a criticism of Parnell, and also O'Brien, *Life of Charles Stewart Parnell* (1899), who credits the Irish parliamentarians Joseph Biggar and Joseph Ronayne (1822–76) with the invention of obstructionism (i. 83–4, 92–3); he credits Sir Charles Gavan Duffy with the foundation of the Irish Party (ii. 229); and he credits Davitt's priority in the Land League (i. 194).

10. The use of Moses as a figure for Irish political independence is used by Joyce in *U* 7. 845–70, where he embellishes the parallel he had heard from the orator John F. Taylor at a University debate in 1901. See *JJ* 91.

11. 'You must have a certain fascination: Parnell. Arthur Griffith is a square-headed fellow but he has no go in him for the mob' (*U* 8. 462).

12. For a description of Parnell's 'cold-blooded, businesslike speeches' and their effect on his audience see O'Brien (1899) i. 193.

13. The Parnell Tribute of 1883 raised over £37,000.

14. Parnell put his finger on the S, 'as if it were a matter of the utmost indifference: "I did not make an S. like that since 1878"' (O'Brien (1899)

ii. 198–9). For the forged letter and the role played by *The Times* see *Parnellism and Crime: reprinted from The Times, second series, Including the Facsimile of Mr Parnell's Letter* (London, 2nd edn., 1887).

15. Richard Pigott (1828–89) forged letters, which he sold to *The Times*, in an attempt to implicate Parnell and his party in agrarian crime and in the Phoenix Park murders. The exposure of Pigott and his suicide is told in O'Brien (1899), ii. 217. Pigott's sons were pupils at Clongowes Wood College with Joyce.

16. Gladstone declared, 'Parnell was the most remarkable man I ever met. I do not say the ablest man; I say the most remarkable and the most interesting. He was an intellectual phenomenon' (O'Brien (1899), ii. 357).

17. 'The title that the people gave him—the "uncrowned King of Ireland".' (O'Brien (1899), i. 105). The wag and the orator are, respectively, Disraeli and Gladstone.

18. Disraeli published a large number of novels, including *Coningsby* (1844) and *Sybil* (1845); Gladstone's copious writings include his *Studies on Homer and the Homeric Age* (1858) and eight volumes of *Gleanings of Past Years* (1879–90).

19. For Parnell's description of Gladstone as 'an unrivalled sophist' see O'Brien (1899), ii. 279.

20. Gladstone objected to O'Connell's pact with Lord Melbourne during the Tithe War of 1834.

21. Nathan, Baron Rothschild (1840–1915), the first member of a Jewish family to become a peer.

22. At the battle of Majuba Hill in February 1881, during the first Boer War, a British force was annihilated. In August 1881 the Pretoria Convention ended the war. By this agreement Britain recognized the independence of the Transvaal.

23. Abdul Hamid II, sultan of Turkey, denounced for 'inhumanity' in a letter of Gladstone, 13 March 1897, later published as a pamphlet, *Letter to the Duke of Westminster*, the issue of which was the behaviour of the Turks during the Greco–Turkish war.

24. The Kilmainham Treaty of April 1882 was an agreement between Parnell and Gladstone, designed to defuse the increasingly violent situation in Ireland.

25. See 'Ireland, Island of Saints and Sages', p. 116.

26. John Morley (1838–1923), English politician, man of letters, and Chief Secretary of Ireland, to whom Gladstone addressed his letter requiring the Irish Parliamentary Party to dismiss their leader after Parnell was cited in the divorce case between Captain William O'Shea (1840–1905) and Mrs Katherine (Kitty) O'Shea (1845–1921), whom Parnell married in June 1891. How Gladstone's letter, when made public, was seen as an ultimatum to Irish MPs by an English minister is described in O'Brien (1899), ii. 248–52.

27. The vote in Committee Room No. 15 of the House of Commons was forty-four against and twenty-six for Parnell's continuing as leader.

28. A revisionist account of this episode, reported without reference to quick-lime by O'Brien (1899), ii. 300–3, and immortalized by Joyce in 'Gas from a Burner', lines 19–20, runs as follows: 'Parnell was to speak in the square of Castlecomer, Co. Kilkenny, and Michael Davitt, who had split with Parnell over the Kilmainham Treaty and opposed his leadership after the divorce case, was to speak there too on the same day. Davitt, the town's favourite, urged his supporters not to attend the Parnellite meeting: to the crowd this sounded like a call to battle, the battle being what was familiarly known in the locality as a "croosting match", "croost" being Irish for pelting or throwing missiles'; in the event bags of plaster-of-paris were thrown at Parnell and 'some of the powder entered Parnell's eye. Dr Hackett, who accompanied Parnell, applied customary first aid by licking the powder from Parnell's eye. When they got clear of the town they stopped at the cottage of the good lady who supplied a folk eye-wash based on white of egg to soothe the irritated eye. Dr Hackett dramatized the affair by referring to the powder as "quick-lime" and Parnell put the drama to good effect by wearing an eye cloth at future meetings. Some allege that he would not put on the cloth until nearing the approach of venue' (Tom Lyng, *Castlecomer Connections*, Castlecomer (1984), 132–3).

29. 'He looked like a hunted hind,' a remark recorded on a visit by Parnell to Cork after his defeat in Committee Room 15 (O'Brien (1899), ii. 298). Yeats recalled that 'During the quarrel over Parnell's grave a quotation from Goethe ran through the papers, describing our Irish jealousy; "The Irish seem to me like a pack of hounds, always dragging down some noble stag"' (*Autobiographies*, New York (1953), 190). The same figure recurs in Yeats, 'Parnell's Funeral'. The common source appears to be: 'The Catholics, though they do not agree among themselves, will always unite against a Protestant. They are like a pack of hounds who will be biting one another until a stag comes in view, when they all unite to run it down' (Johann Eckermann, *Conversations with Goethe*, 7 Apr. 1829). See also Joyce's poem 'The Holy Office' (1904), line 88 (*Poems and Exiles*, 105).

30. *Psalms* 45: 13–14, 'girded with fringes of various golds', found also in 'The Little Office' designed to honour the Blessed Virgin, recalled in *Portrait* 88.

31. The comparison is between Judas and Timothy Healy (1855–1931), nationalist politician and first Governor-General of the Irish Free State, a leader of the opposition to Parnell's leadership, and the victim of Joyce's first publication, 'Et Tu, Healy'.

32. 'Was he now to be thrown to the "English wolves" because an English-man forsooth had cast the first stone' (O'Brien (1899), ii. 273). 'Do not flingamejig to the twolves!' (*FW* 479. 14). Parnell himself inaugurated the phrase in his manifesto of 1890, *To the People of Ireland*: '. . . under-stand the measure of the loss with which you are threatened unless you consent to throw me to the English wolves now howling for my destruction.'

THE CITY OF THE TRIBES

Translated from the Italian, 'La città delle tribù; Ricordi italiani in un porto irlandese', *Il Piccolo della Sera* (11 Aug. 1912).

A considerable amount of the information arranged here by Joyce is taken from James Hardiman, *The History of the Town and County of Galway* (1820). Joyce embellishes the Italian connection, whereas a main theme of Hardiman is the Spanish connection. This and the following article about Aran were sent by Joyce from Galway, where he was staying at Nora's mother's house during his last visit to Ireland, July to September 1912. Galway is described as the 'city of the tribes', according to Hardiman, 'an expression first invented by Cromwell's forces, as a term of reproach against the natives of the town, for their singular friendship and attachment to each other, during the time of their unparalleled troubles and persecutions, but which, the latter afterwards adopted, as an honorable mark of distinction between themselves and those cruel oppressors' (*History of Galway*, 6–7).

1. Compare the description of Bray Head in *U* 1. 181–2.
2. Hardiman in fact cites Henry Cromwell (1628–74), son of Oliver Cromwell and Governor-General of Ireland: '*noe towne or port in the three nations (London excepted) was more considerable*' (*History of Galway*, 25). Neither Cromwell nor Hardiman refers to Italy.
3. 'The trade of the town was so much impeded that Andrew Gerrard, a Florentine merchant, who was keeper of the customs in 1310, had a considerable abatement'; in the lists of mayors, bailiffs, and sheriffs of the seventeenth century there is no Giovanni Fante to be found, but the lists include a Martin Founte, an Adam Faunte, and a Geffry Font (*History of Galway*, 56–7, 218, 219, 221).
4. St Nicholas (*fl.* 340), bishop of Myra, whose relics were stolen thence in 1087 by merchants from the sea port of Bari. The church of St Nicholas in Galway stands opposite the junction of Lombard Street and Bowling Green where Nora's mother lived and Joyce stayed at the time he wrote this article.
5. Giovanni Battista Rinuccini (1592–1653), papal nuncio, came to Ireland with money and weapons to support the Catholic revolt in the reign of Charles I, the 'martyr king'. Hardiman's account of Rinuccini's efforts in Galway includes all these details and concludes: 'In a fit of rage he ordered their bell to be pulled down and placed two priests at the entry to their chapel, to keep the people from resorting there to prayers' (*History of Galway*, 129).
6. Hardiman identifies two bulls issued by the Borgia, Pope Alexander VI (1431–1503) (*History of Galway*, 237).
7. 'The annals relate, that an Italian traveller, induced by its fame in foreign parts visited the town, and that he carefully remarked and noted its situation and extent, the style of its buildings, the manners and customs of the inhabitants, and every other particular worthy of attention. They further state, that being at mass in a private house, (its celebration in

public having been in that year, 1568, first prohibited) he saw, at one view, the blessed sacrament in the hands of the priest, boats passing up and down the river, a ship entering the port in full sail, a salmon killed with a spear, and hunters and hounds pursuing a deer; upon which he observed, that although he had travelled the greater part of Europe, he had never before witnessed a sight which combined so much variety and beauty' (*History of Galway*, 89).

8. 'We had our trade with Spain and the French and with the Flemings before those mongrels were pupped, Spanish ale in Galway, the winebark on the winedark waterway' *(U* 12. 1296–9).

9. 'The Hollanders, as the story goes, contracted to cover over as much ground, as they wished to obtain, with a certain species of silver coin . . . This glittering proposal was at first agreed to by the town's-people; but, upon further reflection, they prudently considered that these industrious settlers might monopolize all their trade, and injure the town, and they accordingly had recourse to a most ingenious artifice to get rid of the agreement when it came to be carried into effect, by insisting that the ground was to be covered with the coin, placed not on the sides, as had been supposed, but close on the edges. This unexpected turn created so material a difference, that it soon put an end to the treaty, which, if the entire be not, as is most likely, a fable, might have been a service to the country' (*History of Galway*, 107).

10. 'There were fourteen families . . . found in the following verse:

> Athy, Blake, Bodkin, Browne, Deane, Darcy, Lynch,
> Joyes, Kirwan, Martin, Morris, Skerrett, French.'

The fourteenth family was Ffont (*History of Galway*, 7, n. 21)

11. 'In the year of 1651 the Marquis of Clanricarde, then Lord Deputy of the kingdom, entered into a treaty with the Duke of Lorrain, to obtain twenty thousand pounds for the King's [i.e. Charles II] service in Ireland; for this sum, he agreed to give the City of Limerick and town of Galway as security; and directed his Commissioners . . . "particularly to describe unto the Duke, the value of the security, the strength and situation of the places and the goodness and conveniency of the harbours, &c." For this purpose, a map of the town was made, which, after the restoration, (when the antient inhabitants were restored by the Crown, to their freedoms and estates,) was finished blazoned and described by the Rev. Henry Joyce, then warden; and afterwards elegantly engraved, at the expense of the Corporation, and dedicated to King Charles II' (*History of Galway*, 25). A copy of Henry Joyce's map is included in Hardiman's *History of Galway*; the original is held in the Library of Trinity College Dublin.

12. This analysis of the map abbreviates the elaborate description of its symmetries, based on lists of seven and of fourteen items, concluding with the pigeon house, in *History of Galway*, 25–33. The following lines of verse translated from the map are also given:

> Rome boasts sev'n hills, the Nile its sev'n-fold stream,
> Around the pole sev'n radiant planets gleam;
> Galway, Conation Rome, twice equals these.

13. This story is told by Hardiman (*History of Galway*, 75–80).

14. That is, Lynch's Castle at the junction of Shop Street and Abbeygate Street.

15. 'He embraced his unfortunate son and launched him into eternity!' (*History of Galway*, 79).

16. The Armorial Ensigns of the fourteen ancient families of Galway are given in *History of Galway*, 8–9. The Roman wolf that fed Romulus and Remus is not included. The two-headed eagle of the Hapsburgs is part of the arms of both the Browne and the Joyce families.

17. 'As described by Lord Clanricarde in 1641 they "were not without a large proportion of pride"'; there is no mention of lust, although Joyce may have in mind 'The following extract [which] is taken from the observations of a lively French traveller . . . "There are public assemblies daily, at a moderate price. Sometimes the ladies are dressed, sometimes half-dressed, and sometimes undressed; and, according to these different degrees, these meetings arc called assembly, drum, or promenade. The price of entrance differs according to the name"' (*History of Galway*, 325, 326–7, n. 18).

18. Nora Barnacle had worked at the age of 12 as porteress in the Presentation Convent.

THE MIRAGE OF THE FISHERMAN OF ARAN

Translated from the Italian, 'Il miraggio del pescatore di Aran: La valvola dell'Inghilterra in caso di guerra', *Il Piccolo della Sera* (5 Sept. 1912). Mr Deasy makes reference to the Galway Harbour Scheme in his letter on foot and mouth disease (*U* 2. 326); and a brief account of the *Il Piccolo* article on Aran and the Galway harbour scheme 'by Mr James Joyce, an Irish-Italian journalist' appears under Joyce's own editorial on 'Politics and Cattle Disease', *Freeman's Journal* (10 Sept. 1912).

Joyce's title makes reference first to Hy-brasil, the illusory western land imagined by the Aran islander, and second to the new Galway harbour scheme, which is described in the prospectus booklet (with map attached), *Galway as a Transatlantic Port* (n.d. [1912]), a copy of which Joyce consults on his boat journey to and from the island. A copy of this booklet and map is in the archive of the Galway Harbour Commissioners. The booklet emphasizes the eventuality of war: '*The Question from an Imperial Standpoint* . . . the expenditure on Galway would in that respect alone be not only recommendable but to most persons seem a work of absolute Imperial necessity . . . The construction of the works projected at Galway for a pier at Mutton Island would, with little, if any, additional outlay make invulnerable defences for that coast. A fort at Mutton Island could protect the whole Bay and any fleet inside it . . . The German fleet recently visited Galway in the course of its strategic cruise around Ireland [which] . . . shows what is in the mind of that astute rival of British trade and commercial supremacy' (*Galway as a Transatlantic Port*, 30–2).

1. Hardiman supplies the basis of Joyce's account of the Claddagh village and its ceremonies (*History of Galway*, 302–7).

2. A reference to Mutton Island in Galway Bay, a proposed site since 1852 of a new harbour.

3. Joyce closely summarizes arguments and statistics put forward in *Galway as a Transatlantic Port*, which include the importance to England of alternative shipping routes to those monopolized by America and the control of naval strategy: 'More than all, perhaps, in this question of new routes is the wonderful and rapid developments of Canada. Its recent industrial growth into becoming the granary of Great Britain makes the Dominion in self-interest seek new openings and better trade routes'; 'Galway stands on the highway to America, which is the great industrial storehouse of the future. It is the nearest part of Europe to that great and prosperous land. Communications between Newfoundland, New York, or Boston and Galway is nearer by two days of time and many hundred miles of distance than either Liverpool or Queenstown. The consequent saving in time and money would be of incalculable advantage to British and American commerce, yet because it is Galway and in Ireland, this benefit which God intended as a blessing is of no avail to them' (*Galway as a Transatlantic Port*, 1–4).

4. Joyce is comparing the recurrent historical aspiration of Galway to be a great transatlantic port with the mythical sighting of Hy-brasil. St Brendan (484–577), author of the *Navigatio* (Brendan's Voyage), charts the discovery of the 'land of promise of the saints', which is often identified both as the mythical island of the west and as America.

5. Inis Mór, the largest of the three islands which, according to Hardiman, 'were anciently overshadowed with wood, of which there are still very evident remains' (*History of Galway*, 332).

6. St Enda (*fl.* 550) is patron of Aran, where he was the teacher of Brendan, Fursa (or Fursey), and Finnian. The identification of St Brendan's *Navigatio* as a precursor both of Dante's *Divine Comedy* and of Columbus's choice of his route to America is made in Le Comte de Montalembert, *Les Moines d'Occident*, 6 volumes (Paris, 1860–77), iii. 90–1. The 'hagiographic calendar' is that of the Very Rev. Canon John O'Hanlon, *Lives of the Irish Saints, with special Festivals, and the Commemoration of Holy Persons. Compiled from Calendars, Martyrologies and various sources*, 10 volumes (Dublin: James Duffy, 1875–1903). O'Hanlon states that 'Fursey had angelic apparitions during his lifetime. The sublime Dante has even borrowed the plot of his Divina Commedia from the celebrated vision of this saint' (i. 223). For the identification of St Finnian with St Frigidianus, bishop of Lucca, see p. 315, n. 19.

7. Synge's description of the Aran islander, so different in its values from that of Joyce, coincides in the matter of dress: 'their flannel shirts and the piquant colour and [shape] of their tam-o-shanters and pampooties' (*The

Aran Islands (1907), in J. M. Synge, *Collected Works*, 4 volumes, London: Oxford University Press (1966), ii. 54). See also, 'The tramper Synge is looking for you, he said, to murder you. He heard you pissed on his hall-door in Glasthule. He's out in pampooties to murder you' (*U* 9. 569–71).

8. See p. 148.

9. St Columba who, according to legend, discovered on Aran the grave of an abbot of Jerusalem.

10. Contrast Synge's more naïve account of a storyteller on Aran: 'He told me that he had known Petrie and Sir William Wilde, and many living anti-quarians, and had taught Irish to Dr Finck, and Dr Pedersen, and given stories to Mr Curtin of America . . . As we talked he sat huddled together over the fire, shaking and blind, yet his face was indescribably pliant, lighting up with an ecstasy of humour when he told me of anything that had a point of wit or malice, and growing sombre and desolate again when he spoke of religion or the fairies. He had great confidence in his own powers and talent, and in the superiority of his stories over all other stories in the world' (Synge, *The Aran Islands*, in *Works*, ii. 50).

11. Joyce introduces an Italian neologism, *'fumolento'*. (Translator's note.)

12. This is an oblique self-reference by Joyce. According to Hardiman's detailed description of the 1657 map of Galway, Henry Joyce had inscribed among the armorial bearings of the four Irish provinces, *'Quasi terebinthus extendens ramos suos'*, and among the names of such colonies as Virginia, Jamaica, and Montserrat, *'Quasi lilium germinans germinabit, et laetabuntur deserta et invia'* (*History of Galway*, 267). Joyce runs these together and allows also for a visual comparison with the curved lines on the map (illustrated p. 202). 'It will flourish like a lily growing and like a terebinth tree spreading its branches' (Ecclesiasticus 24).

POLITICS AND CATTLE DISEASE

Freeman's Journal, (10 Sept. 1912). The text is unsigned but two factors identify it as by Joyce: a letter from Charles Joyce to Stanislaus Joyce, 6 September 1912 (Cornell University Library), states that Joyce wrote a sub-editorial on foot and mouth disease in the *Freeman's Journal*; a short article beneath this sub-editorial summarizes Joyce's article on Aran and the Galway harbour scheme and identifies Joyce as its author.

The history of Joyce's interest in solutions to the problem of foot and mouth disease in Irish cattle is available in *JJ* 325–7 and *Letters* ii. 300. See also *U* 2. 321–420, 12. 831–45).

1. Irish Members of Parliament (often anti-Parnellites) who continued to remain outside the Irish Parliamentary Party of John Redmond.

2. John Dillon (1851–1927), Irish politician and supporter of John Redmond.

3. Henry Chaplin, first Viscount Chaplin (1840–1923), and Charles Bathurst, first Viscount Bledisloe (1867–1958), both English politicians and spokesmen for agricultural interests.

4. Walter Runciman, first Baron Runciman (1847–1937), English shipowner opposed to the protectionist policies of Chaplin and Bathurst.
5. The *Globe* was a conservative London newspaper.
6. The *Irish Times*, a newspaper which had supported the Unionist interest since its foundation in 1859.
7. An eleven-months' man is one who, under the conacre system, rents land without full tenant's rights on an annual eleven-month lease.
8. George Russell, 'AE', editor of the *Irish Homestead* which (besides publishing Joyce's first three short stories) devoted most of its space to agricultural economy.

PROGRAMME NOTES FOR THE ENGLISH PLAYERS

CW 250–2. These programme notes date from 1918/1919. Joyce wrote to his friend Georges Borach that he composed them for the English Players (*JJ* 446–7, 454), an acting group formed by Claud Sykes, an English actor, and by Joyce himself. The group put on these and other plays in Zurich. In June 1918 they presented a triple bill (by Barrie, Synge, Shaw), and in March 1919 on Joyce's advice a single play (by Edward Martyn).

1. *The Twelve Pound Look* (1910) by James Matthew Barrie (1860–1937), Scottish novelist and playwright.
2. Joyce had read the manuscript of Synge's play in Paris in 1902 and condemned it to Stanislaus: 'It is tragic about all the men that are drowned in the islands: but thanks be to God Synge isn't an Aristotelian' (*Letters* ii. 35). Joyce collaborated in an Italian translation of the play and attempted to organize a production in 1909 for which the Synge estate refused to give the rights.
3. That is, the Greek for 'necessity'.
4. Joyce is reported to have said (5 May 1907) that Synge's art 'is more original than my own' (*JJ* 267).
5. George Bernard Shaw, *The Dark Lady of the Sonnets* (1911).
6. Mary Fitton (*fl.* 1600), maid of honour to Elizabeth I, identified as the 'dark lady' of Shakespeare's sonnets by Thomas Tyler, in his facsimile edition of the *Sonnets* (1886); Frank Harris (1856–1931), Irish journalist, author of *The Man Shakespeare* (1909).
7. 'To the onlie begetter of these insuing sonnets Mr W. H. all happiness . . .'—the dedication to Shakespeare's *Sonnets* (1609).
8. Edward Martyn, *The Heather Field* (1899). For Joyce's earlier relation to Martyn's work see 'The Day of the Rabblement', p. 51.

FROM A BANNED WRITER TO A BANNED SINGER

The New Statesman and Nation, NS, 3/53 (27 Feb. 1932), 260–1. Also published in *Hound and Horn*, 1932. See also *JJA* 2. 310–30 for MSS variants. Joyce published this piece, a model of devices complicated and refined in *Finnegans Wake*, in order to further the declining career of John Sullivan, an

Irish-French tenor whom Joyce befriended in Paris in 1929. *The New States-man and Nation* provides an introduction to Joyce's text:

> In this remarkable document, Mr. James Joyce gives his impressions of his friend, Mr. Sullivan of the Paris Opera, in several of his leading roles. Many competent critics regard Mr. Sullivan as the most extraordinary dramatic tenor that Europe has listened to for the last half century. Mr. Joyce complains that Mr. Sullivan is 'banned' or at least unknown in England. The reflections written here were sent in a letter to Mr. Sullivan by Mr. Joyce after an occasion on which the singer was carried shoulder high by his Marseilles admirers after an astonishing performance in 'Guillaume Tell'. One knows of no other similar documents, no letters in a tone of intense admiration and sardonic banter sent by, say, Manzoni to Rubini, or by Flaubert to Gilbert Duprez, or by Ibsen to the Swedish Nightingale. Lovers of grand opera will recognise the operatic situations and phrases with which the text is studded and detect under the mask of their Christian names the three divi who figure in the final quartette. The document which the singer has kindly placed at our disposal is published with Mr. Joyce's permission.

1. Gioacchino Rossini (1792–1868), *William Tell* (1829), an opera in which Sullivan sang the role of Arnold. 'Fidelion' is a pun on Fido, on Beethoven's *Fidelio*, and on the emblem of the faithful lion of Zürich. 'Mastiff' is a pun on *His Master's Voice*, a trade mark of RCA Victor recording company.

2. Sullivan's family came from Co. Cork and, originally, from Co. Kerry. Collard is a manufacturer of grand pianos. The Macgillicuddy Reeks are mountains in Co. Kerry. In *William Tell*, Act IV, Arnold sings an aria on visiting his paternal home 'for the last time'.

3. The 'Bantry gang', named from Bantry in Co. Cork, opposed Parnell after the divorce case. It included Timothy Healy and his uncle Timothy Daniel Sullivan, who set his ballad 'God Save Ireland' to the tune of 'Tramp, tramp, tramp, The boys are marching'. Philip O'Sullivan Beare (*c.*1590–1660) served in the army of the king of Spain. John ('Jay') L. Sullivan (1858–1918), American heavyweight boxer. Barry Sullivan (1821–91) was a 'barnstorming' actor from Cork. Arthur Sullivan (1842–1900), whose varied works include a *Te Deum* (1872) and 'The Lost Chord', and who created with W. S. Gilbert in their light opera, *Pinafore*, a gallant captain who cannot utter the 'great big D——'.

4. Hector Berlioz (1803–69), *The Damnation of Faust* (1846). 'Parigot' is the argot of Paris. The Trocadéro was the concert hall of Paris. Balaclava is the Crimean town which gives its name to the battle of the 'Charge of the Light Brigade', and puns on *klavier*, German for piano. The 'Impressario' is Mephistopheles in *Faust* and the 'garden in the cool of the evening' parodies Genesis 3: 8. 'Thank you, gentle twilight' is the devil's aria in Act III of *The Damnation of Faust*.

5. Camille Saint-Saëns (1835–1921), French composer in whose opera *Samson et Delila* (1877) Joyce imagines Sullivan taking the part of Samson. In

the opera's last scene Samson is led by a child, as is the virtuous king in Isaiah 11: 6. Simpson's is a restaurant in the Strand, London. Timnath is the city of Samson's first wife. Joyce alludes to the prophet's treading in the winepress, Isaiah 63: 3–4, and to Samson's destruction of the temple. B flat is the last note sung by Samson in Saint-Saëns's opera.

6. 'Laib' is German for 'loaf' and proposes a pun on *Leib*, german for 'body', and *Leben*, German for 'life'. 'Dr' is an abbreviation for 'debit'. 'Braun' and 'Brot' are German for 'meat' and 'bread'. Liebfraumilch is a German white wine.

7. Sullivan sang Verdi's *Otello* in Dublin on 27 April 1930 and, afterwards, was urged to make a speech. Daniel Sullivan (*c.*1739–64), Irish counter-tenor, and Daniel O'Connell, orator and politician from Co. Kerry, pro-vide a pun on Dan, the native land of Samson. Muskerry is a barony in Sullivan's Co. Cork and provides a pun on the final lines of Shakespeare's *Love's Labour's Lost*: 'The words of Mercury are harsh after the songs of Apollo.' Compare also the motto of the Irish-French family, Rohan: '*Roy ne puys, Duc ne daygne, Rohan suys*': 'I cannot be king, deign not to be duke, I am a Rohan.'

8. *Durch diese hohle Gasse muss er kommen*: 'He will have come through this narrow pass' (J. C. F. von Schiller, *William Tell*. IV. iii). Melckthal is a valley in Switzerland and the name of Arnold's father in Rossini's *William Tell*. 'Wartemal' is German for 'let's see'. '*Gewittermassen*' is a pun on the German for 'in a certain way' and for 'storm'. '*Heimat*' is German for 'home'. The 'ritzprinz' is César Ritz (1850–1918), founder of the Ritz hotel chain. 'Chyberschwitzerhoofs' includes among its puns 'low-class Swiss hotels'. The '*Feuerzauber*' is the fire music in Richard Wagner's *Die Walküre*. '*Pass auf*' is German for 'pay attention'. Thalwil is a Swiss com-mune. Rossini's *William Tell* ends with the words: '*Liberté redescend des cieux*': 'Liberty comes down again from heaven'. Calville is a kind of apple.

9. Richard Wagner, *Tannhäuser* (1845). Castle Wartburg was Tannhäuser's home before Venus dominated him and its name is the same as the castle in which Luther sought refuge after the Diet of Worms. '*Montagne de passe*' puns on *maison de passe*: 'a brothel' and Venus' mount. 'Casheselks' derives from '*cachesexe*': 'G-string'. '*Pierreuse*' is French for 'street-walker'. 'The harp that once thro' Tara's halls' is by Thomas Moore. '*Puttana madonna*', a Triestine curse meaning 'God's whore of a mother', recurs in *U* 16. 14. '*Simplicissima*' means 'a very naïve girl'. *Salve Regina* is the prayer 'Hail Holy Queen' addressed to the Madonna. Elizabeth was Tannhäuser's first love and, at the end of the first act, he exclaims 'My hope rests in Mary!' 'Bilk' means 'cheat' and 'blak' means 'unchaste'.

10. '*Ecco trovato*': 'There he is revealed.' Lucius Licinius Lucullus (*c.*110–56 BC), a Roman notorious for gluttony. Tarbert is a village in Co. Kerry. Château Kirwan refers to the wine of a vineyard near Bordeaux. Contrary to Ellmann's claim that Joyce intends 'a poor Irish imitation of French wine' (*CW* 265), the vineyard developed by the Kirwan family of Galway is considered to produce one of the premier wines of Bordeaux.

'Thuriferant' translates as 'carrying like a thurible or censer'. '*Nullo modo*': 'in no way'. 'Muftimummed' translates as 'dressed in civilian clothes'. 'Up to mighty London came an Irishman one day', a line from the popular song 'It's a Long Way to Tipperary'.

11. Jakob Liebmann Beer, pseudonym Giacomo Meyerbeer (1791–1864), composer, most famous for his spectacular operas, including *Les Huguenots* (1836) about the St Bartholomew's Day massacre of Protestants in Paris. Joyce adapts the nursery rhyme 'Oranges and lemons, say the bells of St Clement's', and inserts the names of churches in Paris instead of in London. The churches referred to are St André, St Barthelémy, Notre Dame, St Clotilde, St Sulpice, and St Germain l'Auxerrois. In authorizing the massacre Charles IX is reported to have declared, 'If they are to be killed, let them all be killed.' '*Pour la foi*': 'for the [Catholic] faith'. 'Supplice' means 'torture' and puns on St Sulpice.

12. '*Pardie*': 'by God'. In the third act of Meyerbeer's *Les Huguenots* Raoul de Nangis, the part sung by Sullivan, observes: 'Look! the Seine is full of blood and bodies.' Valentine is the Catholic beloved of de Nangis and 'swhipstake' is a pun on the Irish Sweepstake, a lottery famous in the 1930s. 'Piffpaf' is the anti-Catholic aria sung by Marcel in *Les Huguenots*. The Dominican order were known both as *Domini canes* (hounds of the lord) and as *frères prêcheurs* (friars who are preachers). Joyce puns, with 'friers pecheurs', on frying and on sinners.

13. Enrico Caruso (1873–1921), Giacomo Lauri-Volpi (1892–1979), and Giovanni Martinelli (1885–1969), famous tenors. A 'claque' is an opera hat. '*Somnium*' means 'sleep' or 'dream'. A '*Portugais*' is a type of oyster. '*Tes gueules*' means 'your mouths' or 'shut your gobs'. '*Primi assoluti*' means 'star performers'. The three Italian tenors parody 'God Save the King' in praise of Sullivan.

[ON THE MORAL RIGHT OF AUTHORS]

Translated from the French, *XV⁴ Congrès International de la Fédération PEN* (Paris, 1937), 24. Joyce delivered this speech at the 15th International PEN Congress in Paris, 20–7 June 1937. Samuel Roth, through his magazine *Two Worlds Monthly*, had pirated *Ulysses* in the USA. Joyce successfully contrived an international protest and secured an injunction against Roth's continued publication. In this speech Joyce concentrates on the judicial consequences of that injunction for all writers. However, he was disappointed in the response he received: 'I wanted the PEN to take an interest in the pirating of *Ulysses* in the United States but this was brushed aside. It was politics all the way' (*JJ* 704). The chairman had Joyce's speech incorporated in the minutes.

INDEX

The Oxford World's Classics Website

www.worldsclassics.co.uk

- Information about new titles
- Explore the full range of Oxford World's Classics
- Links to other literary sites and the main OUP webpage
- Imaginative competitions, with bookish prizes
- Peruse the Oxford World's Classics Magazine
- Articles by editors
- Extracts from Introductions
- A forum for discussion and feedback on the series
- Special information for teachers and lecturers

www.worldsclassics.co.uk

American Literature

British and Irish Literature

Children's Literature

Classics and Ancient Literature

Colonial Literature

Eastern Literature

European Literature

History

Medieval Literature

Oxford English Drama

Poetry

Philosophy

Politics

Religion

The Oxford Shakespeare

A complete list of Oxford Paperbacks, including Oxford World's Classics, Oxford Shakespeare, Oxford Drama, and Oxford Paperback Reference, is available in the UK from the Academic Division Publicity Department, Oxford University Press, Great Clarendon Street, Oxford OX2 6DP.

In the USA, complete lists are available from the Paperbacks Marketing Manager, Oxford University Press, 198 Madison Avenue, New York, NY 10016.

Oxford Paperbacks are available from all good bookshops. In case of difficulty, customers in the UK can order direct from Oxford University Press Bookshop, Freepost, 116 High Street, Oxford OX1 4BR, enclosing full payment. Please add 10 per cent of published price for postage and packing.